Tupolev Tu-144

Tupolev Tu-144
The Soviet Supersonic Airliner

Yefim Gordon
Dmitriy Komissarov
Vladimir Rigmant

4880 Lower Valley Road • Atglen, PA 19310

Copyright © 2015 by Yefim Gordon, Dmitriy Komissarov and Vladimir Rigmant.

Library of Congress Control Number: 2014957675

All rights reserved. No part of this work may be reproduced or used in any form or by any means—graphic, electronic, or mechanical, including photocopying or information storage and retrieval systems—without written permission from the publisher.

The scanning, uploading, and distribution of this book or any part thereof via the Internet or via any other means without the permission of the publisher is illegal and punishable by law. Please purchase only authorized editions and do not participate in or encourage the electronic piracy of copyrighted materials.
"Schiffer," "Schiffer Publishing, Ltd. & Design," and the "Design of pen and inkwell" are registered trademarks of Schiffer Publishing, Ltd.

Book Design by Polygon Press Ltd., Moscow.
Cover Design by Matt Goodman
Type set in Times New Roman/Square 721 BT

ISBN: 978-0-7643-4894-5
Printed in China

Published by Schiffer Publishing, Ltd.
4880 Lower Valley Road
Atglen, PA 19310
Phone: (610) 593-1777; Fax: (610) 593-2002
E-mail: Info@schifferbooks.com

For our complete selection of fine books on this and related subjects, please visit our website at www.schifferbooks.com. You may also write for a free catalog.

This book may be purchased from the publisher. Please try your bookstore first.

We are always looking for people to write books on new and related subjects. If you have an idea for a book, please contact us at proposals@schifferbooks.com.

Schiffer Publishing's titles are available at special discounts for bulk purchases for sales promotions or premiums. Special editions, including personalized covers, corporate imprints, and excerpts can be created in large quantities for special needs. For more information, contact the publisher.

Contents

Acknowledgments... 6

Introduction... 7

    Chapter 1. The Tu-144 is Born... 11

    Chapter 2. Take One: The Tu-144 Prototype... 65

    Chapter 3. The Prototype in Detail... 101

    Chapter 4. Take Two: Back to the Drawing Board... 113

    Chapter 5. The Production Versions in Detail... 179

    Chapter 6. The Tu-144 in Aeroflot Service... 199

    Chapter 7. The Accidents... 219

    Chapter 8. The Tu-144 in Uniform? (Projected Military Versions)... 231

    Chapter 9. East vs. West, or 'Concordski' vs. Concorde: The Two SSTs Compared... 243

    Chapter 10. A New Lease of Life: the Tu-144LL Testbed... 249

Appendix. Production List... 272

Acknowledgments

The authors wish to express their gratitude to the Tupolev Public Limited Co. which supplied documentary materials on the Tu-144, as well as to Mikhail Gribovskiy and to Nigel Eastaway who provided access to the materials of the Russian Aviation Research Trust (RART).

The book is illustrated by photos by Yefim Gordon, Dmitriy Komissarov, Peter Davison, Alexander Beltyukov, Vladimir Nazarov, Sergey Sergeyev, as well as from the archives of the Tupolev PLC, the M. M. Gromov Flight Research Institute (LII), RART, ITAR-TASS, Novosti Press Agency (APN), NASA, Flieger Revue, the personal archives of Yefim Gordon, Sergey and Dmitriy Komissarov, and from Internet sources.

Colour artwork by Aleksandr Gavrilov. Line drawings by the Tupolev PLC.

Holding a model of the Tu-144, Andrey N. Tupolev discusses the programme's progress with his son and future successor Aleksey A. Tupolev.

Introduction

The advent of turbojet engines revolutionised first and foremost military aviation. The first attempts to adapt the new powerplant to combat aircraft were undertaken in the late 1930s, and the first viable jet fighters and bombers appeared in time to see action in the Second World War. In the immediate post-war years, aircraft designers in the world's leading aircraft manufacturing countries were able to take on the task of introducing jet propulsion in commercial aviation as well. This took air travel to hitherto unimaginable levels of comfort and speed. Work on jet airliners went ahead both in the West and in the Soviet Union.

It should be noted that in spite of the pre-war development work on jet engines undertaken in the Soviet Union, the nation was not in a position to test and field any actual combat jets during the war – unlike Germany, Great Britain and the USA. However, the Soviet designers learned fast and did their best to catch up with their Western colleagues – even if German and British jet engines had to be used initially until indigenous ones could be created.

Yet, it takes more than simply jet engines to build a jet aircraft. In the Soviet Union, fundamental research into the aerodynamics of high-speed flight started back in the early 1940s. In 1946-47 a team of scientists headed by Sergey A. Khristianovich at the Central Aero- and Hydrodynamics Institute named after Nikolay Ye. Zhukovskiy (TsAGI – *Tsentrahl'nyy aero- i **ghidrodinamicheskiy** institoot*) made a series of experiments in the T-106 transonic wind tunnel which yielded valuable results, making it possible to outline a number of fundamental laws pertaining to the aerodynamics of high-speed flight. This led to the development of the first Soviet straight-wing jets; the first indigenous turbojet-powered aircraft – the Mikoyan/Gurevich MiG-9 and Yakovlev Yak-15 fighters (NATO reporting names *Fargo* and *Feather* respectively) – took to the air on 24th April 1946, followed in short order by other designs from the Lavochkin, Sukhoi and Alekseyev design bureaux. TsAGI contributed a lot to the development of transonic and supersonic aircraft by conducting important research on swept wings which made it possible to resolve the principal aerodynamics, stability, aeroelasticity and structural strength issues of swept-wing aircraft. At that time Soviet aviation developed at a very rapid pace. In 1947 the OKB-155 design bureau headed by Artyom I. Mikoyan (OKB = ***opytno-konstrooktorskoye byuro*** – experimental design bureau; the number is a code allocated for security reasons) created the I-310 fighter with wings swept back 35° at quarter-chord which first flew on 30th December and entered production in 1948 as the MiG-15 *Fagot*. It became the first Soviet operational swept-wing aircraft – albeit not the first Soviet swept-wing jet (this honour goes to the Lavochkin '160' fighter prototype which first flew on 23rd July 1947). On 26th December 1948 Semyon A. Lavochkin's OKB-301 achieved another 'first' for Soviet aircraft design when the La-176 fighter prototype with wings swept back 45° at quarter-chord attained Mach 1.02 in a shallow dive; in February 1950 the Mikoyan OKB 'responded' when the MiG-17 *Fresco-A* production fighter – again with 45° wing sweep – exceeded the speed of sound in level flight.

The creation of supersonic wind tunnels was a huge contribution to the supersonic aircraft development effort. At TsAGI this was initially done by upgrading the T-112 wind tunnel when the institute's researchers discovered the beneficial effect of perforations in the tunnel's working section. Building on this experience, in 1953 TsAGI commissioned a supersonic wind tunnel with a 2.25 x 2.25 m (7 ft $4^{37}/_{64}$ in x 7 ft $4^{37}/_{64}$ in) working section making its possible to test models at speeds between Mach 0.6 and Mach 4.0 and variable dynamic pressure. This research made it possible to determine a number of new aerodynamic laws affecting swept wings during the transition to supersonic flight. TsAGI also looked into the use of low aspect ratio wings with thin airfoils as a means of attaining supersonic performance; this research paved the way for the development of such delta-wing fighters as the Mikoyan MiG-21 *Fishbed* and Sukhoi Su-9/Su-11 *Fishpot-B/C*.

Meanwhile, the designers of commercial aircraft wasted no time either. In the late 1940s British and American companies already had jet airliners on the drawing boards; the 44-seat, four-turbojet de Havilland DH.106 Comet 1 first flew on 27th July 1949 and commenced scheduled services on 2nd May 1952. Of course, the Soviet Union joined the race as soon as it was able. The creation of an indigenous jet airliner was not only meant to reduce the time needed to take passengers from A to B – important though this objective was, given the Soviet Union's vast territory and underdeveloped surface transport network – but was also a matter of national prestige. This politically important task was entrusted to the nation's leading designer of commercial aircraft – OKB-156 led by Andrey Nikolayevich Tupolev, the doyen of Soviet heavy aircraft construction. (In 1991 OKB-156 became the Aviation Scientific & Technical Complex named after Andrey N. Tupolev (ANTK imeni Tupoleva – *aviatsionnyy naoochno-tekhnicheskiy **kompleks***), often referred to as ANTK Tupolev in the West. Today it is known as the Tupolev Public Limited Company (OAO Tupolev – *otkrytoye aktsio**ner**noye obshchestvo*).)

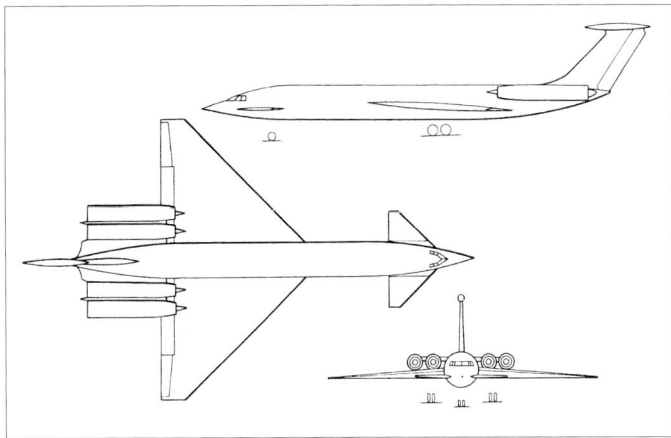

A three-view of the projected Il'yushin IL-66 supersonic airliner.

The first Soviet commercial jet was the Tu-104 *Camel* medium-haul airliner. To save time Andrey N. Tupolev opted for maximum structural and systems commonality with the Tu-16 *Badger* twin-turbojet medium bomber – in effect, only the fuselage was new. Though not the world's first jet airliner to fly (the maiden flight took place on 17th June 1955) and carry fare-paying passengers, the Tu-104 took Aeroflot Soviet Airlines, the sole national air carrier, into the jet age and became the world's first jet airliner in sustained commercial service following the forced withdrawal of the Comet 1 after a series of fatal accidents.

Several years later the original scenario of jet aircraft technology development was repeated. As supersonic flight became reality in the 1950s, military aviation was the first to benefit from this progress, but almost immediately aircraft designers on both sides of the Iron Curtain began preparing projects of supersonic airliners – or, to use a term coined shortly thereafter, supersonic transports (SSTs) – as well. As might be imagined, the first of these projects were based on supersonic bombers.

The early SST projects developed in the Soviet Union warrant a brief description – just to show the different approaches taken by different OKBs.

The OKB-240 design bureau headed by Sergey V. Il'yushin made its only known foray into supersonic airliner design in 1959

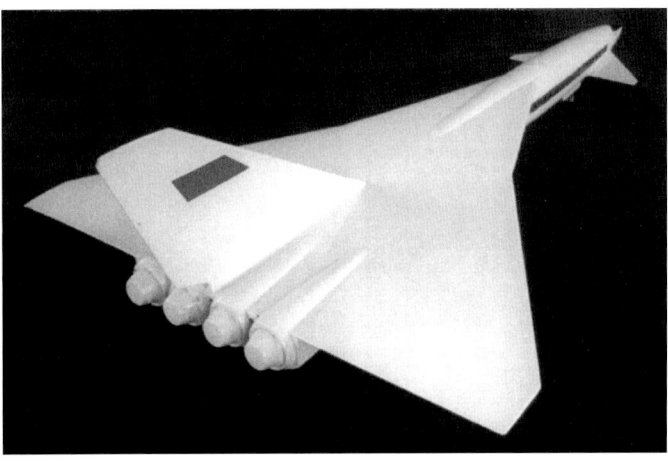

This model shows the final configuration of the M-53 with high-set cranked-delta wings, canards and the engines located all together.

at the initiative of its leader. Designated IL-66, the projected SST had a tail-first configuration with large low-set cropped-delta wings and low-set all-moving cropped-delta canard foreplanes; the sharply swept tail terminated in a large cigar-shaped fairing. The twin-wheel nose landing gear unit retracted forward and the four-wheel main gear bogies inward into the fuselage. Four turbojets having axisymmetrical air intakes with shock cones were mounted in pairs on the aft fuselage sides, echoing the layout of the subsonic IL-62 *Classic* long-haul airliner. Il'yushin expected engines of the required thrust class to be available; at that time the engine design bureaux led by Vladimir Ya. Klimov (OKB-117) and Sergey K. Tumanskiy (OKB-300) were hard at work on afterburning turbojets (the VK-15B and the R15-300 respectively) which could prove suitable for the IL-66. The VK-15B had a take-off rating of 15,600 kgp (34,400 lbst), and the R15-300 was rated at 11,200-13,500 kgp (24,700-29,770 lbst).

According to preliminary design studies, the IL-66 was expected to carry 60-100 passengers to distances of up to 7,300 km (4,537 miles) at a cruising speed of 3,000 km/h (1,865 mph). The aircraft could be used on long-haul routes, such as the Moscow-Khabarovsk service to the Soviet Far East. In the designers' opinion, putting an SST into operation on that route would offer a considerable time saving for passengers and would be economically viable.

In the spring of 1960 Sergey V. Il'yushin approached the Soviet Council of Ministers (that is, government) with a proposal that the IL-66 project be included in the prototype construction plan drawn up annually by the State Committee for Aviation Hardware (GKAT – *Gosudarstvennyy komitet po aviatsionnoy tekhnike*). GKAT was the name by which the former Ministry of Aircraft Industry (MAP – *Ministerstvo aviatsionnoy promyshlennosti*) was known in 1957-65 before reverting to its original name and 'rank'. However, the Committee's leaders took a justifiably sceptical view of the project, which was obviously far too ambitious and clearly beyond the technological capacity of the Soviet aircraft industry at that time. Il'yushin was advised to study the feasibility of an airliner with a lower supersonic speed, featuring an airframe made of the usual aluminium alloys (the IL-66 project was based on the use of heat-resistant steel alloys).

Following these instructions, OKB-240 brought out a completely reworked project redesignated IL-72. Its design specifications were more realistic – the seating capacity was reduced to 40-60 passengers, the cruising speed target was Mach 2.2. Lower speed made it possible to choose aluminium alloys as construction materials. The range was expected to be 4,000-4,500 km (2,486-2,797 miles). On 14th February 1961, these design targets were discussed at the OKB's Technical council. However, the OKB was unable to proceed with this project, its resources being overtaxed by work on the IL-18 *Coot* turboprop airliner, the IL-38 *May* anti-submarine warfare aircraft and by the construction of the IL-62 prototype. No information is available on the layout of the IL-72.

Studies in this field were also made by Vladimir M. Myasishchev's OKB-23 which came up with several unusual SST projects. Designated M-53, the aircraft came in a variety of project configurations based on OKB-23's strategic bombers/missile-carriers. One version shared the layout of the M-50/M-52 *Bounder* experimental bombers, featuring high-set cropped-delta wings with two engines on underwing pylons and two at the tips, conventional tail surfaces and a bicycle undercarriage. Another similar version called M-53A had four underwing engine nacelles and a tricycle undercarriage. Other versions derived from the unbuilt M-56/M-57 bombers were more radical, featuring a tail-first layout with cranked-delta wings and four underwing engines in spaced nacelles (M-53B) or paired lifting-body nacelles (M-53V). The most exotic variant was the M-53G using a tail-first layout with four engines housed in a common nacelle so that the nozzles were located between the twin vertical tails (this necessitated the use of a bicycle undercarriage). Various engines were considered, including the 11,000-kgp (24,250-lbst) Dobrynin VD-7K turbojet developed by OKB-36 in Rybinsk (Yaroslavl' Region, central Russia) and the projected 18,500-kgp (40,780-lbst) Zoobets RD16-17P turbojet developed by OKB-16 in Kazan', Tatar ASSR.

The ultimate version of the M-53, powered by four 17,000-kgp (37,480-lbst) Zoobets RD16-23 turbojets, was 51.3 m (168 ft 3^{11}/$_{16}$ in) long, with a wingspan of 27 m (88 ft 7 in) and a height on ground of 10.8 m (35 ft 5^{13}/$_{64}$ in). The aircraft was to have a take-off weight of 165 tons (363,760 lb) and a payload of 12 tons (26,455 lb), being flown by a crew of three and carrying 130 passengers. Range with maximum fuel was 6,000 km (3,726 miles), the cruising speed 2,200 km/h (1,366 mph) and the cruise altitude 16,000-17,000 m (52,490-55,770 ft). This version was submitted to GKAT for review on 29th August 1960, but the liquidation of the Myasishchev OKB two months later (for the second time in its history) brought all further work to an end.

Before describing the Tupolev OKB's early work in this field, it should be mentioned that two distinct design schools, or scientific methods, existed in the Soviet Union with regard to high-speed flight. One was headed by Professor Vladimir V. Stroominskiy at TsAGI, who was an avid proponent of swept wings; the other was led by Professor Pyotr P. Krasil'shchikov, who favoured delta wings. Being a member of the Soviet Academy of Sciences, Stroominskiy enjoyed great authority; also, he had an assertive personality and had a way of ramming his point home. Therefore most of the contemporary Soviet fighters and bombers, including such Tupolev types as the Tu-16 and the supersonic Tu-22 *Blinder* bomber, had swept wings. Yet this layout was inferior to the delta-wing layout in certain situations, limiting the designers' possibilities; foreign practice – primarily the French company Dassault Aviation's experience – showed that delta-wing fighters had an advantage over swept-wing designs with a high aspect ratio. Incidentally, the Mikoyan OKB had arrived at the same conclusion by testing the swept-wing Ye-2 prototypes and the similarly sized delta-wing Ye-4/Ye-6 series; the latter won, evolving into the MiG-21. It was much the same story in Pavel O. Sukhoi's OKB-51 – albeit the swept-wing Su-7 *Fitter-A* and the very similar delta-wing Su-9 both received the go-ahead, filling two different roles.

Now, the Tupolev OKB had been searching for the optimum layout of a heavy aircraft since 1948; General Designer Andrey N. Tupolev favoured swept wings, sharing Stroominskiy's views on the subject. Yet, this did not prevent the OKB's designers from exploring alternative layouts, including delta wings, and combining the OKB's own design features with them. This was influ-

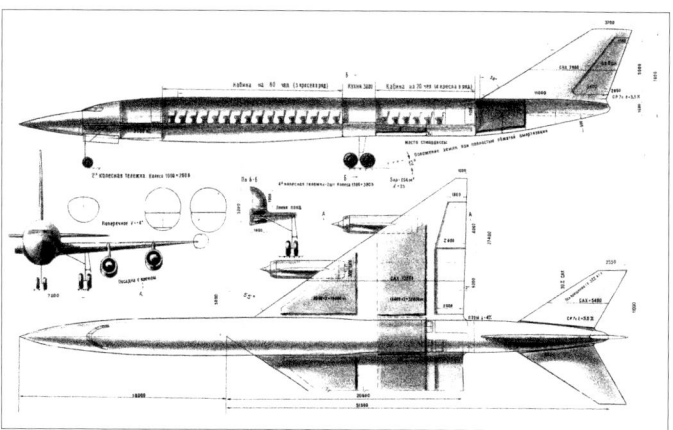

Above: One of the Myasishchev M-53's many project configurations featuring simple delta wings, conventional tail surfaces and spaced engine nacelles. The front view shows the alternative wingtip placement of the outer engines. The forward cabin seats 80 passengers five-abreast; the rear one seats 20 four-abreast.

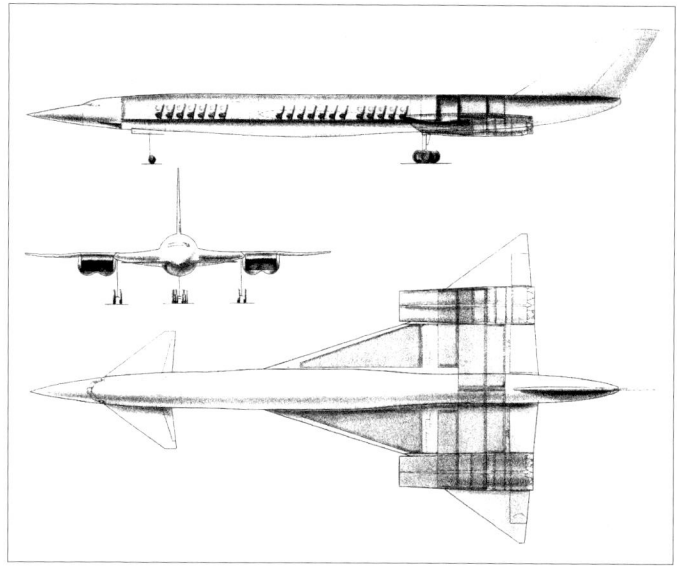

Another project configuration of the M-53 with a tail-first layout, double-delta wings, paired engines and a bicycle undercarriage.

enced by such aircraft as the British Avro 707 experimental aircraft, the Avro 698 Vulcan strategic bomber (for which, incidentally, the Avro 707 was a proof-of-concept vehicle), the American Convair F-102 Delta Dagger fighter and other types. The results of preliminary calculations were in favour of the tailless-delta layout; yet, in keeping with TsAGI's (read: Stroominskiy's) recommendations the '105' (the Tu-22's immediate precursor) and '106' (a stillborn derivative of the Tu-22) were designed along conventional swept-wing lines. The Tupolev OKB's first delta-wing bomber project, the '103', was shelved at the preliminary design (PD) stage; it was not until development of the aircraft which is the subject of this book – the Tu-144 SST – commenced that the ideas embodied in the '103' project were dusted off.

The event that led Tupolev to change his attitude to delta wings came in late 1955, when some serious discussions on supersonic aircraft design took place in the Soviet and foreign aviation press. (Here 'Soviet aviation press' refers to specialised trade publications which were distributed on a need-to-know basis.) Numerous publications in the trade press gave proof positive that the area rule reducing harmful interference between airframe components and hence drag works not only at high subsonic speeds but also at supersonic speeds, making it possible to create an aircraft designed for speeds up to Mach 2.5 with an acceptably high lift/drag ratio. Yet, the optimum layout had to be chosen in order to implement this rule. Here, delta wings gave the designers wide scope for work, making it possible to carry enough fuel, accommodate equipment, provide a spacious cabin offering the passengers a high degree of comfort, and fit into the existing airport infrastructure and air traffic control (ATC) system.

By 1955 the Soviet aircraft designers were able to research materials on the tailless aircraft of the German designer Alexander Lippisch, the piston-engined Northrop XB-35 Flying Wing bomber prototype and its turbojet-powered YB-49 Flying Wing derivative, the technical reports of the Northrop Corporation and Messerschmitt AG, as well as the tailless aircraft projects developed in the Soviet Union by Roberto Bartini, Aleksandr S. Moskalyov and other designers. Yet, all of these aircraft were subsonic; no trustworthy materials could be found on how the tailless layout would behave at supersonic speeds, or in take-off and landing modes.

Although built with conventional swept wings and conventional tail surfaces, the Tu-22, which entered flight test on 21st June 1958, provided invaluable practical experience of resolving the stability and control problems of heavy multi-mode aircraft. Equally important was the experience gained with the Tu-121 supersonic ground-launched cruise missile, which was likewise tested in 1958, and its production derivative, the Tu-123 *Yastreb* (Hawk) reconnaissance drone, which first flew in 1961, as they had delta wings.

In the early 1960s the Tupolev OKB embarked on its first SST project provisionally designated '134' (Tu-134) – the first aircraft to bear the designation. In accordance with the OKB's practice, the project was based on a bomber design – the '106A' project – and became the responsibility of the Tupolev OKB's PD projects section headed by Sergey M. Yeger.

Two layouts were considered (with shoulder-mounted and low-set swept wings), each with two alternative powerplants – two 21,500-kgp (47,400-lbst) Kuznetsov P-6 (NK-6) afterburning turbofans or four 14,200-kgp (31,300-lbst) Dobrynin VD-19R2 afterburning turbojets in wing-mounted nacelles. The low-wing version was 45.9 m (150 ft 7 in) long and 10.5 m (34 ft $5^{25}/_{64}$ in) tall, while the high-wing version was 42.15 m (138 ft $3^{29}/_{64}$ in) long and 9.3 m (30 ft $6^{4}/_{64}$ in) tall. Both versions had a wing span of 23.6 m (77 ft $0^{59}/_{64}$ in), a maximum payload of 8,000 kg (17,640 lb), a cruising speed of 2,100 km/h (1,304 mph) and a seating capacity of 50-70 passengers. Estimated range was 3,000-3,500 km (1,863-2,173 miles) supersonic and 4,000-4,500 km (2,484-2,795 miles) subsonic. The work proceeded no further work than the PD stage and the Tu-134 designation was reused in 1963 for a twin-turbofan subsonic short-haul airliner (NATO reporting name *Crusty*).

A further impetus to the Tupolev OKB's work on SSTs came when the Council of Ministers issued directive No.1057-437 on 3rd October 1960. Pursuant to this directive the Myasishchev OKB was closed down, being absorbed by Vladimir N. Chelomey's OKB-52, which spelled the end for the Myasishchev M-56 missile strike aircraft project. With the competitor thus eliminated, the Tupolev OKB was tasked with developing a long-range supersonic reconnaissance/strike aircraft, the project receiving the designation '135' (Tu-135). A large number of alternative layouts were considered, the ultimate one being a tail-first layout with delta wings, a single vertical tail, high-set canard foreplanes and paired engines in underwing nacelles, which provided high design performance by the standards of the day. The large amount of wind tunnel work (six versions of the wings alone were tested, including take-off and landing modes) gave ample material which was used later in the development of the Tu-144 SST – even though the Tu-135 itself again remained a paper project.

Also, in the early 1960s TsAGI began exploring a new type of lifting surfaces – compound-sweep wings consisting of basic wings having a moderate aspect ratio and low aspect ratio leading-edge root extensions (LERXes). Both parts could have various planforms; the basic wings could be trapezoidal, swept-back or of delta (or cropped-delta) planform, whereas the LERXes could be delta-shaped, ogival or even rectangular. As early as 1959, TsAGI aerodynamicist Leonid Ye. Vasil'yev had demonstrated that by choosing the optimum combination of basic wing shape and LERX shape it was possible to create wings with any required difference in the aerodynamic centre's position at low subsonic speeds and supersonic speeds – even wings where the aerodynamic centre does not shift at all as the aircraft goes supersonic. This took care of the longitudinal trim problem for any tailless aircraft (or aircraft with a small horizontal tail) without entailing a significant deterioration of the lift/drag ratio at supersonic speeds.

Further calculations and practical experiments conducted by Leonid Ye. Vasil'yev, V. S. Kuznetsov and Yu. A. Chirkov at TsAGI revealed a whole range of other important fundamental characteristics of compound-sweep wings. Specifically:

• at subsonic speeds the lift of such wings has a non-linear, benign characteristic – wing lift is retained up to high angles of attack (AOAs); thus, such wings generate considerably more lift than the basic wings minus LERXes;

• the extremely broad chord at the root (thanks to the LERXes) makes it possible to use airfoils with a very low thickness/chord ratio, which reduces wave drag and improves the lift/drag ratio above Mach 1 and allows a large portion of the internal volume to be used for fuel tankage;

• the lift is generated along a considerable length as the slipstream flows across compound-sweep wings, which reduces the intensity of the sonic boom;

• thanks to the broad chord, compound-sweep wings have a low friction drag coefficient at both subsonic, transonic and supersonic speeds;

• compound-sweep wings ensure a high lift/drag ratio at supersonic speeds;

• compound-sweep wings have favourable structural and strength characteristics.

That said, it's not surprising that compound-sweep wings have found large-scale use both in the Soviet Union/Russia and elsewhere. It deserves mention that much of the information obtained experimentally by TsAGI was obtained using wind tunnel models developed by the Tupolev OKB.

Chapter 1

The Tu-144 is Born

The initial attempts to create an SST by simply adapting the design of a supersonic bomber – an approach tried successfully by the Tupolev OKB with its subsonic airliners of the 1950s – showed that this 'quick fix' approach did not work. This was because the early heavy supersonic combat jets, which could in theory have served as the basis for an SST, were only intended for a brief supersonic dash over the target, with their airframes and systems designed accordingly, whereas an SST had to be capable of sustained cruise at a speed of at least Mach 2.0. Additionally, the character of airline operations, with their more frequent flights as compared to a combat aircraft, placed higher demands on the reliability of all of the airliner's structures and systems, especially considering the longer duration of supersonic cruise. Little by little, having analysed all options open to them, aircraft designers on both sides of the Iron Curtain became convinced that a supersonic airliner had to be a 'clean sheet of paper' design if it was to be economically efficient.

In the early 1960s the British Aircraft Corporation (BAC) and the French consortium Aérospatiale teamed up to begin practical design work on a supersonic airliner aptly named Concorde. Cruising at Mach 2+, the Concorde was to carry 120-140 passengers over a distance of 6,000-6,500 km (3,730-4,040 miles). Concurrently, proceeding from their perspective of the world market for supersonic airliners, all of the major US transport aircraft manufacturers (Boeing, Lockheed and Douglas) started work on much larger SSTs designed to carry 250-300 passengers over 7,000-8,000 km (4,350-4,970 miles) with a cruising speed of up to Mach 3. Even making allowances for America's huge financial resources and technological potential, these were 'pie in the sky' projects which were 30 or even 40 years ahead of their time; in fact, they were close in their ideology to the second-generation supersonic transport (SST-2) concept whose prospects, even now, are nebulous.

An assessment of the future SST's operating conditions made by Soviet experts (with due regard to the national aircraft indus-

Looking like a collection of prizes, these simple 'stick with wings' models served for exploring the delta wing shape and variations thereof (pure delta, more-or-less cropped delta and double delta with different leading-edge sweep angles) in TsAGI's supersonic wind tunnel.

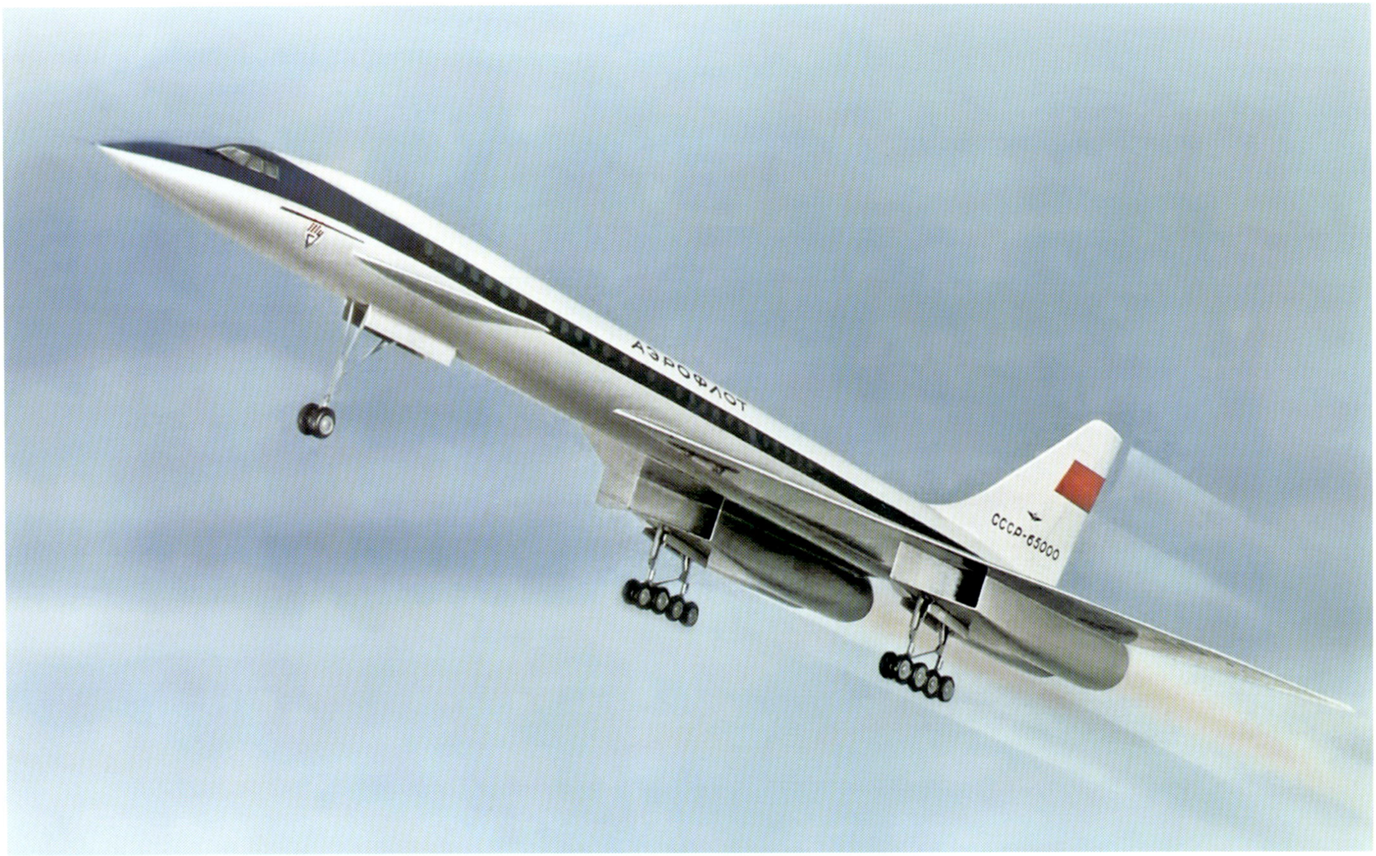
АЭРОФЛОТ
СССР-65000

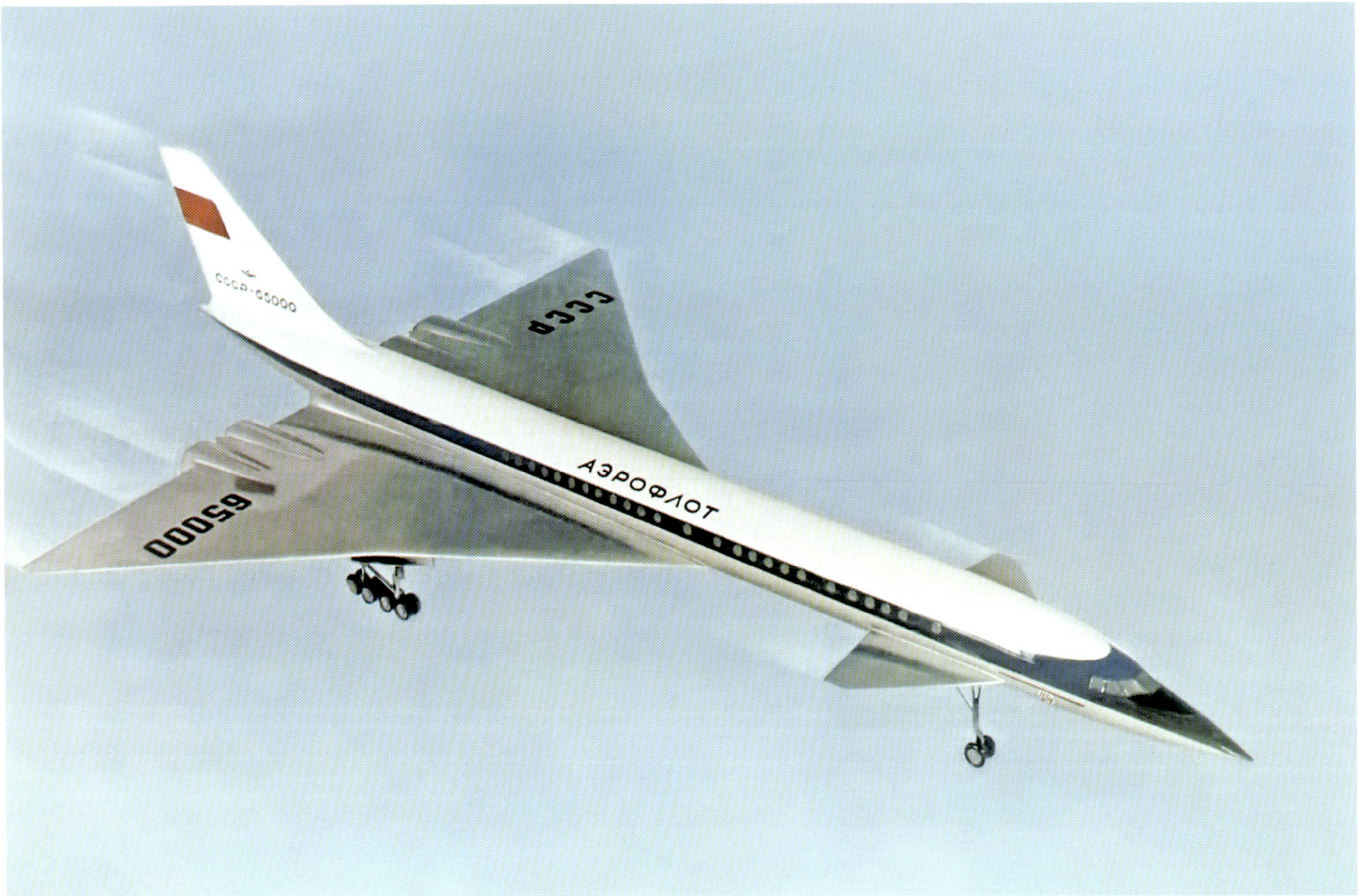
СССР-65000
СССР
АЭРОФЛОТ
65000

Chapter 1 - The Tu-144 is Born

Left and below left: These pictures from the project documents show one of the Tu-144's earliest project configurations based on the unbuilt Tu-135. It retains the bomber's tail-first layout, its cranked-delta wings and engine nacelles whose upper portions are angled upwards. Note the complex eight-wheel main gear units featuring tandem pairs of struts with four-wheel bogies. The registration CCCP-65000 may hint at the year of development (1965) and would eventually be worn by a production Tu-134A in late 1975.

Above right: Three-quarters rear view of the same desktop model. The shape of the engine nozzles suggests Kuznetsov NK-6 turbofans.

Right: One more aspect of the same model. The nose is conventional (not drooping).

Below: A three-view of a very similar Tu-144 project configuration having shoulder-mounted (rather than low-set) canards and clipped wingtips. The figures in the centre denote the take-off weight, seating capacity, cruising speed, effective range, take-off run and wing area for the normal (left) and high gross weight configurations.

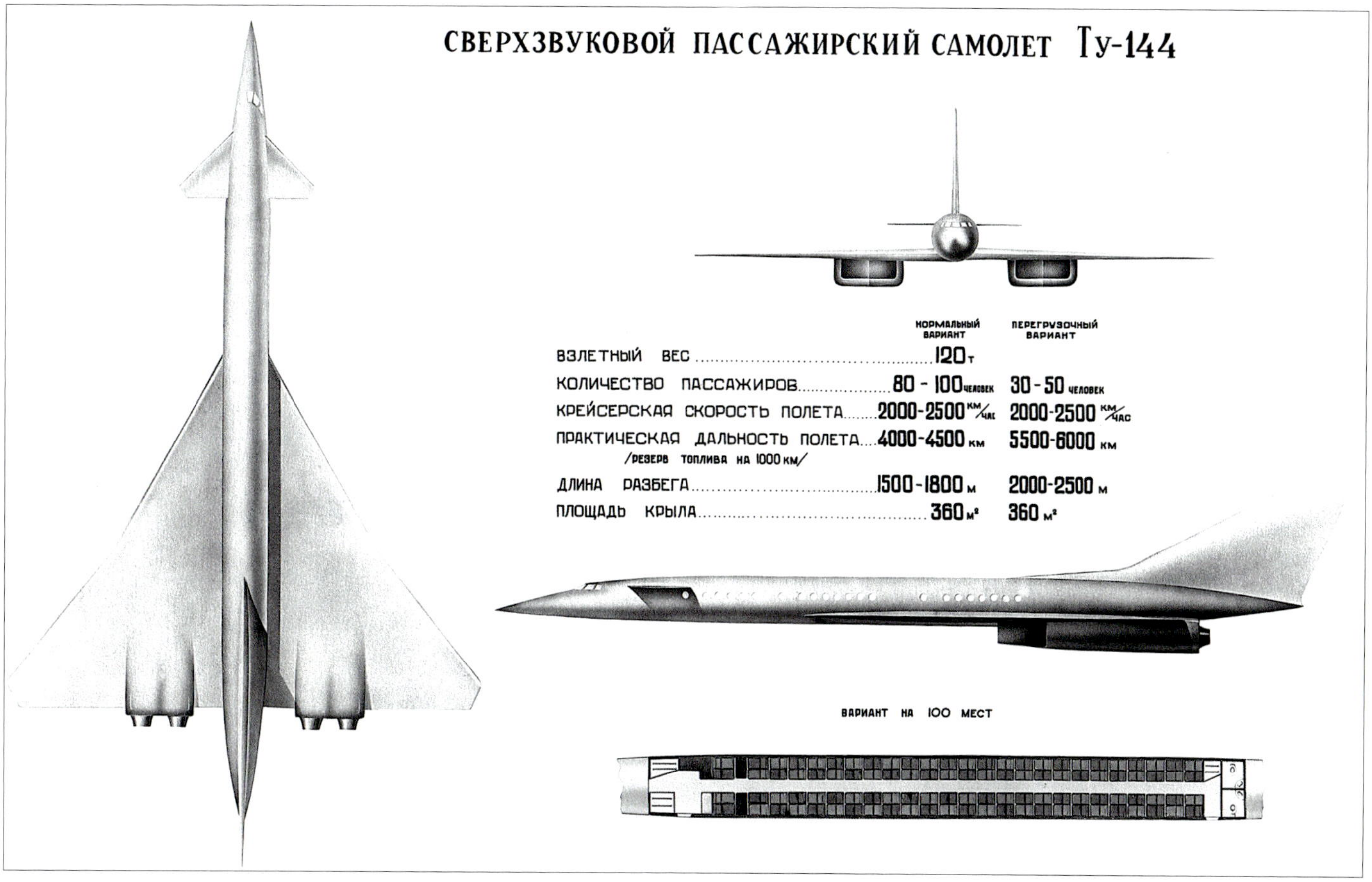

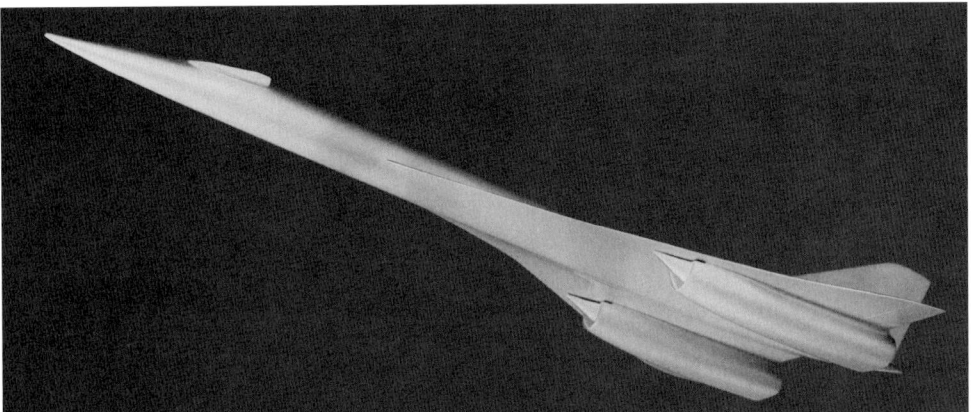

A desktop model depicting an early PD project configuration of the Tu-144 featuring near-ogival wings, fixed canards and widely spaced nacelles with a common 'Mirage-style' semi-circular air intake for each pair of engines. Note the vertical tail with sweepback on both leading and trailing edges.

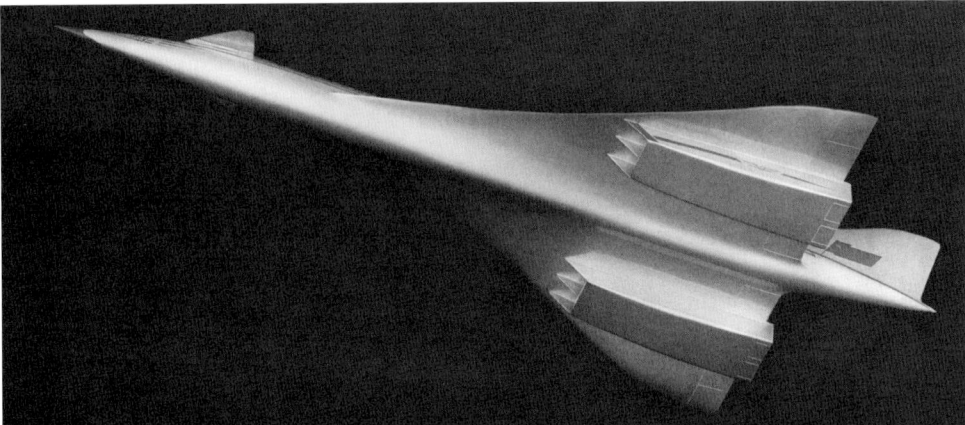

A very similar model showing two-dimensional intakes with vertical splitters, horizontal airflow control ramps and what appears to be clamshell thrust reversers on all four engines. This view shows that the wings are not quite ogival, featuring straight leading-edge sections.

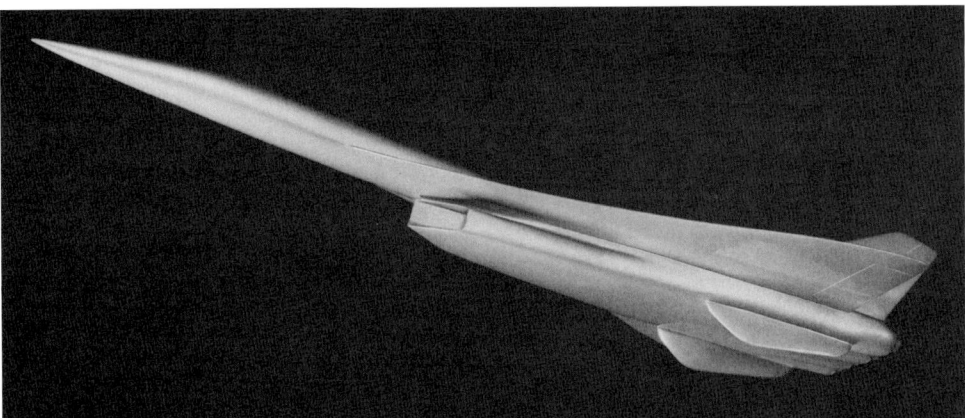

This model shows one of the tailless-delta PD project versions with twin vertical tails augmented by twin ventral fins. The engines are grouped in a common nacelle with an XB-70 style V-shaped front set apart from the wing undersurface and vertical intake ramps.

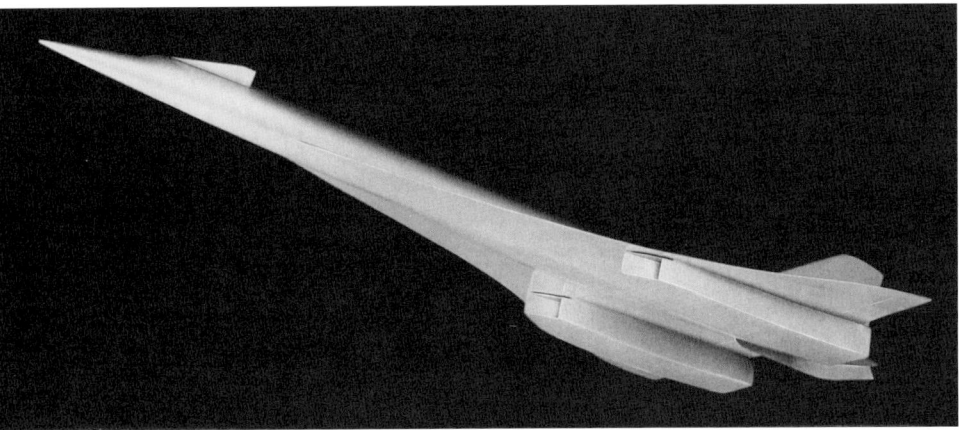

Another variation on the project form with fixed canards and spaced nacelles. Here the intakes have vertical airflow control ramps. Note the addition of a ventral fin on the centreline.

Chapter 1 - The Tu-144 is Born

This model in Aeroflot livery has a single vertical tail and a similar common engine package with a 'Valkyriesque' intake, but the wing leading edge acts as the boundary layer splitter and the engine nozzles are enclosed by a boxy structure. The registration CCCP-72000 was later used in real life for a prototype of the Antonov An-72 *Coaler-A* STOL tactical transport.

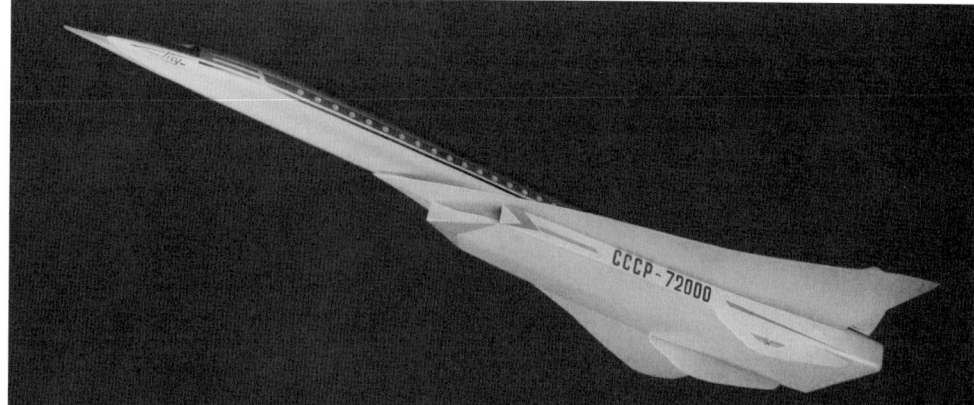

This model wearing the same registration CCCP-72000 combines twin tails with canards and has an air intake divided into four channels with horizontal airflow control ramps. Note the slight difference in wing shape and the teardrop-shaped housing for the nose gear unit.

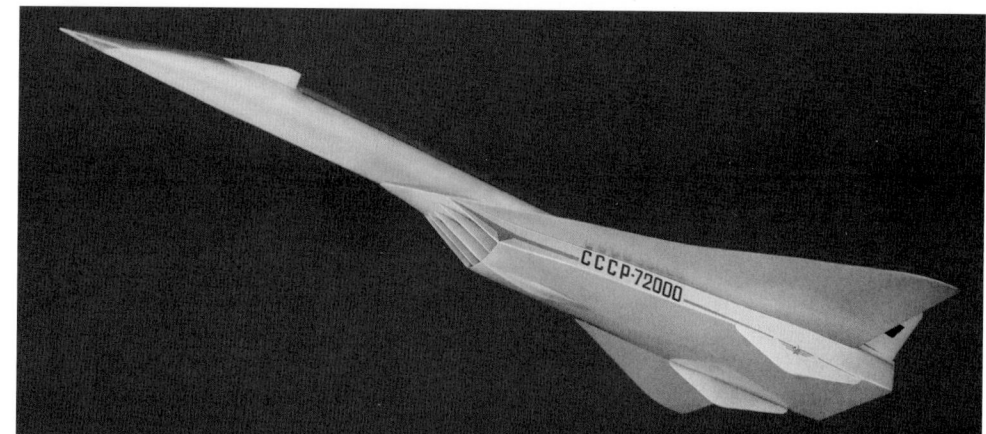

Another variation on the common nacelle theme; the model has one vertical tail and wings of almost classic delta shape, with no perceptible leading-edge kink. This time the intakes are grouped in pairs flanking a so-called centrebody which houses the nose gear unit; note the bulges outboard of the nacelle for the main gear units.

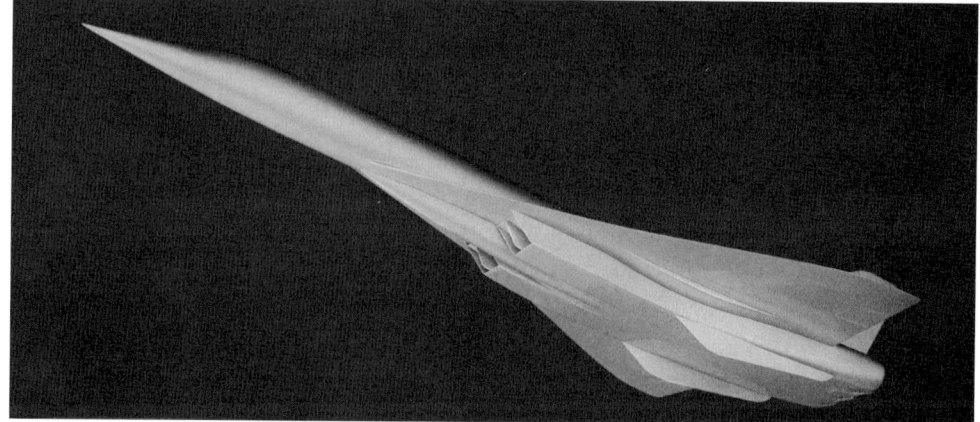

A similar model differing in having cranked-delta wings with long LERXes and outward-canted twin tails. The centrebody appears smaller because the intakes are placed further forward, with longer inlet ducts. Note how the rear end of the nacelle curves upwards.

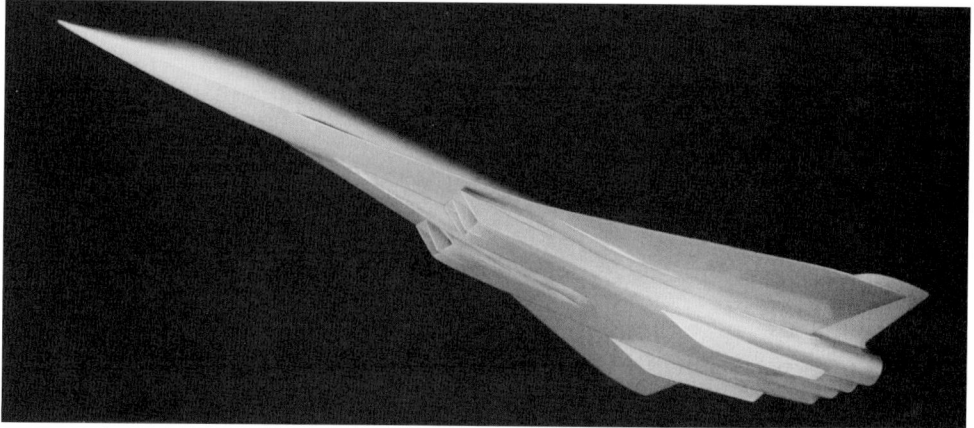

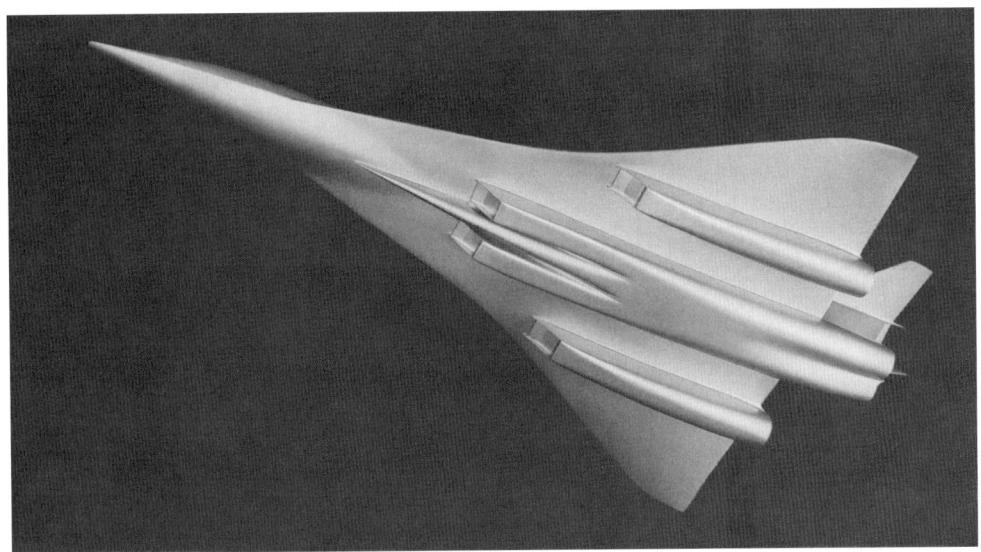

Left: This model depicts one of the most unorthodox configurations, with quasi-ogival wings, a T-tail, two engines in the fuselage and a further two in individual nacelles, all with horizontal intake ramps.

Below and below left: Four display models of PD project configurations of the Tu-144. The difference in wing planform and in fuselage fineness ratio is clearly visible.

Right and below right: Several early sketches of the Tu-144.

Bottom right: This model marked CCCP-7200 is one step closer to the final configuration.

try's current technological level and its prospects for the near future, as well as to the capabilities of the Soviet economy and to Aeroflot's needs) showed that the best way to go for the Soviet designers was to develop an aircraft similar to the Anglo-French Concorde in its design performance. The Soviet aircraft industry's research establishments and manufacturing enterprises were now facing a whole range of scientific and technical challenges which neither subsonic commercial aviation nor supersonic military aviation had had to deal with before. First of all, the supersonic airliner's lift/drag ratio at Mach 2.0-2.2 needed to be improved radically in order to obtain the specified 6,500-km (4,040-mile) range with 100-120 passengers in supersonic cruise. The target figure was a lift/drag ratio of 7.5-8.0 or better, which was much higher than anything hitherto achieved with Soviet supersonic

Chapter 1 - The Tu-144 is Born

bombers and missile strike aircraft in the same flight conditions. By comparison, the design lift/drag ratio values at Mach 2.0 were 4.4 for the Tu-22, 5.5 for the Myasishchev M-50, 5.6 for its unflown M-52 derivative and 6.4 for the projected Tu-135 and M-56 missile strike aircraft.

The problems of a heavy aircraft's stability and handling at subsonic, transonic and supersonic speeds and practical methods of balancing the aircraft in these conditions with minimum aerodynamic losses had to be addressed. Sustained flight at Mach 2+ involved research to achieve the necessary structural strength at airframe temperatures close to 100-120°C (212-248°F); heat-resistant structural materials, lubricants and sealants had to be created, as well as airframe structures able to withstand prolonged kinetic heating, including heating/cooling cycles and the attendant expansion and contraction of the airframe. The engines had to meet very stringent requirements, being powerful, fuel-efficient and able to run stably in sustained supersonic cruise; the engine air intakes needed to be adjustable for a wide range of altitudes and speeds. The parameters of the engines and their intakes had to be harmonised, with due regard for area-ruling, ensuring the required airflow with the lowest possible aerodynamic losses.

Sustained supersonic cruise was best performed at high altitude; thus, new life support systems had to be devised to provide a comfortable environment for the passengers and crew at altitudes up to 20,000 m (65,620 ft) under kinetic heating conditions. New avionics enabling automated flight, accurate navigation in sustained supersonic cruise and automatic landing were needed. To ensure the SST's seamless integration into the existing air transport systems, the peculiarities of Soviet and foreign airline transport practice, as well as those of existing airports and air traffic control (ATC) systems, also had to be taken into account.

All these factors, as well as progress made on SST programmes in the West, were carefully studied at TsAGI, in the Tupolev OKB

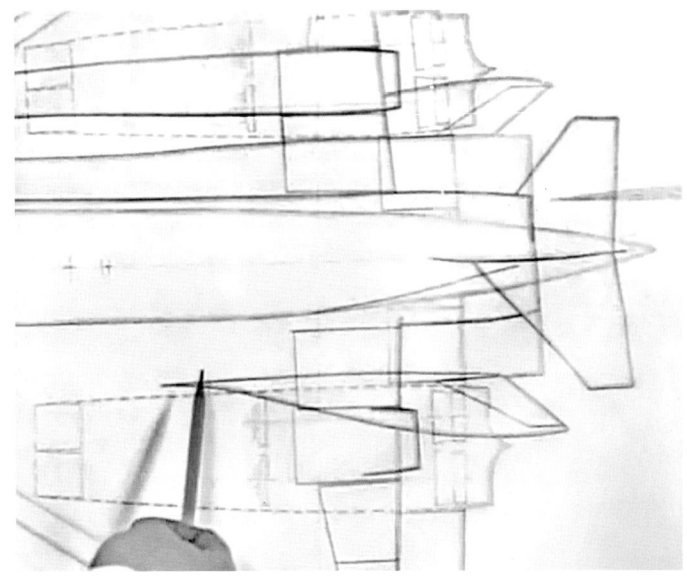

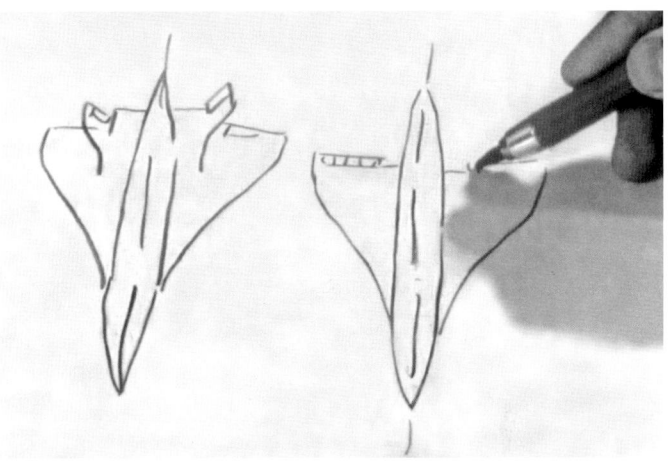

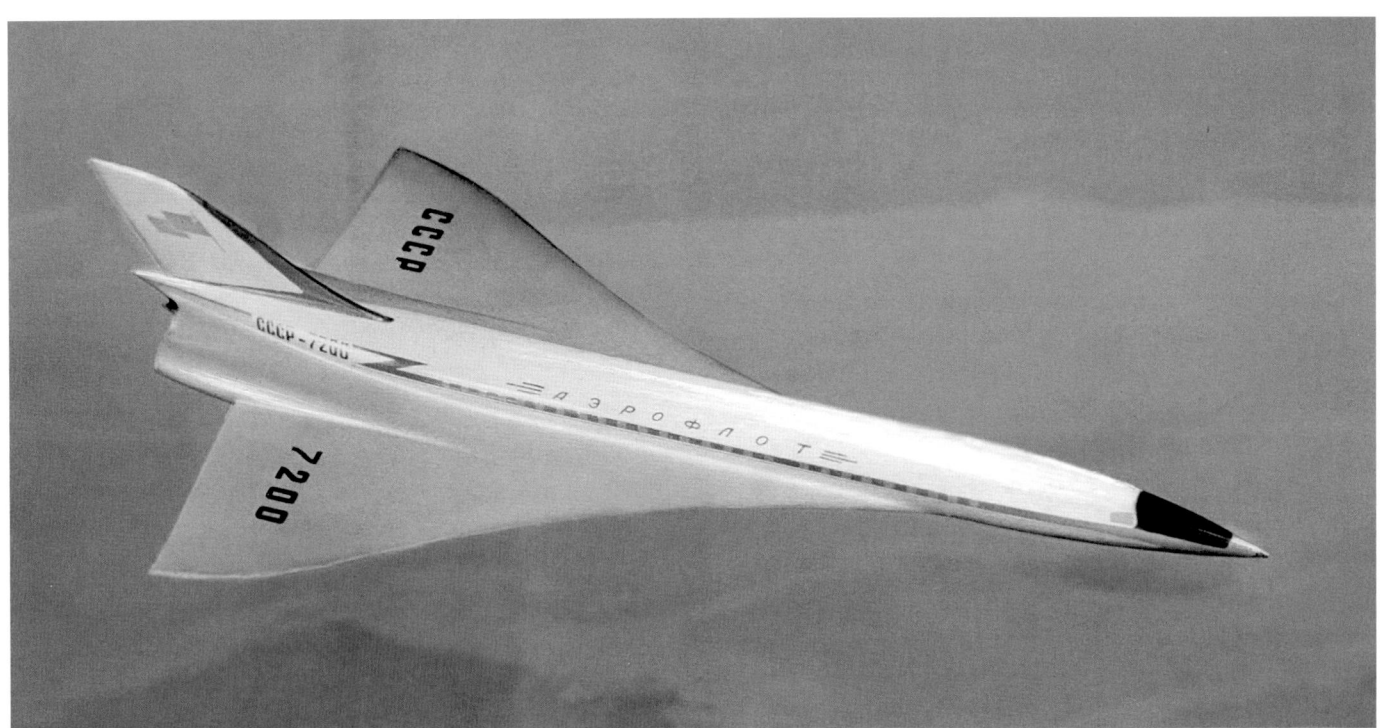

Left and below left: Two more views of the model depicted on the preceding page. The model has ogival wings and a vertical tail with strong sweepback on both leading and trailing edges. Note the very short rear fuselage and the way how the engines are located well aft, the long inlet ducts curving upwards to 'blend through' the wings; the paired air intakes are divided by a centrebody housing the nose gear unit. The nose features a short drooping nosecone with a large anti-glare panel.

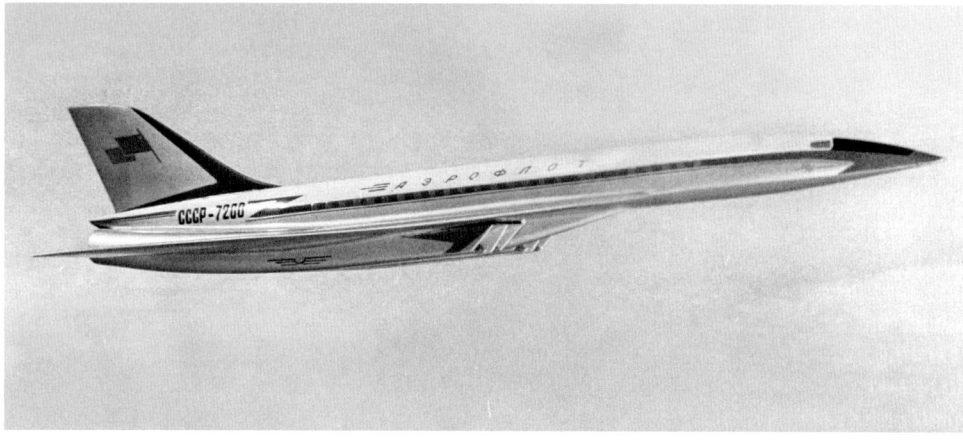

Bottom: The forward fuselage of a similar model with the nose visor drooped for take-off/landing. The upper side of the visor incorporates narrow windows affording a degree of forward visibility when the visor is raised. Note the different location of the nose gear unit (well ahead of the engine air intakes) and the 1950s-style circular Tupolev OKB logo on the nose.

and other research and design establishments involved. The Soviet supersonic airliner programme named SPS-1 (*sverkhzvookovoy passazheerskiy samolyot pervovo pokoleniya* – first-generation supersonic airliner, or SST-1) was officially kicked off by Council of Ministers/Communist Party Central Committee joint directive No.798-271 issued on 16th July 1963, MAP order No.276 to the same effect following ten days later. The aircraft was designated Tu-144; this followed the tradition established with the Tu-104,

according to which the Tupolev OKB's post-war airliners were designated in the 1x4 series – much like Boeing's 7x7 system.

In accordance with the Council of Ministers directive and MAP order the Tupolev OKB was to develop an aircraft with the following performance:
• cruising speed, 2,300-2,700 km/h (1,428-1,677 mph);
• seating capacity, 80-100 passengers;
• range with a 120,000… 130,000-kg (264,550… 286,600-lb) normal take-off weight, 4,000-4,500 km (2,480-2,795 miles);
• range in maximum TOW configuration with 30-50 passengers and external fuel tanks (! – *Auth.*), 6,000-6,500 km (3,730-4,040 miles).

With a normal take-off weight the Tu-144 was to operate from Class A airfields; this means a runway length of 3,250 m (10,660 ft). In maximum TOW configuration a so-called unclassed airfield with a runway in excess of 3,250 m was required.

The Tupolev OKB was asked to look into the possibility of giving the Tu-144 intercontinental range, which would enable non-stop flights to the USA. The CofM directive and the MAP order called for the construction of five Tu-144s in 1966-67, including two static/fatigue test airframes.

As will be seen from the above, the Tu-144 did not meet Aeroflot's requirement of being able to operate the 6,280-km

Chapter 1 - The Tu-144 is Born

Top: Almost there: This model – again marked CCCP-65000 – shows a higher fuselage fineness ratio, larger wings of different planform and a different vertical tail with no trailing-edge sweep. Note how the engine nacelle terminated in line with the wing trailing edge.

Above: Another model with the same registration which is even closer to the real thing. Note the longer rear fuselage and the more pointed nose-cone.

Right: Three-quarters rear view of the model at the top of the page. Note the structure around the engine nozzles.

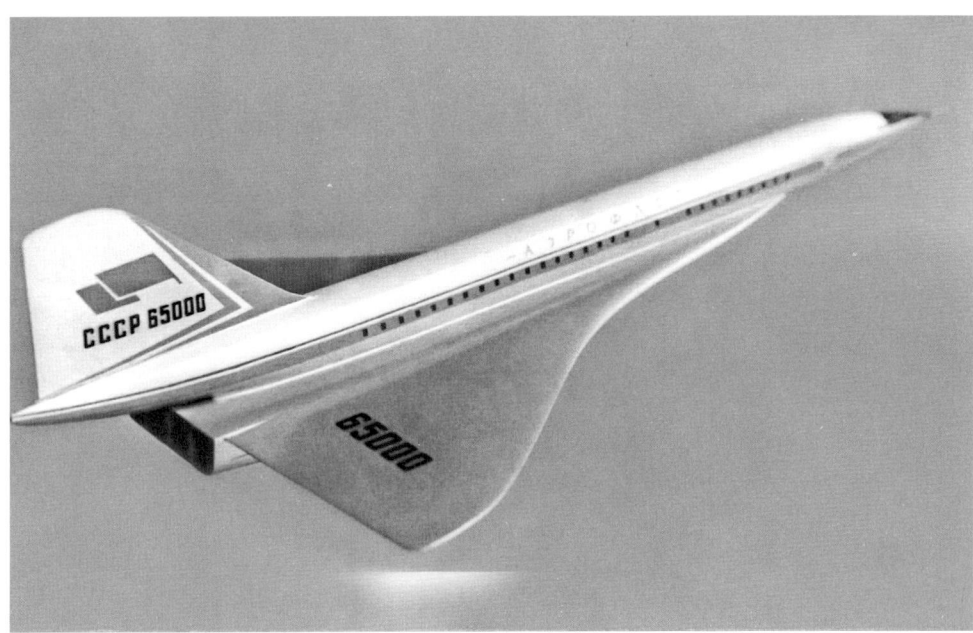

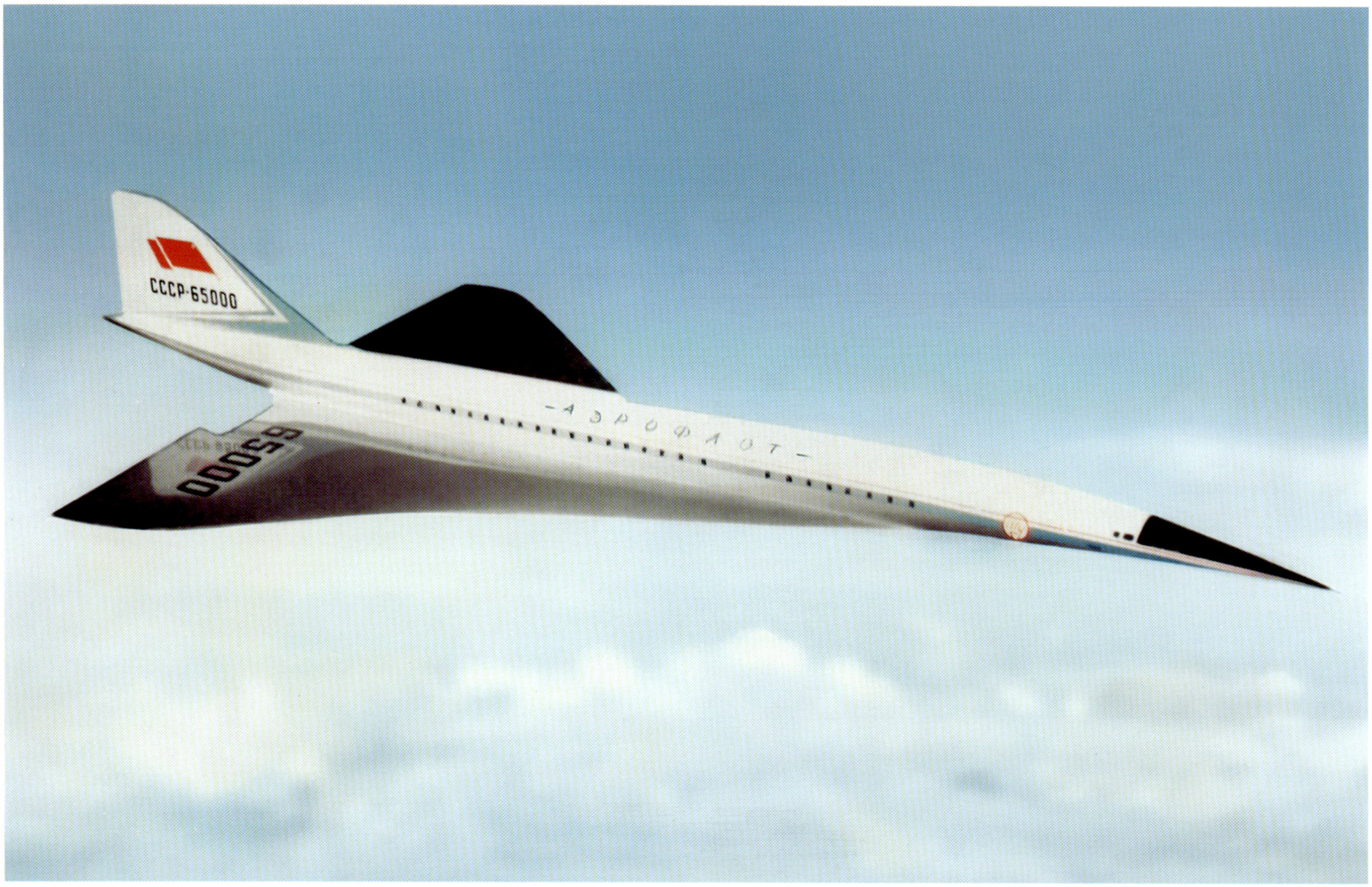
СССР-65000
65000
–АЭРОФЛОТ–

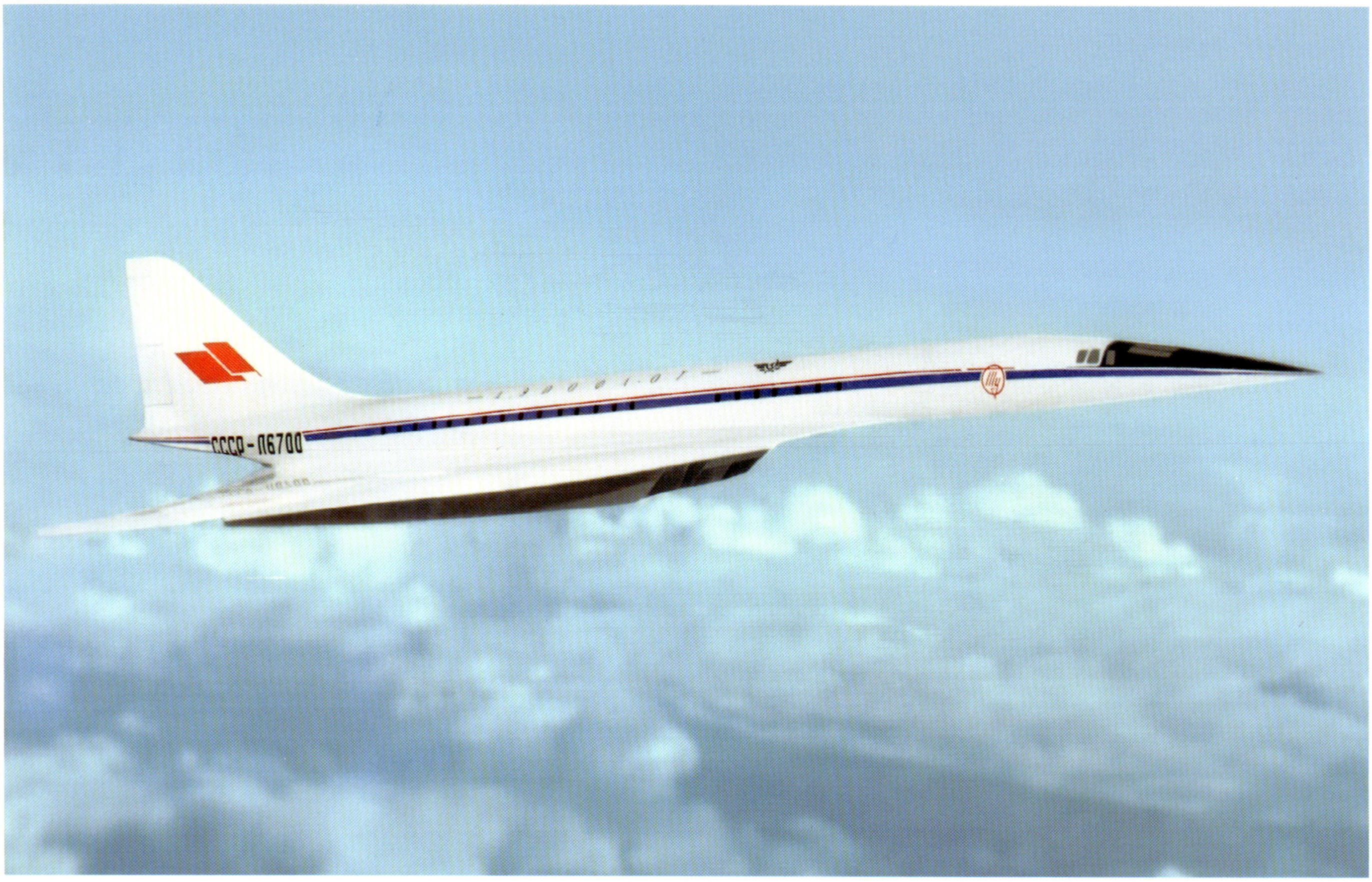

Chapter 1 - The Tu-144 is Born

Left: A different angle on the model depicted in the second photo on page 19. The engine nozzles are actually located short of the wing trailing edge.

Below left: This model shows the definitive *izdeliye* 044 version of the Tu-144. Oddly enough, it wears the old-style registration CCCP-Л6700 (SSSR-L6700 in Cyrillic characters) under a system that was no longer in use, having been discontinued in 1958.

Right: This view of the same model shows the bulges on the wings' upper surface over the mainwheel wells.

Below right: A metal desktop model similar to the *izdeliye* 044; the ventral strakes are still there and the aircraft appears to have a stepped nose.

(3,900-mile) Moscow-Khabarovsk service non-stop with a normal payload. Also, the speed specified in the abovesaid documents exceeded the maximum design speed at which relatively cheap and easy-to-use ordinary aluminium alloys with a low heat resistance could be used. Aware of the technical problems (notably those associated with achieving the range required for flying non-stop from Moscow to Khabarovsk), the government authorised the designers to proceed in two stages; an operating range of 4,000-4,500 km was to be achieved initially and extended to 6,500 km during the second stage.

During the time it took to design and build the Tu-144, four Council of Ministers/Communist Party Central Committee directives were passed and more than ten rulings issued by the CofM Presidium's Commission on Defence Industry Matters (VPK – *Voyenno-promyshlennaya komissiya*). These documents either revised the design specifications and programme schedule or contained instructions to various enterprises and institutions participating in the SPS-1 programme. More often than not, the deadlines set forth in the documents signed by even the highest-ranking officials were not met – for perfectly legitimate reasons, not because someone was trying to sabotage the programme. With a task of such a grand scale and unprecedented complexity, such delays were inevitable.

There have been claims that the Tu-144 was created entirely by up-and-coming young specialists. Nothing could be farther from the truth; with all due credit to young innovators, you cannot beat experience. As was his wont, General Designer Andrey N. Tupolev personally picked the people who would handle the most complex and high-priority tasks, not trusting anyone else to do it; he tried to find that optimum combination of young talent and maturity that had always assured success in the past. Until his death in harness in 1972 he personally supervised the key aspects of the Tu-144 programme and liaised with the government, ensuring support for the project at the top level. The actual design work was supervised by his son Aleksey A. Tupolev. The latter had by then been working in the aerodynamics department of OKB-156 for nearly 20 years and had performed a large amount of aerodynamic calculations. In 1958 Tupolev Jr. was put in charge of a new line in the OKB's work – exploration of supersonic flight with UAVs; by the time the OKB started work on the Tu-144 six programmes dealing with supersonic flight had been developed and implemented under Aleksey A. Tupolev's direction. Moreover, his team was the only one with practical experience of testing an aerial vehicle in sustained Mach 2.5 flight of more than 1 hour's duration (the Tu-123 UAV). Therefore, before one feels inclined to accuse Tupolev Sr. of nepotism (although the father-and-son relationship undoubtedly was a key factor), one has to admit that Aleksey A. Tupolev was one of the best men for the job from a professional standpoint.

Andrey N. Tupolev decided to entrust the design work on the Tu-144 to the OKB's Section K which had hitherto been responsible for unmanned aerial vehicles (UAVs). Section K had accumulated adequate experience of designing aircraft capable of

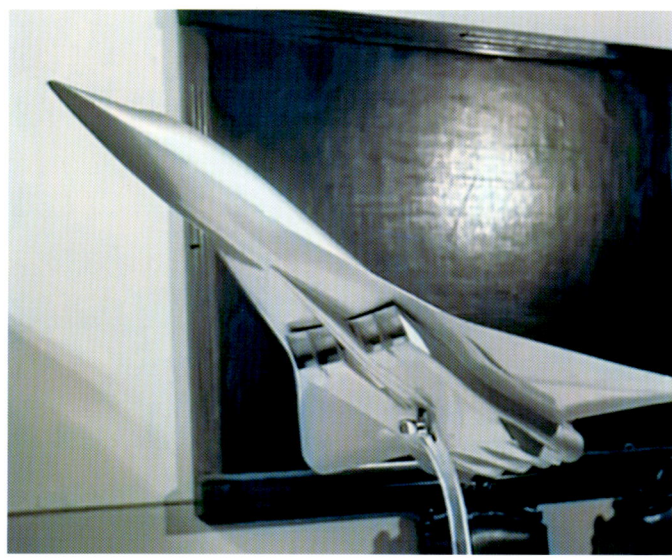

This page: This desktop model looks identical to the one in the second photo on page 15, except for the removal of the canards (the black blotches aft of the flight deck show their former location). The nose appears to be conventionally designed, with no drooping section. These views accentuate the fat fuselage tapering off into a 'beaver tail' at the rear extremity, the small twin tails (the combination of these features makes the aircraft looks rather unwieldy), the curved underside of the common engine air intake, which is divided into four lobes, and the shape of the wings with a slight leading-edge kink and curved tips. Given the location of the nose gear unit aft of the air intake lip, the wheelbase would have been quite short. The rear view illustrating the boxy aft end of the engine nacelle shows the fins and ventral strakes are strictly vertical.

Opposite page, left-hand row: A broadly similar desktop model which differs primarily in having paired air intakes with horizontal airflow control ramps divided by a large centrebody/nose gear fairing with a raked front end. This suggests a somewhat longer wheelbase. The wing leading-edge kink is even less pronounced.

Opposite page, right-hand row: Four more aspects of the model shown in the third photo on page 15. Note that the single vertical tail has a large root fillet, the similarly fat centrebody/nose gear fairing has a parabolic front end and there are gaps on either side between it and the intakes. There is slight forward sweep on the wing trailing edge. In common with the model shown on page 18, the rear end of the engine nacelle is angled upwards, but there are 'pen nib' fairings between the engine nozzles.

Chapter 1 - The Tu-144 is Born

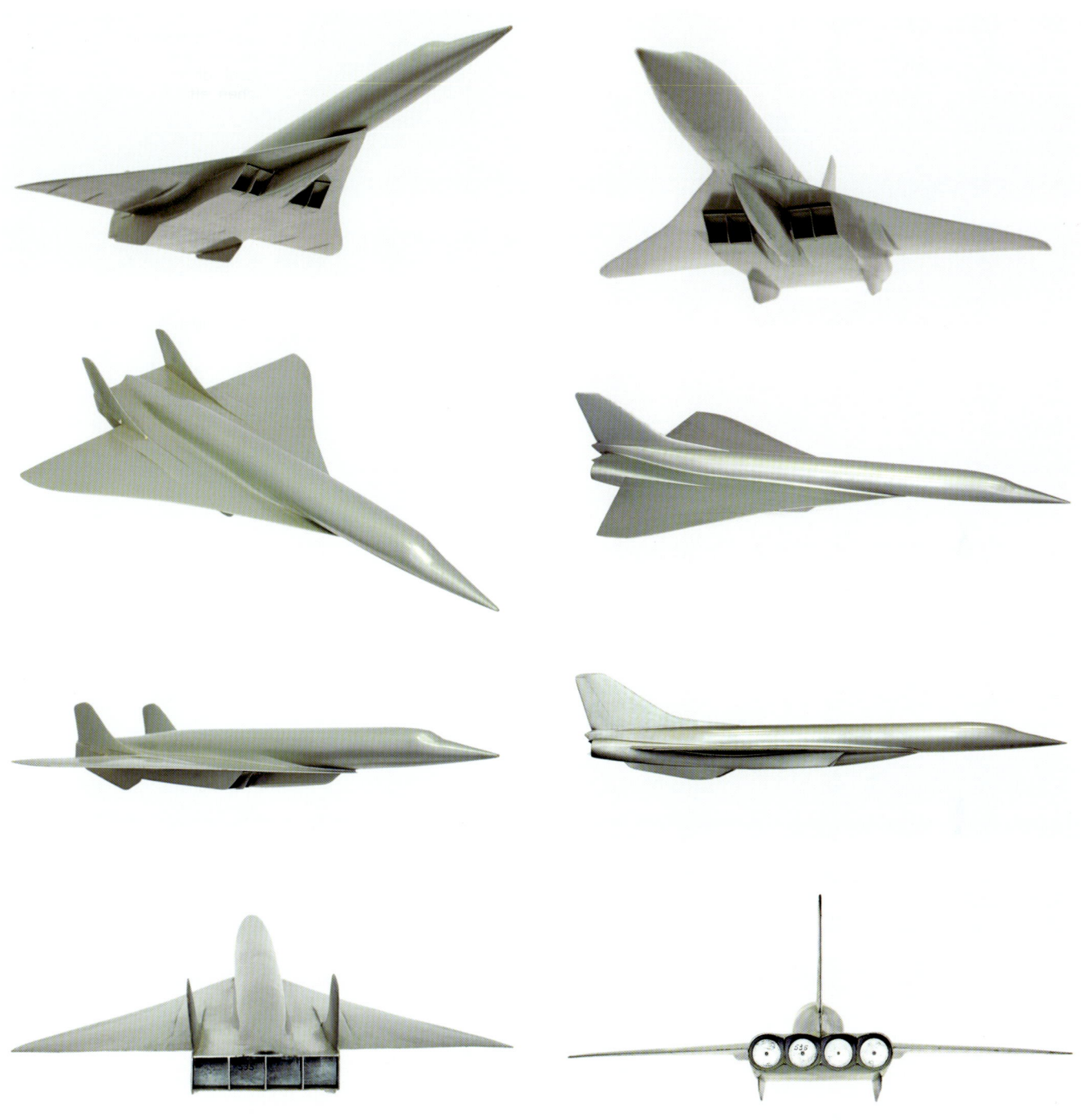

sustained flight at speeds in excess of Mach 2, having worked on the Tu-121 ground-launched cruise missile and its reconnaissance drone derivatives – the semi-expendable Tu-123 (DBR-1 Yastreb-1) and the fully recoverable Tu-139 (DBR-2 Yastreb-2); their mission profiles were broadly similar to the Tu-144's envisaged flight profile. Aleksey A. Tupolev, the General Designer's son, became the Tu-144's project chief. It was under his leadership and with the aid of other gifted designers that the concept and future shape of the Tu-144 took shape. After Andrey N. Tupolev's death in 1972 and the appointment of Aleksey A. Tupolev as head of OKB-156, Yuriy N. Popov and Boris A. Gantsevskiy headed the Tu-144 programme. Later, overall responsibility for the Tu-144 passed to Aleksandr L. Pookhov who, as a young engineer, had made a major contribution to the design effort in the 1960s.

Work in key areas of design was done by Ye. I. Kholopov, V. I. Kozlovskiy, V. D. Vostroknootov, V. I. Korneyev and Ye. I. Schekhterman. Later, a team of engineers (V. P. Lebedev, M. A. Fazylov, V. V. Teryoshin, M. Ye. Kalmanovich *et al.*) was formed at the OKB to promptly resolve the issues arising during preparation of the manufacturing drawings and subsequent trials and production of the aircraft.

Gradually, as the scope of the design work widened, other sections of the Tupolev OKB were called upon to participate in the project. Soon the Tu-144 became one of the OKB's (and generally MAP's) most important programmes for the decade that followed.

The choice of the general arrangement and aerodynamic layout, the placement of the basic systems and other highly complex issues were efficiently handled by the PD section under Valentin I. Bliznyuk, who later became famous as the programme chief of the Tu-160 *Blackjack* strategic missile strike aircraft. A team under Gheorgiy A. Cheryomukhin (who later became the Tupolev OKB's chief aerodynamicist) was responsible for the Tu-144's aerodynam-

The photos on this page depict the first of the two MiG-21I subscale demonstrators for the Tu-144 (the MiG-21I/1), registered CCCP A-144, showing to advantage its tailless-delta layout and wing shape. Note the large elevon actuator fairings on the underside of the wings.

Chapter 1 - The Tu-144 is Born

ics, working in close contact with their colleagues at TsAGI; the latter establishment was closely involved in the Tu-144's development throughout, providing invaluable scientific and practical support. At the early design stage the principal work on the Tu-144's aerodynamics was performed by K. N. Baboorin-Bel'chikov, K. F. Naboyshchikov, Arsik A. Rafaelyants-Agayan (the daughter of the Armenian-born aircraft designer Aram N. Rafaelyants), M. I. Blinchevskiy, Pyotr M. Leshchinskiy and Yuriy L. Strizhevskiy. Aleksandr E. Sterlin, the OKB's most experienced aerodynamicist, gave valuable advice.

The wider an aircraft's speed envelope is, the harder the task of the designers who inevitably have to make compromises when choosing the aerodynamic layout. In the case of the SST the compromises are particularly difficult because of the fundamental difference in the aircraft's aerodynamics in subsonic and supersonic flight. Hence several research institutes contributed their expertise to the shaping of the Tu-144's aerodynamics; TsAGI co-ordinated the work and had the final say in order to avoid a 'too many cooks' situation.

It is a universal truth that any aircraft – including SSTs – should be balanced, stable and adequately controllable in flight. In the Tupolev OKB there was a long-standing tradition – a 'house rule', if you like – that stability and controllability are to be ensured by the aircraft's geometry without resorting to automatic stability augmentation systems; using the latter is only justified if the required cruise lift/drag ratio or field performance cannot be obtained by other means. Thus, creating a unique control system was never a goal in itself.

General Designer Andrey N. Tupolev looks through an aeronautical magazine together with his colleague at OKB-155 Artyom I. Mikoyan, very probably discussing the MiG-21I in the process. Both men wear two Gold Star Medals that went with the Hero of Socialist Labour title.

Here, MiG-21I/1 CCCP A-144 is examined at Zhukovskiy by a French delegation visiting the USSR as part of the Soviet-French co-operation during the development of the Tu-144.

Basically, the task facing the designers boiled down to five items: obtaining the highest possible lift/drag ratio in all flight modes (and thus maximising range); obtaining adequate wing lift quotients to allow the aircraft to operate from runways of the stipulated length; obtaining stability and handling characteristics that would meet airworthiness standards and be agreeable from the pilots' point of view; achieving high weight efficiency in order to improve range and field performance; and achieving high fuel efficiency in cruise flight and the required take-off and cruise thrust to ensure the required range, field length and climbout gradients in the event of a single or multiple engine failure on take-off. The best longitudinal trim method also needed to be chosen. The last three items were not purely aerodynamics issues, yet the required performance could not be obtained without them.

At the time when development of the Tu-144 got under way, the designers had the choice of the following aerodynamic layouts which had been tried on supersonic aircraft:

• conventional swept-wing layout (exemplified in the Soviet Union by the Mikoyan/Gurevich MiG-19 *Farmer* fighter, the Su-7 fighter-bomber and the Tu-22 bomber);

• tailed-delta layout with delta wings and conventional horizontal tail surfaces for pitch control (exemplified by the MiG-21 and Su-9/Su-11 fighters, the M-50 bomber and the Tu-108 bomber project, the Tu-121 and Tu-123 UAVs);

• tailless-delta layout with combined trailing-edge surfaces for pitch/roll control called elevons (exemplified by the Convair F-102 Delta Dagger and Convair F-106 Delta Dart interceptors, the Dassault Mirage III tactical fighter, the Dassault Mirage IV tactical bomber – and the BAC/Aérospatiale Concorde);

• tail-first or canard layout – again with delta wings and canard foreplanes for pitch control (exemplified by the North American XB-70 Valkyrie bomber and the Myasishchev M-56 project).

At the PD stage, when the Tu-144's aerodynamic layout was being selected, the designers had to rely not so much on their previous experience with supersonic aircraft but rather on the huge scope of experimental and theoretical data that was pouring in exactly as the SST was being designed. Several research institutes and OKBs were working almost in parallel, verifying theoretical research on transonic and supersonic flight and undertaking numerous wind tunnel tests. Various wing shapes were explored, wing airfoils and their optimum thickness/chord ratios determined.

The Tu-144's aerodynamic layout was largely determined by the need to achieve the stipulated range in supersonic cruise while ensuring adequate stability and handling and providing the required field performance. Taking the advertised specific fuel consumption (SFC) of the intended engines as the starting point, the designers strove to achieve a maximum cruise lift/drag ratio of 7 at Stage A of the programme. Considering the financial, technological and weight factors, the cruising speed was to be above Mach 2.05. A value of Mach 2.35 at a cruise altitude of 18,000 m (59,055 ft) was selected initially; with these parameters the airframe could still be made largely of aluminium alloys.

MiG-21I CCCP A-144 was finished in two shades of grey, with blue trim along the wing/fuselage joint line and the Soviet flag in typical 1960s 'flying' style. The registration was repeated on the underside of the wings. Note how the port LERX merges with the AOA sensor fairing. Note also the data link aerial aft of the nose gear unit.

Chapter 1 - The Tu-144 is Born

The Tupolev OKB and TsAGI considered several dozen alternative layouts at the PD stage. One of the Tu-144's earliest project versions – we will call it Version 1, purely for reference purposes – was rather unusual, featuring low-set compound delta wings, a swept T-tail and four engines. Two of the engines were housed in a common ventral nacelle so that the nozzles were at the aft extremity of the fuselage, while the other two were housed in individual nacelles under the outer wings; all four engines had individual two-dimensional air intakes with horizontal airflow control ramps. The intakes of the Nos. 2 and 3 engines were spaced and a large fairing – the so-called centrebody – was located between them, housing the nose gear unit. The conventional layout was rejected because the horizontal tail would generate up to 20% of the overall drag.

Another early project version – we will call it Version 2 – was based on the abovementioned '135' (Tu-135) project. It had a tail-first layout with low-set cranked-delta wings (the leading-edge kink was very subtle), fairly large low-set cropped-delta canard foreplanes and a single vertical tail of trapezoidal shape. The circular-section fuselage had a high fineness ratio and a sharply pointed nose (apparently of conventional fixed geometry), the cabin seating up to 100 passengers four-abreast. The engines were arranged in side-by-side pairs under the wings inboard of the leading-edge kink (that is, fairly close to the fuselage), breathing through two-dimensional air intakes with vertical airflow control ramps (the engine nacelles adhering directly to the wing undersurface had V-shaped front ends in plan view). The twin-wheel nose gear unit was located well forward (in line with the canards' leading edge) and retracted aft, while the main gear units consisted of tandem pairs of struts with four-wheel bogies retracting into the engine nacelles (into the space between the curved inlet ducts).

A slightly different version (let's call it Version 3) had shoulder-mounted canards and a vertical tail with a swept trailing edge. The wing area in this version was 360 m² (3,875 sq ft). The aircraft had a take-off weight of 120,000 kg (264,550 lb) and a cruising speed of 2,000-2,500 km/h (1,242-1,552 mph). Two payload/range options were envisioned; in the normal version the aircraft carried 80-100 passengers over a range of 4,000-4,500 km (2,485-2,796 miles) and had a take-off run of 1,500-1,800 m (4,920-5,910 ft), while the long-range version carried 30-50 passengers over 5,500-6,000 km (3,417-3,728 miles) and had a take-off run of 2,000-2,500 m (6,560-8,200 ft). Fuel reserves for a 1,000-km (621-mile) diversion were included in both cases.

One of the preliminary design project versions (Version 4) looked like a Concorde that had sprouted shoulder-mounted cropped-delta canards – the similarity was unbelievable. Yet, despite the general similarity, the wing shape was different; unlike the Concorde, which had wings with an ogival leading edge, the Soviet version had more pronounced straight leading-edge sections with smooth transitions in between. The rear ends of the engine nacelles had a rectangular cross-section and all four engine nozzles incorporated clamshell thrust reversers.

Version 5 was also 'Concordesque', but the pairs of engines had common semi-circular air intakes with adjustable shock cones – or rather half-cones (a similar intake design was used on the Dassault Mirage series). The tail-first layout was eventually rejected because of the adverse effect the canards would have on the wings.

A model of the Tu-144 with ogival wings pictured during tests in TsAGI's water tunnel, with streams of dye visualising the airflow (or should we say water flow?) patterns.

Five other PD project models were markedly different in appearance, featuring a tailless-delta layout with all four engines grouped in a common ventral nacelle so that the nozzles were at the aft extremity of the fuselage; small twin vertical tails were located at the outer ends of this engine package, with shallow ventral fins to augment them. The landing gear was reworked – at any rate, the wheelbase was shorter, the nose gear being located aft of the air intakes to avoid foreign object damage (FOD).

The common engine package offered several advantages over the widely spaced twin-engine nacelles used on the Concorde. Cross-section area was minimised, the long inlet ducts required to ensure adequate surge resistance could be incorporated quite easily, the location of the engines close to the centreline reduced the yaw caused by thrust asymmetry in the event of an engine failure, and the wing downwash in the area of the intakes was reduced. Placing the intakes well forward made it easier to ensure FOD protection. Flutter resistance was improved, the control runs and piping for the engines could be made shorter, and a greater proportion of the wing trailing edge was available for the control surfaces. On the minus side, the long inlet ducts incurred a weight penalty, the considerable thickness of the turbulent boundary layer required the air intake lips to be set far apart from the wing undersurface. Also, flight tests revealed subsequently that the rear

Right: A rather schematic gliding model of the Tu-144 with quasi-ogival wings suspended nose-down.

Far left and left: The model is taken aloft by a Mil' Mi-4 helicopter and released with a parachute.

Below left and below: The model propped up on trestles; note the sectional 'shish kebab on a spit' design.

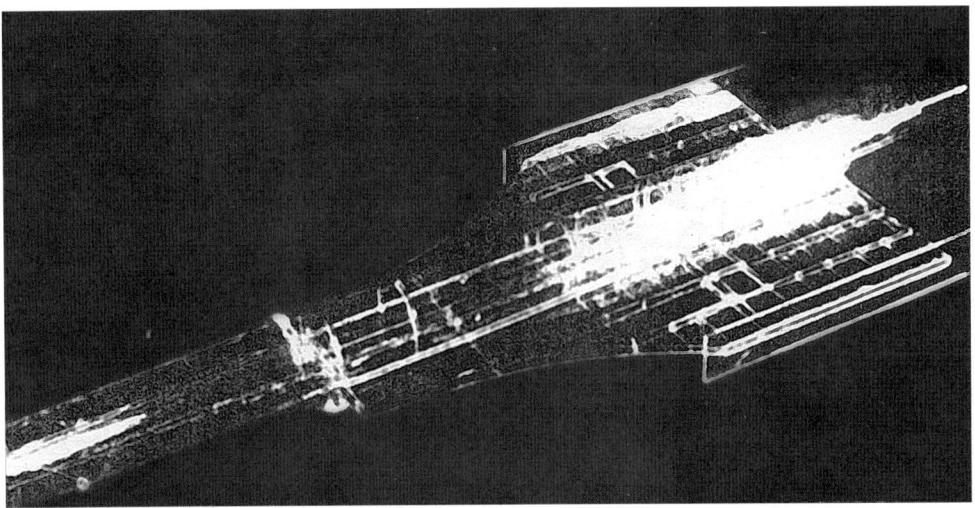

Left: A transparent model of the Tu-144 made of Perspex and used for photometric tests.

Below left: This model of the Tu-144 served for thermal (kinetic heating) tests. Note the double-delta wings resembling the eventual production version (*izdeliye* 004).

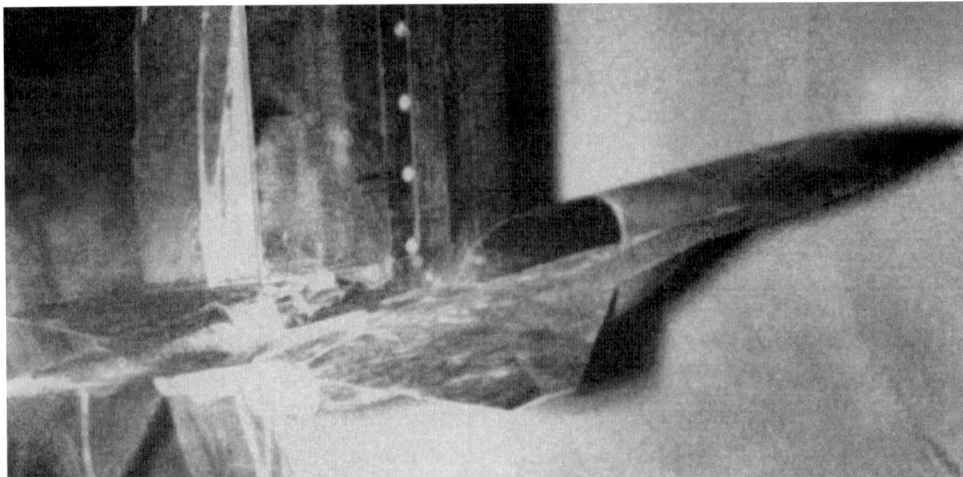

Bottom left: This picture from a wind tunnel using a special photography technique visualises the shock wave patterns generated by the aircraft in supersonic flight.

Right: A model of the *izdeliye* 044 demonstrator using oil for airflow pattern visualisation.

Far right: Here, for comparison, is a model of the *izdeliye* 004 in the wind tunnel, showing the different wing shape. Note how the streaks of dye visualise the powerful vortices generated by the LERXes.

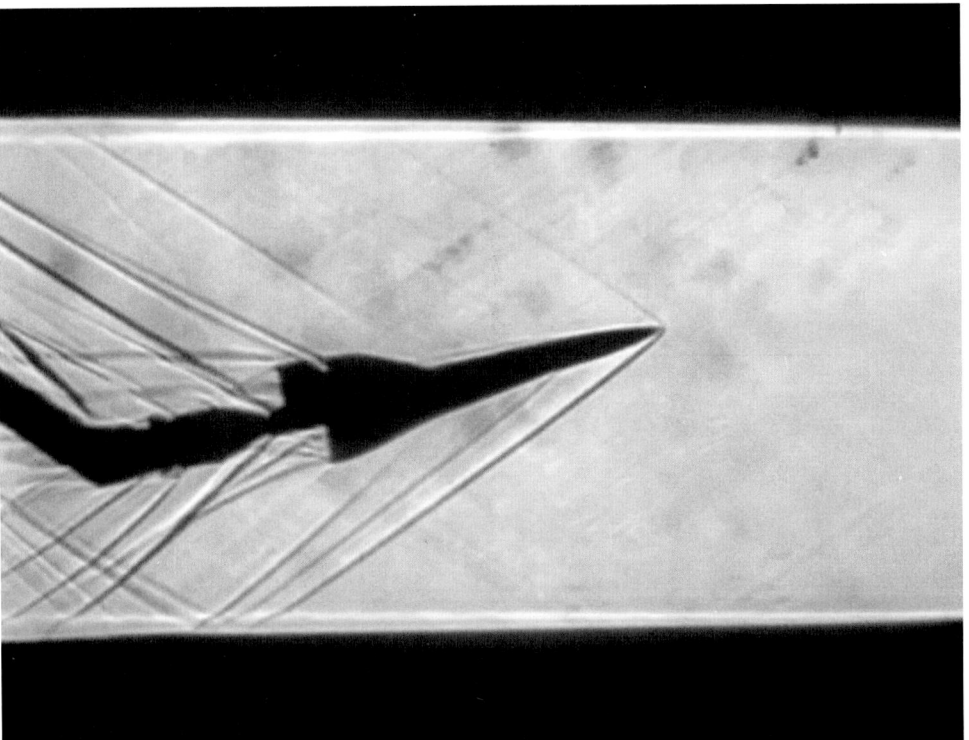

Right and below right: Two shots from the water tunnel showing a model of the *izdeliye* 004 at extreme angles of attack with the nose visor drooped. The engine nacelles are not reproduced.

Far right: Two more shots from the water tunnel. The partial model on the left is the production-standard Tu-144 while the one on the right appears to be the projected Tu-160M bomber (see Chapter 8).

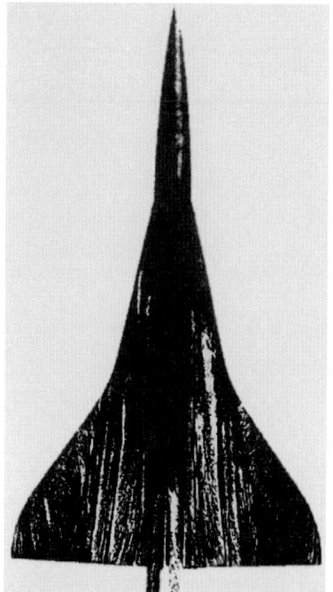 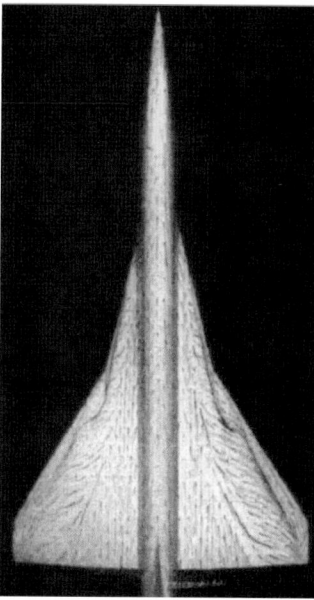

fuselage tended to get excessively hot because of the engines being located so close to it and required a heat shield.

Version 6 was similar in appearance to the XB-70, except for the absence of canards; the engine nacelle had a V-shaped front end in plan view and vertical airflow control ramps, the intakes being set apart from the wing undersurface. Version 7 was also 'Valkyriesque', but here the intakes adhered directly to the wing undersurface; the wing leading edge was kinked, not curved, and the wing LERXes did not blend with the fuselage – instead, they were set apart from it to act as a boundary layer splitter, meeting in a V shape! Another difference from Version 6 was that the rear end of the nacelle was boxy, not showing individual engine nozzles.

Version 8 was basically similar but had a raked 'big grin' air intake featuring four inlets in a row, with horizontal airflow control ramps; again, the wing LERXes doubled as a boundary layer splitter. Since there was no room in the centre splitter for the nose gear unit, the latter was enclosed by a teardrop fairing. Version 9 had almost cropped-delta wings with a very slight leading-edge kink and a single vertical tail; the engines breathed via two pairs of two-dimensional air intakes with horizontal airflow control ramps which were divided by a large centrebody housing the nose gear unit. Version 10 was similar but had a curved wing leading edge, twin vertical tails canted outward and different proportions (notably, the engine inlet ducts were longer and the intakes were positioned further forward, making the centrebody less conspicuous).

Eventually the designers opted for a low-wing tailless-delta layout with a single vertical tail and four engines in a common nacelle. The wings had a near-ogival planform, the leading-edge sweep being 78° on the inboard portions and 55° on the outboard ones. The wing planform was dictated by the need to minimise the shift of the wings' aerodynamic centre during the transition from subsonic to supersonic flight and back again. The vertical tail had a similar shape. As in the twin-tailed project versions, all four air intakes with sharply raked leading edges were grouped together, with three vertical splitters in between; the air intakes featured horizontal airflow control ramps. Version 11 was similar to Version 10, except for the single vertical tail with a swept trailing edge. Version 12, however, had the engine nozzles immediately aft of the wing trailing edge so that the rear fuselage protruded considerably beyond them, and the vertical tail had no trailing-edge sweep; this was fairly close to the definitive configuration.

World aircraft design practice and the results of the Tupolev OKB's own research performed by the early 1960s indicated that the tailless-delta layout was the best choice for a supersonic airliner. However, this layout had many influential opponents in high places. Hence MAP deemed it necessary to build a subscale proof-of-concept vehicle for the Tu-144 with a scaled-down version of the Tu-144's wings in order to check the stability and handing of the ogival-wing, tailless-delta aircraft in all flight modes and work out the optimum piloting techniques. Using his friendship with General Designer Artyom I. Mikoyan, head of the OKB-155 'fighter maker' design bureau, Andrey N. Tupolev asked him to build such an aircraft. The Mikoyan OKB's head office in Moscow was not in a position to do the job, having higher-priority programmes to take care of. Therefore, development of the technology demonstrator was entrusted to the special design office of the Gor'kiy aircraft factory No.21 where the MiG-21 tactical fighter

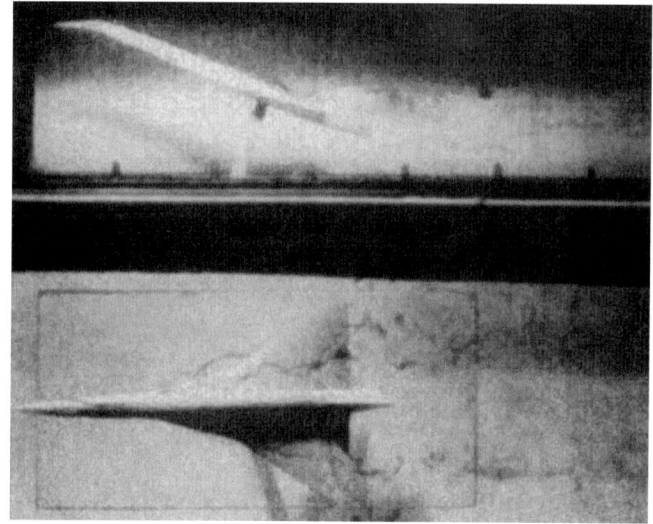 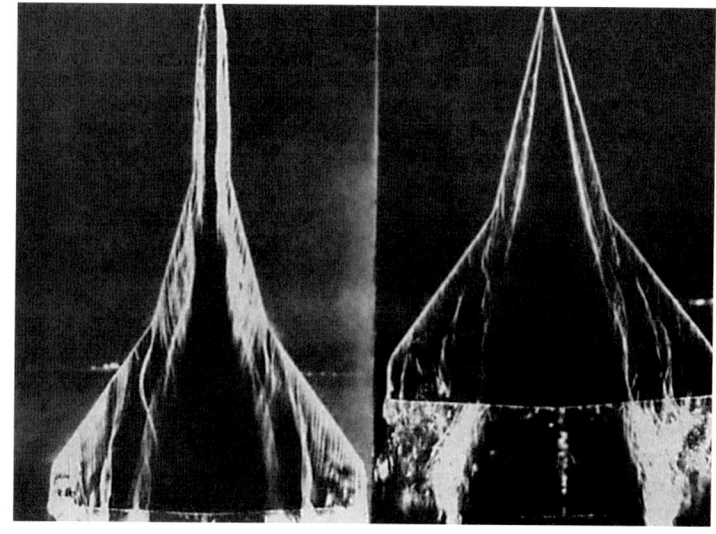

Split personality... or what? This photo of a structural model of the Tu-144 (*izdeliye* 004) with designer Aleksandr L. Pookhov in four copies having a debate among themselves is really a humorous collage made by Pookhov's colleagues at the Tupolev OKB as a gift to him.

was being produced. An MAP order to this effect was issued on 1st August 1964. At OKB-155 the programme was supervised by I. V. Froomkin (the MiG-21I project chief), while Yevgeniy I. Mindrov (head of the special design office) headed the design effort in Gor'kiy. The scientists Maks A. Taïtz, Arseniy D. Mironov and V. Grachov, as well as project engineer V. Startsev (representing LII), participated actively in drawing up the specifications to which the technology demonstrator would be designed.

The demonstrator was officially designated MiG-21I (for *imitahtor* – 'simulator', that is, in-flight simulator) and bore the in-house product code *izdeliye* 21-11. (*Izdeliye* (product) such-and-such is a code for Soviet/Russian military hardware items commonly used in paperwork to confuse outsiders.) Unofficially the machine was known as the *Analog* (Analogue); this was a reference to its similarity to the Tu-144 in layout and wing planform. Some sources erroneously referred to the aircraft as the 'A-144', which supposedly stood for 'analogue of the Tu-144'.

The machine was based on the production MiG-21S *Fishbed-J*. The fighter's fuselage and landing gear were mated with new thin wings of ogival planform; changes were made to the control system,

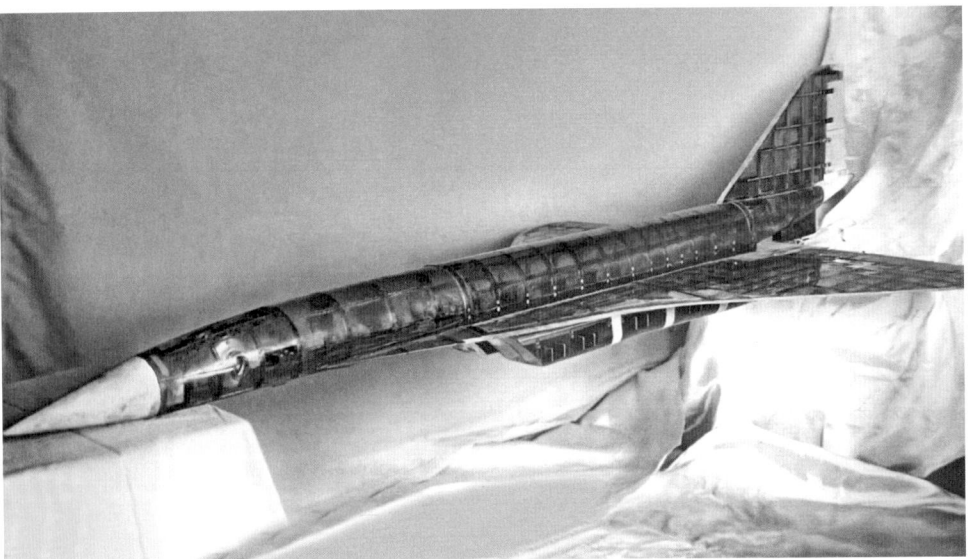

Left: A scaled-strength model of the Tu-144 (*izdeliye* 044) built for tests in the supersonic wind tunnel.

Top right: Another scaled-strength model in the working section of TsAGI's T-109 supersonic wind tunnel. Note the opaque LERXes.

Centre right: The same model in the midst of a test session. The 'flight speed' increases and the wings flex...

Right: ...until they go BANG! The aftermath of the model disintegrating due to wing flutter.

and the armament, weapons control system and part of the equipment were deleted. The Gor'kiy factory's design office prepared the blueprints for the new airframe components and equipment items in 1965-66; N. A. Limanov was the aircraft's project chief.

Since the MiG-21I's wings represented a scaled-down version of the Tu-144's wings, the design team made use of the Tu-144 blueprints supplied by the Tupolev OKB. A wind tunnel model of the MiG-21I was tested at TsAGI; this made it possible to determine the machine's principal aerodynamic parameters in all flight modes and issue recommendations for the test pilots long before the demonstrator actually flew.

The new wings had a gross area of 41.1 m² (442.4 sq ft) and an aspect ratio of 1.62. The leading-edge sweep was 78° on the LERXes and 55° on the outer portions. The wings utilised a thin symmetrical airfoil with a sharp leading edge; the thickness/chord ratio varied from 2.3% to 3.5%. There were no high-lift devices. The entire trailing edge was occupied by two-section elevons with individual actuators; the travel limits were +7°/–20° in elevator mode and +15°/–28° in aileron mode. All control surfaces were operated by irreversible hydraulic actuators. The pitch control circuit incorporated a device allowing the pilot to select the stick-to-elevons gearing ratio between 0.735 and 1.59. The roll control circuit featured a non-linear gearing ratio between stick travel and elevon travel, just like on the MiG-21S. Spring-loaded artificial-feel devices were provided to emulate the aileron/elevator forces on the stick. The control system included a three-channel (pitch/roll/yaw) damper which could be selected on or off in flight. With the damper in operation, the elevon and rudder deflection limits were ±0°30' in the pitch channel, ±1°12' in the roll channel and ±4° in the yaw channel.

As compared with the standard MiG-21S, the fuselage of the MiG-21I was 0.75 m (2 ft 5^{17}/$_{32}$ in) shorter; in contrast, the wing span was 60% greater. The Analogue was powered by a Tumanskiy R13F-300 turbojet delivering 6,490 kgp (14,310 lbst) in full afterburner. Jumping ahead of the story, we may say that this aircraft flew well, and any remaining doubts about the suitability of the tailless-delta layout were dispelled.

The next task was to ensure that the tailless-delta aircraft would be balanced in the pitch channel in all flight modes in such a way that, with the CG in the normal position, no elevon deflection (or extremely small deflection) would be required for longitudinal trim. The designers knew this could be done by introducing wing camber; however, TsAGI advised against it, stating this would entail a reduction of the lift/drag ratio. Therefore the OKB also considered other options. Option 1 was to bend the forward fuselage upward. However, in this case the nosecone ahead of the flight deck needed to be relatively short to ensure a good field of view on landing approach, which would inevitably cause higher drag in cruise flight; also, the drag increase would be greater than the lift increase, spoiling the lift/drag ratio.

Option 2 was to angle the rear end of the engine nacelle upwards (one of the early project models showed the rear end of the nacelle protruding above the wings' upper surface). This led to an even greater reduction of the lift/drag ratio and was rejected.

Option 3 was to optimise the planform of the delta wings according to the linear theory and sharply increasing the root

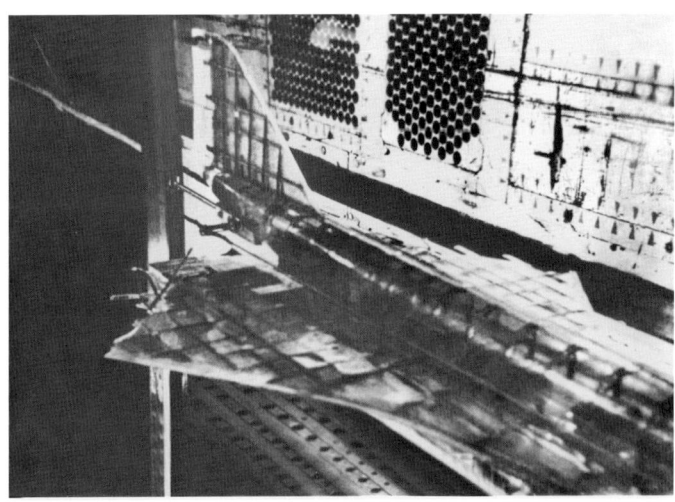

chord. Yet, this required the engine nacelle to be angled downwards, entailing the risk of a tailstrike during rotation, which in turn required a taller landing gear to prevent this.

The requisite lift/drag ratio could be obtained and the aircraft balanced with minimum aerodynamic losses by selecting the correct wing planform and airfoils. No theory explaining how to choose them existed yet, and the quest for the Tu-144's optimum wing planform and airfoils was guided by the following considerations. Sharply swept LERXes would extend acceptable stability and handling over a wider range of speeds, create an upwash on the main portions of the wings, reduce the overall thickness/chord ratio at the roots while retaining the same depth of the wing structure and help to accommodate the fuel tanks in such a way that their aggregate centre of gravity would coincide with the aircraft's requisite CG position. The spanwise distribution of the lift across the wings should be as close as possible to an elliptical pattern; so should the distribution of the lift along the aircraft's length. The lengthwise distribution of the cross-section area should be as close as possible to a minimum-drag axisymmetrical object (this is known as the 'area rule').

Left: A large and accurate model of the Tu-144 (izdeliye 044) – incidentally, designated 'object 044' – in TsAGI's T-101 subsonic wind tunnel. The model is in a take-off/landing attitude with the nose visor lowered.

Below left: Upper front view of the same model during the experiment, showing the many wool tufts.

Right: Another angle on the same model, with the T-101's fan section in the background.

Below: This view of the model shows the intake design and the 12-wheel main gear bogies.

More than 30 models of the Tu-144's wings were tested in TsAGI's T-112, T-113 and T-114 wind tunnels in co-operation with the institute's researchers (Rafaïl I. Shteinberg, Leonid Ye. Vasil'yev, Viktor M. Shoorygin and Sergey M. Belotserkovskiy). Together with different versions of the LERXes, this gave a total of more than 200 variants. Further tests were made in the T-313 wind tunnel of the Theoretical & Applied Mechanics Institute of the Soviet Academy of Sciences' Siberian Division (ITPM – *Institoot teoreticheskoy i prikladnoy mekhaniki*) in Novosibirsk when the Tupolev OKB's aerodynamicists disagreed with TsAGI; later, TsAGI accepted the results of these additional tests as a reference material. ITPM also helped to design the optimum deformation of

Chapter 1 - The Tu-144 is Born

Left and far left: As these views show, the 'object 044' wind tunnel model was painted a vivid turquoise colour. The working section of the wind tunnel was illuminated from all sides by floodlights.

Below, far left: The model in the T-101 could be filmed from all sides during the experiment.

Below left: This view shows how the gap between the pairs of air intakes disappears towards the rear of the nacelle.

Right and below right: Rare colour photos of Andrey N. Tupolev holding a model of the Tu-144.

Bottom right: Another view of the model showing the penultimate project form.

the wings in flight caused by aerodynamic loads. Occasionally the Tupolev OKB called on the Moscow State University named after Mikhail V. Lomonosov, the Moscow College of Technology named after Nikolay E. Baumann (MVTU – *Moskovskoye vyssheye tekhnicheskoye oochilishche*) and the Riga Institute of Civil Aviation Engineers (RIIGA – *Rizhskiy institoot inzhenerov grazhdahnskoy aviahtsii*). As often as not, however, the necessary results could be obtained in the OKB's own wind tunnel.

Interestingly, not only wind tunnels but also water tunnels (basically the same but using water as the working medium and dyes instead of wool tufts) were used in the development of the Tu-144. The first such water tunnel with a 150 x 150 mm ($5^{29}/_{32}$ x $5^{29}/_{32}$ in) working section was installed right in the Tupolev OKB aerodynamicists' workroom at the initiative of Ye. Ya. Pivkin and worked for many years. Later, similar water tunnels were built at TsAGI and the Moscow Aviation Technology Institute (MATI), using Tupolev OKB drawings. Still later, TsAGI's Section 5 designed and built an even bigger water tunnel with a 400 x 400 mm (1 ft 3¾ in x 1 ft 3¾ in) working section, which allowed unique experiments in extreme flight modes to be undertaken. Photos obtained in the water tunnel were often used for analysing the aerodynamic parameters obtained in wind tunnels.

Having found proof positive of their ideas, the OKB's aerodynamicists (Gheorgiy A. Cheryomukhin, Aleksandr L. Pookhov, Arsik A. Rafaelyants-Agayan, Anatoliy B. Koshcheyev, Zhookova, Govor, Strizhenov *et al.*) developed the future Tu-144 prototype's wing planform and camber. Their main objective was to obtain a cruise lift/drag ratio in excess of 8 without compromising field performance. After Andrey N. Tupolev had made some revisions to the wing design for technological reasons, detail design of the wing structure began. (On the actual prototype the lift/drag ratio turned out to be somewhat lower – about 7.)

Of course, since the theory of wing design for an SST was still in the making and the OKB's aerodynamicists had insufficient experience in designing low aspect ratio wings, they carefully studied the information on western SST projects (first and foremost the Concorde) that came their way. Yet they made the final choice of the wing shape and airfoils on their own. As early as 1963, the Tu-144 and the Concorde met face to face for the first time at the 25th Paris Air Show – in model form, of course. The

Concorde model was made of Plexiglas, which gave at least some idea on the wing airfoils; in contrast, the Tu-144 model was made of wood and revealed nothing of the sort.

Much effort was spent on optimising the fuselage contours. For instance, the fuselage had a high fineness ratio; in particular, the forward and rear fuselage sections had a fineness ratio of 6 and 7 respectively in order to ensure low drag in supersonic cruise. However, the long needle-shaped nose did not tie in with the requirement to ensure a good field of view on take-off and landing – which was a must, since the low aspect ratio wings resulted in a high AOA on approach. Therefore, in common with the Concorde the Tu-144 had an unpressurised nosecone which was hinged at the bottom and could be lowered by an electric actuator to improve the field of view. This drooping nose was painstakingly tested in TsAGI's wind tunnels to select the optimum deflection angles, improving the overall lift/drag ratio.

Choosing the optimum contours and internal layout of the engine nacelle turned out to be no easy task either. The engine makers placed high demands on the stability of the airflow at the compressor faces, which necessitated the use of long inlet ducts and required the engine nacelle to fit within the width of the wing LERXes. In the early project version the nacelle was area-ruled, widening towards the rear where the engines were (this was done for nacelle/main landing gear integration reasons as well), and the four air intakes were grouped together.

Later the intakes were divided into two pairs to reduce the engines' mutual influence in the event of surge and provide a more convenient location for the nose landing gear unit. As a result, the front portion of the engine nacelle became wider and a fairing of triangular cross-section between the two pairs of intakes accommodated housing the nose landing gear unit, the cleft gradually vanishing aft of this fairing. The integration between the engine nozzles and the wing trailing edge turned out to be poor, and a special boxy structure with air ejection was designed around the nozzles to reduce boattail drag.

The airframe structure was designed under the supervision of Iosif F. Nezval' and Boris A. Gantsevskiy, old hands with a wealth of experience. As was customary at the Tupolev OKB, after the airframe had been divided into basic subassemblies these were worked on in parallel by separate design teams and sections headed by Konstantin P. Sveshnikov, S. I. Petrov, Ivan S. Lebedev, Aleksandra S. Prytkova, V. T. Zhvakin, Nikolay T. Kozlov, O. N. Golovin, A. V. Gorbachov, Vladimir A. Chizhevskiy *et al*. Along with the head office in Moscow, some other branches of the Tupolev OKB (notably the one in Tomilino township south of Moscow headed by V. Yu. Shaltuper) were involved in designing the airframe. Specifically, the wing design section was responsible for the detachable outer wings outboard of ribs 20L and 20R; Section F-2 designed the forward fuselage up to frame 25; Section F-1 designed the rear fuselage aft of frame 96; the wing design team of the OKB's Section K was responsible for the wing centre section; the design office of the Tomilino branch was responsible for the centre fuselage (frames 25-96), the engine nacelle and the wing LERXes ahead of the front spar. The wing centre section incorporated the aforementioned centrebody which alleviated the bending loads on the lower skin of the centre section. Since Aleksandra Prytkova was responsible for this element of the structure, local wits promptly amended its name to 'Shoorochka's centrebody'.

The choice of structural design features was dictated by the following peculiarities of the SST's layout and operations: a long and relatively thin fuselage mated with thin delta wings; tall wing-mounted main landing gear units; kinetic heating causing temperature differences between structural elements or even major airframe components and hence local expansion/contraction and the attendant stresses; higher-than-usual weight efficiency requirements; and a long design service life. The wings were the hardest part, as they incorporated a number of integral fuel tanks, which would be filled with a varying quantity of fuel, and there would be a sizeable temperature differential between the upper and lower skins. The wing/fuselage joint also presented a problem because of the exceptionally broad root chord.

Structural strength and fatigue life issues assumed special importance when the Tu-144 was being designed. By the time the Tupolev OKB embarked on its first-generation SST programme it had accumulated a lot of practical experience in calculating the required strength of airframe structures. This stemmed from the development and service introduction of both commercial and military aircraft, including supersonic bombers and heavy interceptors. Still, the very nature of the SST programme demanded enhanced reliability and hence a more exacting approach to structural strength.

Chapter 1 - The Tu-144 is Born

Left: The hot end of the NK-144 engine during bench tests; the nozzle is coated with special heat-sensitive paints to determine the hottest areas.

Below left: A ground test article of the *izdeliye* 044's rear fuselage and engine nacelle, showing how the aluminium skin melted in the hot exhaust stream. A titanium heat shield had to be designed to cure the problem.

Right: Tu-144 project chief Aleksey A. Tupolev (left) and OKB-36 Chief Designer Pyotr A. Kolesov having a discussion about the RD36-51A engine.

At first this aspect of the design process was supervised by the Tupolev OKB's structural strength department chief Aleksandr R. Bonin; actual design work was headed by Aleksey P. Gannushkin (dynamic strength section) and Vyacheslav V. Soolimenkov (static strength section). TsAGI drew up a set of structural strength norms specifically for the Tu-144, and these were subsequently included into the Provisional Airworthiness Regulations for Supersonic Aircraft according to which the Tu-144 was certificated.

Despite the OKB's long history, creating a supersonic airliner involved situations lying outside the designers' prior experience. Besides, Soviet computer technology was at an early stage of development in the 1960s, forcing the designers to use then-current mathematical analysis methods for calculating the structural strength; however, these methods quickly showed themselves to be inadequate. This led the structural strength norms to be amended and new calculation methods to be developed. The airframe had to be designed in such a way as to ensure high weight efficiency by correctly choosing the design structural loads. Also, structural materials having adequate strength and creep resistance parameters when exposed to high temperatures and dynamic loads for extended periods had to be chosen (more about this later).

One of the challenges facing the designers was the calculation of the external loads applied to the aircraft on take-off, in cruise flight and on landing; they determined the aircraft's static strength and service life, and its actual strength and weight efficiency depended on whether the loads had been calculated correctly. Vyacheslav V. Soolimenkov, who was then chief of the external loads calculation team, headed this work (he subsequently became head of the Tupolev OKB's structural strength department). F. A. Kocharyan took an active part in analysing the loads and working out standard loads for static and fatigue tests. Other Tupolev OKB employees who contributed a lot to developing the load calculation/measurement techniques were B. L. Merkoolov, A. F. Pcholkin, I. Ya. Borovaya, I. A. Golovnya, V. N. Perel'shtein, V. G. Yoodovich *et al.*; TsAGI specialists Yuriy A. Stoochalkin,

Teodor A. Frantsooz and B. D. Frank. The Siberian Aviation Research Institute (SibNIA – *Sibeerskiy naoochno-issledovatel'skiy institoot aviahtsii*) in Novosibirsk also contributed to the research in this area, developing static and fatigue test techniques which took the peculiarities of supersonic flight into account. The Tu-144's peculiarities included its airframe loading at the moment of touchdown, during taxying and during the take-off and landing runs when the landing gear wheels ran over the imperfections of the runway surface (and the runways and taxiways at Soviet airfields were generally far from perfect). Because of the Tu-144's fairly flexible airframe, the jolts occurring in these conditions created sizeable structural loads applied to the fuse-

Project specifications of the Tu-144 issued by GosNII GA in 1964		
	Normal TOW	**Maximum TOW**
Seating capacity	120	70-80
Payload, kg (lb)	12,000 (26,455)	7,000-8,000 (15,430-17,640)
Range, km (miles)	4,500 (2,795)	6,300 (3,910)
Take-off run, m (ft)	1,800-2,000 (5,900-6,560)	2,100-2,500 (6,890-8,200)
Take-off weight, kg (lb)	130,000 (286,600)	n.a.
Speed, km/h (mph)	2,100-2,300 (1,304-1,428)	2,100-2,300 (1,304-1,428)
Airfield class	Class A	Unclassed

The definitive version of the MGA's specifications for the Tu-144 issued in 1965		
	Stage 1	**Stage 2**
Range, km (miles)	4,500 (2,795)	6,500 (4,040)
Payload, kg (lb)	14,000-15,000 (30,860-33,070)	11,000-13,000 (24,250-28,660)
Seating capacity	150 (F16CY134)*	110 (F16CY94)
Take-off weight, kg (lb)	150,000 (330,690)	180,000 (396,825)
Required runway length, m (ft)	2,600 (8,530) (Class B airfield)	3,250 (10,660) (Class A airfield)

* F = first class seating; CY = tourist class seating

lage; this wreaked havoc with the aircraft's service life and had to be taken into account.

The designers spent a lot of effort on determining the airframe's structural design (the optimum location of the load-bearing elements) and optimising specific structural details. This work proceeded under the direction of Valeriy P. Shoonayev, who went on to become the company's structural strength department chief. The choice of the optimum structural design and the calculation of in-flight structural stresses and deformations called for calculation methods for which no software existed yet in the 1960s; therefore, In parallel with the calculations of the airframe's stress and strain conditions, the possible structural design layouts were compared, using scaled-strength and structurally similar models.

Initially a model of the Myasishchev M-50 bomber was used for these experiments; later several scaled-strength models of the Tu-144 made of Plexiglas and a structurally similar metal model to 1/3rd scale were designed and built. A lot of research on structural stress was done using static test articles. The Plexiglas models rigged with stress sensors allowed photoelasticity methods to be used during the tests. It should be noted that the use of structurally similar and scaled-strength models became a mandatory part of the Tupolev OKB's working practice for many years after the Tu-144 programme. The day's only computerised method of calculating structural strength was available in the form of a programme designed by Yuriy Ye. Il'yenko; actually this software had been designed for aeroelasticity calculations of the M-50 when Il'yenko was still working at the Myasishchev OKB but, as a bonus, could also be used to determine structural stress. Three aeroelastic conditions of the airframe had to be taken into account: theoretical (that is, when the wings are in the assembly jig in a no-load condition), ground (when the wings droop under their own weight) and in-flight (when the wing flex upward due to

Above left: The modified Tu-134 fuselage which served as a test rig for the Tu-144's dynamic heat insulation system. Note the air ducts and the passage with an air lock leading to the entry door.

Above: A prototype of the Tu-144's air conditioning system being installed in the high-altitude chamber.

Left: Such dummies with light bulbs inside were installed in the cabin of the Tu-134 fuselage serving as the test rig to simulate the heat emitted by the passengers.

Chapter 1 - The Tu-144 is Born

wing lift); it was this latter condition that was of most interest to the aerodynamicists.

This was, so to say, the pebble that started the avalanche; from then on the Tupolev OKB began actively exploring computerised structural strength calculation methods, an effort that culminated in the development of a powerful multi-function computer system named Diana under the supervision of V. L. Glezer and A. V. Stasevich. Noteworthy research was done to explore thermal loads, thermal stresses and their effect on the airframe's functioning (this included not only structural strength but also metal creep and durability). This work directed by Igor' B. Ginko and A. A. Kozlov was performed jointly with TsAGI's Research Section No.3 (NIO-3 – *naoochno-issledovatel'skiy otdel*) under Vladimir F. Koot'yinov.

Additionally, TsAGI and SibNIA tested a number of specially manufactured wing sections with spars and ribs of various design (with corrugated sheet webs or truss-type) to assess the effect of varying temperatures on stress and strain levels. TsAGI specialists Aleksandr I. Makarevskiy, Andrey F. Selikhov, Yuriy A. Stoochalkin *et al.* made a major contribution at this stage. At the Tupolev OKB, engineers Igor' B. Ginko, Alfred M. Davtyan, I. K. Kulikov, F. A. Kocharian, B. L. Merkoolov, V. L. Glezer, V. A. Shvilkin, I. Ya. Borovaya, V. N. Perel'shtein, V. G. Yoodovich, L. P Chool'skiy, Valeriy P. Shoonayev and I. A. Golovnya developed the calculation methods and calculated the Tu-144's actual design loads, determining the strength norms and setting the loads to be applied to the static test airframe.

Eventually the designers settled for multi-spar wings with upper and lower skins featuring integrally machined stiffeners of complex shape; at the OKB these panels were jocularly called 'wafer panels'. As compared to conventional panels with riveted stringers, such panels offered better heat transfer characteristics and lower thermal stresses, as there were no rivets that would be subjected to shearing loads due to different expansion/contraction of the skin and the stringers. After machining, such panels were thermally treated; initially, when the technology was still immature, this caused severe cracking of the integral stiffeners.

As a Russian saying goes, 'new things are thoroughly forgotten old ones'; to stop thermal expansion/contraction cycles from causing structural deformation impairing the airframe's functioning, girder-type beams and corrugated sheets, just like in the early days of aviation. These were used for the wing spars and ribs, as a conventional design with sheet webs was unsuitable because of strong thermal stresses in the webs. Of course, again modern technologies were used – the truss-type beams and corrugated webs were integrally machined. Subsequent static tests and fatigue tests fully confirmed the validity of these design features.

The wings were built in five pieces – the forward sections (which were the LERXes), the centre section and the detachable outer wings, which were attached to it by bolts and flanges. The centre section was a one-piece subassembly with no centreline manufacturing break and was attached to the fuselage structure via fittings; it incorporated the mainwheel wells. The forward sections were attached to the fuselage by special fittings allowing some longitudinal travel in order to reduce the stress caused by heating/cooling cycles. The fin had a similar multi-spar structure and the leading-edge section was again attached by fittings allowing some longitudinal travel. The engine nacelle was attached to the wing centre section from below; the inlet ducts were built in three sections and attached in such a way that wing flexure did not cause deformation of the inlet ducts (and thus potentially disrupt engine operation). The fuselage was of semi-monocoque construction with frames and stringers supporting the skin; for the first time in Soviet practice, the fuselage structure included panels with integrally machined stiffeners in addition to traditional riveted ones.

Fighting the dangerous manifestations of aeroelasticity (flutter and control surface reversal) is a difficult enough task even when designing a conventional subsonic aircraft; with a supersonic airliner, the task becomes monstrous. It is tackled by means of scaled-strength models tested in wind tunnels. Such a model of the Tu-144 for flutter tests was created by the OKB, using a software package developed by Vladimir G. Boon'kov at TsAGI. Calculations made with the help of this model helped to determine the aircraft's own oscillation frequencies. The traditional technology of manufacturing such models involves using weighted foam plastic sections that are assembled like shish kebab on a spit (hence the Russian slang term for such models, *shashlychnaya model'* – 'shish kebab model'). However, 'shish kebab' turned out to be unsuitable for the Tu-144. Eventually several dozen structurally similar scaled-strength models made of carbonfibre reinforced plastic (CFRP) or Plexiglas were manufactured for wind tunnel tests. The engineers' task was further complicated by the need to simulate differing fuel loads on these models. This research was done in TsAGI's T-109 wind tunnel. Tupolev OKB specialists O. I. Poltavtseva, Vyacheslav V. Soolimenkov, V. A. Shvilkin, B. Ya. Choodayev, V. N. Pappe and L. K. Zvyagin, as well as TsAGI specialists B. A. Kirshtein, V. V. Lyshinskiy, Lev S. Popov and Ye. I. Sobolev, participated in the flutter and controllability research programmes.

Even before the Tu-144 had been developed, the Soviet structural strength norms for aircraft had contained clauses about aero-elastic stability; these meant that under no circumstances should the interaction between an elastic airframe and the aircraft's automatic flight control system result in oscillations. However, it was the Tu-144 that became the first aircraft on which the methods of dealing with such oscillations were tried out in earnest.

The landing gear was developed by a special department headed by Yakov A. Livshitz, a top-notch 'gear man' who had been responsible for the undercarriages of the Tu-16, Tu-95, Tu-22 and other Tupolev aircraft. The designers working under his command included M. T. Ivanov, V. S. Gorbunov and V. K. Rezaykin. The need to ensure an adequate rotation angle on take-off and adequate ground clearance for the air intakes (in order to prevent the engines from hoovering up foreign objects from the ground) resulted in a tall landing gear. The twin-wheel nose unit retracted aft into a fairing between the pairs of air intakes, its position relative to the latter being chosen in such a way as to prevent snow/slush ingestion.

The main gear units could only be stowed in the wings outboard of the common engine housing; considering the low thickness/chord ratio and the limited space within the wings, this turned into a real problem. Yet, the designers came up with an ingenious solution, making a virtue out of necessity. In order to fit inside the thin wings each main gear bogie had no fewer than 12 small wheels in three rows of four, with a wide track; this gave the additional benefit of increasing the landing gear footprint and reducing the runway loading. During retraction the bogies somersaulted forward to lie inverted in the wheel wells. This did the trick, albeit the wings in the area of the wheel wells still had to be suitably bulged. Additionally, to minimise the required space the main gear struts had a cunning 'knee-action' design, the small upper segment swinging aft and the rest of the oleo forward (a similar solution had been used on the Grumman F8F Bearcat, the Fokker F-27 Friendship and several Soviet transport aircraft projects); the bogies were hinged close to the rear axle so that most of the bogie lay against the oleo, reducing the overall length when stowed.

One of the toughest problems when designing a supersonic aircraft is the development of a suitable powerplant – and that means not only the engine(s) proper but also the supersonic air intake(s). In the case of a commercial aircraft (SST), specially stringent reliability, fuel efficiency and service life requirements apply, and there are also environmental protection regulations to contend with. This requires a host of design, technological and operational tasks to be solved.

By the early 1960s turbofan engines had become common, including afterburning turbofans for military applications (especially for supersonic combat jets). Soviet and western calculations of the parameters of non-afterburning jet engines required to give an SST a cruising speed of Mach 2.0-2.2 showed that the optimum bypass ratio of such engines ranged from 0 (pure turbojets) to 1.5. This figure depended on the aircraft's lift/drag ratio, weight efficiency and, importantly, the proportion of the fuel used for the subsonic sections of the flight (take-off/climbout, descent/landing) and the fuel reserves for a diversion to an alternate airfield. Additionally, the subsonic sections could include cruise flight over populated areas for noise abatement reasons (more will be said about this later).

Thus, General Designer Andrey N. Tupolev was faced with the all-important question of choosing the correct engine type to power the Tu-144. After assessing the capabilities of the Soviet aero-engine design bureau he selected two which were then working on engines in the required thrust class (the other OKBs could only offer engines that were too small for the Tu-144). One of the two, OKB-276 in Kuibyshev headed by General Designer Nikolay D. Kuznetsov, was a long-standing partner of the Tupolev OKB, having supplied the NK-12 turboprop engines for the Tu-95 *Bear* strategic bomber, its Tu-114 *Rossiya* (Russia; NATO reporting name *Cleat*) long-haul airliner derivative and the latter's Tu-126 *Moss* airborne early warning & control (AEW&C) derivative. (The city is now renamed back to Samara, and the company is now called SNTK Trood (*Samarskiy naoochno-tekhnicheskiy kompleks* – 'Labour' Samara Scientific & Technical Complex named after Nikolay D. Kuznetsov).)

Kuznetsov offered a two-spool afterburning turbofan aptly designated NK-144, with a bypass ratio of 0.6, a take-off (maximum afterburner) rating of 17,500 kgp (38,580 lbst), a minimum-afterburner cruise rating of 3,970 kgp (8,750 lbst) and a non-afterburning cruise rating of 3,000 kgp. It was based on the core of the 10,500-kgp (23,150-lbst) NK-8 commercial turbofan powering the IL-62 *sans suffixe* airliner; incidentally, the NK-8 had also been selected for the Tu-154, which was then under development. As originally conceived the NK-144 was to have a 12-stage compressor (this was eventually changed to a three-stage low-pressure compressor, or fan, and a three-stage high-pressure compressor) and make use of heat-resistant materials optimised to withstand the kinetic heating in supersonic cruise. For the first time in Soviet practice, the afterburner (which had smoothly adjustable thrust) was located downstream of the core/bypass flow mixer; this was to improve fuel efficiency 2-3% as compared to separate core and bypass flow nozzles.

The other design bureau was the aforementioned OKB-36 in Rybinsk, alias RKBM (*Rybinskoye konstrooktorskoye byuro motorostroyeniya* – Rybinsk Engine Design Bureau), which was headed by a new Chief Designer, Pyotr A. Kolesov, since 1960. Kolesov offered the RD36-51A single-spool non-afterburning turbojet having a take-off rating of 20,000 kgp and a cruise SFC of 1.23 kg/kgp·hr (lb/lbst·hr) at Mach 2.2. Development of this engine began in 1967 pursuant to a Council of Ministers directive which, again, had been issued at Andrey N. Tupolev's initiative. Tupolev decided that early Tu-144s would be powered by NK-144 engines, intending to replace them with RD36-51As on later production aircraft when the latter engine had reached an adequate reliability level. (However, it was a long time before this intention could be implemented – see Chapter 4, Tu-144D section.)

In keeping with the aforementioned directive No.798-271, in 1964 the State Civil Aviation Research Institute (GosNII GA – *Gosudarstvennyy naoochno-issledovatel'skiy institoot grazhdahnskoy aviahtsii*) issued specifications for the Tu-144; these were duly reviewed and approved by other branches of Ministry of Civil Aviation (MGA – *Ministerstvo grazhdahnskoy aviahtsii*). The document envisaged the following performance for the airliner's normal and maximum take-off weight configurations:

The specifications were submitted to General Designer Andrey N. Tupolev for approval. On receiving the specs the Tupolev OKB prepared an advanced development project (ADP) reflecting the Tu-144's two-stage development strategy and submitted it to GosNII GA for review. Stage A envisioned a powerplant consisting of four Kuznetsov NK-144 afterburning turbofans. With these engines the Tu-144 would offer the following performance:
- take-off weight, 150,000 kg (330,690 lb);
- payload, 14,000-16,000 kg (30,860-35,270 lb);
- seating capacity, 150;
- crew, 5;
- service altitude, 18,500-20,500 m (60,695-67,260 ft);
- cruising speed, 2,500 km/h (1,552 mph);
- range, 4,515 km (2,804 miles);
- take-off run, 1,720 m (5,640 ft);
- landing run, 1,330 m (4,360 ft);
- unstick speed, 350 km/h (217 mph).

Stage B envisaged extending the Tu-144's range and installing a new powerplant consisting of four Kolesov RD36-51A axial-flow non-afterburning turbojets developed by OKB-36. This version was expected to have the following performance:
- take-off weight, 180,000 kg (396,825 lb);
- payload, 8,000 kg (17,640 lb);
- seating capacity, 80;

Chapter 1 - The Tu-144 is Born

A test rig for testing the Tu-144's systems for resistance to static electricity.

Right: A large-scale test rig for testing the Tu-144's structure in kinetic heating conditions.

Below: The same rig, showing a chunk of the Tu-144's fuselage in the working section.

The propulsion test rig featuring the air intakes and NK-144 engines.

- airframe weight, 78,000 kg (171,960 lb);
- fuel load, 94,000 kg (207,230 lb);
- range, 6,510 km (4,043 miles);
- service altitude, 18,500-20,500 m (60,695-67,260 ft);
- cruising speed, 2,500 km/h (1,552 mph);
- take-off run, 2,370 m (7,775 ft);
- landing run, 1,440 m (4,720 ft);
- unstick speed, 380 km/h (236 mph);
- fuel burn, 24-25 tons/hr (52,910-55,115 lb/hr).

It has to be said, however, that many of the performance figures stated above changed considerably as the programme advanced to the detail design stage.

Having carefully studied the ADP, in 1965 GosNII GA drew up a report which basically approved the project, except for the payload stated for Stage B; the customer (MGA) saw it as inadequate and insisted that the Kolesov-engined version should have a payload of 11,000-13,000 kg (24,250-28,660 lb). In 1966 the OKB built a wooden full-size mock-up of the Tu-144 which was duly examined and approved by an MGA commission.

At the Tupolev OKB, the Tu-144's powerplant integration was initially the department of Kurt V. Minkner, one of the Soviet Union's most prominent specialists in the field of aircraft propulsion technology. After his death in harness in 1972, Vladimir M. Vool' took over the job in March 1972. Other Tupolev OKB employees involved in the development of the Tu-144's powerplant included Aleksandr P. Balooyev, Ye. M. Mindlin, Donat A. Kozhevnikov, Boris S. Ivanov, A. A. Koor'yanskiy, V. A. Tveretskiy, M. Ya. Gol'dman, Ye. Ye. Kooz'min, Nina N. Foorayeva, Valentin V. Malyshev, Yefim R. Goobar', V. A. Leonov, V. N. Nikitin, Ye. V. Voroshilin, V. M. Proshin, V. F. Novikov, F. N. Kuleshov and A. N. Golovnya who participated in the development of the engines proper, the air intakes and the fuel system, as well as in the ensuing aerodynamic, bench and flight tests.

Now, since the NK-144 was selected for Stage A, it is worth describing the powerplant based on it in more detail. Generally it takes longer to develop an aero engine from scratch than it takes to design an all-new airframe, and the common wisdom is that you design an aircraft around the engines, not vice versa. Therefore, it is easy to see why Tupolev accepted Kuznetsov's idea of developing the NK-144 as a derivative of the NK-8 – an idea supported by the Central Aero Engine Institute (TsIAM – *Tsentrahl'nyy institoot aviatsionnovo motorostroyeniya*) and TsAGI. The proven core of the NK-8 meant that the NK-144 would be a reliable engine with ample thrust reserves – exactly what the Tupolev OKB needed for testing and perfecting the SST. Also, Nikolay D. Kuznetsov had made his mark as a gifted designer and a good co-ordinator in the early 1950s by designing the NK-12. Now he had a chance to prove this image once again by overcoming the many organisational and technical problems that would inevitably arise when creating such an engine. Hence on 16th July 1963 the Council of Ministers issued a directive officially tasking OKB-276 with developing the NK-144 engine; the directive had been drafted at Andrey N. Tupolev's initiative.

Throughout the development of the NK-144 engine a considerable contribution was made by TsIAM, the main Soviet authority in this field since 1930. TsIAM's leading specialists – Gheorgiy P. Svishchev, Robert S. Kinasoshvili, Sergey M. Shlyakhtenko, Isaak A. Birger, Boris F. Schorr, Nikolay Ya. Litvinov, Aleksey A. Shevyakov, Vladimir M. Akimov, Gorimir G. Chornyy, L. I. Sorkin, L. Ye. Ol'shtein, Mikhail M. Tskhovrebov, Sergey A. Sirotin *et al.* – worked in close co-operation with the Kuznetsov OKB, undertaking a huge scope of research work on the engine's components and the engine as a whole. This included testing of the complete NK-144 engine in a thermovacuum chamber emulating the operational conditions in supersonic cruise.

TsAGI's Section 1, whose domain is the gas dynamics of powerplants, also had a hand in the matter. TsAGI specialists Lev A. Simonov, Vladimir I. Vasil'yev, Viktor T. Zhdanov, Aleksandr V. Nikolayev, Gersch L. Grodzovskiy and Viktor D. Sokolov conducted a large scope of work on the aerodynamics of air intakes and engine nozzles. Shortly afterwards, the Flight Research Institute named after Mikhail M. Gromov (LII – *Lyotno-issledovatel'skiy instituut*) joined in – the NK-144 was put through its paces on the institute's Tu-95LL engine testbed (*letayushchaya laboratoriya* – lit. 'flying laboratory') converted from the second prototype *Bear-A* bomber (the '95/2'). (In Russian the term *letayushchaya laboratoriya* is used indiscriminately to denote any kind of testbed or research/survey aircraft.) The development engine was installed in the bomb bay in a special nacelle which could be raised or lowered hydraulically on a system of levers; the nacelle was semi-recessed for take-off and landing to give adequate ground clearance, extending clear of the fuselage into the slipstream before start-up. A large amount of work was done to check the engine's start-up reliability, its operation at constant and variable rpm, its surge resistance, the reliability of afterburner light-up and operation and so on; engineer S. V. Petrov was in charge of this work.

Prior to installation in the Tu-144 prototype the NK-144 was rigorously tested according to all standards then in force for commercial and military aircraft and in all anticipated flight modes.

At the design cruising speed of Mach 2.2 and a cruise altitude of 18,000 m (59,060 ft), where the ambient temperature was as low as −56.5°C (−69.7°F), the impact temperature at the engine compressor faces was 153°C (307°F); at Mach 2.35 and 20,000 m (65,620 ft) it rose to 183°C (361°F). Tests at increased rpm (to simulate engine overspeeding), turbine temperatures and vibrations were undertaken; the efficiency of the fire suppression system was checked, as was the engine's FOD resistance in the event of birdstrike or ice ingestion (the birds weighed up to 1.5 kg/3.3 lb).

Since jet engines cannot operate in a supersonic airflow for structural strength reasons, the incoming air has to be slowed down before it reaches the engine's compressor face, and the NK-144's operation with highly complex fully adjustable supersonic air intakes was another area that received much attention, as it was crucial for the powerplant's reliability and efficiency. A peculiarity of the air intakes of a supersonic aircraft is that the range of functions performed by the air intake increases as the Mach number grows.

As regards air intake design, the Tu-144 project included the following points. Each engine was to have its own individual intake so as to minimise the engines' mutual influence in the event of surge and during start-up. (The latter bit is not a trifle, as one might be inclined to believe. Remember the MiG-19 fighter: the airflow parameters of the common air intake divided by a splitter into two inlet ducts were such that the wind direction on the hardstand had to be taken into account – the downwind engine had to be started first, otherwise the upwind engine would literally rob it of breath, making start-up impossible!) The air intakes had four distinct modes of operation: take-off/climb/subsonic cruise, acceleration beyond Mach 1.3, supersonic cruise at Mach 2.0-2.2 and deceleration/descent. Tupolev OKB designers Aleksandr P. Balooyev, Ye. M. Mindlin, V. S. Timofeyev, N. P. Leonov, N. N. Pershin, Ye. Ye. Kooz'min, V. A. Gusarov, V. I. Roganov, Yu. S. Yegorov, Donat A. Kozhevnikov, E. S. Berezanskiy, N. I. Fedoseyev, M. I. Goosikhin, A. S. Sidorov, A. V. Verem'yeva and V. Yu. Shaltuper invested a lot of effort into the development and refining of the Tu-144's air intakes.

The tests began with scale models of the air intakes and wing/intake combinations in TsAGI's supersonic wind tunnel, the largest models (to 1/15th scale) featuring functional (remote-controlled) inlet ramps, spill doors and engine simulators altering the mass flow. These tests confirmed the results of the theoretical research on the intakes' design, making it possible to issue recommendations concerning detail design of specific features to enhance the intakes' efficiency. They culminated in two series of tests of the full-size intake in a thermovacuum chamber at TsIAM and at the Kuznetsov OKB (aka NPO Trood; NPO = *na**ooch**no-proiz**vod**stvennoye obyedineniye* – Research & Production Association). At Andrey N. Tupolev's initiative the TsIAM branch office in Toorayevo (an industrial area of Lytkarino township in the south-east of the Moscow Region) built the special Ts1-A gas dynamics research rig. This had a supersonic nozzle from which a stream of air at Mach 2.2 was

The Tu-144's fuel system test rig featuring duel tanks on an articulated platform of comparable size to the aircraft's wings.

Above: A subscale model of the Tu-144's fuselage and wings undergoing preliminary static tests.

Right: Another view of the same model, with a test engineer providing scale. Note the plethora of rods and beams transferring the loads to the test article.

directed at a full-size version of the Tu-144's air intake assembly, entering the air intake and the running NK-144 engine.

The tests proved that the air intake and the powerplant as a whole worked as it should in supersonic cruise. They also made it possible to adjust the control laws of the air intake's movable airflow control ramp, assess the pressure losses in the inlet duct and the deformation of the velocity and pressure fields upstream of the engine's compressor face. Andrey N. Tupolev frequently visited the Toorayevo branch and provided assistance to the team constructing the Ts1-A rig.

The tests at NPO Trood, where another rig was built to explore the operation of the NK-144 and the full-size air intake on take-off and in subsonic flight, also yielded valuable results. It was quickly discovered that the engine's surge resistance in take-off mode was insufficient and engine operation was disrupted by the inevitable airflow separation at the sharp air intake lips typical of supersonic air intakes in this mode. This was true for the prototype NK-144 engines having a two-stage fan; the problem was eventually cured by adding a third fan stage, which also allowed the engine to be uprated to 20,000 kgp (44,090 lbst) in the NK-144A version. As a temporary remedy, profiles altering the air intake lip profile to a more rounded one were fitted to create a more agreeable airflow pattern, pending delivery of the revised engines. It was also decided to use auxiliary blow-in doors on the production Tu-144 instead of movable lower intake lips as a means of preventing surge.

Development of the Tu-144's flight control system initially proceeded under the guidance of Lazar' M. Rodnyanskiy, who had worked in the Myasishchev OKB until its liquidation and had accumulated valuable experience of designing automated control systems. After his untimely death in 1971 at the age of 56, this direction of work was headed by Aleksandr S. Kochergin. The OKB's aerodynamics section headed by Gheorgiy A. Cheryomukhin also provided some ideas on the system's features. Tupolev OKB personnel involved in developing the control system included B. I. Lyubetskiy, V. I. Goniodskiy, N. I. Martynov, Yu. N. Kashtanov, Vadim M. Razumikhin and A. I. Nefyodov. A series of control system test rigs, including an 'iron bird'/flight simulator, was built at the initiative of Boris N. Sokolov.

Chapter 1 - The Tu-144 is Born

(Speaking of which, the total number of test rigs built in the course of the Tu-144 programme exceeded 80. These included static electricity and lightning protection rigs, a landing gear test rig and so on. All of this made it possible to evolve a system of hardware failure assessment, reducing the number of simulated failures to be tested in actual flight conditions.)

For a supersonic aircraft, be it commercial or military, thermal loads – primarily due to the strong kinetic heating at supersonic speeds – are a key factor dictating the choice of the structural materials, general arrangement, flight trajectory and flight modes. The higher the cruise Mach number, the more acute this problem becomes. Nearly 50 years ago the Tupolev OKB – first and foremost a small design team under Vladimir A. Andreyev (who later became the Tupolev PLC's Chief Designer for cryogenic-fuel aircraft) – came face to face with these problems for the first time. Therefore a special section headed by Andreyev and Cand. Tech.

One of the test rigs used during the Tu-144's development.

Sc. Galina T. Koovshinova was set up at the OKB to calculate the thermal loads and work out the parameters of the heat insulation/protection systems.

A further complication is that when the aircraft accelerates to supersonic speed the skin gets hot quickly, whereas the underlying structure takes a while to soak up the heat; the process is reversed during deceleration/descent, with additional internal stresses arising in both cases. In cruise flight a temperature equilibrium is reached. (Actually, in the case of the wings it is not reached – the cold fuel inside the tanks warms up but it is also used up, the wetted area growing smaller.) The task of determining the airframe structure's equilibrium temperatures (with due regard to the air conditioning system's operation and the fuel's thermal capacity) was one of the toughest. Proceeding from the work done by various research institutes, the OKB developed calculation techniques and undertook experiments allowing it to calculate the Tu-144's equilibrium and gradient temperatures (that is, temperatures rising and falling during the climb to/descent from cruise altitude); these figures tallied well with the results obtained in actual flight tests.

Protecting the rear fuselage from the hot jet exhaust turned out to be another major challenge. It transpired that nobody in the Soviet Union had taken on this issue before; there had been no need to, as the supersonic aircraft developed by the Tupolev OKB and other design bureaux had the engine nozzle(s) positioned either at the aft extremity of the fuselage or well away from the fuselage sides. (Similarly, the jet efflux issue was not critical for the Concorde whose rear fuselage was unaffected by the heating problem because the engine nacelles were placed well away from the fuselage.) Hence there was no ready-made solution. The problem was aggravated by the fact that in sustained supersonic cruise the skin temperature of the primary structure (including the hottest areas of the airframe) came close to the limit beyond which aluminium alloys started melting, compromising structural integrity. At the Mach 2.35 cruising speed originally envisaged, the Tu-144's skin temperature was expected to reach 140°C (284°F). However, the decision to use NK-144 afterburning turbofans with nozzles of 1.7 m (5 ft $6^{31}/_{32}$ in) diameter led to an increase in the speed and temperature of the efflux – the core of the jet could get as hot as 1,500°C (2,732°F) – and increased dynamic and thermal loads on the rear fuselage. The location of all four engines in a common nacelle on the prototype only made the problem worse, as it took the exhaust jets dangerously close to the fuselage skin, creating the risk of overheating and structural failure.

The specialists of the Tupolev OKB and other R&D establishments began large-scale theoretical and practical research effort spearheaded by Galina T. Koovshinova to explore the exhaust jet dynamics and the interaction of the jet efflux with the airframe. The maximum temperature of the rear fuselage structure aft of the engine nozzles recorded on a test rig was 360-450°C (680-842°F), which was unacceptably high even for a titanium structure – especially a highly stressed one. To remedy this, a hollow heat shield consisting of a titanium sheet skin and a basalt fibre filler was fitted to the rear fuselage; special evaporative-action radiators were installed inside the rear fuselage to cool the structure. Yet, subsequently the Tu-144's cruising speed was reduced to Mach 2.2 in order to reduce the thermal loads.

The production of such a radically new aircraft as the Tu-144 created a spate of technological problems that had to be tackled by all branches of industry having to do with aviation. This especially concerned the new structural materials, instruments and equipment used and the manufacturing technologies involved; the technological leap for the Soviet aircraft industry brought about by the Tu-144 was comparable to the one when the Tupolev OKB reverse-engineered the Boeing B-29 Superfortress in 1945-46 as the Tu-4 *Bull*. Numerous research establishments of the aircraft industry, as well as Tupolev OKB specialists (A. A. Kozlov, Nikolay T. Kozlov, Alfred M. Davtyan, V. A. Zaslavskiy, Vladimir M. Shitov, Igor' B. Ginko *et al.*), took part in selecting the structural materials for the Tu-144.

Andrey N. Tupolev, who always cared a lot about aviation technologies, personally co-ordinated the efforts to introduce new materials and production methods as part of the Tu-144 programme. Much of this burden was shouldered by the brilliant technologist Isaak B. Iosilovich (during the Great Patriotic War of 1941-45 he had organised production of the Tu-2S bomber at Moscow-Fili in his capacity as Director of plant No.23), MMZ No.156 chief engineer Aleksey V. Meshcheryakov, chief technologist Semyon A. Vigdorchik, chief metallurgist Ivan L. Golovin and deputy chief engineer Vladimir P. Nikolayev. Mention should be made of coordinator/procurement specialist Mikhail

Chapter 1 - The Tu-144 is Born

A. Bormashenko, who often worked wonders in procuring hard-to-obtain structural materials for MMZ No.156, the dielectric materials section chief Boris A. Peshekhonov, the plant's Director Viktor I. Borod'ko and many others working as a close-knit and dedicated team.

Given the Tu-144's intended cruising speed of Mach 2.35 (later Mach 2.2), it was possible to utilise aluminium alloys as the primary structural material, which gave a considerable cost reduction as compared to titanium or stainless steel and increased the airframe's service life – not to mention the fact that aluminium alloy structures are much easier to manufacture. Incidentally, the Concorde, too, was originally designed to cruise at Mach 2.2 but in the course of airline service the cruising speed was limited to Mach 2.05.

The D16 series duralumin alloys widely used by the Soviet aircraft industry in the early 1960s were unsuitable for an aircraft with a long service life (30,000 hours) operating at skin temperatures of 100-130°C (212-266°F) and designed with a high weight efficiency. Specifically, the D16T version was unsuitable for sustained temperatures in excess of 80°C (176°F); the D16T1 version had better heat resistance but had poor fatigue resistance. New aluminium alloys with greater heat and fatigue resistance that would ensure structural integrity had to be developed and the technologies of processing them devised. This included creep resistance – that is, resistance to residual permanent deformations arising in the course of operation.

A major R&D effort was undertaken. At first, the All-Union Institute of Aviation Materials (VIAM – *Vsesoyoozny institoot aviatsionnykh materiahlov*; specifically, the institute's laboratory chief Iosif N. Friedlander) offered the brand-new VAD-23 aluminium-lithium alloy (*vysokoprochnyy alyuminiy deformeeruyemyy* – deformable high-strength aluminium; the 'deformable' bit refers to parts manufacturing processes) as the primary structural material for the airframe. Tupolev OKB specialists – structural strength department chief Aleksandr R. Bonin, chief metallurgist Ivan L. Golovin and chief technologist Semyon A. Vigdorchik – supported him, recommending the VAD-23 alloy to General Designer Andrey N. Tupolev, as it was strong, light and able to withstand high temperatures for extended periods. Its actual properties were still unknown, and it was offered on the strength of the authoritative VIAM's recommendations. However, considering that the VAD-23 was still untried in operational conditions, the OKB's specialists also offered an alternative – the AK4-1 aluminium alloy, which was by then used in aero engine manufacturing. (It should be noted that Vigdorchik was not only a man of initiative but an extremely learned man and always ready to share his knowledge with anyone who showed genuine interest; therefore, unsurprisingly, he enjoyed great authority in the aircraft industry.)

Considering that the wing spars were among the most complex elements of the Tu-144's airframe, sample spars of various designs were manufactured and tested. It turned out that the VAD-23 alloy was inferior to the AK4-1 as regards durability and resistance to cracking, belying the 'deformable' bit of its name – samples of this material shattered like glass during testing; therefore it was rejected and the AK4-1 was selected as the primary structural material. However, when the OKB's experimental plant started working with the first samples of this alloy, the engineers were in for a nasty surprise again: all its advantages notwithstanding, the AK4-1 turned out to have a low critical deformation rate. This was a major liability when manufacturing stamped parts, as it led to a severe deterioration of fatigue resistance and corrosion resistance. Careful analysis revealed that the core of the problem lay in the alloy's excessively grainy structure leading to inter-crystalline stress and corrosion. To improve fatigue resistance the alloy's chemical composition had to be altered by sharply reducing the silicone content, and a two-stage sheet metal rolling process was invented, improving the material's mechanical stability. To enable the manufacture of wings with a high load ratio the Soviet metallurgical industry had to master production of AK4-1 alloy parts up to 9 m (29 ft 6$^{11}/_{32}$ in) long, up to 2 m (6 ft 6$^{3}/_{4}$ in) wide and up to 65 mm (2$^{9}/_{16}$ in) thick. Such items were rolled from slabs of up to 800 mm (2 ft 7$^{1}/_{2}$ in) diameter weighing up to 3 tons (6,610 lb), with a uniform chemical composition. It proved necessary to use a new uniform alloying technology and a homogenisation technology to alleviate linear stresses (the slabs were forged consecutively from several directions to modify the grain structure and make the slabs more suitable for the ensuing rolling process). Moreover, the need to machine such panels led to the development of computerised numerically controlled (CNC) machine tools.

Another aluminium alloy, VAL-10 (*vysokoprochnyy alyuminiy liteynyy* – high-strength aluminium optimised for casting), was developed to meet a Tupolev OKB requirement. VAL-10 castings had mechanical properties similar to those of stamped parts; therefore a sizeable number of half-finished parts for the Tu-144 were manufactured by casting instead of stamping, making production less labour-intensive.

A new technology of stretching the half-finished articles after the rolling process was introduced to prevent machined skin panels from warping. At the Tupolev OKB's request a stretching machine delivering a force of 6,000 tons (13,227,500 lbf) was created and commissioned at the metal foundry in the town of Verkhnyaya Salda (Sverdlovsk Region, southern Urals).

Considerable success was achieved with introducing titanium alloys for areas of the airframe which were exposed to temperatures in excess of 160°C (320°F). Titanium was used on an unusually wide scale in the Tu-144's design. As late as 1958 the share of titanium in a typical Soviet aircraft's airframe was less than 0.5%; on the Tu-144 it rose to an unprecedented 15% of the airframe weight.

The new alloys' properties, which were not stated in available literature, had to be studied. Hence the OKB set up a new division called Technological Laboratories Section (OTL – *Otdel tekhnicheskikh laboratoriy*). This section worked in close contact with such notable research establishments as VIAM, the All-Union Institute of Light Alloys (VILS – *Vsesoyoozny institoot lyohkikh splavov*), the Central Research Institute of Ferrous Metals (TsNIIChM – *Tsentrahl'nyy naoochno-issledovatel'skiy institoot chornykh metahllov*), the Aviation Technology Research Institute (NIAT – *Naoochno-issledovatel'skiy institoot aviatsionnykh tekhnologiy*) and so on. For example, VILS developed technologies for mass production of the new alloys used in the Tu-144's structure, while the institute's experimental production facility supplied these materials for prototype construction. This co-operation

helped a lot to introduce the titanium alloys that are indispensible for a supersonic aircraft. Titanium alloys are stronger and stiffer than aluminium (and even steel, in some circumstances) and can withstand temperatures up to 400°C (752°F); they also have high corrosion and fatigue resistance. Also, titanium lends itself well to welding, allowing rivet or bolted joints to be eliminated and a weight saving achieved. The VT-6 (*vysokoprochnyy titahn* – high-strength titanium), VT-20, OT-4 (*ognestoykiy titahn* – fireproof titanium) and OT-4-1 alloys were best suited for constructing the airframes of supersonic jets.

Titanium alloy parts are generally harder to manufacture than aluminium alloy parts due to the physical properties of titanium; also, machining titanium parts is more expensive. Thus, in order to cut production costs it was necessary to improve the manufacturing technologies associated with titanium parts. The first attempts at manufacturing welded titanium sheet structures in open-air conditions gave unsatisfactory results; the chemical reaction of the titanium with the atmosphere during the welding, coupled with different thermal treatment modes, caused adsorption of atmospheric hydrogen, which led to a marked reduction of the material's viscosity and ultimately to profuse cracking. It became clear that titanium structures had to be welded and thermally treated in an inert medium (such as argon) or in vacuum. None of the Soviet aircraft factories had appropriate equipment for such operations. For the purpose of welding small titanium parts and perfecting the technology at the same time, the OTL designed and built an experimental argon welding chamber with argon purity monitoring; this chamber is still in use today. Refinement of the titanium welding technology was the responsibility of A. P. Svetovidov, V. S. Sytnikov, K. I. Petrov, O. N. Sankov and other NIAT and Tupolev OKB engineers. However, this first chamber was only good for manufacturing several dozen parts for the Tu-144 prototype; it was not until 1968 that NIAT designed the first full-size argon-arc welding/annealing chamber and had it manufactured for the Tupolev OKB's experimental shop in Moscow – MMZ No.156 'Opyt' (*Moskovskiy mashinostroitel'nyy zavod* – Moscow Machinery Plant; opyt translates as either 'experiment' or 'experience'). Jumping ahead of the story, it may be said

Far left: A wooden mock-up of the Tu-144's (*izdeliye* 044) nose section with the nose visor drooped, showing the main windshield and the twin windows in the visor's upper side.

Left: the underside of the mock-up's radome; a strip of plywood is still missing, exposing the internal structure.

Above right: The mock-up with the nose visor in the cruise position. The visor carries a ventral blade aerial and has a further antenna marked immediately aft of the radome joint line.

Right: The lowered visor shows the curved joint line. Note the open direct vision window on the captain's side and the fuselage frame numbers (15, 16, 17 and so on)

that most of the large titanium components for the prototype and production Tu-144s were welded and annealed at the Ministry of Defence Industry's ***Severnyy Zavod*** (Northern Plant) in Leningrad, the only plant in the Soviet Union which had the requisite industrial-standard equipment.

Another temporary problem was the manufacture of titanium sheet parts, angle pieces and other small items for the prototype's airframe, as the Soviet aircraft industry could not supply such items ready-made. Again, these parts had to be manufactured in house. For the first time in Soviet practice, Tupolev OKB specialists used gas chromatographs to check the argon purity in the welding/annealing chamber, precluding the presence of oxygen, hydrogen and nitrogen which might impair the welding quality.

A technology for manufacturing titanium honeycomb structures by diffusion welding was developed jointly with NIAT and its Voronezh branch, as well as the Academy of Sciences' Institute of Metallurgy and Material Science named after Aleksandr A. Baykov (IMET – *Institoot metalloorghiï i materialovedeniya*) and the Moscow-based Problem Solution Scientific Research Laboratory of Vacuum Diffusion Welding (PNILDSV – *Problemnaya naoochno-issledovatel'skaya laboratoriya diffoozionnoy svarki v vahkuume*).

The Tupolev OKB also developed a whole set of technological guidelines for working with titanium that were later adopted by the Soviet aircraft industry. Among other things, MMZ No.156 developed a method of manufacturing honeycomb-core titanium panels with a filler of VT-15 titanium foil 0.08 mm (0.0031 in) thick, which was supplied by the Verkhnyaya Salda Metal Foundry. Panels up to 1,000 mm (3 ft 3⅜ in) long, 500 mm (1 ft 7¹¹⁄₁₆ in) wide and 80 mm (3⁵⁄₃₂ in) thick were manufactured by diffusion welding in a vacuum furnace at 950-1,050°C (1,724-1,922°F). The technologies of bending and welding honeycomb-core titanium panels and installing fasteners in them were also verified.

The Tu-144 also triggered the wide use of the following alloys and parts made thereof:

• AK4-1 aluminium alloy – sheets 0.5-1.0 mm (0.019-0.039 in) thick, up to 1.5 m (4 ft 11³⁄₆₄ in) wide and up to 7 m (22 ft 11¹⁹⁄₃₂ in) long, extruded profiles up to 150 mm (5²⁹⁄₃₂ in) deep and up to 10 m

Far left: The port main gear unit of the Tu-144 (*izdeliye* 044) mock-up in mid-retraction, showing the 'knee-action' strut and 12-wheel bogie. The cowling of the No.1 engine is incomplete.

Left: The mock-up's flight deck interior. The distinctive push-button control boxes on the control wheels of the real aircraft are absent.

Below left: The centre fuselage of the Tu-144 (*izdeliye* 044) mock-up, showing the second entry door (which would open differently on the actual aircraft) and the inflated emergency slide beside it resting on the port LERX. The numbers of the wing spars are given below some of the fuselage frame numbers; note the lights shining through the cabin windows to illuminate the interior with simulated natural light in the darkened hangar.

Right: Andrey N. Tupolev ponders design issues as he sits beside a different mock-up – that of the production version. Three members of the design team are standing behind, with PD section chief Valentin I. Bliznyuk on the right.

(32 ft 9⁴⁵⁄₆₄ in) long, forged and rolled slabs up to 63 mm (2³¹⁄₆₄ in) thick and measuring up to 9 x 1.6 m (29 ft 6²¹⁄₆₄ in x 5 ft 3 in);
• VAD-23 aluminium alloy extruded profiles and stamped panels;
• V93 aluminium alloy stampings;
• VAL-10 aluminium alloy and ML-10T6 magnesium alloy castings (ML = **mahgniy liteynyy** – magnesium optimised for casting);
• OT-4 and OT-4-1 titanium alloys – sheets 0.3-12.0 mm (0.0118-0.47 in) thick, up to 1.2 m (3 ft 11¹⁵⁄₆₄ in) wide and up to 4 m (13 ft 1³¹⁄₆₄ in) long, extruded profiles up to 3.5 m (11 ft 5⁵¹⁄₆₄ in) long, slabs 35-60 mm (1³⁄₈ to 2²³⁄₆₄ in) thick and stamped parts);
• VT-22 titanium alloy (precision stamped parts);
• VT-5 titanium alloy (stamped profiles);
• VT-16 titanium alloy (cold- and hot-rolled rods for making fasteners);
• VT-5L titanium alloy castings measuring up to 0.8 x 1.2 m (2 ft 7³¹⁄₆₄ in x 3 ft 11¹⁵⁄₆₄ in); again, the L stands for *liteynyy*.

That was not all. The temperatures at which the Tu-144 would operate necessitated a large amount of research on a new generation of non-metallic materials, such as glassfibre reinforced plastic (GRP) for the weather radar radome and other antenna fairings, glass and Perspex for the flight deck and cabin windows, rubber for tyres and various seals, heat-resistant bonding agents, sealants working in hot air and hot fuel or fuel vapour mediums, foam plastics and other heat insulating materials, plastics for cabin wall liners and other interior parts and so on. All of these materials were to withstand prolonged exposure to temperatures ranging from –40°C (–40°F) to 130°C (226°F) without deteriorating. Here, again, VIAM was heavily involved. It should be noted that in order to achieve high weight efficiency the designers increased the share of non-metallic materials in the Tu-144's structure to 23% by weight – again an unprecedentedly high figure by Soviet standards.

Among other things, the Tupolev OKB's non-metallic materials laboratory headed by Boris A. Peshekhonov joined forces with VIAM to develop and assess two types of heat-resistant sealants intended for the fuel system – fluoride silicone and fluoride rubber. It turned out that in normal temperatures fluoride rubber sealants were less prone to deterioration over time; also, fluoride silicone sealants tended to become excessively brittle in high-temperature

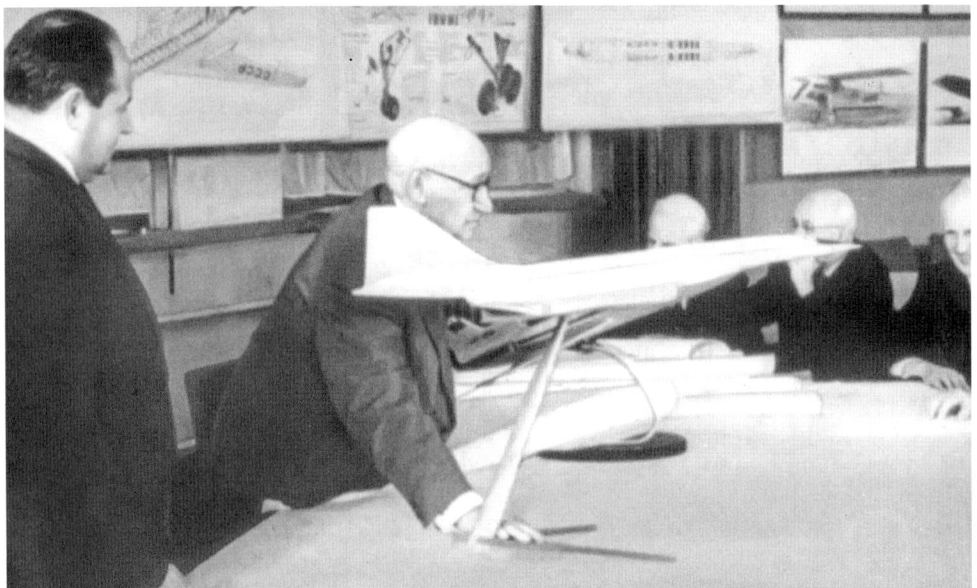

Left: General Designer Andrey N. Tupolev speaks at a session of the OKB's technical council devoted to the Tu-144 and the Tu-154, as the two models on the desk suggest. The poster on the wall beyond pertains to the Tu-134, however.

Below left: A scene from the same session; Andrey N. Tupolev and Tu-144 project chief Aleksey A. Tupolev listen as a designer delivers a report on the SST's control system. Posters showing the Tu-144's interior layout and its air conditioning system are also visible here.

Right: Aleksey A. Tupolev makes a report in front of the interior layout poster. The latter shows a 120-seat all-economy layout with basically five-abreast seating (40+80), with a scrap view of the three-abreast 18-seat first class cabin of the 98-seat version.

Right: ANT mulls over what he has just heard, while Tupolev Jr. stands by, awaiting a reaction to the reports. The latter could occasionally be quite harsh – Old Man Tupolev was never shy to speak his mind.

conditions. On the other hand, fluoride rubber sealants were not flexible enough, which created considerable difficulties when applying them to the fuel tanks. Together with VIAM (represented by Ya. I. Mindlin), the Rubber Industry Research Institute (NIIRP – *Naoochno-issledovatel'skiy institoot rezinovoy promyshlennosti*, represented by R. Ya. Smyslova) and the Academy of Sciences' Physical Institute named after P. N. Lebedev (FIAN – *Fizicheskiy institoot Akademii naook*), the OKB's non-metallic materials laboratory created the 51G series of modified fluoride rubber sealants which eventually found use on the production Tu-144 (but not the prototype) and was superior to foreign counterparts.

The Research Institute of Technical Glass (NIITS – *Naoochno-issledovatel'skiy institoot tekhnicheskovo stekla*; in this context 'technical' means special-purpose) succeeded in creating new-generation GRP able to withstand strong heating at high speeds and strong UV radiation at high altitude. This allowed the designers to resolve some complex problems, reconciling the requirements of the aerodynamicists (who demanded the lowest possible drag) and the avionics specialists (who demanded minimum interference with the antennas' operation). Designing the nose radome turned out to be an unexpectedly difficult task; moulding it in the usual way from a wide glassfibre strip proved impossible, and eventually the radome was fashioned from pieces of glassfibre cut to shape. The radome was shaped according to the same laws as the entire forward fuselage. It took the designers quite a while to select the optimum materials for the radome; the best results were

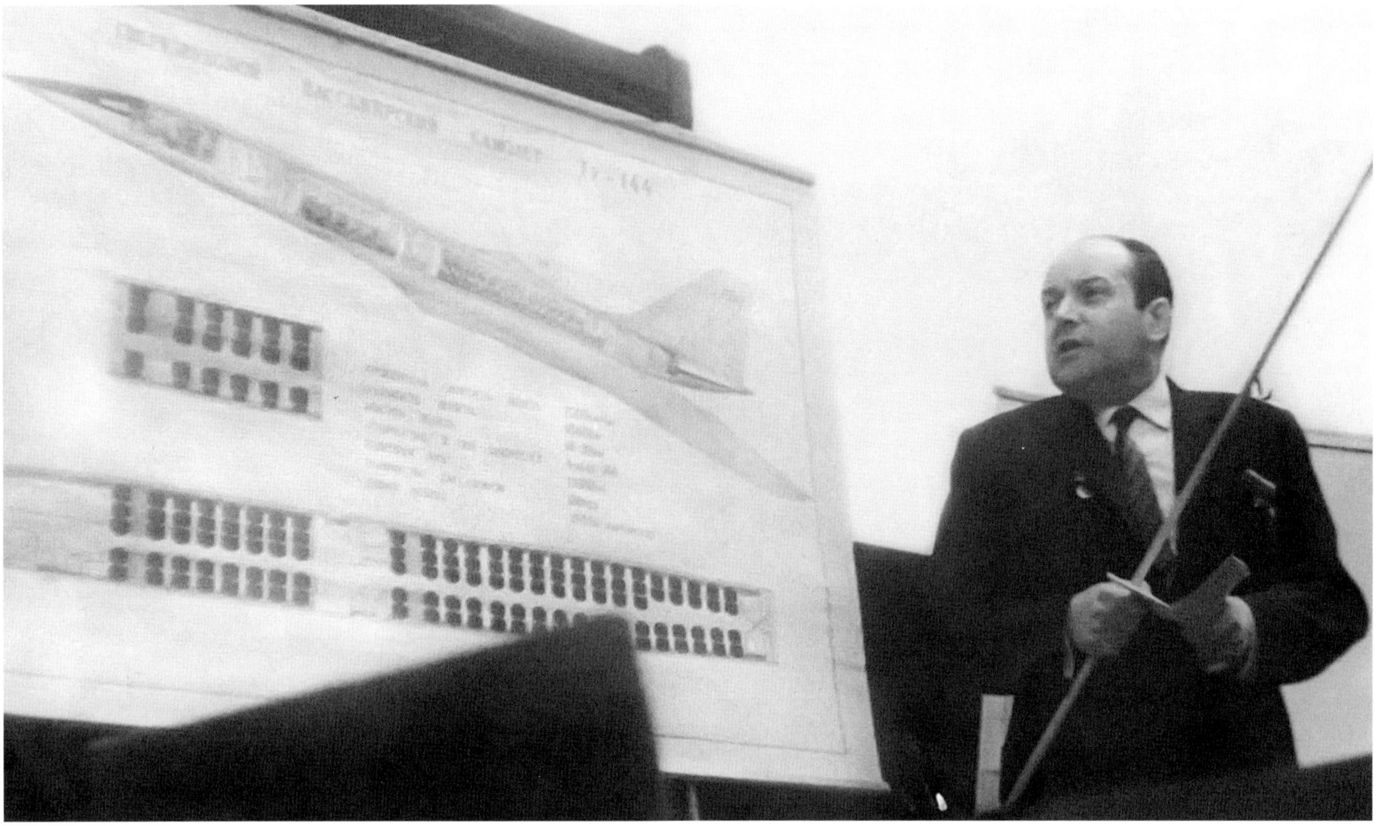

Chapter 1 - The Tu-144 is Born

obtained with EDF grade epoxy/phenol resin as a binder. However, it was even harder to design and manufacture the dielectric tailcone housing an antenna array because the tailcone was located in the area where the acoustic loads and heat from the engine exhaust were at their highest. A special technology had to be devised – the tailcone was moulded, using the specially formulated K-917 silicone-organic binder, and then given a coat of U2-28B sealant ensuring heat resistance.

The Tu-144 introduced cabin and baggage compartment floor panels of GRP honeycomb construction that were much lighter than traditional ones. As often as not, simple solutions could be found to seemingly complex engineering tasks. For example, a technology was devised (and appropriate equipment designed) for coating metal surfaces with polyurethane foam, which cured at normal temperatures and had excellent heat insulating properties. It was used in the avionics/equipment bays, parts of the cabin, on the cabin doors and in the wheel wells; box-type structures made of polyurethane foam were used in pressurised areas.

For the first time, new E-2 grade heat-resistant Plexiglas (likewise developed by NIITS) was used for the windows incorporated into the Tu-144's hinged nose visor – the glazing panels subjected to the highest thermal and dynamic loads. This was no mean achievement; had the designers had to use heat-resistant silicate glass for these transparencies, this would incur a sizeable weight penalty. Still, putting E-2 Plexiglas into production proved to be no easy task.

On the Tu-144 the OKB used a completely new approach to designing the cabin windows with their multi-layer glazing. Each pane in the set had its specific function but could withstand the entire load for a short time if any of the other panes failed. The outer pane was non-stressed (that is, it did not normally absorb the pressure differential), acting as a heat shield. The cold centre pane absorbed the pressure differential, while the inner pane had a decorative function but also organised the cooling air flow, making it possible to include the windows into the cabin cooling system. This approach made it possible to use Plexiglas for all three panes, making the design much simpler and cheaper as compared to a design using glass. The flight deck windshield was made of triplex glass ensuring the required heat resistance, birdstrike resistance and resistance to the elements.

New grades of rubber had to be developed for the Tu-144's door perimeter seals, rubber hoses, gaskets and the like. Non-metallic materials were also used for special fittings in order to reduce the heat transfer to various equipment items from the hot skin.

Together with other research and development institutions, the OKB did a huge scope of work on the Tu-144's systems and equip-

Top left: Aleksey A. Tupolev chairs a technical meeting devoted to the Tu-144; note the model on the desk depicting an early twin-tail PD project version.

Above left: An early mock-up of the Tu-144's nose section (note the three-piece windscreen instead of the definitive V-shaped one).

Left: The Tupolev OKB's mock-up shop, with large cutaway models of the Tu-144 and Tu-154, plus the Tu-144 (*izdeliye* 044) nose mock-up shown earlier.

ment. The tailless-delta layout with low aspect ratio wings offered optimum performance in sustained supersonic cruise but was characterised by instability in a number of other flight modes (poor pitch and roll stability and airspeed fluctuations during the landing approach). Besides, the SST had higher unstick and approach speeds as compared to subsonic airliners. All of this necessitated a huge amount of R&D work on the Tu-144's control system, including the ABSU-144 automatic flight control system (*avtomaticheskaya bortovaya sistema oopravleniya* – AFCS). The new nature of the tasks led the Tupolev OKB to use new design features. In particular, the AFCS had to remain activated throughout the flight, ensuring the required stability and handling. Hence the control channels were quadruply redundant for maximum reliability, and quick-action electro-hydraulic control surface actuators were used. To overcome the approach speed problem the AFCS included an autothrottle which stabilised the airspeed during final approach.

The Tu-144's control system offered easy and comfortable control thanks to the automated features maintaining constant (and good) control characteristics in all flight modes and thanks to the G load/AOA limiter. The multiple redundancy of the control system hydraulics made sure that the flight envelope was unaffected by the failure of one hydraulic system, certain limits being imposed for flight safety reasons if any two systems failed.

The ABSU-144 was designed from scratch and enabled the following automatic control modes:
• automatic programmed course selection, using input from the navigation suite;
• automatic ICAO Cat II landing approach (decision altitude 30 m/100 ft, horizontal visibility 400 m/1,300 ft) and, if required, automatic go-around;
• automatic Mach number stabilisation in cruise flight;
• automatic stabilisation of barometric altitude, pitch, heading and desired track;
• alteration of pitch, heading, desired track and execution of co-ordinated turns;
• automatic stabilisation and alteration of the indicated airspeed by adjusting the engine thrust;
• presentation of flight and navigation data on the flight director and the artificial horizon.

The ABSU-144 AFCS was an integrated suite comprising the SAU-144 automatic control system (*sistema avtomaticheskovo oopravleniya*), the STU-75 approach/landing system (*sistema trayektornovo oopravleniya* – trajectory control system), the SUU-144 stability and control system (*sistema oostoychivosti i oopravlyayemosti*), the AT-6 autothrottle (*avtomaht tyaghi*) and the SVK-144 built-in test equipment (*sistema vstroyennovo kon-*

Top right: Another discussion at the OKB concerning the Tu-144, with project aerodynamicist Gheorgiy A. Cheryomukhin at far left.

Above right: Aleksey A. Tupolev with members of the Tu-144 design team, including Valentin I. Bliznyuk on the right.

Right: Tupolev Jr. and Tupolev Sr. at a session of the technical council.

trolya – BITE). All systems had back-up features activated automatically in the event of a failure.

For starters, the electronic components of the suite were developed and verified on a test bench by the Moscow Institute of Electromechanical and Automatic Equipment (MIEA – *Moskovskiy instıtoot elektromekhaniki i avtomahtiki*). Next, the ABSU-144 was put through its paces at Zhukovskiy on a Tu-104B airliner with the non-standard registration CCCP-06195 No.1 (it should have been CCCP-42484 in the Tu-104 registration sequence; construction number 021502) which had been converted into an avionics testbed by the Tupolev OKB. The flight deck was standard; a test engineer's workstation in the cabin featured a Tu-144 instrument panel with the controls of the NK-144 navigation suite (about which more will be said later); the suite underwent certification trials on this aircraft. Jumping ahead of the story, it deserves mention that the OKB used Tu-104B CCCP-06195 extensively for training Tu-144 aircrews until the testbed was transferred to LII in 1974.

While we are on the subject of flight control systems, it may be mentioned that the Tu-144's flight deck ergonomics received considerable attention. This work initially proceeded under the supervision of Leonid L. Kerber and Iosif M. Sklyanskiy; later, Vladimir P. Sakharov took over in this capacity. O. S. Arkhangel'skiy made a significant contribution to choosing the layout of the Tu-144's flight deck in general and the instrument panels in particular. By the time the flight deck mock-up was built, LII's flight test personnel had accumulated considerable experience as regards cockpit ergonomics. After assessing the test results obtained with the *Polyot-1* (Flight-1) automatic navigation system – the first one of its kind in the Soviet Union – Andrey N. Tupolev gave orders that LII test pilot Nikolay V. Adamovich-Iodko, the system's project test pilot, be called upon to help with the Tu-144's ergonomics issues. Assistance from Adamovich-Iodko, as well as from Tupolev OKB test pilots Eduard V. Yelian (the Tu-144's project test pilot) and Ivan K. Vedernikov, made it possible to incorporate design features reducing the pilot workload.

Much attention was paid to the reliability and operational safety of the fuel system. In particular, the correct grade of jet fuel had to be chosen with regard to the kinetic heating in sustained Mach 2.35 cruise; towards the end of the flight the fuel temperature would reach 100°C (212°F) or even 140°C (284°F) for the residual fuel at the bottom of the tanks, and the temperature was further increased by 40-60°C (104-140°F) at the engines' fuel nozzles in the combustion chambers. The designers chose to use T-8 or T-8V grade thermally stable hydrotreated jet fuel with a specific gravity of 0.79 kg/litre versus 0.775 kg/litre for the standard T-1 and TS-1 jet fuels. T-6 grade hydrogenated jet fuel was chosen as the alternate grade; it had a specific gravity of 0.83 kg/litre, which offered longer range with the same fuel capacity. The fuel load (up to 100,000 kg/220,460 lb) was to be housed in seven main tanks and four service tanks (one for each engine). The usual centrifugal pumps were to be augmented by jet pumps transferring fuel from the bottom of the tanks and acting as a back-up.

The designers went to great lengths to reduce the fire hazard in kinetic heating conditions. At an early stage it was decided to pressurise the fuel tanks with inert (non-combustible) gas, by analogy with military aircraft featuring an inert gas pressurisation system to reduce the risk of fire and explosion if the tanks were pierced by enemy projectiles. A large scope of research work was done, resulting in a decision to use so-called nitrogenated fuel. During the refuelling procedure, nitrogen under pressure would be forced through the fuel to substitute the oxygen dissolved in it; during the climb and in cruise flight this 'sparkling drink' would give off gaseous nitrogen, automatically filling the empty space in the fuel tanks as the fuel was used up.

The use of nitrogenated fuel necessitated development of special fuel nitrogenation equipment (including mobile and man-portable equipment) for processing the fuel at airport fuel depots, in refuelling bowsers and on board the aircraft. Tupolev OKB engineers Boris S. Ivanov, A. A. Koor'yanskiy, Valentin V. Malyshev, V. A. Tveretskiy, V. D. Borisov, V. A. Nadey, N. Ya. Borovoy, E. N. Krasnovskiy and A. F. Chervyakov took an active part in the development of the Tu-144's fuel system and associated equipment.

While we are on the subject of the Tu-144's fuel system, it should be mentioned that the OKB built a test rig to determine the fuel transfer algorithm for the purpose of longitudinal trim (maintaining the correct CG position) and to verify the fuel metering and fuel tank venting systems. The rig featured a hydraulically actuated platform with two degrees of freedom on which the Tu-144's actual fuel tanks holding a total of 110 tons (242,500 lb) of fuel were mounted; the platform could be tilted in two directions at once to emulate the aircraft's pitching and rolling motion. The tanks were connected to a vacuum system, and fuel 'usage' and transfer took place in a pre-programmed sequence. Heaters were installed to emulate kinetic heating. This and other test rigs were used to simulate various hardware failures, including a situation when the main electric system failed and the fuel pumps were operated from the emergency power distribution bus. The tests made it possible to issue recommendations on minimising fuel pressure fluctuations and develop sensors for measuring these fluctuations during the flight tests; the pumps, valves and other fuel system components were also verified.

In parallel, the fire suppression system catering for the engines and the equipment bays was tested at the OKB's engine test facility. Special fire protection coatings which foamed when exposed to flames were verified, as were fire protection features for the engines' throttle cable runs, and the durability of the firewalls was checked. All these features were found to be in conformity with then-current standards.

However, fire protection is not limited to engines and such. For the first time in the Soviet Union, all materials used for the interior (cabin wall liners, seat upholstery and the like) were tested for fire resistance. The OKB built a special rig for integral evaluation of the fire propagation/toxic fumes emission hazard of the cabin and the adjacent avionics/equipment bays. It represented a section of the Tu-144's cabin (with typical seating layouts), equipment bay and baggage compartment, replicating the placement of various materials and making it possible to check their mutual influence in the event of a fire. By changing the power of the flame source and the heating/cooling modes the testers were able to ascertain the effect of natural and enforced convection in the cabin on the spread of the flames and establish how the consequences of the fire depended on

Chapter 1 - The Tu-144 is Born

Minister of Aircraft Industry Pyotr V. Dement'yev, General Designer Andrey N. Tupolev, Minister of Civil Aviation Lt.-Gen. Boris P. Boogayev and project chief Aleksey A. Tupolev during an inter-department meeting concerning the SST programme.

the power of the flame source and the mass of the combustible materials. Later, this rig came in handy for training crews in emergency evacuation procedures in a smoke-filled flight deck/cabin.

The hydraulic system was a lot different from that of subsonic aircraft, as this crucial system catered for many other systems – first and foremost the flight controls. Thus, in order to maximise the efficiency of the hydraulic actuators while keeping their size and weight to a minimum the OKB had to commission hydraulic pumps and drives with a working pressure of 200 kg/cm² (2,857 psi) capable of working at temperatures up to 170-200°C (338-392°F). The following novel features were also introduced into the hydraulic system:

• a combined hydraulic reservoir pressurisation system using compressed nitrogen bottles as the primary source and the air conditioning system as a back-up. This operating algorithm significantly improved the pressurisation system's reliability, precluding ingestion of dust and moisture into the hydraulic system;

• a hydraulic fluid cooling system featuring a fuel/hydraulic fluid heat exchanger and thermostatic valves (the latter allow the fluid to reach the required operating temperature quickly at low ambient temperatures and maintain the correct temperature in all flight modes);

• all-new resonance-type pulsation dampers featuring no movable parts, which makes for high efficiency, reliability and a long service life;

• all-new hydraulic line tension/deformation compensators;

• an emergency turbine pump unit fed by compressed air from the auxiliary power unit (APU), allowing all hydraulic equipment to operate even with all four engines inoperative;

• a hydraulic pump monitoring system featuring a cross-feed valve, a flow meter and a pressure gauge with a remote sensor;

• a system maintaining pressurisation of a hydraulic reservoir shared by two hydraulic systems if one of them is ruptured;

• combined hydraulic modules reducing the number of modules and piping connections.

The hydraulic system operated the control surface actuators, landing gear actuators, wheel brakes and the airflow control ramps in the engine air intakes. Hence special attention was paid to reliability; the system comprised four completely separate subsystems, vital hydraulic actuators being fed by two subsystems each.

The Tu-144 programme called for the development of a new generation of avionics and electric equipment, which were computerised to a considerable degree. Many of the electric and electronic equipment items were unique to supersonic aircraft. The Tu-144's avionics and electric equipment incorporated the latest know-how developed by numerous research and production enterprises. These included the Ramenskoye Instrument Design Bureau (RPKB – ***Ra***menskoye ***p***riborno-***k***onstrooktorskoye ***byuro***), the MKB *Voskhod* (*Moskovskoye konstrooktorskoye byuro* – 'Sunrise' Moscow Design Bureau), MMKB ***Rodina*** (*Moskovskoye mashinostroitel'noye konstrooktorskoye byuro* – 'Motherland' Moscow Machinery Design Bureau), *Rubin* (Ruby), *Kristall* (Crystal) and AKB *Dzerzhinets* design bureaux, and others. For example, the Kiev-based *Kommunar* (Commune worker) Production Association was responsible for the Groza-M144 weather radar – the version of the widespread *Groza* (Thunderstorm) radar optimised for the SST – and the identification friend-or-foe (IFF) and ATC transponders. The Electric Products Design Bureau in

Left: Andrey N. Tupolev and his associates standing behind him (left to right: V. Cherenko, V. Korneyev, Vladimir M. Vool', Ye. Zaslavskaya, Valeriy A. Vishnevskiy, A. Krylov, Valentin I. Bliznyuk, Viktor P. Sakharov and Ivan S. Lyulyushin) with the first large display model of the Tu-144, which was first shown in Paris and is now at the Central Russian Air Force Museum in Monino. The Tu-144 full-size mock-up can be discerned in the background.

Right: 'We told you we could do it – and we did it!' Andrey N. Tupolev with the Tu-144 (*izdeliye* 044) demonstrator shortly before the first flight.

Sarapul (Udmurtian Autonomous SSR) developed the Tu-144's landing and taxi lights, navigation lights, anti-collision beacons and power distribution/overload protection devices. The *Yakor'* (Anchor) design bureau supplied the DC batteries.

Extremely stringent requirements applied to the reliability of the power generating equipment, control/actuating systems and the electric components of the fuel system, necessitating development of asynchronous electric motors. The Soviet electric systems of the day using generators with pneumatic/mechanical drives were unsuitable for an SST as far as both power output and electric current parameters were concerned. Therefore a large amount of research had to be undertaken and new standards and regulations developed. 60-kVA stable-frequency three-phase AC generators with hydromechanical constant-speed drives (CSDs) were designed as the Tu-144's primary power source. Jointly with LII (which provided scientific support from V. N. Soochkov, V. P. Shcholkin, V. L. Aparov *et al.*), AKB Dzerzhinets (where the generators were designed under the leadership of A. F. Fedoseyev, A. V. Delektorskiy and A. N. Mironov) and the Rubin design bureau (where the CSDs were developed under the leadership of I. I. Zverev) a state-of-the-art 115 V/400 Hz and 200 V/400 Hz AC electric system with a nominal output of 240 kVA was created. (AKB = *agregahtnoye konstrooktorskoye byuro* – equipment item design bureau; Dzerzhinets means 'Dzerzhinskiy's comrade-in-arms', Feliks E. Dzerzhinskiy being the founder of the notorious KGB.) No Soviet aircraft had used such a system before, although such systems were by then common in the West, so the Tupolev OKB was breaking new ground once again. The generators were oil-cooled and worked in parallel pairs. Also for the first time in Soviet practice, sparkless electric equipment was developed to minimise the fire and explosion hazard. The increased operating temperatures throughout the airframe made it imperative to develop and put into production a new generation of heat-resistant electric wires, which had been imported until then; these included wires designed for strong currents, which allowed the cross-section (and hence the weight of the wiring) to be reduced.

The Tu-144 was the first Soviet aircraft to make large-scale use of computers and processors in various systems, and it is a well-known fact that voltage spikes or power failures can damage processors. Hence the electric system included power supply monitoring devices which automatically (and promptly) switched the processor to a different power distribution bus if the current one failed. The need to ensure a safe landing in the event of an electrics failure in supersonic cruise led the designers to rethink the electric system structure completely, separating the AC and DC subsystems by function. This structure later became universally accepted and is used on all present-day aircraft.

Long-range supersonic flight necessitated development of a new-generation navigation suite on whose reliability and accuracy flight safety depended, and the complexity of the navigation suite also increased perceptibly as compared to subsonic aircraft. This suite, which, like the engine, was designated NK-144 (in this case the NK stood for *navigatsionnyy **kompleks***, not Nikolay Kuznetsov), was developed by LNPO *Elektroavtomatika* ('Automatic Electric Devices'; LNPO = *Leningrahdskoye na**ooch**no-proiz**vod**stvennoye obye**din**eniye* – Leningrad Scientific & Production Association). The suite was intended for flights along designated airways and outside them, in any geographical conditions and in any season, day or night. The navigation suite enabled the following modes:

• non-stop automatic computation and indication of the aircraft's current co-ordinates and heading in the geographical and orthodromic co-ordinate systems;

• automatic and manual course and co-ordinate correction;

• computation and indication of the estimated time of arrival (ETA) and the minimum distance remaining to the destination point and any of other pre-programmed points;

• computation and indication of the current flight altitude and audiovisual warning of departure from the designated flight level;

• computation and indication of the pitch and roll angles, current magnetic and gyroscopic headings;

• computation and indication of the indicated airspeed (IAS), true airspeed (TAS), Mach number and outside air temperature and entering these data into the AFCS;

• shaping and indication of the ground speed and drift angle;

• shaping and indication of the desired track and track angle error (for the purpose of automatic control) and entering these data into the AFCS to enable automatic flight along a pre-programmed route;

• non-stop automatic indication of the aircraft's current position on a moving-map display (MMD).

The NK-144 suite was developed by the Tupolev OKB under the supervision of Leonid L. Kerber; later he left the OKB and was succeeded by Viktor P. Sakharov as the suite's project chief. Like The ABSU-144 AFCS, it was tested on the aforementioned Tu-104B CCCP-06195 No.1. (As an aside, the registration passed

to a quasi-civil Mil' Mi-26 *Halo* heavy-lift helicopter when the Tu-104B testbed was struck off charge as time-expired.)

Due to the kinetic heating, in cruise flight the boundary layer temperature reached 150-180°C (302-356°F), the aircraft's skin having a temperature of 110-130°C (230-266°F). As a result, the requirements applied to the air conditioning system (ACS) were totally new; the ACS of a typical subsonic airliner was required to heat the cabins because of the extreme cold outside the aircraft at cruise altitude, delivering 10,000-20,000 kcal/hr, whereas an SST's air conditioning system was required to *cool* the cabins, delivering cold at a rate of 60,000-80,000 kcal/hr! Also, consider that, since the SST's cruise altitude was up to 20,000 m (65,620 ft), the cabin pressure differential would be far greater than that of a typical subsonic airliner cruising at around 11,000 m (36,090 ft). Far from being just a system providing creature comforts for the passengers, the ACS turned into a life support system for the occupants and a system ensuring the normal functioning of the aircraft's avionics in supersonic cruise; without it, everyone and everything inside the fuselage would be literally cooked.

The Tu-144's ACS was developed by a special section of the OKB headed by Aleksandr S. Kochergin (later succeeded by G. A. Sterlin) in close co-operation with NPO *Naooka* ('Science'

Research & Production Association). It incorporated many unusual features, and the result was truly impressive. The actual design work proceeded under the supervision of I. V. Ponomaryov (thermal laboratory chief), V. S. Zonschain, V. A. Piskunov (development of the ACS proper and the engine air bleed system) and V. T. Klimov (calculations group chief); they succeeded in finding solutions that ensured high weight efficiency. Development and testing of the ACS took several years of research and development work. The parameters of the heat insulation and the reliability parameters of the system's components had to be determined, the optimum location of the air distribution ducts chosen, the pressure control algorithm worked out and so on.

First, at Andrey N. Tupolev's initiative the Odessa Food & Refrigeration Industry Technology Institute developed an experimental cooling machine charged with chlorofluorocarbon for cooling the engine bleed air that was fed into the ACS. Shortly afterwards, in January 1963 the OKB's specialists teamed up with NPO Naooka to propose an air/air cooling system in which engine bleed air was cooled in several stages from 600°C to –25°C (from 1,112°F to –13°F); for the first time in Soviet practice, heat exchangers with buffer zones were used. This system was developed by Grigoriy I. Voronin, Aleksandr S. Kochergin, G. A. Sterlin, Yakov M. Itskovich, Valentin T. Klimov and G. V. Novikov. TsIAM participated in the testing and refining of the system, using its test rigs.

The most noteworthy part of the ACS was the so-called dynamic heat insulation – the first of its kind in world aircraft design practice. Calculations showed that the heat gain from the Tu-144's hot skin in cruise flight would exceed 50,000 kcal/hr. If conventional heat/soundproofing mats were to be used for absorbing this heat, they would have to be about 130 mm (5$^{7}/_{64}$ in) thick, weighing an aggregate 1,000-plus kg (2,200-plus lb) and taking up a volume of more than 50 m³ (1,765.73 cu ft); this would severely reduce cabin space – or require the fuselage diameter to be increased. Therefore, building on their experience with supersonic UAVs, the Tupolev OKB designers developed a multi-layer structure consisting of an outer glassfibre layer (the static layer), porous inner panels and air ducts. In the cabins this 'sandwich' was concealed from view by porous wall liner panels. Cold air from the ACS at –30°C (–22°F) would be distributed in the cabin via overhead spreader ducts, warming up to 22-24°C (71.6-75.2°F). Then, the air exited the cabin interior via the porous panels and was forced between the layers, absorbing the heat coming from outside in cruise flight. Such a 'sandwich' could be a mere 20 mm (0$^{25}/_{32}$ in) thick and weigh three times less than conventional heat insulation with similar characteristics.

As compared to conventional heat insulation, the dynamic heat insulation system offered several advantages. Agreeable temperatures were maintained throughout the flight envelope in the pressurised and unpressurised sections of the fuselage alike (the unpressurised areas were cooled by cabin bleed air); the heat penetrating the insulating layer was reduced by a factor of 2.0-2.5, allowing the capacity of the ACS to be reduced, and the equipment in the unpressurised bays was adequately cooled.

Calculations and tests of models and full-size specimens showed that the ACS worked as it should. Yet, the system could not go on the Tu-144 unless the General Designer said so, and Old Man Tupolev was wary of pioneering ideas. First, he had his trusted aides Aleksandr R. Bonin, Aleksandr E. Sterlin, Kurt V. Minkner and Semyon A. Vigdorchik carefully examine the project materials of the ACS; when the 'jury' returned a positive verdict, Andrey N. Tupolev still was not satisfied and demanded full-scale hardware tests. In 1966 or 1967 the dynamic heat insulation was put through its paces, using the appropriately modified fuselage of a Tu-134 *sans suffixe* (probably the static test airframe) converted into a test rig at Tupolev's orders. This rig was developed by a team led by Ye. Ya. Blinov and D. M. Koondin. The fuselage featured a scaled-down version of the 'sandwich' walls and a parabolic metal fairing replacing the navigator's station glazing in the extreme nose. The cabin was outfitted with wall trim panels and other equipment; the passengers were represented by non-anthropomorphic dummies featuring 75-watt light bulbs to emulate the heat radiated by the human body, and heat-emitting cabin equipment was similarly emulated.

The fuselage was placed in a rectangular chamber with polyurethane foam insulated walls; hot air was blown into this chamber via two overhead ducts, heating the fuselage skin to the anticipated temperature of 160°C (320°F), while two further ducts at the bottom collected the air and returned it to the heaters/blowers. The other components of the ACS were installed in a special high-altitude chamber next door emulating flight at up to 20,000 m (65,620 ft) and were connected to the fuselage by ducts. A system of air locks allowed the testers to enter the Tu-134 fuselage and 'make themselves at home' in the cabin, checking out the operation of the ACS from a passenger's point of view. Several thousand hours of tests on this rig proved that the dynamic heat insulation worked perfectly.

Incidentally, the other ACS components (such as the cooling turbines) were also unique, as the system had a variable cycle, heating the cabin on the ground (in the cold season) and at subsonic speeds and cooling it in supersonic cruise and on the ground (in the summer season). Consider that the temperature of the engine bleed air used for pressurisation/air conditioning could reach 530-570°C (986-1,060°F). Most of the air conditioning system's features had no equivalents in indigenous or foreign aircraft design practice and were duly patented.

A section headed by Konstantin V. Yanvaryov and L. D. Doobrovin was responsible for the cabin pressurisation system, the oxygen system and soundproofing solutions. The OKB's experience with subsonic and supersonic military aircraft was used when designing the Tu-144's oxygen system. The KKO-5 oxygen equipment set (*komplekt kislorodnovo oboroodovaniya*) was recommended for the Tu-144 prototype's flight tests, as it catered for all possible emergencies – including bailing out. After LII testers had undertaken a series of tests with a mock-up of the Tu-144's flight deck in a high-altitude chamber involving bailing out via an emergency hatch (without ejection seats), the KKO-OS-1 version (*obleg**chon**noye snaryazheniye* – lightened gear) was developed. Work was also under way on an automated oxygen system for the passenger cabin; LII specialists V. M. Yevdokimov, A. T. Zverev, V. K. Kordinov, B. A. Nartsissov and V. A. Shangin took an active part in this work.

Chapter 1 - The Tu-144 is Born

The passenger service equipment (galleys, lavatories and the like) and the emergency equipment (inflatable rescue slides and so on) was the responsibility of the sections headed by S. V. Drozdov, L. A. Korovin, Igor' B. Babin, A. I. Matus, A. V. Rovitskiy and Yu. I. Vukolov.

In designing the Tu-144 the Tupolev OKB was confronted for the first time with the need to take ecological problems and the world community's growing environmental awareness into account. This concerned first and foremost noise pollution and, in particular, the so-called sonic boom – sudden loud bangs resembling thunderclaps or explosions which are caused by the shock waves generated by a jet travelling above Mach 1 (depending on configuration, speed and other factors, occasionally the aircraft may create a double or even triple 'boom'). Quite apart from the fact that the dreadful bangs frightened people and animals in the areas where test flights (or practice flights of combat aircraft) were taking place, the shock waves could shatter windows and cause other minor damage. Studies of this phenomenon had begun in the world's leading aircraft-building nations more than a decade before the first flights of the SSTs, and the latter were developed at a time when the regulations concerning the environmental impact of commercial aircraft were tightened dramatically.

Once the decision to develop the Tu-144 had been taken in 1963, the sonic boom phenomenon became the subject of systematic theoretical and practical research in the Soviet Union. In 1964 LII worked out requirements for special equipment measuring the intensity of the sonic boom and then undertook flight experiments near Bronnitsy (Moscow Region), using a Su-9 interceptor. All suitable types of sensors available at LII and TsAGI (including imported ones) were involved, and the experiments showed that the measuring equipment needed refining.

In 1965 the sonic boom research programme was included into the Soviet Union's 8th Five-Year Economic Development Plan (1966-70), testifying to the importance attached to the problem at the top level. LII worked out an inter-department short-term research plan for the purpose of measuring the sonic boom parameters of all Soviet supersonic combat aircraft (including the MiG-19 fighter and the Tu-22 bomber), studying the shock wave's interaction with the ground and ground structures and its effect on people and animals. The experiments showed that the intensity of the sonic boom depended on the atmospheric conditions, the flight mode and the aircraft's size and layout. When environmental protection movements became increasingly vocal, lobbying against SSTs, this served as an incentive for more detailed research into the problem; Sukhoi Su-15 *Flagon*, Mikoyan MiG-21 and MiG-25 *Foxbat* interceptors were used at this stage, and later the MiG-21I proof-of-concept vehicle as well. Jumping ahead of the story, it may be said that the Tu-144's flight test programme included special acoustic measurements along the flight track. These allowed the most 'offensive' flight modes to be defined, namely acceleration and the early phase of cruise flight; the pressure increase at the forefront of the shock wave in these modes was 11-13 kg/m² (2.25-2.66 lb/sq ft) at Mach 1.3 and 10-11 kg/m² (2.05-2.25 lb/sq ft) respectively.

Similar research was done in the USA (which summed up the first results in 1965), France and Sweden; opinion polls were held in areas regularly 'boomed' by supersonic military jets. In 1967 Soviet researchers of the sonic boom established contacts with their French colleagues under the auspices of the Commission for Soviet-French Co-operation in Aircraft Industry Matters; the first session of the joint expert panel in Moscow took place in July 1967. At the second session, which was held in Paris in February 1968, Gheorgiy P. Svishchev, Gheorgiy S. Büschgens (both representing TsAGI), Arseniy D. Mironov (LII) and M. L. Mogilevskiy made reports on TsAGI's research and the flight tests made by LII and GosNII GA to record the sonic boom and its effect on people and animals. The French presented interesting data on the development of measurement systems, including those which were activated automatically in anticipation of the approaching shock wave, and on the measurement results obtained in the focus area of the sonic boom created by low-flying aircraft. In 1968 LII specialists A. V. Rodnov, Yu. A. Zavershnev, V. S. Grachov and V. A. Kholodkov teamed up with V. N. Ivanov from the Institute of Experimental Meteorology and TsAGI specialist Yu. V. Lavrov to conduct a large-scale flight experiment with the main purpose of studying the transformation of the sonic boom in the ground layer of the atmosphere and in clouds. Concurrently, GosNII GA conducted research on how the sonic boom was transformed by residential buildings and how it affected healthy and diseased humans and animals (dogs and rabbits); this research was spearheaded by Yu. N. Kulagin. Meanwhile, engineers M. Ya. Blinchevskiy and L. N. Isakova took on the problem at the Tupolev OKB; later they took an active part in analysing the results of the Tu-144's sonic boom measurements.

After much discussion at the international level the International Civil Aviation Organisation (ICAO) officially acknowledged that sonic boom was permissible – but only on overwater flights. It was recommended that each member nation should decide for itself whether to permit or ban supersonic operations on overland flights. Most of the ICAO member nations imposed bans on SST operations over land, but the Soviet Union and India refused to toe the line.

Knowledge of the problem accumulated by then suggested that the sonic boom could not be eliminated completely, as an aerial vehicle travelling at speeds above Mach 1 inevitably generated shock waves and areas of vacuum. The correct way to go was 'if you can't beat 'em, cheat 'em': the flight routes of SSTs had to be plotted over water or sparsely populated areas, circumventing built-up areas, and a composite subsonic/supersonic flight profile was to be used. Furthermore, the force of the sonic boom could be reduced somewhat by optimising the aircraft's shape (a 'low-boom aircraft').

Still, the ambient noise issue (the first ICAO noise regulations were introduced concurrently with the development of the first-generation SSTs) were clearly not the decisive factor affecting the choice of the aircraft's layout. The cost factors associated with the engines powering a supersonic airliner require the engines to have the lowest possible bypass ratio; this, in turn, results in a higher exhaust jet velocity and hence higher noise. Now since an SST's field performance is inevitably worse than that of a similarly sized subsonic airliner (because of the SST's low aspect ratio delta wings), their noise levels cannot be equivalent; an SST needs more thrust, taking off in afterburner mode, and is thus inherently noisier. This is especially true for the noise levels alongside the runway, which are almost entirely determined by the engines' efflux. Taking all of this into consideration, after a number of work sessions the ICAO's Noise Committee deemed it possible to permit operation of the first-generation SSTs (the Tu-144 and the Concorde) with the noise levels which their designers had managed to obtain ('they did the best they could').

Since the SSTs were to cruise at 16,000-18,000 m (52,490-59,050 ft) instead of the 10,000-11,000 m (32,810-36,090 ft) typical of subsonic airliners, the possible effect of solar (ultraviolet) and space radiation on the aircraft and its occupants was another cause for concern, as exposure to radiation increases the risk of cancer. At the initial stage of the SST programme this issue was quite acute and was studied both at the national level and by international organisations – ICAO and the International Commission on Radiological Protection (ICRP). The Tu-144's development and test programme included a special effort to develop an onboard radiation metering kit and ground-based systems for predicting dangerous solar radiation levels. Subsequent events, however, showed that the fears were exaggerated; on the routes chosen for the SSTs the radiation levels were not so high as to damage the health of the crew and passengers. Any real danger could only arise in the event of a sudden burst of solar activity, especially during operations in high latitudes. In that case the only chance to get out of harm's way was to execute an emergency descent, and the procedure was duly developed and verified by the Tupolev OKB.

In addition to the research institutions and design bureaux already listed in this chapter, the Tu-144 programme involved many others – virtually the entire R&D potential of the Soviet Union. For example, the Aircraft Instrument Engineering Research Institute (NIIAP – *Naoochno-issledovatel'skiy instítoot aviatsionnovo priborostroyeniya*) assisted with the integration of the navigation suite and the bench testing of the electric system. The aforementioned MIEA and LNPO Elektroavtomatika developed the electronics components used in the avionics modules; the aforementioned RPKB was responsible for the flight director, the horizontal situation indicator and the **Raduga** (Rainbow) gyro-inertial navigation system. MMKB Rodina was responsible for the hydraulic control surface actuators, the air intake ramp actuators and the nose gear steering actuator/shimmy damper. NPO Naooka supplied not only the ACS and cabin pressurisation system components but also the fuel tank pressurisation and venting system components. Apart from the primary electric system's CSDs, the Rubin design bureau supplied the hydraulic pumps, the wheels and the wheel brakes. MMZ *Zvezda* (Star) developed the crew rescue system (more will be said about it in Chapter 2), the crew gear, the fire warning system and quick-action oxygen equipment (the latter was produced under foreign licence).

The Kristall design bureau supplied sparkless centrifugal fuel pumps and jet pumps for the main and service tanks, as well as the air turbine-driven emergency hydraulic pump. The Leningrad Fuel Metering Systems Design Bureau developed fuel metering and fuel transfer systems. The Kuibyshev-based *Armatoorproyekt* (= Fixture Design) design bureau developed the master fuel shut-off cocks, other fuel system valves and connectors, and hydraulic line connectors. A plant in Kirov developed and supplied the principal electric drives, including the actuator of the drooping nose visor.

The Oxygen Equipment Design Bureau (KBKO – *Konstrooktorskoye byuro kislorodnovo oboroodovaniya*) in the town of Orekhovo-Zooyevo (Moscow Region) supplied oxygen systems of its own design and ensured licence production of certain foreign-made items. The *Ghidravlika* (Hydraulics) plant in Ufa, the capital of the Bashkir ASSR, developed fluoride plastic (similar to Teflon) and metal hoses for the flight control system, the landing gear and the air intake ramps. The Moscow-based *Voskhod* (Sunrise) design bureau and its branch office in Khar'kov, the Ukraine, developed the SVS-30-3 air data system (*sistema vozdooshnykh signahlov*) and aneroid flight instruments. The Ul'yanovsk Instrument Design Bureau (UPKB – *Ool'yanovskoye priborno-konstrooktorskoye byuro*) supplied the principal flight instruments and the AOA sensors. The Stoopino Machinery Design Bureau (OKB-120, or SKBM – **Stoopinskoye konstrooktorskoye byuro mashinostroyeniya**) in the town of Stoopino (Kaluga Region, central Russia) developed the TA-6A auxiliary power unit (*toorboagregaht* – 'turbine unit') for self-contained engine starting, power supply and air conditioning on the ground.

The Tu-144 programme required a complete shake-up of the Soviet aircraft industry's metallurgical, structural material and machine tool branches. For instance, the use of milled panels required the development and introduction of computer-controlled milling machines, which were created by the Savyolovo Machinery Plant (Moscow Region). The Verkhnyaya Salda Metal Foundry Production Association (VSMPO – **Verkhnesaldinskoye metallurgicheskoye proizvodstvennoye obyedineniye**) supplied titanium sheet, cast, forged and stamped parts. The Kuibyshev Metal Foundry supplied similar parts made of aluminium alloys; the *Elektrostal'* ('Electric Steel') plant in the town of the same name in the Moscow Region furnished stainless steel components. The Nikopol' Metal Foundry (Dnepropetrovsk Region, the Ukraine) and the Perm' Metal foundry supplied tubes and pipes made of various metals; the Balashikha Foundry & Mechanical Plant (BLMZ – *Balashikhinskiy liteyno-mekhanicheskiy zavod*, Moscow Region) and the Rzhev Foundry & Mechanical Plant (Kalinin Region, now Tver' Region, Russia) supplied titanium and aluminium castings respectively. Shot peening technologies were introduced as a means of shaping and reinforcing the surface of skin panels.

As mentioned earlier, computer technology was underdeveloped in the Soviet Union in those days. Nevertheless, the Tupolev OKB used its computing resources to the full when designing the Tu-144. The computer section headed by Boris N. Sokolov and Boris P. Beloglazov (and its team chiefs I. P. Sandrykin, A. D. Toozov, A. V. Stasevich and A. N. Smirnov) took an active part in issuing the project documents with high quality.

It deserves mention that other aircraft industry design bureaux – notably the Il'yushin OKB and Oleg K. Antonov's GSOKB-473 in Kiev – were also called upon to assist with issuing the manufacturing drawings for the Tu-144. But then, there was no open competition between state-owned enterprises in the Soviet Union.

Chapter 2

Take One: the Tu-144 Prototype

Tu-144 first prototype/demonstrator (*izdeliye* 044)
Because of the many problems arising in the course of the Tu-144's development the Tupolev OKB decided to begin the hardware stage of the programme with what, in today's terminology, could be described as a full-scale demonstrator. Because the OKB was breaking new ground, this aircraft – known in house as *izdeliye* 044 – would verify the fundamental aerodynamic features, structural strength solutions, systems and equipment devised for the Tu-144, helping the OKB to create a viable SST. Even at the design stage it was clear that *izdeliye* 044 would be an experimental aircraft – the production Tu-144 would be very different, and its design features were being developed in parallel. Actually it was not a case of 'the first pancake coming out wrong', as Russian folk wisdom goes. Remember that Soviet and western designers were in a neck-to-neck race and the unofficial objective was to be the first to fly an SST, and *izdeliye* 044 would serve that purpose. Importantly, in the course of its flight tests the demonstrator would provide the answers that would require more time and greater expenditures to obtain with the help of ground test rigs – notably, it would prove the validity of the calculation methods used.

Meanwhile, as already mentioned, at Andrey N. Tupolev's initiative the OKB-155 'fighter maker' design bureau led by Artyom I. Mikoyan was developing a subscale proof-of-concept vehicle that would verify the airliner's tailless-delta layout in actual flight – the MiG-21I, or Analogue. Even with all necessary information provided by the Tupolev OKB, the design work on the MiG-21I was making slow progress and was holding up the Tu-144 programme as a result. Legend has it that Andrey N. Tupolev became the bane of Mikoyan's existence for a while, urging him to complete the aircraft as soon as possible. Each morning he would posi-

A model of CCCP-68001, the Tu-144 (*izdeliye* 044) demonstrator aircraft.

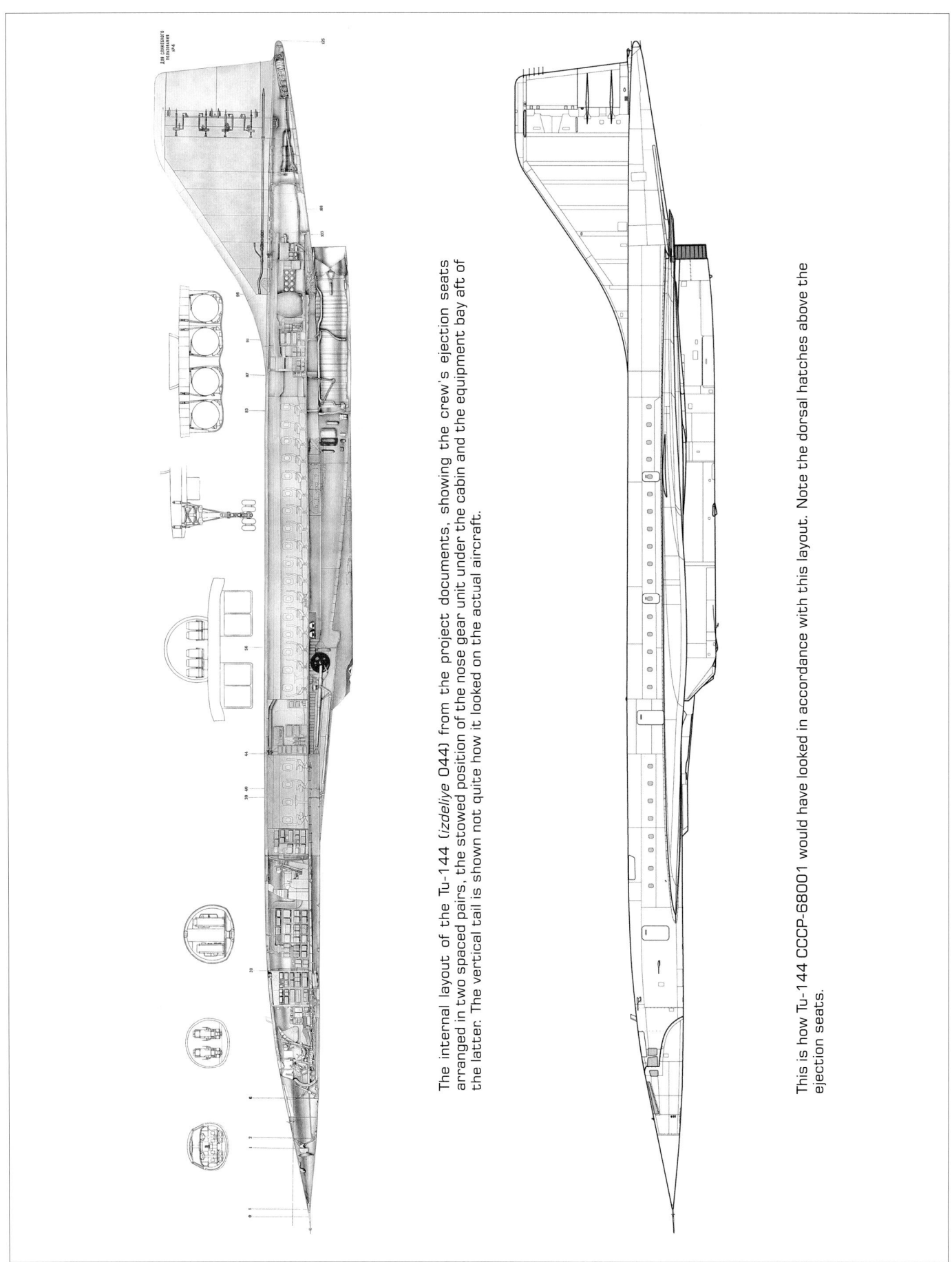

The internal layout of the Tu-144 (*izdeliye* 044) from the project documents, showing the crew's ejection seats arranged in two spaced pairs, the stowed position of the nose gear unit under the cabin and the equipment bay aft of the latter. The vertical tail is shown not quite how it looked on the actual aircraft.

This is how Tu-144 CCCP-68001 would have looked in accordance with this layout. Note the dorsal hatches above the ejection seats.

Chapter 2 - Take One: the Tu-144 Prototype

Right: The Tu-144 (*izdeliye* 044) static test article. It was built and tested in parallel with the *izdeliye* 044 demonstrator.

Below right: Another view of the static test airframe. Note the 'cages' with load transfer rods and pressure sensors over the starboard wing and the rear fuselage.

Bottom right: One more aspect of the static test article's starboard wing.

tion himself under the window of Mikoyan's apartment and call out loudly in an exceptionally plaintive voice: *'Artyom Ivanovich, **whe-e-en** are you going to give me my Analogue?'*, much to the amusement of everyone who happened to be within earshot – except Mikoyan himself.

Manufacture of the *izdeliye* 044 prototype (construction number 0) began in 1965; because of its c/n the aircraft was colloquially known at the OKB as *noolyovka* – 'Aircraft Zilch' (some sources, though, state the c/n as 001). The prototype and the static test airframe (c/n 00) were built by the OKB's experimental plant, MMZ No.156, some subassemblies being supplied by the OKB's other branches. By the early 1960s MMZ No.156 had become a powerful production facility that allowed the manufacturing process to be organised in parallel with the design work. In so doing the engineers looked into the possibility of retaining at least some of the existing production technologies for the Tu-144 and worked out what new manufacturing equipment should be ordered.

The large-scale use of titanium in the Tu-144's airframe necessitated the acquisition of additional welding equipment and machine tools, which had to be designed from scratch in some cases. The introduction of large CNC milling machines necessary for manufacturing the wing skins and spars opened up a whole can of worms. The first such

Left: This photo of the Tu-144 (*izdeliye* 044) static test article shows the dorsal ejection hatches at the same location as on the flying prototype.

Below left: Three-quarters rear view of the static test article.

Right: The forward fuselage section of the *izdeliye* 044 prototype in the assembly jig at MMZ No.156. Note that the ejection hatches are already there but the apertures for the glazing are still missing; also, the nose radome appears to be made of metal, not GRP. The rear fuselage section and the rear pressure dome are also visible. The slogan on the wall beyond reads: 'Aircraft industry workers! Be bold in introducing the latest achievements of science and technology on the production lines!'

Below right: The Tu-144 prototype takes shape in the final assembly shop of MMZ No.156. The flight deck windows are temporarily papered over to avoid scratches.

machines, which (as already mentioned) were designed by the Savyolovo Machinery Plant, turned out to be extremely troublesome, and it took the workforce a lot of time to learn to use them. The risk of ruining the expensive half-finished articles was very high, and the air in the workshops of MMZ No.156 literally crackled with tension. Designing the assembly jigs and fixtures turned out to be another complex issue, as the designers placed extremely high demands as to manufacturing accuracy and surface finish.

Shop 2 of MMZ No.156 was the principal metal cutting facility equipped with CNC milling machines; it was headed by G. I. Solomatin, with I. P. Sandrykin in charge of the computing facility. Shop 6 headed by N. G. Sharlygin was the electrochemical coating and chemical milling facility; the chemical milling technology devised there subsequently found use at production plants.

Shop 10 was the airframe subassembly build-up and final assembly shop. It also manufactured control system, fuel system and ACS/pressurisation system components and installed the engines; G. F. Volkov, N. V. Ptitsyn, M. P. Goozanov, A. I. Shabanov, I. I. Grigor'yev, B. Ye. Bogdanov, A. M. Zadudayev and many others made a significant contribution at this stage.

Shop 12 was responsible for the hydraulic systems (including control system actuators) and landing gear installation/checks. I. F. Shabanov, A. A. Valevin, Ye. N. Krasnyy, A. A. Babanin, V. V. Rodin, V. N. Borisov, I. P. Zotov and many others were involved in these operations. Shop 13 was the electric equipment shop; specific areas of work were headed by A. V. Khakhanov, M. A. Treibman, K. S. Belinov, I. G. Anan'yev and I. S. Yefanov. The new types of wiring and other electric equipment forced the

Chapter 2 - Take One: the Tu-144 Prototype

Above: The Tu-144 prototype, now painted and registered CCCP-68001, in hangar No.2 of the OKB's flight test facility in Zhukovskiy (ZhLliDB) in August 1968. The aircraft is trestled for a landing gear check and the underside is illuminated by portable lights.

Left: The same hangar, with the aircraft surrounded by work platforms; note the flight engineer's ejection hatch amidships. The ZiS-151 or ZiL-157 6x6 army lorry with a van body visible on the left is probably a systems test lab, while the GAZ-51A 4x2 general purpose lorry on the right is a UPG-250M hydraulics test vehicle.

Left: The forward fuselage of CCCP-68001 as the preparations for the rollout are almost completed.

Above right: Front view of the painted prototype at Zhukovskiy, showing the windows in the nose visor and the anti-glare panel around them.

Right: The prototype's port outer wing panel is moved into position by an overhead crane before being mated with the centre section.

shop to introduce new technologies and hire additional personnel. Shop 19 was the model shop headed by V. I. Vorob'yov, which manufactured unique and complex wind tunnel models and scaled-strength models on schedule. Shop 36 was the non-metallic materials and sealants shop headed by V. E. Yagnatinskiy.

A decision taken by the Minister of Aircraft Industry to organise broad co-operation between the plants that were to participate in series production of the Tu-144 did a lot to speed up the work. Many of the Tu-144 prototype's airframe components and assembly jigs were supplied by production aircraft factories. A large group of workers from these plants took special training and participated in the construction of the prototype. In accordance with the plan approved by Vice-Minister of Aircraft Industry Aleksandr A. Belyanskiy – a crack production man who had been director of aircraft factory No.18 during the Great Patriotic War – production of components for the *izdeliye* 044 prototype was assigned as follows. MMZ No.156 in Moscow manufactured the forward fuselage (flight deck section) and the wing centre section; it was also responsible for final assembly of the fuselage and mating it with the wings, this work taking place in Shop 10. The OKB's Tomilino branch, which included a newly-constructed manufacturing shop, built the centre fuselage (designed locally), the rear fuselage (designed by the OKB's head office) and the movable nose visor. Another experimental plant in Moscow manufactured the engine nacelle and the air intake assembly, including the inlet ducts. The manufacturing shop of the Tupolev OKB's flight test facility in the town of Zhukovskiy south of Moscow (ZhLIiDB – *Zhukovskaya lyotno-ispytahtel'naya i dovodochnaya bahza*, Zhukovskiy Flight Test & Refinement Base) also manufactured certain parts. Production plant No.18 in Kuibyshev was subcontracted to supply the rudder, the elevons and the

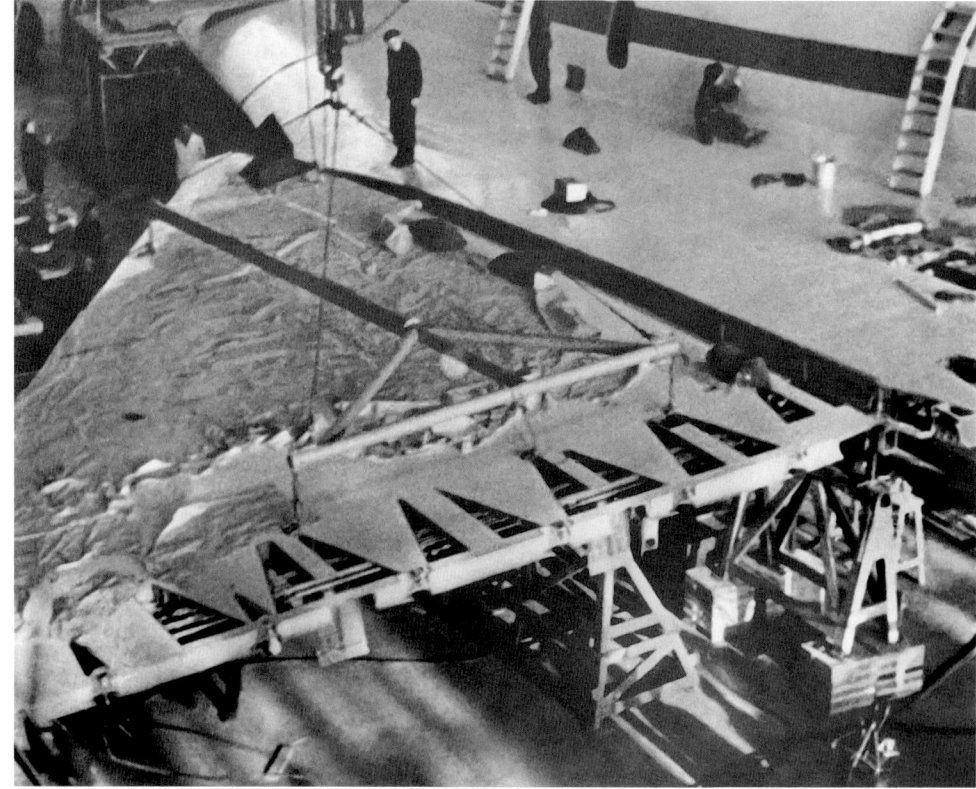

Above: A YaAZ-210D prime mover modified as an airfield tug (Moscow Region licence plate 21-73 YuAU) pushes CCCP-68001 back into the hangar at the Zhukovskiy flight test facility.

Below: Tu-144 project test pilot Eduard V. Yelian in full flying attire familiarises himself with the flight deck of Tu-144 CCCP-68001 while the aircraft is still in the hangar.

main gear units. Another production plant, No.64 in Voronezh, manufactured the outer wings, the nose gear unit, and various labour-intensive parts; the outer wings were delivered to Moscow as a slung load by a Mil' Mi-10 *Harke* heavy-lift helicopter captained by Mil' OKB test pilot Vasiliy P. Koloshenko. It was plant No.64 that would eventually produce the Tu-144 in series (plant No.18 envisaged originally was too busy with Tu-95 production).

Airliner and transport aircraft prototypes are always provided with devices allowing the crew to parachute to safety if things go terribly wrong. However, since bailing out conventionally was unthinkable at supersonic speeds, the designers took the unprecedented decision to equip the Tu-144 demonstrator with ejection seats. In keeping with then-current Soviet practice, the seats were developed in house, but not specifically for the SST; these were KT-1 seats (**kreslo Toopoleva** – 'Tupolev seat') created for the Tu-22M *Backfire* supersonic bomber.

Wearing the eloquent registration CCCP-68001 (that is, 1968, Tu-144 No.001), the demonstrator was completed in early 1968. Next, it was disassembled and transported in pieces to Zhukovskiy. Getting the Tu-144 there was something of a problem in itself due to the aircraft's large size. Preparations for the move went on throughout prototype construction, and a special section of the OKB took care of this problem. It was tasked with designing and building custom-made four-wheel transportation dollies that were used first for transporting the centre and rear fuselage sections by road to Moscow and then for transporting the partially assembled aircraft to Zhukovskiy. All four wheels of each dolly were steerable, and each wheel was adjusted manually for manoeuvring the outsize load through the narrow driveways of the MMZ No.156 compound. After passing between the buildings the fuselage was wheeled out through the gate into Radio Street running along the Saltykovskaya Embankment of the Yauza River (in 1977 this was renamed Academician Tupolev Embankment). Many of Moscow's municipal services were called upon to assist with this special

Chapter 2 - Take One: the Tu-144 Prototype

transport operation; this involved removing obstacles (such as temporarily taking down lamp standards) in tight spots and raising the overhead wires for trams and trolleybuses to allow the Tu-144 fuselage to pass under them. The operation was accomplished in the course of one night; the time was chosen both in order to avoid creating traffic jams and for security reasons. Final assembly took place in Hangar 2 of ZhLIiDB.

Here it should be noted that the flight test facility in Zhukovskiy began preparing for the Tu-144's trials programme well in advance. The ZhLIiDB was a fully-fledged branch of the OKB headed by Aleksey S. Blagoveshchenskiy and comprising several sections; the flight operations facility proper headed by Yevgeniy K. Stoman, the calculations and experiment section responsible for test result analysis (headed by Daniil S. Zosim) and the above-mentioned manufacturing shop headed by S. S. Kooz'min were the most important ones.

The flight test facility also included a test range section (SIP – *sloozhba ispytahtel'novo poligona*) headed by Boris N. Grozdov, which had accumulated considerable experience with UAVs, including the aforementioned Yastreb series, which was not only supersonic but also utilised the tailless-delta layout – just like the Tu-144. This section also claimed a leading role in the testing of the SST, which resulted in fierce in-house rivalry.

Leonid T. Kulikov, a participant of the Tu-144's flight tests, reminisced: *'From its inception the flight test operations service was headed by Yevgeniy Karlovich Stoman, with Boris Nikolayevich Grozdov as his all-time deputy. [...] Despite their difference in age and character, they were perfectly matched. As a rule, Ye. K. Stoman did not say much; he always weighed his opinions carefully and was calm and unhurried. His friend B. N. Grozdov was just the opposite – merry and seemingly carefree, an amiable man who could not live five minutes without cracking a joke. Yet, when it came to important work, he was instantly transformed from a joker into a serious and sober-minded engineer who could quickly tackle complex tasks. These two brilliant specialists laid the foundation of the preparation, conduct and analysis of flight tests [at the Tupolev OKB] in the post-war period. [...] In 1952 a young Air Force captain, Vladimir Nikolayevich Benderov, came from GK NII VVS to join the already established team of the flight test facility. Almost immediately he started testing heavy military aircraft as a test engineer. [...] Benderov quickly moved up the career ladder in the test work and was even head of the flight test facility for a while. By the time the preparations to test the Tu-144 began he had been appointed deputy director of the ZhLIiDB with responsibility for test work. Boris Nikolayevich Grozdov and Vladimir Nikolayevich Benderov quickly formed a strong bond. It was a bond between two equal colleagues, and even a father-and-son relationship to a certain degree. [...] At that time B. N. Grozdov was appointed head of the Special Test Division (SIP) which was responsible for testing UAV, first and foremost the Yastreb reconnaissance drone. (This is how Kulikov deciphers this acronym: spetsiahl'noye ispytahtel'noye podrazdeleniye – Auth.) His team had amassed enough experience in testing supersonic aerial vehicles in flight modes hitherto unknown to us; the Yastreb had a maximum speed of 2,700 km/h [1,680 mph] and a cruise altitude in excess of 20,000 m [65,620 ft]. It gave a practical insight into*

Above: Mikhail V. Kozlov, the Tu-144's assigned co-pilot, in the flight deck of CCCP-68001.

Below: Flight engineer Yuriy T. Selivyorstov at his workstation. Curiously, here he is wearing an old-fashioned leather helmet, not a ZSh-5 'bone dome'.

Chapter 2 - Take One: the Tu-144 Prototype

Left: This front view of CCCP-68001 with the nose visor raised underscores the area-ruling of the engine nacelle.
Above and below: Two more views of *izdeliye* 044 with the nose lowered.

the issues of thermal loads [caused by kinetic heating], the operation of the cruise engine's fuel system, and stability and handling throughout the speed and altitude envelope; most importantly, however, the unusual tailless delta layout had been verified in actual flight. Unlike most of the facility's test personnel, the SIP worked in close contact with the OKB's specialists. The crew conducting the tests was mixed, consisting of flight test facility and OKB representatives. This co-operative work practice had proved its usefulness. [...]

By the time preparations for testing the Tu-144 got under way – that was in early 1962, – the close-knit collective of the SIP and OKB test personnel had accumulated sufficient experience, and the [Yastreb] reconnaissance drone's flight modes were similar to those of the Tu-144's. (Sic – Kulikov states the year as 1962, even though development of the Tu-144 began in 1963! One can only guess what the actual year of the event was – *Auth.*) All this warranted drawing up a proposal to Aleksey Andreyevich Tupolev, the Tu-144's project chief (who was also the Yastreb's project chief), that the SIP/OKB team be entrusted with testing the Tu-144. The issue was discussed by a limited number of test work chiefs – B. N. Grozdov, G[heorgiy] M. Gofbauer, V[ladimir] V. Kulinskiy, L[ev] A. Lanovskiy and L. T. Kulikov. It's hard to tell now who floated the idea first, but after discussing it we were positive that we could tackle the job. It was then that we decided to state our

Above: CCCP-68001 shortly after the maiden flight; a maintenance platform was used for boarding/deplaning for want of a proper gangway that was tall enough.

Left: History in the making as the Tu-144 takes off for its maiden flight on 31st December 1968, raising a pall of snow obscuring everything behind the aircraft.

Above right: A fine study of Tu-144 CCCP-68001 in 'clean' configuration. Note the open excess air spill doors under the pairs of air intakes.

Right: The Tu-144 in 'dirty' configuration, with a MiG-21U trainer acting as a chase plane.

Chapter 2 - Take One: the Tu-144 Prototype

Chapter 2 - Take One: the Tu-144 Prototype

Left and below left: These excellent pictures of Tu-144 CCCP-68001 in its first flight, with the MiG-21I/1 (CCCP A-144) flying chase, were taken from a Tu-124 airliner used by the Tupolev OKB as a support aircraft. The nose visor is raised but the landing gear is down, showing the slight nose-up position of the main gear bogies in no-load condition. The low speed accounts for the visibly high angle of attack. Note that all control surfaces retain their natural metal finish, the titanium skin appearing almost black.

Above: Eduard V. Yelian in the captain's seat of the Tu-144 as it taxies out for a test flight.

Above right: Mikhail V. Kozlov in the co-pilot's seat. The position of the ejection hatches in the roof above the pilots' heads suggests that the seats would slide all the way aft before ejection if need arose.

Right: Yelian is joyfully tossed into the air after the successfully accomplished first flight of the Tu-144 – a Russian custom which puzzles foreigners a lot.

Below and below right: Yelian receives a hug and congratulations from General Designer Andrey N. Tupolev after the first flight.

ideas to A. A. Tupolev in an informal atmosphere at the Aragvi restaurant, "washing them down with a glass of, er, tea", as the popular saying goes. (This expression implies drinking strong drinks. The original sounds like za ryumkoy chayu – a corruption of za chashkoy chayu ('with a cup of tea'); ryumka is Russian for 'wine glass' or 'vodka glass' – Auth.)

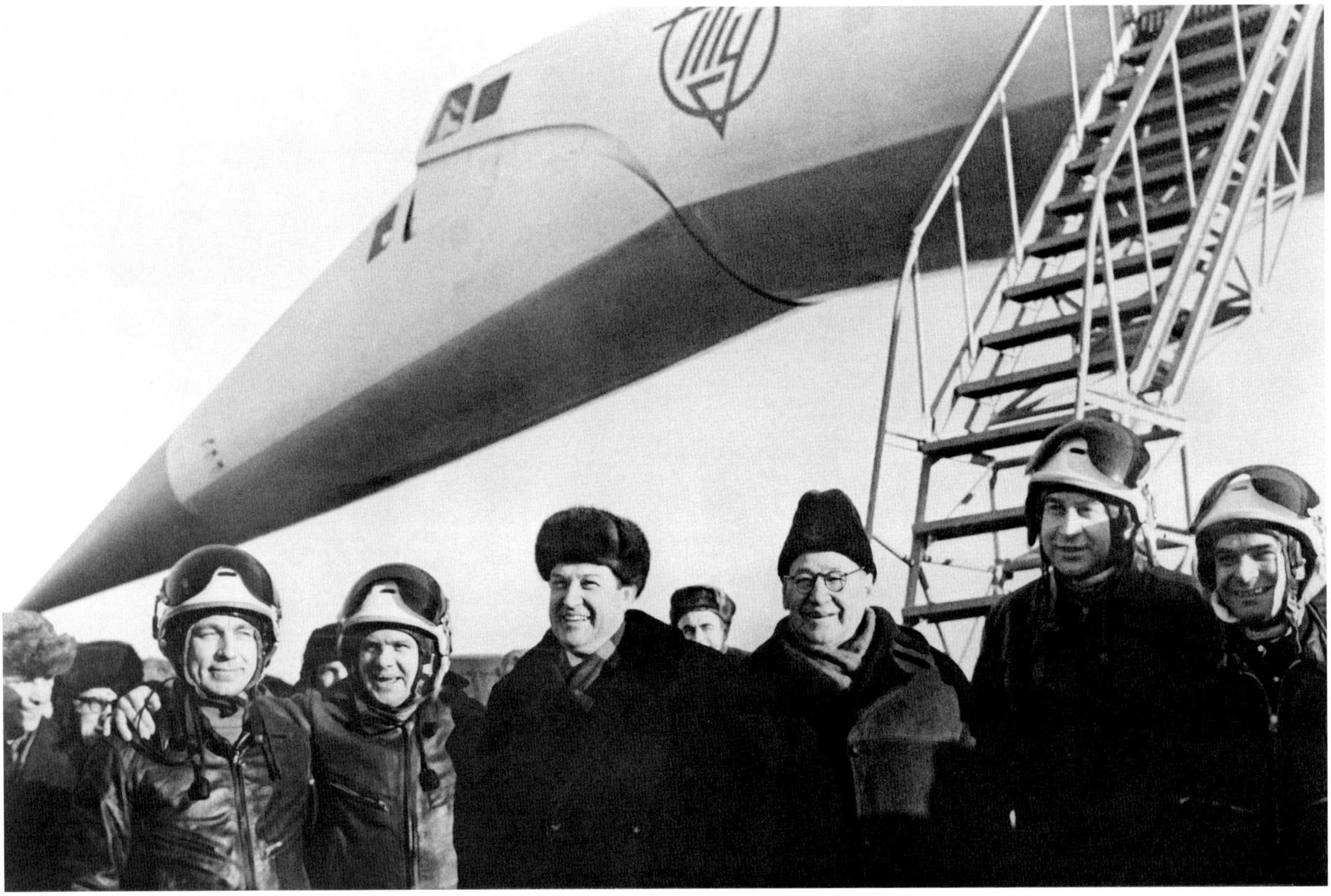

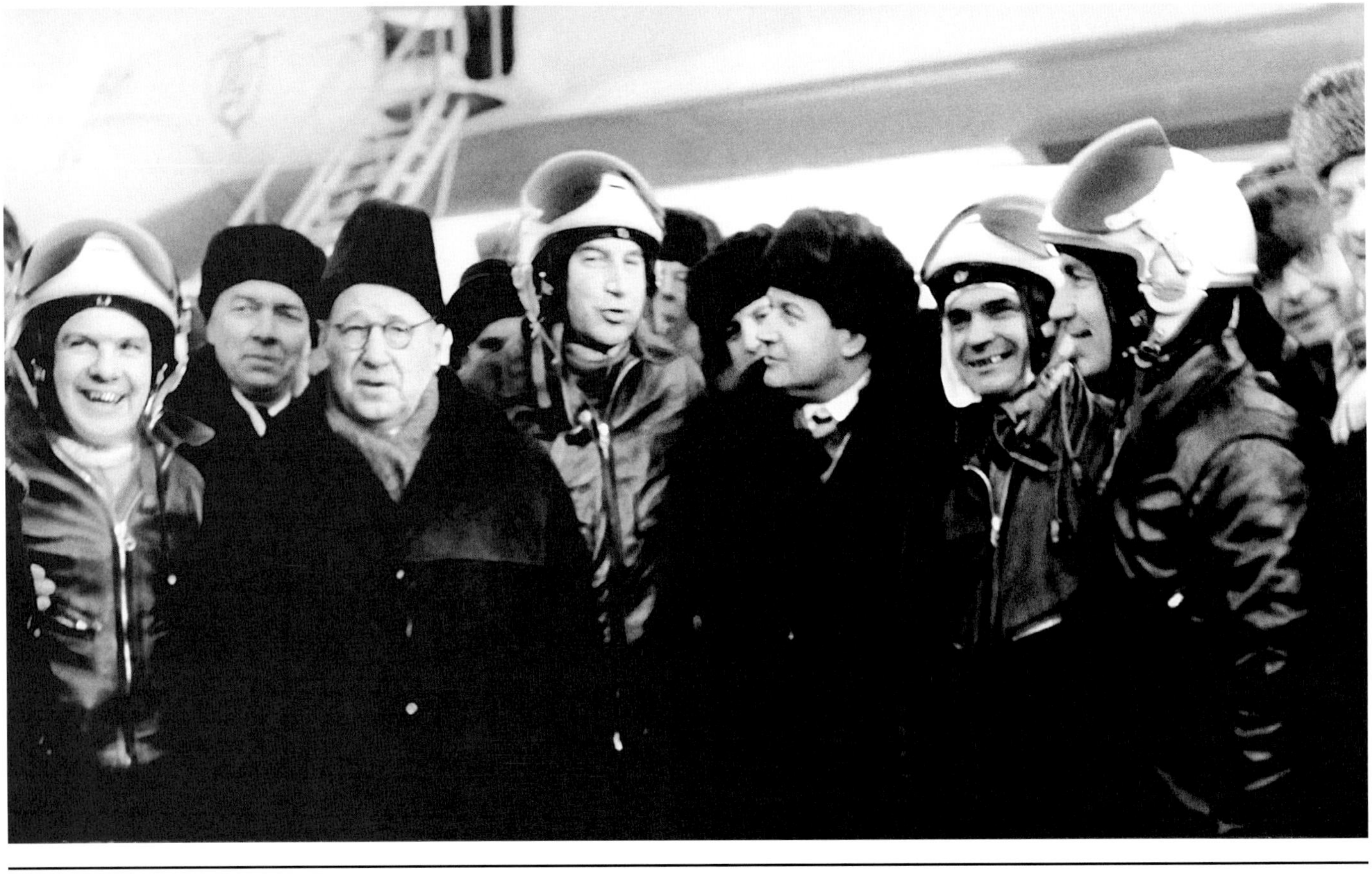

Chapter 2 - Take One: the Tu-144 Prototype

*In those days we would celebrate important events in our lives in this fashion quite often, and it was a time-honoured tradition. The choice of the Aragvi restaurant was apparently dictated by B. N. Grozdov's Georgian descent; it was he who was responsible for organising the event. (The Aragvi is a river in Georgia, and a restaurant of that name would obviously have Georgian cuisine – Auth.) And so, one evening in June or July 1962 our group forgathered on the first floor of the Aragvi restaurant; A. A. Tupolev came, too. Everyone was in high spirits (no pun intended – Auth.) We started making speeches, trying to convince A. A. Tupolev to entrust the joint SIP/OKB team with the tests so that the already established arrangement could be used. Incidentally, this would **not** require a new, separate team to be set up specifically for testing the Tu-144. Right in the midst of the discussion, just when G. M. Gofbauer and L. A. Lanovskiy had stated their points of view, the door of the room where we were having our private function opened and V. N. Benderov walked in, accompanied by his beautiful wife Roza. For a few seconds there was dead silence; it was like the grand finale in [Nikolay V. Gogol's play] "The Inspector General" (that is, when the arrival of the real Imperial Inspector General is announced*

Above left: A photo-shoot after the first flight. Left to right: Mikhail V. Kozlov, Eduard V. Yelian, Aleksey A. Tupolev, Andrey N. Tupolev, Vladimir N. Benderov and Yuriy T. Selivyorstov. ANT is rarely seen smiling in photos, but here he has every reason to.

Left: Another post-flight shot showing Yelian, one of the designers, Tupolev Sr., Benderov, Tupolev Jr., Selivyorstov and Kozlov.

Above right: The Tu-144's first crew – left to right: Kozlov, Benderov, Selivyorstov and Yelian.

Right: Eduard V. Yelian reports on the Tu-144's first flight, with ANT (nearest) and other OKB-156 designers listening.

and everybody is struck speechless, realising that the previous one they had been courting in various ways is an impostor and now they are in deep trouble – *Auth.*). Then V. V. Kulinskiy, with typical single-mindedness, spoke up: "You were not invited! And you have no business being here!" It was rude, but it was getting right to the point. Benderov, like the well-mannered person he was, said "Thanks everyone", turned and left. The ambiance was ruined; the conversation could no longer proceed in the intended way, and the meeting did not give the result we wanted. The invited ones stayed until the end, of course, but the mood was rotten.

The following day, after putting two and two together, we realised what had happened. The adorable B. N. Grozdov, who was torn between "allegiance" to us and to V. N. Benderov, had double-crossed us. He had told Benderov of the impending meeting with

Top: CCCP-68001 on the north apron at Moscow-Sheremet'yevo airport, with the old control tower (adorned with Lenin's portrait) in the background, on 20th May 1969 during a new civil aviation hardware display staged for the Soviet and foreign media.

Above left: Vladimir N. Benderov, Mikhail V. Kozlov and Eduard V. Yelian were present at the display, wearing Aeroflot uniforms for the occasion.

Above: A very happy-looking Andrey N. Tupolev (with a model of the Tu-144 behind him) at a press conference in the Sheremet'yevo concourse on 26th May 1969.

Above right: CCCP-68001 is towed by a KrAZ-214 6x6 prime mover during a presentation at Moscow/Vnukovo-2 on 17th May 1971.

Right: The Tu-144 with an APA-50M ground power unit connected.

Chapter 2 - Take One: The Tu-144 prototype

A. A. Tupolev and specifically what we were going to discuss with the latter. Of course, Vladimir Nikolayevich had wanted the Tu-144 test programme for himself; he had his own ideas of how it should be performed, and the SIP – much less the SIP+OKB team – did not fit into his plans at all. And, before we could discuss the issue with A. A. Tupolev, Grozdov had divulged it to Benderov. The latter immediately started taking steps [against us], using his clout with A. A. Tupolev in order to "stake his claim" and make sure that only ZhLIiDB specialists be allowed to test the aircraft. Thus ended the abortive attempt to have the tests of the Tu-144 performed by an alternative team which, in our opinion, was in a better position to tackle the highly complex task.'

Unfortunately the designers did not succeed in achieving one of their main goals – high weight efficiency. All due measures notwithstanding, CCCP-68001 had an operating empty weight of 84 tons (185,185 lb), which was about 20 tons (44,090 lb) higher than expected! That was the price to pay for the absolute newness of the aircraft and its systems.

At Zhukovskiy the aircraft was reassembled; by June most of the systems had been prepared for

Above left: The Tu-144 departs from runway 25 at Moscow-Sheremet'yevo on 21st May 1969 past the small government apron on the south side where a Tu-104A and an IL-14S are parked.

Left: This shot of the departing Tu-144 shows the shape of the engine nacelle (note how the area around the nozzles is sculpted), the open auxiliary intake doors, the open rear end of the nose gear fairing and the gaps between the elevon sections compensating wing flexure.

Top right: Another shot of CCCP-68001 at the moment of lift-off.

Above right and right: Publicity photos of Aleksey A. Tupolev and the crew of CCCP-68001 (taken in the rear and front cabins respectively).

Above: Tu-144 CCCP-68001 at Hannover during the ILA '72 airshow. Note that the rudder is now painted white.

Bottom: CCCP-68001 at Sheremet'yevo, with Polar Aviation aircraft (An-12B transports and an IL-18 airliner) in the background.

Above right and right: More views of CCCP-68001 at Sheremet'yevo.

Below: The aircraft is towed by a purpose-built MAZ-541 tug past the trademark 'mushroom' concourse at Sheremet'yevo in May 1969.

Below right: The Tu-144 lands at Prague-Ruzyne during its first visit abroad on 23rd May 1971 (en route to Paris-Le Bourget).

Chapter 2 - Take One: The Tu-144 prototype

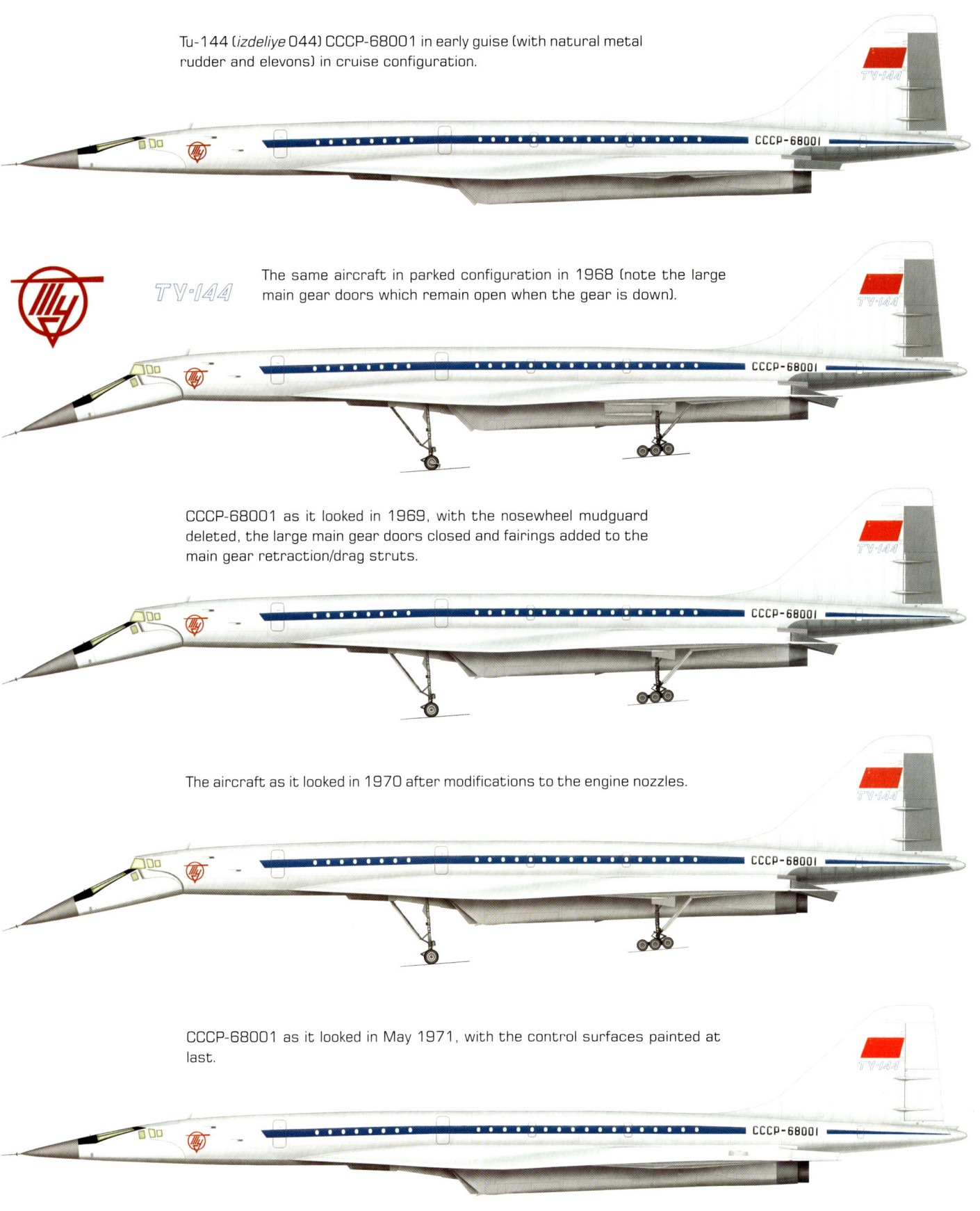

Tu-144 (*izdeliye* 044) CCCP-68001 in early guise (with natural metal rudder and elevons) in cruise configuration.

The same aircraft in parked configuration in 1968 (note the large main gear doors which remain open when the gear is down).

CCCP-68001 as it looked in 1969, with the nosewheel mudguard deleted, the large main gear doors closed and fairings added to the main gear retraction/drag struts.

The aircraft as it looked in 1970 after modifications to the engine nozzles.

CCCP-68001 as it looked in May 1971, with the control surfaces painted at last.

Chapter 2 - Take One: the Tu-144 Prototype

Above: An air-to-air of CCCP-68001 flying over an industrial area near Moscow in 1969 or 1970.

Right: The test crew (left to right: Mikhail V. Kozlov, Yuriy T. Selivyorstov, Vladimir N. Benderov and Eduard V. Yelian) heads to the Tu-144, which is being worked on by the ground crew (note the open cowlings).

ground checks. The assembly teams toiled around the clock, working in three shifts. The ZhLIiDB test team joined the action in August. Vladimir N. Benderov, who had been promoted to the facility's Deputy Director for added responsibility, coordinated the overall effort; project engineers Vyacheslav Borsuk, Vitaliy M. Koolesh and Boris A. Pervookhin were in charge of specific area. The finishing touches were applied by October and the aircraft was basically ready to commence trials.

One of the most important phases of the ground tests following reassembly was the first power-on test, which nearly ended in an

Above: Wearing the exhibit code 826, Tu-144 CCCP-68001 is seen here at Le Bourget on 25th May 1971.

Below: Aleksey A. Tupolev and Bulgarian leader Todor Zhivkov (fourth from left) during the Tu-144's visit to Sofia in September 1971.

Above right: CCCP-68001 in the static park of the 29th Paris Air Show together with IL-62M CCCP-86673 and the Mil' V-12 heavy-lift helicopter (CCCP-21142). Note the open APU air intake door.

Right: The Tu-144 is welcomed at Sofia-Vrazhdebna airport.

Chapter 2 - Take One: the Tu-144 Prototype

Left: CCCP-68001 pictured during its visit to Berlin-Schönefeld airport on 13th-17th June 1971. The 'tin can' on the nose pitot is a cover protecting the pitch/yaw vanes.

Right: Another view of the aircraft at Berlin-Schönefeld on 13th June 1971.

Below: CCCP-68001 pictured during one of its airshow appearances.

accident. The reassembled aircraft was jacked up – apparently because a landing gear check was planned, among other things. When electric power was switched on and the hydraulic system powered up, the aircraft suddenly started shaking – so badly that the testers feared it would tip over the jacks and fall down. Everything was shut down and the engineers started searching for the cause of the problem. It turned out that they had – for the first time – encountered auto-oscillations on an aircraft with an aeroelastic airframe and an AFCS.

Meanwhile, two MiG-21I (Analogue) proof-of-concept vehicles were built; the airframes were largely manufactured in Gor'kiy, but the ogival wings were 'subcontracted out' to aircraft factory No.64 in Voronezh. Final assembly of the MiG-21I/1 (c/n N010104) took place in Moscow at MMZ No.155. Wearing the eloquent and very non-standard civil registration CCCP A-144, this aircraft performed its maiden flight at Zhukovskiy on 18th April 1968 at the hands of LII test pilot Oleg V. Goodkov, the MiG-21I's project test pilot. The first flight was preceded by a short hop to an altitude of 1-2 m (3-6 ft). It was during this hop that Goodkov discovered that the Analogue was reluctant to land, bouncing several times as the pilot tried to bring it down to terra firma. The reason was the air cushion effect created by the large wings. By the end of 1968, when Tu-144 CCCP-68001 was due to enter flight test, MiG-21I CCCP A-144 had made 64 flights; 57 of them were performed by Goodkov.

The MiG-21I reached a maximum altitude of 12,000 m (39,370 ft) and was flown at indicated airspeeds from 212 km/h (131 mph) at 3,000 m (9.840 ft) to 1,205 km/h (748 mph) at 11,500 m (37,730 ft); it attained a maximum speed of Mach 2.06. The CG range in these flights was 40.2% to 47.7% mean aerodynamic chord; the CG position was selected by installing ballast weights in the nose or rear fuselage. The first aircraft had an all-up weight of 6,550-7,930 kg (14,440-17,480 lb) and a wing loading of 160-193 kg/m² (32.8-39.5 lb/sq ft). The corresponding figures for the second aircraft (MiG-21I/2) were 6,260-7,640 kg (13,800-16,840 lb) and 152-186 kg/m² (31.16-38.13 lb/sq ft).

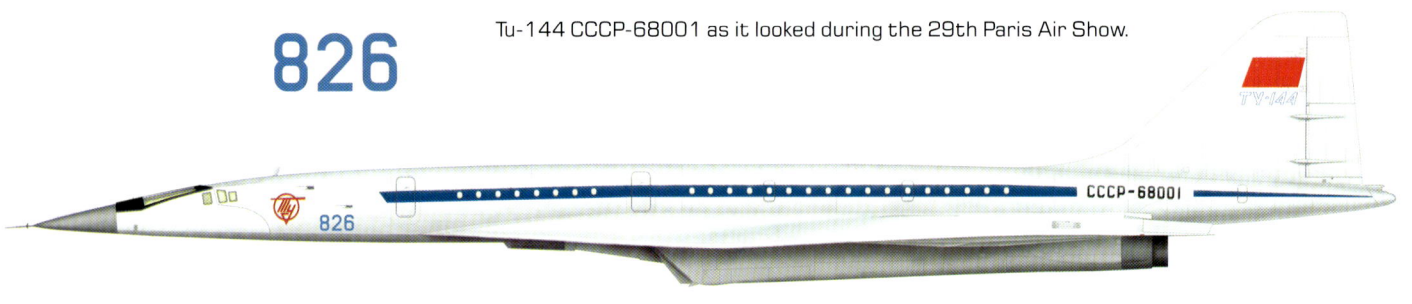

Tu-144 CCCP-68001 as it looked during the 29th Paris Air Show.

Chapter 2 - Take One: the Tu-144 Prototype

The test results provided a virtually complete picture of a tailless-delta aircraft's flight dynamics and control characteristics within a wide range of AOAs and speeds (up to Mach 2). The machine's stability and control characteristics were determined, its handling in subsonic and supersonic flight at varying speeds and altitudes was assessed, and the aircraft's stall and spinning characteristics were explored. A total of 16 test pilots flew the Analogue, including Tupolev OKB test pilots Eduard V. Yelian, Mikhail V. Kozlov and Sergey T. Agapov. By July 1969 these pilots had made 142 flights in the first MiG-21I alone; eight of these were performed by Yelian and Kozlov. Thus, among other things, the Analogue served as a trainer.

Being fairly easy to fly, the Analogue was popular with the pilots. Eduard V. Yelian commented thus: *'I had flown straight-wing aircraft before, and I have to say that in take-off and landing mode swept wings have provided the pilot largely with a lot of inconvenience, such as all manner of stalls and oscillations. [...] Well, at subsonic speeds the tailless MiG-21 derivative proved to be quite similar in handling to straight-wing aircraft; it possessed absolutely brilliant controllability. Its landing speed was around 220 km/h [136 mph] versus the MiG-21's 320 km/h [198 mph]. I had a really good time flying the Analogue. Oh, there were a few minor complications in supersonic flight – the machine was prone to Dutch roll up to Mach 1.7, but that was easily corrected.'*

Gradually, as the ground checks proceeded, the ground crew for the Tu-144's flight tests was formed. It consisted of experts who had participated in the testing of the Tupolev OKB's combat aircraft – technicians N. S. Kopylov, V. M. Mikhaïlov and R. M. Kvitsiniya, electrics engineers N. V. Fandeyev and V. M. Fetisov, equipment engineers S. Smol'skiy, N. Kolosov *et al.*

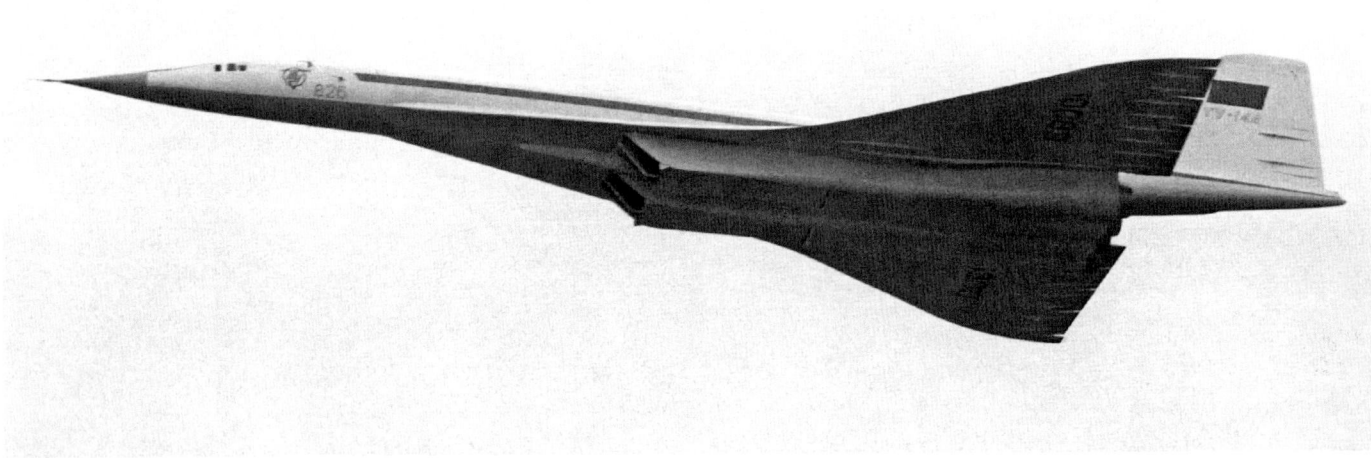

Generally the ground tests went well – albeit not without incident; the emergency hydraulic pump driven by an air turbine (using compressed air supplied by the auxiliary power unit) suffered an uncontained failure on one of its first runs, injuring N. S. Kopylov.

Selecting the flight crew, especially the project test pilot, was far more difficult. The reason was that the Tupolev OKB was experiencing a generation change. Such prominent test pilots of the older generation as Ivan M. Sookhomlin, Aleksey P. Yakimov, Mikhail A. Nyukhtikov (all of them holders of the Merited Test Pilot title) and others had reached an advanced age, while the young test pilots who had recently joined the Tupolev OKB still lacked the necessary experience. True, there were pilots of a generation in between these two, who were both young enough and experienced enough, but they were engaged in other high-priority programmes. For example, Aleksey D. Kalina was the project test pilot of the Tu-134, which first flew on 29th July 1963 and entered service in 1967; its testing was far from over. Yuriy V. Sookhov was the project test pilot of the Tu-154 *Careless* three-turbofan medium-haul airliner which first flew on 4th October 1968; Vasiliy P. Borisov was assigned as project test pilot to the as-yet unflown Tu-22M0 *Backfire-A* supersonic bomber which would enter flight test on 30th August 1969.

Above: Here CCCP-68001 is probably shown making a demonstration flight at Le Bourget on 5th June 1971.

Left: Here we have a minor malfunction: the smaller doors of the port mainwheel well have failed to close after gear retraction due to broken linkages.

Above right: A large delegation of US Communists visiting the Soviet Union, including Communist Party USA Chairman Gus Hall (eight from left) and CPUSA National President Henry M. Winston (sixth from right, with cane) examines the Tu-144 during a trip to Zhukovskiy.

Right: Gus Hall (accompanied by his wife) shakes hands with Andrey N. Tupolev.

Far right: Henry M. Winston shakes hands with Andrey N. Tupolev; Aleksey A. Tupolev is in the middle.

The first flight date was drawing inexorably close – the Tu-144 had to fly before the end of the year by all means. After much deliberation and discussion the crew was finally assigned, comprising captain (project test pilot) Eduard V. Yelian and first officer Mikhail V. Kozlov, plus Valeriy M. Molchanov as a back-up pilot. This was a procedure similar to that in the Soviet Cosmonaut Detachment: should Yelian be unable to fly the aircraft for whatever reason, Kozlov would back him up as captain and Molchanov would become first officer. The choice of project test pilot was no matter of chance – Eduard Yelian (holder of the Hero of the Soviet Union and Merited Test Pilot titles) was the pilot who knew the Tu-144 and its systems best, having spent much time at the OKB's

design office; he had done a lot of work on the 'iron bird' test rig, contributing a lot to the shaping of the Tu-144's flight deck and its control algorithms.

Yelian was an ideal candidate for taking the Tu-144 up on its maiden flight, but Merited Test Pilot Mikhail Kozlov was equally well trained; this talented pilot had some experience with supersonic aircraft, having tested the Tu-22 bomber, and had been nominated for the HSU title for this highly complex programme. Valeriy Molchanov was a young pilot, one of the first aerobatic pilots to graduate from LII's Test Pilot School. The three of them started 'flying' the Tu-144 on the 'iron bird' and flying the MiG-21I, taking the latter to the limits of its flight envelope.

Apart from the pilots, there were two other crew members. Yuriy T. Selivyorstov was the most experienced flight engineer at the Tupolev OKB's flight test facility; together with his colleagues A. I. Dralin and M. V. Laponogov he had studied the Tu-144's systems down to the smallest detail. Finally, Vladimir N. Benderov, the engineer in charge of the test programme, would fly as test engineer.

Engine runs, taxying tests and final ground checks went on for a month. By 20th December 1968 CCCP-68001 was finally ready to fly but the weather was inclement, with fog and low cloud, leaving no chance for the flight. Being anxious about the flight test schedule (the Soviet SST had to make its maiden flight ahead of its Anglo-French counterpart by all means, as a matter of national prestige), the Ministry of Aircraft Industry went so far as to enlist the services of a special Aeroflot detachment operating 'sky cleaner' aircraft to improve the weather over Zhukovskiy. Still, Mother Nature refused to play ball. When the 'sky cleaners' had done their job and the weather was acceptable, the go-ahead was given to tow the Tu-144 to the runway holding point. However, even as the aircraft moved, so thick a fog descended suddenly, so that the visibility dropped to 15-20 m (50-65 ft); a take-off was out of the question, and the Tu-144 was gingerly towed back to the hardstand.

A harrowing week or so followed; the flight and ground crews involved in the Tu-144 programme were on tenterhooks, coming to the flight test facility in the early morning hours day after day in the hope of a change in the weather. The bad weather persisted until New Year's Day; 31st December 1968 dawned with brilliant sunshine at last, but soon afterwards the weather began deteriorating again. Minister of Aircraft Industry Pyotr V. Dement'yev washed his hands of the whole affair, saying *'It's up to you to decide [whether to fly or not]'*, and left the airfield, going back to Moscow. As soon as the sun broke through the clouds again, Andrey N. Tupolev gave the order to proceed. The engines were promptly started and minutes later the Tu-144 left the ground for the first time, 25 seconds after brake release, with the MiG-21I/1 and a Tupolev Tu-124 *Cookpot* twin-turbofan short-haul airliner (a Tupolev OKB support aircraft) flying chase.

The 37-minute maiden flight went without a hitch, except that the weather deteriorated again and the first landing of the world's first SST had to take place in conditions in which many production airliners of the day were obliged to stay on the ground. The pilots reported that the machine flew well and responded well to the controls.

This first flight of the Tu-144 was not just a great New Year present for everyone concerned but an event of world significance and a milestone in the history of Soviet aviation. The objective of being the first past the post had been attained; the Concorde 001 prototype (F-WTSS) flew only on 2nd March 1969.

Here is how Merited Test Pilot Mark L. Gallai (HSU), a LII test pilot, described the events on the day of the first flight:

'At length, everything was ready. The [MAP] Methodical council had held a session at which seasoned test pilots, scientists

Left: US astronaut Neil Armstrong shakes hands with Andrey N. Tupolev as he receives a model of the Tu-144 as a gift in June 1970.

Above right: Another delegation visiting the hangar at Zhukovskiy where the Tu-144 is parked. Front row: Tupolev OKB engineers Andriasov and M. S. Mikhailov, test pilot Mikhail V. Kozlov, Soviet cosmonaut Gheorgiy T. Beregovoy, Neil Armstrong, Andrey N. Tupolev, designer Aleksandr A. Arkhangel'skiy, engineer Smirnov, Vladimir N. Benderov and Aleksey A. Tupolev.

Right: Another scene from the same visit. The rear row includes cosmonaut Gherman N. Titov (centre) and obvious KGB agents on the right. The front row features the wives of Titov and Armstrong, Tupolev Sr., Armstrong, Arkhangel'skiy and Tupolev Jr.

Chapter 2 - Take One: the Tu-144 Prototype

and engineers had discussed in detail all the factors affecting the aircraft's and the crew's readiness for the tests, gone over the plan of the maiden flight, meticulously picked the optimum course of action for the crew in the event anything should go wrong... The verdict was: "It's OK to fly – tomorrow if you want to".

Came tomorrow – and, as one of my colleagues put it, it was not the aircraft but our nerves that were put to the test. For ten long days – 21st to 31st December 1968 – we were forced to wait for favourable weather. Twice the entire airfield was set agog by false alarms: the weather service promised an improvement in the weather, the "action stations" command was given, powerful tugs would tow the aircraft to the holding point, the bosses would arrive... Yet, in spite of the promises, the weather stayed inclement, and when dusk started falling – which would be soon enough (21st December is the shortest day of the year), – there was nothing to do but to call the whole thing off.

Tupolev was the man who showed the calmest reaction to this wearying wait. [...] Meanwhile, the weather kept making fun of us... Actually it is more fitting to say "the weathers" (even though this word is singularia tantum, *if memory serves) because within those ten days we had all imaginable kinds of bad weather except tropical storms. First, there was low cloud; therefore in the days before the first "false alarm" the men in charge of the tests approached the Methodical Council, urging it to authorise the maiden flight if the cloudbase was 500 m [1,640 ft] instead of the stipulated 1,000 m [3,280 ft]. After a deal of haggling, the Council gave the go-ahead to fly if the cloudbase was not less than 700 m [2,300 ft]. Still, the debate on this subject quickly petered out because the cloudbase would not rise above 300 m [980 ft] anyway.*

On 30th December the clouds scattered; the word went out to prepare for the flight, but... just then a crosswind of such gale force swept across the runway that it was hardly thinkable to take off in a production aircraft, never mind a unique new aircraft. And again, the General Designer's figure stood out in stark contrast to all those men who were arguing, cursing the weather and waving their arms. Taking refuge from the wind in his car, he pondered about something with a poker face, the expression giving only the faintest hint of hurt feelings.

In the morning of the 31st [December] there were no clouds and no wind, but there was thick fog. Special aircraft operated by the Hydrometeorological Service were summoned to the rescue; they were reputed to work wonders, scattering clouds like the Lord Almighty himself! Yet, it soon transpired that competing with the Lord Almighty was not easy. For one thing, the circular hole in the fog which these aircraft managed to make would not stay put and promptly drifted away; for another, the fog inside this hole did not clear completely – it merely turned into a fairly thick haze, which was no good. There was nothing to do but wait – again... all the more so because suddenly the weather began improving on its own, without any input from the scientists. Yet, this change in the weather was terribly slow; it was hard to tell if the weather would improve acceptably before dusk fell. The crew – pilots E. V. Yelian and M. V. Kozlov, engineer in charge V. N. Benderov and flight engineer Yu. T. Selivyorstov – took their seats in the Tu-144 in order not to waste precious minutes, should the weather improve sufficiently; we had to count every single minute.

The Tu-124 support aircraft departed on a weather reconnaissance mission; the crew radioed that the situation up there was somewhat more favourable. Hope dawned for us. The six of us – Chief Designer Aleksey Andreyevich Tupolev (the General Designer's son), flight test facility chief Aleksey Sergeyevich Blagoveshchenskiy (formerly a well-known combat pilot and test pilot), air traffic controller Aleksey Petrovich Shelyakin and two or three other men – were sitting in the bright orange-coloured mobile ATC post van. Andrey Nikolayevich's massive black limousine was parked a few metres away. On hearing the report from the weather reconnaissance aircraft [Andrey N.] Tupolev pondered for about 30 seconds. Then he climbed out of the car, walked up to our van, stood in the doorway and asked for the transmitter microphone. It took him a few seconds to get to grips with the mike and earphones. Next came a dialogue which was not quite in conformity with the rules of radio exchange but was quite interesting.

"048 (the Tu-144 prototype's ATC callsign that day – Auth.), this is me" – Tupolev said on the radio without much ado. Apparently Yelian had not the slightest doubt as to who the "me" was, and promptly acknowledged:

"048 here. Roger."

Still, Tupolev considered it necessary to clarify:

"It's me. Andrey Nikolayevich."

"Gotcha. 048 here, awaiting instructions."

"What's your opinion of the situation?"

It was a straight question, and he got a straight answer at once. Apparently the crew, too, had not just been sitting there idly and had made up their minds as to the chief question of the moment ("To fly or not to fly").

"The situation does pose a few problems, but it is possible to fly."

"Well, then let's get rolling, nice and easy" – the General Designer said, unexpectedly quoting a line from a contemporary song ('Let's sit down, friends, before a long journey', performed by Maya Kristalinskaya and recorded in 1962 – Auth.).

"Roger."

"...and don't forget about the song on the way" – Tupolev continued. As it turned out, he – unlike many of the radio audience – knew more than just the first line from the chorus of the popular song.

"You can bet we won't" – said Yelian, picking up the humorous tone of this unusual exchange.

"Good luck, then" – Tupolev said, concluding the conversation.'

(Here an important comment must be made. In this last phrase Tupolev used a well-know Russian idiom for a good luck wish – *Ni **pookha**, ni pera!* (literally, '[May you get] neither down nor feather!', as a wish to a hunter); very much like the German expression *Hals- und Beinbruch!* ('May you break your neck and legs'). The correct answer to this idiom is *K chortu!* ('To the devil!') – 'as the call, so the echo', you know.)

'And then we all stretched our necks like geese, straining to hear what the aircraft captain would answer to the 80-year-old academician, – Gallai continues. – Apparently tradition was stronger than etiquette, because Yelian, on hearing the "feathery" wish, briskly replied: "To the devil!" This phrase, which was

Chapter 2 - Take One: the Tu-144 Prototype

promptly quoted in almost all newspaper and magazine features devoted to the Tu-144's maiden flight, sounded perfectly natural in this conversation whose at-ease tone had been set by Tupolev from the start. The old man was wise; few people were capable of easing the general tension before a difficult mission and creating a good mood with just two or three phrases like this. [...]

After the General Designer's command, things picked up speed. Really, a slower tempo was out of the question because it was a race against the clock – there was not much time left until sundown. On the other hand, there was not much left to do before the take-off – everyone and everything, from the prototype aircraft to the helicopter carrying the medical and rescue teams, was ready.

We drove in our orange van down the runway, closer to the spot where, according to the calculations, the Tu-144 was to become airborne. A flurry of snow, dust and jet exhaust swirled behind the Tu-144 as the engines were started. The crew requested permission to take off and was cleared to do so. After a short 25-second take-off run the aircraft left the ground. The drooped nose – a feature meant to improve the view from the flight deck – gave it a ponderous appearance. Yet, we did not enjoy the sight for too long – after take-off the Tu-144 quickly vanished into the haze.

About half an hour later, having made two circuits of the airfield, it reappeared out of the murk as it came in to land. A few dozen seconds more, and the Tu-144 was rolling down the runway, the engines whining steadily at ground idle.'

Aleksey P. Yakimov, who was then head of the flight department at the flight test facility and thus had to authorise the crew to fly, gives a more restrained account of that memorable day – albeit also including a few devils. 'During the last ten days of December 1968 we worked like devils, towing the aircraft to the runway [in the morning] and back to the hardstand in the evening. Came 31st December. The aircraft was back on the runway; everything seemed to be ready – both the aircraft and the crew. A decision [on whether to fly or not] had to be taken, and the weather was lousy; the cloudbase was at about 300 m. Andrey Nikolayevich sat in his car, while I took turns sitting at the control tower and going to Andrey Nikolayevich (in order to tell him the latest information – Auth.). We sent an aircraft up on a weather reconnaissance mission. Finally, [Nikolay A.] Bessonov (the captain of the Tu-124 weather reconnaissance aircraft – Auth.) *reported: "There is a gap in the clouds; it may be over the airfield in due time". I went to Andrey Nikolayevich again and, with his blessing, authorised the take-off. I drove to the tower, made an appropriate entry in the log book and quoted the [weather] conditions. That's how the flight was carried out. Now, thinking back to it, I recall the torment I was in when pondering whether to give the go-ahead or not. Fortunately everything went well.'*

The following day, on 1st January 1969, all Soviet newspapers ran a news item by the TASS News Agency. It went as follows: *'For the first time in the world, the Tu-144 supersonic aircraft has flown on 31st December 1968. (Sic;* it should have been 'supersonic commercial aircraft' – *Auth.) The Tu-144 will carry passengers at a cruising speed of 2,500 km/h [1,552 mph]. The operation of the aircraft's systems, including the automatic control system, as well*

Another view of Tu-144 CCCP-68001 with the nose raised.

as the equipment and the engines was checked during the flight. The aircraft was flown by captain Merited Test Pilot Eduard Vaganovich Yelian, first officer test pilot Mikhail Vasil'yevich Kozlov (HSU), test engineer Vladimir Nikolayevich Benderov and flight engineer Yuriy Trofimovich Selivyorstov. The aircraft will carry on with the planned test programme. The maiden flight of the Tu-144 supersonic airliner is a new achievement of Soviet science and technology and a major contribution to the development of the Soviet aircraft industry for the purpose of peaceful use of aviation.' The news item was circulated worldwide within a few days.

On 20th-21st May 1969 CCCP-68001 made its public debut at Moscow-Sheremet'yevo airport where it was demonstrated statically to Soviet and foreign media representatives and civil aviation specialists. It was then that the NATO's Air Standards Co-ordinating Committee (ASCC) assigned the reporting name *Charger* to the Tu-144. At the same time, however, a more popular nickname was coined, 'Concordski'; this sobriquet stuck to the Tu-144 for the rest of its life, hinting at the alleged Soviet custom of copying Western designs.

The second MiG-21I (c/n N010103) was not completed until the end of 1969, making its first flight from Gor'kiy-Sormovo (the factory airfield of plant No.21) at the hands of LII test pilot Igor' P. Volk. It served for aerodynamic experiments and differed from the first aircraft in several respects. In particular, the original straight LERXes with 78° leading-edge sweep were replaced by scimitar-shaped ones. A cigar-shaped pod housing a cine camera was installed at the tip of the fin and a small fairing housing a second cine-camera pointing to starboard was added to the fuselage spine. The cine-cameras served for capturing the airflow pattern on the wings; to this end the starboard wing was covered with wool tufts. Additionally, the wings were rigged with air pressure sensors (pitot heads and static ports) and a laser system visualising the airflow over the wings was fitted.

Tragically, MiG-21I CCCP A-144 crashed right in the middle of Zhukovskiy airfield on 28th July 1970 when the main part of the test programme was already completed. LII test pilot Viktor S. Konstantinov was practising a display programme for the 29th Paris Air Show (due in 1971) where he was to fly a production MiG-21; that was to be the first appearance of a Soviet combat aircraft at a major international airshow. He decided to show off, performing an unscheduled series of low-level aerobatic manoeuvres right above the runway – forgetting that the MiG-21I's handling differed from that of the standard tailed-delta fighter. One error on the part of the pilot was enough – the aircraft lost speed and started pancaking. Konstantinov ejected too late and was killed. That left the second MiG-21I to support the Tu-144's tests.

On 1st June 1970 the Tu-144 went supersonic for the first time. A month and a half later, on 15th July, CCCP-68001 attained its maximum speed of 2,443 km/h (1,517 mph) or Mach 2.35. On 17th May 1971 the aircraft participated in a new commercial aircraft display at Moscow-Vnukovo airport. On 23rd May it travelled abroad for the first time, making a two-day stop at Prague-Ruzyne airport. On 25th May – 8th June 1971 the Tu-144 was presented to the Western world 'live' at the 29th Paris Air Show under the exhibit code 826, rubbing noses with the Concorde in real life for the first time; this included a single demo flight on 5th June.

In the winter of 1971 the Tu-144 prototype's sonic boom was measured for the first time in a LII test area near the town of Belo'omut (Ryazan' Region, central Russia); the research team was headed by A. V. Rodnov. Truck-mounted and heliborne acoustic measurement stations with self-contained power sources were used in these experiments; these measurement stations had been developed by LII in anticipation of the Tu-144's flight tests. A small number of test flights provided enough information to allow preliminary conclusions on the intensity of the sonic boom to be drawn. Light structures and properly installed window panes took no damage from the shock wave. As for people, they hardly felt the pressure of the shock wave at all – they were annoyed mostly by the suddenness of the sonic boom; if the test flights took place in the early morning hours, the sudden 'thunderclap' was loud enough to wake up everyone in the nearby villages.

Flight tests and in-flight measurements give the final verdict as to whether the anticipated aerodynamic load figures obtained by calculation and in wind tunnel tests are correct or not. With the Tu-144, the technique lay in measuring the strain fields on the wings' upper and lower skins and measuring the strain levels on the spar webs and the ribs. The wing deformation (caused by structural weight and the fuel load inside the wings and aerodynamic loads) had been calculated and 'designed into' the wings. When tests began, the need arose to compare the estimated deformation with the real picture; this was done in a novel way by placing photo cameras operating in accordance with a certain algorithm at the cabin windows. This new and exciting job was performed by Aleksandr L. Pookhov and I. K. Kulikov, and the real-life deformation matched the estimates exactly.

Subsequently the Tu-144 demonstrator made a series of publicity flights to Berlin-Schönefeld (13th-17th June 1971), Warsaw-Okęcie (17th June 1971), Sofia-Vrazhdebna (6th-14th September 1971), Hannover (the ILA '72 airshow, 19th April – 1st May 1972) and Budapest-Férihegy (30th September – 5th October 1972); the flights from Moscow to Sofia and back were made in supersonic cruise. The test results confirmed the validity of the design principles and the efficacy of the design features incorporated into the aircraft; they were used in the development of the production version described in Chapter 4. Tu-144 CCCP-68001 continued flying test missions until 27th April 1973 when it was struck off charge; at that point it had made more than 120 flights, with a total time since new of 180 hours (including about 50 hours supersonic). On the whole the demonstrator had served its intended purpose well. Sadly, this aircraft was broken up in March 1985, though it really should have been preserved for posterity because it had made history as the first-ever supersonic airliner. Yet, the Soviet Air Force Museum's management showed a lack of interest in this...

The development, construction and testing of the Tu-144 demonstrator (*izdeliye* 044), and the additional research at TsAGI and the Tupolev OKB that followed, furnished invaluable data and experience. This was taken into account when creating the production version – a very different aircraft in which many of the deficiencies discovered on the demonstrator had been designed out. The production Tu-144 differed markedly from the *izdeliye* 044 as regards aerodynamics, structural design and performance.

Chapter 3

The Prototype in Detail

Type: Medium/long-haul supersonic airliner of tailless-delta layout. The airframe is of all-metal construction embodying the fail-safe design principle to enhance reliability and has a 30,000-hour designated service life over 15 years.

Fuselage: Semi-monocoque riveted stressed-skin structure. The fuselage cross-section changes from circular at the forward extremity to quasi-circular (formed by two arcs of different radii with the larger radius at the bottom, so that the underside is flattened) for most of the length and back to circular at the rear. The resulting cross-section enables comfortable five-abreast passenger accommodation while keeping the cross-section area to a minimum. Maximum width 3.25 m (10 ft 7⁶¹⁄₆₄ in), equivalent fuselage diameter 3.039 m (9 ft 11⁴¹⁄₆₄ in), overall fineness ratio 17.92.

The fuselage is largely manufactured of AK4-1 aluminium alloy, and flush riveting is used throughout. Structurally the fuse-

Tu-144 CCCP-68001 (in early guise) at rest, with the nose visor lowered and the elevons fully drooped.

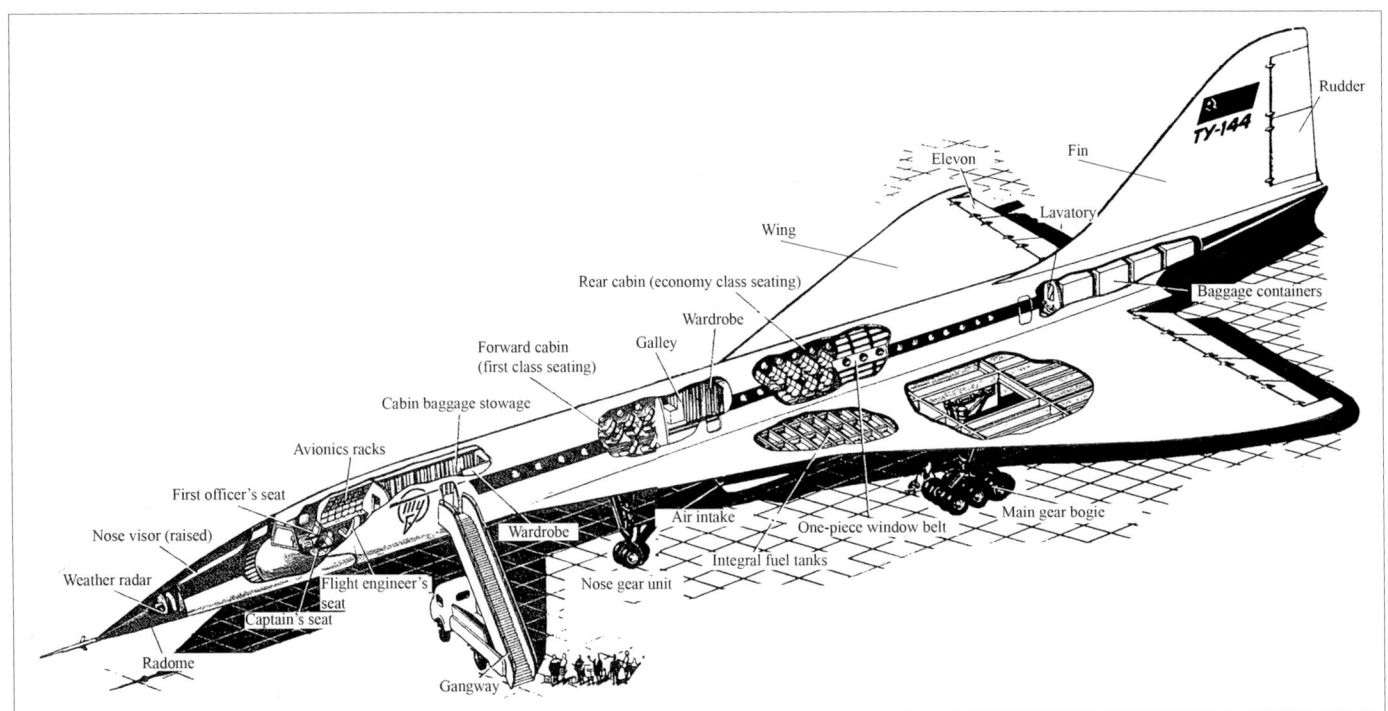

lage is built in three sections: the forward fuselage (Section F-1), the centre fuselage (Section F-2) and the rear fuselage (Section F-3).

The unpressurised *forward fuselage* (frames 1-7) is the sharply pointed movable nose visor which is drooped to improve the forward view on take-off and landing; its fineness ratio is 5.86. The nose visor is hinged to the bottom of fuselage frame 15 and actuated by a duplicated (main and back-up) electrically-driven screw-jack attached to the top of the front pressure dome; the actuator features a hydraulic emergency drive forcing the visor down into an intermediate position if the electric motors fail. When the visor

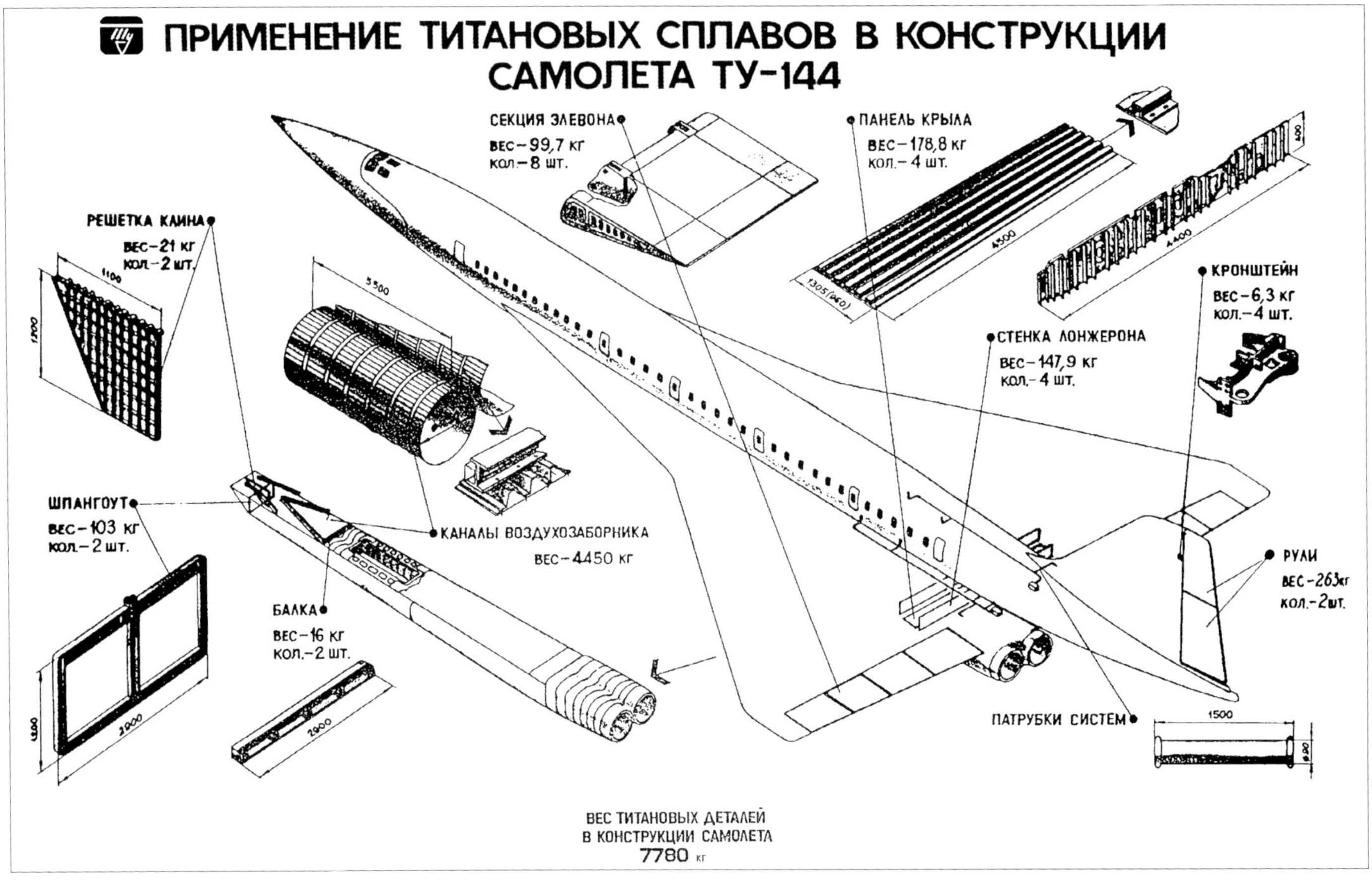

Chapter 3 - The Prototype in Detail

Left: A cut away drawing of Tu-144 CCCP-68001.

Below left: This drawing illustrates the share of titanium in the Tu-144's airframe design.

Right: This upper view shows the trapezoidal shape of the upper windows in the Tu-144 prototype's hinged nose visor. The windshield and the forward pressure dome can just be seen through them.

Below: The fully lowered nose visor reveals the curved joint line, the V-shaped windshield and its wipers. The main pitot at the tip of the radome carries pitch and yaw vanes. Note the three air data system sensors to port aft of the radome and the L-shaped pitot above the Tupolev logo.

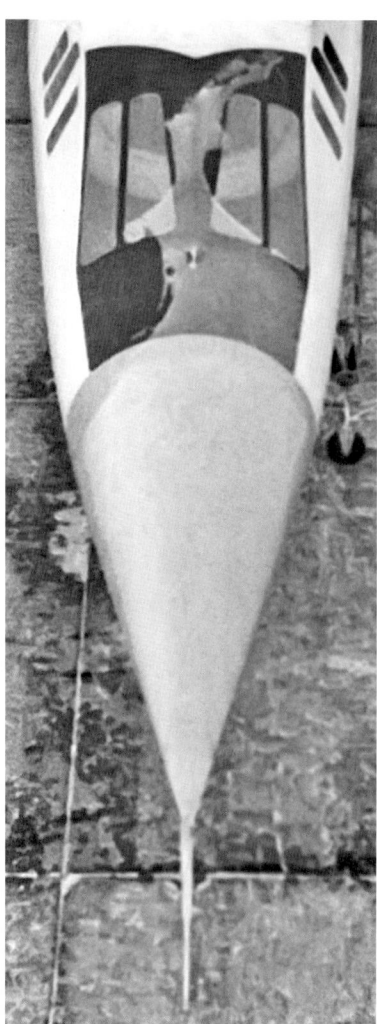

is raised for cruise flight, the upper/lower fuselage contours in the area are unbroken. The nose visor incorporates four dorsal glazing panels and one window on each side aft of them, providing a measure of forward view in cruise flight; it terminates in a conical glassfibre radome 5.8 m (19 ft 0$^{11}/_{32}$ in) long tipped with a pitot.

The *centre fuselage* (frames 8-108) accommodates the flight deck, the passenger cabins and the baggage compartments forming a single pressure cabin. Along nearly half its length the fuselage is permanently attached to the wing centre section forming the cabins' pressure floor. A hefty longitudinal structure (the so-called centrebody) runs along the centreline below the wings, forming the lower load-bearing element of the fuselage and significantly increasing its rigidity.

The flight deck commences with the front pressure dome; it is designed for a crew of three, the flight engineer sitting behind the two pilots, facing to starboard. It features a windscreen of shallow V shape (exposed when the nose visor is lowered) and two side windows on each side; the rear pair are aft-sliding direct vision windows. The two optically flat birdproof windscreen panes are made of boron-silicate triplex glass 51 mm (2 in) thick; the remainder of the glazing is specially formulated E-2 grade Plexiglas.

Located aft of the flight deck is the No.1 avionics/equipment bay (up to frame 20), which is divided into port and starboard halves to permit access to the flight deck; it houses the principal navigation, communication and control equipment. The port half accommodates part of the short-range radio navigation (SHORAN) system, the digital navigation computer, the moving-map display (MMD) modules and the flight control system modules (the trajectory measurement system, the air data system and more). The starboard half houses more SHORAN modules, the Lotos radio, the identification friend-or-foe transponder, the radar set, the Raduga inertial/gyro system and the automatic fuel metering/usage equipment. It also houses oxygen bottles and electric transformers. Further aft is the forward baggage compartment, followed by the forward vestibule with a rectangular entry door to port and a rectangular service door of similar size to starboard for baggage loading and emergency evacuation.

Aft of the forward vestibule is the forward passenger cabin, which was meant to accommodate either 40 passengers in the 120-seat all-tourist version (eight rows of seats five-abreast in a 2+3 arrangement with the aisle offset to port) or 18 first-class passengers in six three-abreast rows (1+2) in the 98-seat version; in both cases the first two rows were to face each other, with tables in between. The cabin is followed by the centre vestibule/galley with a second entry door to port and a service door to starboard for catering and emergency evacuation; these doors are positioned

103

above the wing LERXes. All four doors open outwards, swinging forward on curved arms. Next comes the rear passenger cabin (frames 50-85) meant to accommodate 80 tourist-class passengers on 12 five-abreast rows (the first two rows again facing each other, with tables in between) and five four-abreast rows; it features two spaced pairs of inward-opening (plug-type) rectangular overwing emergency exits. The cabins feature oval windows with triple glazing set into large one-piece longitudinal panels forming part of the centre fuselage structure. The seat tracks and the design of the removable cabin bulkheads and galley units allow the cabins to be reconfigured for different seating arrangements. The interior trim of the cabins and entry vestibules is largely composed of easily detachable panels made of non-combustible synthetic materials.

The toilets are located at the rear of the cabin. Aft of these is the rear baggage compartment, which is accessed via an inward-opening ventral hatch aft of the engine nozzles and terminates in the rear pressure dome. The rear baggage compartment is flanked by the two halves of the No.2 avionics/equipment bay starting at frame 87.

The pressure cabin is faced from inside with a heat insulation material consisting of two layers of KAST-V grade Textolit composite with a layer of glass wool (fibreglass insulation) in between. It also features a dynamic heat insulation system protecting it against kinetic heating during supersonic cruise. The fuselage skin is double, and cooling air from the cabin is forced between the layers.

The unpressurised *rear fuselage* has a fineness ratio of 7.495. It carries the tail unit and accommodates the auxiliary power unit and the brake parachute container enclosed by an upward-hinged tailcone. The rear fuselage underside features a full-length wrap-around heat shield made of titanium.

The actual *izdeliye* 044 prototype (CCCP-68001) has a different interior layout as compared to the project, featuring structural changes associated with its flight test status. The crew is enlarged to four by introducing a test engineer; the flight engineer's workstation is moved aft to the forward cabin and located on the port side just aft of frame 28, with the test engineer's workstation symmetrically to starboard. All four crewmembers are provided with ejection seats; hence two pairs of rectangular dorsal hatches with jettisonable covers are incorporated into the flight deck roof and into the roof of the forward cabin a short way aft of the forward pair of doors, enabling ejection in an emergency. The substitution of normal pilot seats with ejection seats also necessitated relocation of certain controls in the flight deck.

For safety reasons the crew section is isolated from the rest of the pressure cabin by an additional pressure dome at frame 32 to reduce the volume of the depressurised section in the event of decompression. Additionally, a flat bulkhead with a door is installed at frame 20, acting as an airflow damper in this situation.

The No.1 avionics/equipment bay commences immediately aft of the pilots' seats. The space between frames 20-28 is mainly occupied by test equipment; the port side rack holds data recorders for the vibration monitoring suite, while the one on the on the starboard side houses data recorders for the navigation suite, automatic flight control system, electric system and aerodynamic measurements. Further aft is a bay accommodating the flight engineer and test engineer with their workstations (frames 28-32),

Chapter 3 - The Prototype in Detail

Right: Front view of the port wing. Note the large gaps between the elevon sections, all four of which are set at different angles in this view.

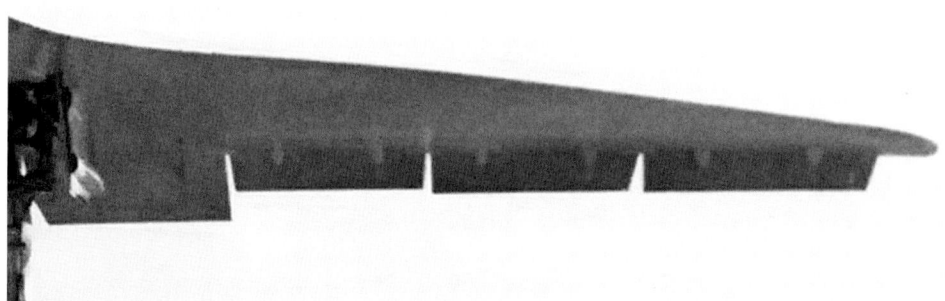

Below right: The port wingtip, showing the leading edge curvature, the navigation light (which is apparently only visible from the side but not from the front) and the elevon actuator fairings.

Bottom right: The outermost portions of the wing trailing edge are fixed and carry six static discharge wicks.

Above left: The rear cabin of Tu-144 CCCP-68001 in 1971 Paris Air Show configuration with five-/four-abreast tourist class seating. Note the open overhead luggage racks with passenger service units and the alternating seat upholstery colours.

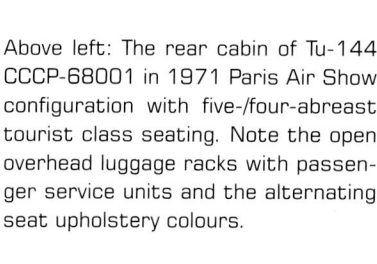

Left: The remnant of the three-abreast first class seating in the front cabin, with tables between the facing first two rows.

followed by a remnant of the forward cabin in representative first-class configuration with nine seats. The flight engineer's main bank of instruments is located at frame 28; there is also a side console and a port side bank of throttles which is linked to the main bank of throttles in the flight deck and the autothrottle by push-pull rods.

The centre vestibule houses test equipment for the hydraulic and air conditioning systems, as well as some items of the aircraft's intended equipment installed there temporarily for lack of space (fire extinguisher bottles, circuit breaker panels and hydraulics modules).

For the initial flight test phase the seats in the rear cabin were replaced by more test equipment (airframe and engine stress measurement systems, fuel system monitoring equipment, a vertical gyro, pitch/yaw/roll rate sensors, G load sensors and a data link system transmitting information to the ground control centre in real time). This was mounted on the starboard side on detachable racks, the power supply cables for the equipment running along

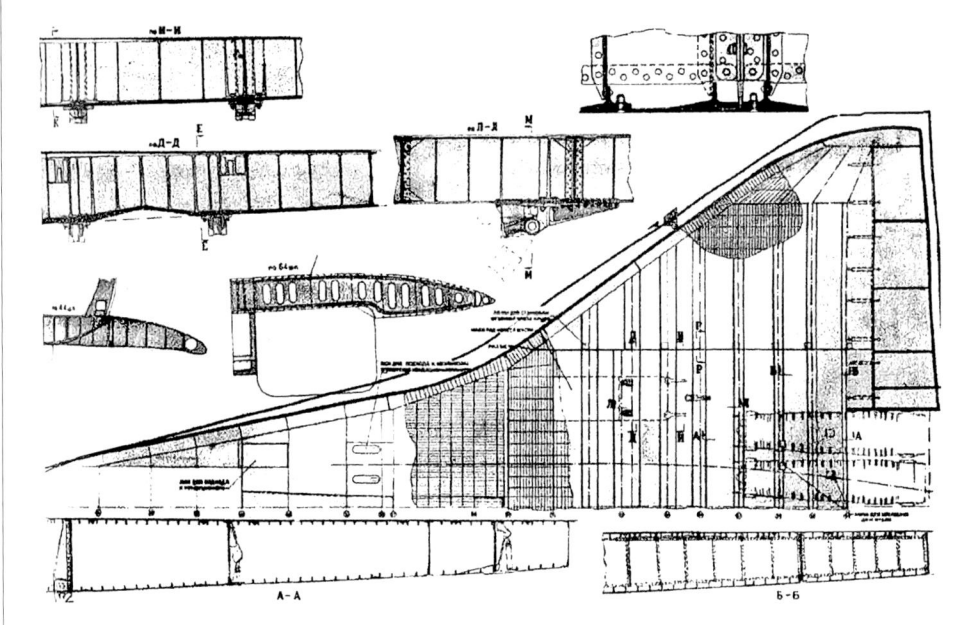

Above: This view illustrates the Tu-144 prototype's wing leading edge shape, with a smooth transition between long straight-edge portions.

Left: A drawing from the project documents showing the Tu-144 prototype's wing design.

Below left: The rear fuselage and tail of CCCP-68001 as originally flown, with an unpainted titanium rudder and a very conspicuous heat shield.

Below: Later, the rudder and the heat shield were both painted white.

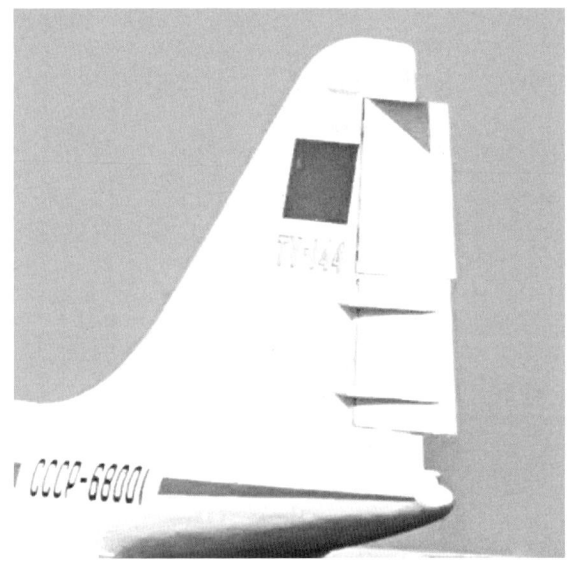

Chapter 3 - The Prototype in Detail

The landing gear of the Tu-144 prototype in early guise, with a nosewheel mudguard and open mainwheel well doors. Note the landing lights mounted on the main gear struts, the area-ruled engine nacelle and the anti-collision light under its starboard half. Note also that the intake upper lips are not parallel to the wing undersurface.

Right: The nose gear of CCCP-68001 in later guise (minus mudguard).

Far right: The main gear in later guise; the main doors are closed.

Below right: This view gives details of the port main gear strut and bogie and the sculpted main gear doors. Note that the retraction ram/drag strut has no fairing yet.

the starboard side of the cabin floor and partly along the overhead luggage racks. The test equipment caters for the fuel system and the strain gauges fitted to various parts of the airframe; the data link system is also installed in the rear cabin and there are provisions for installing cine cameras. The cabin also accommodates some of the AFCS modules attached to the seat tracks (the compact attitude and heading reference system, angle speed sensors and G-load sensors); a special well is provided under the cabin floor at frame 56 for the gyros of the Raduga system.

The front end of the No.2 avionics/equipment bay houses the electrics distribution buses. This bay accommodates the modules of the automatic engine starting and monitoring system, the *Mikron* (Micron) radio set (to port), the radio altimeter and the DC batteries (to starboard), the water tank and the nitrogen bottles. The rear baggage compartment houses more test equipment associated with the powerplant.

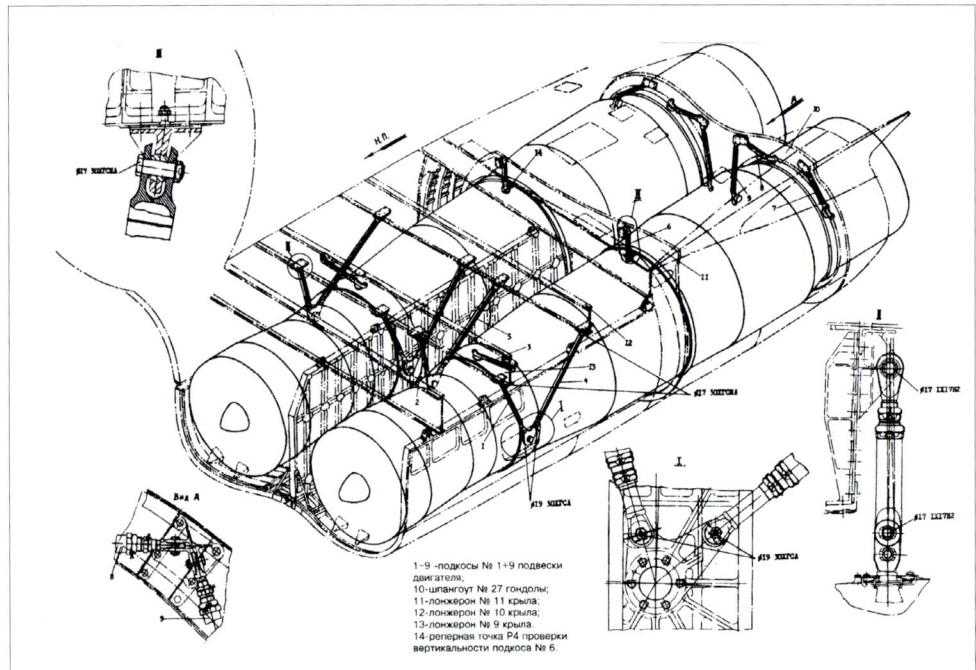

Left: This drawing from the Tupolev OKB documents shows how the demonstrator's NK-144 engines were attached to the airframe by rods and fittings.

Right: The engine nozzles of CCCP-68001 as originally flown, with a boxy structure at the top of the nacelle.

Below right: The same aircraft in later guise with exposed engine nozzle petals.

Below: A cut away example of the Kuznetsov NK-144 turbojet used as a teaching aid.

Wings: Cantilever low-wing monoplane with low aspect ratio compound-delta wings featuring large leading-edge root extensions and an ogival leading edge. The LERXes make up 22.9% of the gross wing area. Leading-edge sweepback 78° on the LERXes and 55° on the outer wing portions; the trailing edge has zero sweepback. Aspect ratio 1.575 if the LERXes are included or 1.935 disregarding the LERXes; wing taper 10.25 or 6.0 respectively. The wings occupy two-thirds of the fuselage length.

The wings are stressed-skin fail-safe structures made predominantly of AK4-1 aluminium alloy. They utilise specially developed airfoils with a mean thickness/chord ratio of 2.46%. Structurally the wings are built in four pieces: the sharply swept forward section combining the two LERXes, the centre section and two detachable outer wing panels. The forward and centre sections permanently attached to the fuselage serve as attachment points for the engine nacelle, the air intake trunks and the landing gear.

Chapter 3 - The Prototype in Detail

The *forward section* comprises two triangular integral fuel tanks flanking the fuselage between frames 28-44 and a centre portion (frames 44-71) which incorporates integral tanks and the nosewheel well; it also carries the air intake assemblies. The structure consists mainly of girder beams supporting the skin panels which are stiffened by spot-welded stringers; the centre portion has five spars attached to fuselage frames 44, 52, 53, 65 and 71.

The *centre section* is a multi-spar structure comprising milled skin panels with integral stiffeners supported by girder spars (spars 5-14) and girder ribs (ribs 0 through 16L/16R). It serves as an attachment point for the engine nacelle. It also incorporates integral fuel tanks, the mainwheel wells and air conditioning system bays; the latter are accessible via removable panels. The portion of the wing centre section above the engine bays is made of heat-resistant steel and titanium.

The detachable *outer wings* are joined to the centre section by bolts and flanges and are structurally similar to it; the manufacturing breaks are at 5.75 m (18 ft $10^{3}/_{8}$ in) from the centreline. They likewise incorporate integral tanks. The wing trailing edge is almost entirely occupied by four-section elevons whose welded structure is made entirely of titanium alloy; the innermost section on each side is attached to the wing centre section and the other three to the outer wing. Each elevon section is suspended on two hinges and has two actuators enclosed by ventral fairings. To allow for the considerable wing flexure under aerodynamic loads, the gaps between the elevon sections widen towards the trailing edge. The outermost portions of the trailing edge are fixed and carry six static discharge wicks each.

Tail unit: Vertical tail only, comprising a large fin and an inset rudder; aspect ratio 0.705, taper 3.52. The vertical tail utilises a TsAGI P-109 symmetrical airfoil; the thickness/chord ratio is 3.5% at the root and 3% at the tip.

The fin is a one-piece subassembly and is similar in planform to the wings, with an ogival leading edge and very slight negative sweepback on the trailing edge; the root fillet terminates ahead of the wing trailing edge. Structurally the fin is similar to the wing centre section, being made of AK4-1 aluminium alloy and featuring a multi-spar stressed-skin structure with milled skin panels; the fin torsion box between fuselage frames 102-114 houses an integral fuel tank used for longitudinal trim in supersonic cruise. The fin cap is dielectric, incorporating an HF radio antenna. The two-section rudder is similar to the elevons, being made of titanium alloy; each section has two actuators with fairings located to port on the lower half and to starboard on the upper half. A curious feature of the rudder is that the hinges are offset to port on the upper half and to starboard on the lower half.

Landing gear: Hydraulically retractable tricycle type, with pneumatic emergency extension; the landing gear is powered by either of two hydraulic systems.

The aft-retracting nose unit located immediately ahead of the engine nacelle has a V-shaped main strut 4.79 m (15 ft $8^{37}/_{64}$ in) tall and a forward-mounted telescopic retraction/drag strut, stowing in a wheel well located in the gap between the pairs of air intakes. It is fitted with twin 1,020 x 300 mm (40.15 x 11.81 in) non-braking wheels and equipped with a flat-plate mud/snow/slush guard. The nose unit features a steering mechanism/shimmy damper and is controlled by the rudder pedals. Steering angles for taxying are ±60°, ensuring adequate ground manoeuvrability.

The main units are located immediately outboard of the engine nacelle and retract forward into the wing centre section. Each unit has a double-jointed 'knee-action' strut 3.628 m (11 ft $10^{53}/_{64}$ in) tall, an aft-mounted telescopic retraction ram/drag strut and a 12-wheel bogie fitted with 730 x 250 mm (28.74 x 9.84 in) wheels in three rows of four. The mainwheels are equipped with disc brakes and built-in electric fans that keep the brakes from overheating.

109

The main gear bogies are attached to the struts via universal joints allowing them to rock both fore-and-aft and sideways. During retraction they are rotated forward through 180° by separate hydraulic rams/rocking dampers to lie inverted in the wheel wells.

All three units have long-stroke oleo-pneumatic shock absorbers and torque links; these, together with longitudinal and transverse damping, ensure a smooth ride during taxying and take-off/landing. The oleo stroke is 540 mm (21¼ in) for the nose unit and 590 mm (23¹⁵⁄₆₄ in) for the main units.

The nosewheel well is closed by two doors positioned well aft and by fairings attached to the nose gear strut. Each main unit has two large and suitably bulged main doors enclosing the bogie, two small clamshell doors in line with the gear fulcrum (enclosing the 'knee-action' joint) and a narrow rear fairing attached to the retraction strut. All doors originally remained open when the gear was down, though the large main gear doors were later revised to open only when the gear was in transit.

For emergencies or wet/icy runway operations the Tu-144 is equipped with twin brake parachutes housed in the tailcone, with a total area of 104 m² (1,118 sq ft). The brake parachute container is cooled by cabin bleed air in cruise flight to prevent deterioration of the parachute fabric due to overheating; the parabolic hinged cover of the brake parachute container is dielectric and incorporates a Pion (Peony; pronounced '*pee on*') antenna/feeder system. The parachute release lock is mounted dorsally.

Powerplant: Four Kuznetsov NK-144 axial-flow afterburning turbofans rated at 17,500 kgp (38,580 lbst) in full afterburner for take-off, with a minimum-afterburner cruise rating of 3,970 kgp (8,750 lbst) at 18,000 m (59,055 ft) and 2,350 km/h (1,460 mph) and a non-afterburning cruise rating of 3,000 kgp (6,610 lbst) at 11,000 m (36,090 ft) and 1,000 km/h (621 mph).

The NK-144 is a two-spool turbofan with a fixed-area subsonic air intake, a two-stage low-pressure (LP) compressor, a three-stage high-pressure (HP) compressor, an annular combustion chamber with multiple burners, a single-stage HP turbine, a two-stage LP turbine, an afterburner (common to the core and bypass flows) and a fixed-area nozzle. Construction is mostly of titanium castings and forgings. The air intake assembly has a fixed spinner and 18 radial struts. A ventral accessory gearbox is driven off the LP compressor shaft. The engine is started by an air turbine starter, using compressed air supplied by the APU, ground supply or cross-feed from the other engines.

Bypass ratio 0.6. Overall engine pressure ratio at sea level 14.2. Turbine temperature 1,360°K. SFC 1.6 kg/kgp·hr at take-off, 1.56 kg/kgp·hr in minimum-afterburner cruise and 0.965 kg/kgp·hr in non-afterburning cruise. Length overall 7.69 m (25 ft 2¾ in). Inlet diameter 1.355 m (4 ft 5¹¹⁄₃₂ in). Dry weight 3,540 kg (7,800 lb).

The engines are controlled from the pilots' central control pedestal and the flight engineer's station by means of push-pull rods and cable runs. An AT-6 autothrottle is provided.

The engines are mounted side by side in a large common nacelle under the centre fuselage/wing centre section; they are separated from each other by titanium firewalls and from the wing structure by a titanium heat shield. The nacelle's cross-section changes from rectangular at the front to quasi-oval at the rear. Despite the engines being grouped as closely as possible, the engine nacelle has a fairly large cross-section area of 12 m² (129.17 sq ft).

The engines breathe through two-dimensional supersonic air intakes featuring horizontal airflow control ramps. The front end of the nacelle is split to provide room for the nosewheel well (the air intakes are arranged in pairs with vertical splitters dividing them into individual inlet ducts); further aft the gap between the intake assemblies gradually narrows and becomes shallower until it vanishes. Each intake is 1.06 m (3 ft 5⁴⁷⁄₆₄ in) wide and 1.2075 m (3 ft 11¹⁷⁄₃₂ in) high. To prevent boundary layer ingestion the intakes are set apart from the wing undersurface so that their upper lips act as a boundary layer splitter plates. A V-shaped fairing spilling

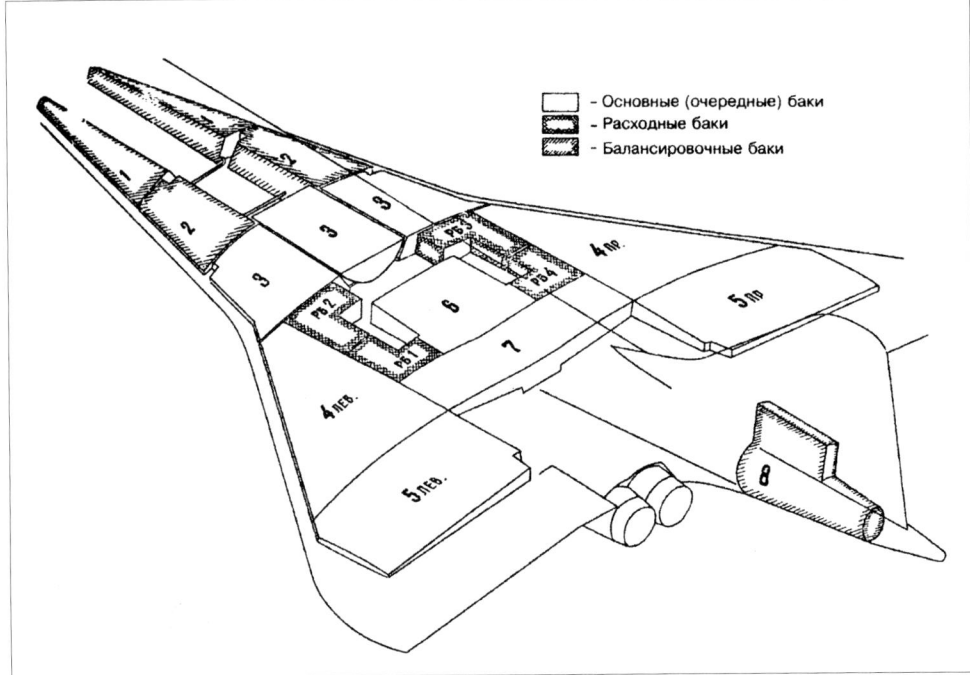

Opposite page: The centre portion of the Tu-144 prototype's main instrument panel with the large round moving-map display on the left and the weather radar display on the right. To the right of the latter, at the co-pilot's station, is a control panel allowing the control surface gearing ratio to be altered.

Left: The layout of the Tu-144 prototype's fuel system. The types of fuel tanks are, top to bottom: main tanks, service tanks and trim tanks. The four service tanks are marked 'РБ' (RB – for *raskhodnyy bahk*); the Nos. 4 and 5 main tanks are subdivided into 4L/4R and 5L/5R.

Chapter 3 - The Prototype in Detail

the boundary layer outward and inward into the abovesaid gap connects the intake lip to the wing undersurface; its shape is optimised for minimum drag. Part of the boundary layer is routed through special channels above the engines, cooling them. Each inlet duct features a ventral bleed door which opens in cruise flight to spill excess air. Further downstream the ducts' cross-section changes to circular; each duct is 13.663 m (44 ft 9^{29}/$_{32}$ in) long.

The Nos. 1 and 4 engines are provided with cascade-type thrust reversers which are part of the airframe, not the engine, and have internal blocker doors. The thrust reverser grids are inclined 15° outward to direct the jet blast away from the main gear wheels.

Access to each engine for maintenance or installation/removal is provided by three outward-hinged ventral cowling panels. Purpose-built dollies are used for engine removal/installation and transportation.

A Stoopino Machinery Design Bureau TA-6A APU is installed in the unpressurised rear fuselage for self-contained engine starting, ground power supply and air conditioning, with an air intake door to port and an exhaust door to starboard. The TA-6A has a three-stage axial compressor, a three-stage axial turbine and a GS-12TO DC generator/starter. Length overall 1,585 mm (5 ft 2^{13}/$_{32}$ in), width 620 mm (2 ft^{13}/$_{32}$ in), height 735 mm (2 ft 4^{15}/$_{16}$ in); dry weight (less generator) 245 kg (540 lb). The TA-6A can operate at ambient temperatures of –60°/+60°C (–76°/+140°F) and altitudes up to 3,000 m (9,840 ft); fuel consumption is 225 kg/hr (496 lb/hr). The air supply rate is 1.35 kg/sec (1.97 lb/sec), bleed air pressure 4.5 kg/cm² (64.28 psi).

Control system: Powered dual controls with twin-chamber irreversible hydraulic actuators in all three control channels; the actuators deliver a force of 13,000 kgf (28,660 lbf). The actuators are powered by four separate hydraulic systems for maximum reliability and are connected to the control columns and rudder pedals by conventional mechanical linkages, mostly passing under the floor. The control runs are mostly rigid (push-pull rods and bellcranks); however, to allow for the airframe's expansion/contraction cycles due to kinetic heating and subsequent cooling, cable runs with tension mechanisms automatically taking up the slack are provided at frames 15 and 96. The mechanism conveying the control inputs to the elevons is located at frame 96; the rudder control runs pass along the cabin roof at the rear. The control circuits feature spring-loaded artificial-feel units. An autopilot linked to the compass system and the navigation suite is fitted.

Pitch and roll control is provided by elevons on the outer wings divided into four sections each for greater reliability and ease of handling at different speeds. The elevon actuators are semi-recessed in the wing structure and partially enclosed by fairings; dampers are also fitted to the outer ends of the elevon sections. Directional control is provided by a two-section rudder; the rudder actuators are completely housed inside the fin.

The controls and instruments in the flight deck are grouped according to their operational use. The instrument panels located in front of the pilots hold the primary flight instruments, the radar display, the MMD and the engine instruments. The central control pedestal carries the bank of throttles (with reverse thrust control levers for the outer engines), the wheel brake control handle, the

nose visor control handle and the control panels for the autothrottle, the AFCS and the digital navigation computer. The side consoles accommodate the switches associated with the communications suite and some other systems. The overhead circuit breaker panel features the controls of the navigation suite, the fire suppression system and other systems. The control wheels incorporate banks of switches and indicator lights for activating certain flight modes.

Fuel system: The wings incorporate a total of 16 integral fuel tanks housed in the LERXes and the centre section/outer wing torsion box, plus a trim tank in the fin torsion box. Total fuel capacity is 102,000 litres (22,440 Imp gal). The transfer pumps in the fuel tanks are powered by hydraulic motors. The fuel transfer and usage sequence is observed automatically to maintain the required CG position throughout the flight.

The rivet joints in the fuel tanks are sealed with VGF-2 heat-resistant fluoride silicone sealant (*vysokotemperatoornyy ghermetik ftorsilikonovyy*) during assembly, whereupon the insides of the tanks are sprayed with a thin coat of VGF-1 sealant. T-8 or T-8V grade kerosene is used; the fuel is nitrogenated to ensure thermal stability and reduce the fire hazard in kinetic heating conditions.

Hydraulics: Four separate hydraulic systems, each with its own reservoir, operating the control surface actuators, the landing gear, nosewheel steering mechanism, wheel brakes, nose visor emergency actuator and fuel transfer pumps. Hydraulic power is provided by eight NP-85 plunger-type pumps (*nasos ploonzhernyy*), two on each engine, and by a 2-NP-85 back-up pump driven by an air turbine; each system includes two pumps driven by different engines. Nominal pressure 210 kg/cm² (3,000 psi). With two or three engines inoperative, available hydraulic power is reduced and limits are imposed on the flight envelope. If all four engines fail, hydraulic power is still available as the engines will be windmilling; at 3,000 m (9,840 ft) and below the APU can be started up to power the air turbine pump.

The hydraulic lines are made of special high-strength steel and incorporate tension compensators to allow for the airframe's expansion/contraction cycles. Hoses are used to connect the hydraulic lines to hydraulic equipment powered by several systems. All systems use special 7-50S-3 grade hydraulic fluid with a high resistance to heating; total capacity is 400 litres (88 Imp gal), including 100 litres (22 Imp gal) in each of the two hydraulic tanks.

Electrics: The primary electric system uses 208 V/400 Hz and 120 V/400 Hz three-phase stable-frequency AC supplied by four 60-kVA oil-cooled engine-driven brushless generators. The oil-cooled generators and their hydromechanical CSDs are built as integral units with a common oil system; the CSDs ensure a stable generator speed (and thus AC frequency) at accessory gearbox output shaft speeds between 320 and 6,500 rpm. The APU features a 40-kVA GT-40PCh6 three-phase AC generator and a 12-kW GS-12TO DC generator. Backup 24 V DC power is provided by two lead-acid batteries located in the No.2 avionics/equipment bay.

The distribution buses are located at the front end of the rear baggage compartment, with circuit breaker panels amidships (in the centre vestibule) and in the crew section and with transformers in the No.1 avionics/equipment bay. The main wiring bundles run along the cabin roof. Ground power receptacles are provided on the underside of the engine nacelle's rear portion, offset to port.

Pneumatic system: The pneumatic system controls the crossfeed valves in the fuel system, pressurises the hydraulic tanks, deploys and releases the brake parachutes. In the event of ejection it also jettisons the hatches above the crew's ejection seats. The system is charged with nitrogen at a nominal pressure of 150 kg/cm² (2,142 psi); the nitrogen bottles with a total capacity of 150 litres (33 Imp gal) are located in the No.2 avionics/equipment bay.

Fire suppression system: Fire extinguisher bottles charged with 114V₂ grade chlorofluorocarbon (CFC) are provided for fighting fires in the engine bays and in the APU bay. As mentioned earlier, the fire extinguisher bottles were temporarily installed in the centre vestibule. In the event of an engine fire the flow of cooling air through the bay of the affected engine is shut off to prevent flame propagation.

Oxygen system: The crew is provided with breathing apparatus and oxygen masks in case of decompression; the oxygen bottles are installed in the No.1 avionics/equipment bay. In the event of ejection the crew uses the KP-27 breathing apparatus (*kislorodnyy pribor* – oxygen set) and oxygen bottles built into the seats.

Air conditioning and pressurisation system: The entire fuselage between frames 8-108 is pressurised by engine bleed air. The air conditioning system (ACS) temporarily located at the rear of the forward cabin behind the additional pressure dome during the initial flight tests ensures an agreeable microclimate for the occupants throughout the flight envelope; the heat insulation system ensures that the cabin wall temperature in supersonic cruise does not rise above 25°C (77°F). The ACS includes four air/air heat exchangers. Most of the envisaged six air conditioning subsystems were deleted on the prototype as surplus to flight test requirements, leaving an empty bay in the centrebody between frames 56-65 where coolers charged with CFC should have been.

Avionics and equipment: The Tu-144 is fully equipped for day/night operation in visual meteorological conditions (VMC) and instrument meteorological conditions (IMC), including automatic flight assisted by an autopilot.

a) navigation and piloting equipment: This includes a compass system enabling automatic route following, an instrument landing system (ILS) including localiser, glideslope beacon and marker beacon receivers, a short-range radio navigation system, a *Biryuza* (Turquoise) radio altimeter, a Groza-144 weather radar in the movable nose visor and other equipment.

b) communications equipment: Mikron HF communications/command link radio (located in the No.2 avionics/equipment bay) and a Lotos (Lotus) radio for short-range air-to-air and air-to-ground communications, plus an intercom.

c) IFF system: an *izdeliye* 020M ATC/IFF transponder.

d) data recording equipment: MSRP-12-96 primary flight data recorder (*magnitnyy samopisets rezhimov polyota* – flight mode magnetic recorder) on the port wall of the rear baggage compartment, plus test equipment suite data recorders.

Crew rescue system: On the *izdeliye* 044 prototype the four crew members are provided with upward-firing Tupolev KT-1 ejection seats permitting safe ejection at altitudes from ground level to the aircraft's service ceiling and at speeds of 130 km/h (80 mph) or higher. Each seat has a two-stage ejection gun, ground handling safety pins, a PS-T three-stage parachute system (two stabilising drogue parachutes and a 50-m²/538-sq ft pilot's parachute), a KP-27 breathing apparatus and an NAZ-7 survival kit (*nosimyy avareeynyy zapahs* – portable emergency supply). The fully armed seat weighs 155 kg (341 lb). In high-altitude test flights the crew wore VKK-6 pressure suits (*vysotnyy kompenseeruyushchiy kostyum* – altitude compensation suit) and GSh-6 full-face pressure helmets (*ghermoshlem*) allowing them to survive an ejection at high altitude.

Chapter 4

Take Two: Back to the Drawing Board

Tu-144 supersonic airliner (production version, *izdeliye* 004)
As mentioned in the preceding chapters, even as *izdeliye* 044 was being designed it became clear that the first Tu-144 had a number of incurable shortcomings. In particular, the close proximity of the engine exhausts to the rear fuselage caused strong vibration and heating which not even the titanium elements in the airframe could withstand; also, the location of all four engines in a common nacelle complicated maintenance access and engine removal. The cruise lift/drag ratio turned out to be inadequate (about 7 instead of 8+), making it impossible to achieve the desired range. Thus, the OKB decided to build no more *izdeliye* 044 aircraft and embarked on a major redesign.

The development work took two directions: refinement of the powerplant and substantial improvements to the airframe structure and aerodynamics. As early as 12th December 1966 the VPK issued ruling No.290 requiring General Designer Andrey N. Tupolev to work out proposals on improving the Tu-144's flight performance and economic parameters jointly with TsAGI, TsIAM

At this angle the production Tu-144 with the nose drooped looks eerily like a giant bird pondering whether to give the photographer a peck.

Above: An interesting wind tunnel model at TsAGI combining the old wing shape of *izdeliye* 044 with canards. Note that the latter have zero anhedral (unlike the real thing).

Below: A view from the wind tunnel showing the airflow around the canards with their double-slotted leading-edge slats and flaps.

Below right: A test article replicating the canards' airfoil in the wind tunnel.

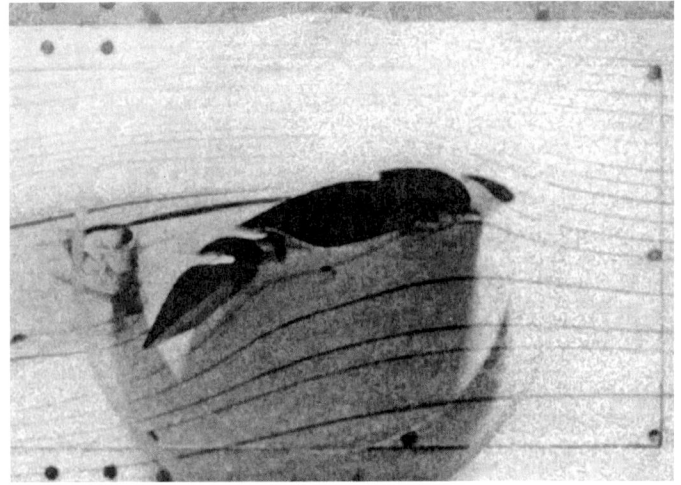
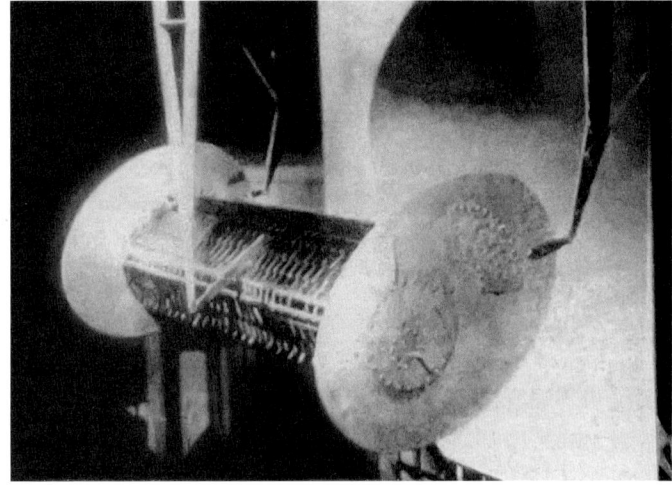

Chapter 4 - Take Two: Back to the Drawing Board

Above: A scaled-strength model of the Tu-144 (*izdeliye* 004) suspended on steel cables in TsAGI's wind tunnel.

Below: This lower front view of the model accentuates the new wing shape with a sharply kinked leading edge.

Below right: Another view of the same model; the transparent skin shows the internal structure.

Chapter 4 - Take Two: Back to the Drawing Board

Above left: A 'hairy head with horns' – a model of the *izdeliye* 004's nose section with canards covered in wool tufts – in TsAGI's T-101 wind tunnel. Here the nose visor is raised; note the extreme AOA.

Left: The same model (called Model 115MD) with the nose visor down and a more normal flight attitude.

Above: A full model of the *izdeliye* 004 in the T-101 wind tunnel. Unlike the partial model shown on the preceding page, the canards are functional (retractable); the control surfaces appear to be movable as well.

and the Ministry of Civil Aviation. On 30th June 1967 the VPK issued another ruling titled 'On the construction of Tu-144 aircraft with improved flight performance'.

The resulting aircraft was different enough to warrant a new in-house product code, *izdeliye* 004; in fact, from a structural standpoint it was a completely new design. The fuselage was longer and featured a circular cross-section (the flattened underside and characteristic chines of the *izdeliye* 044 demonstrator were gone), the maximum diameter being increased from 3.039 m (9 ft $11^{41}/_{64}$ in) to 3.3 m (10 ft $9^{59}/_{64}$ in). The design of the drooping nose was altered; in particular, the shape was optimised for minimum drag (this work was headed by Prof. Gersch L. Grodzovskiy at TsAGI) and the end result was a fuel burn reduction that amounted to 1-2% of the total fuel capacity. The four dorsal glazing panels on the demonstrator's nose visor gave way to two additional side windows (that is, three windows on each side), but when the nose visor was raised into cruise position the pilots' forward field of view was still very limited. The shape of the rear fuselage section, the design and placement of the entry and service doors and emergency exits were also changed (the rearmost exits were now at the aft end of the main cabin). The centrebody was retained, accommodating certain equipment items and associated piping runs.

The wings of *izdeliye* 004 had marginally bigger span and greater area, pronounced camber and a very different planform. Whereas the *izdeliye* 044 had featured a smooth transition between the straight edges of the LERXes and the outer wings, the new version had a pronounced leading-edge kink; this was because research at TsAGI and the OKB had shown that the smooth transition had a negative effect on longitudinal stability at high AOAs. In so doing the leading-edge sweepback was changed from 78° on the LERXes and 55° on the outer wings to 76° and 57° respectively, reducing interference drag in cruise flight; the wing camber axis was moved from the rearmost wing spar to the foremost spar and the wings were given negative incidence. These changes made it

Tupolev Tu-144

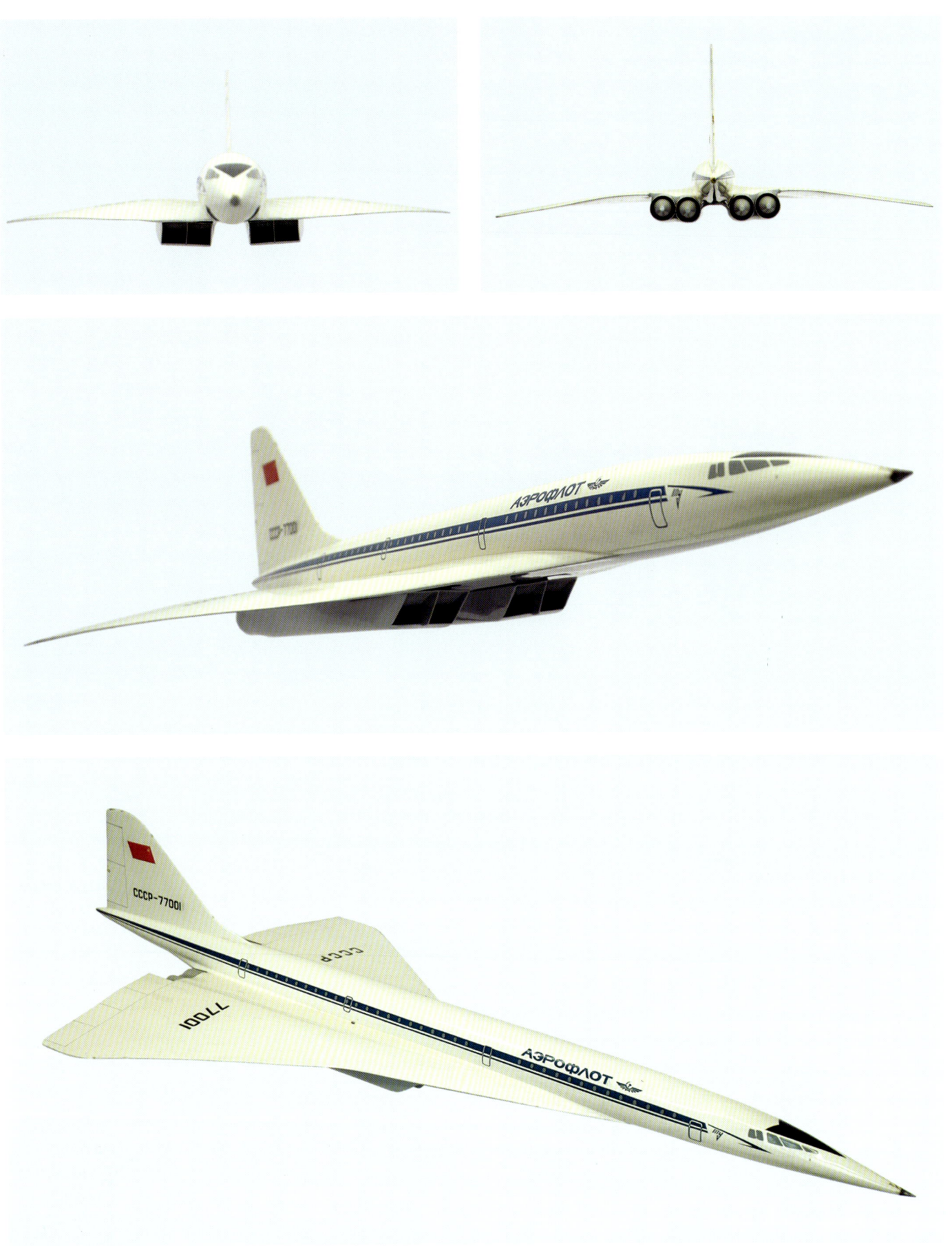

Chapter 4 - Take Two: Back to the Drawing Board

Left: This desktop model of the Tu-144 (*izdeliye* 004) sporting the non-existent registration CCCP-77001 features engine nozzles with conical centrebodies indicative of RD36-51A turbojets, which were planned for the Tu-144 all along.

Right: A landing gear test rig with the main gear units of the production-standard Tu-144. Here a hydraulic ram on the inboard side tilts the starboard bogie into a vertical position before the 'knee-action' strut folds, the N-shaped upper segment swinging aft and the oleo strut swinging forward. Note the wheel brake housings.

Below right: The flight simulator of the Tu-144 (*izdeliye* 004).

possible to attain the coveted lift/drag ratio of 8 on the production model. This work proceeded under the guidance of TsAGI aerodynamicists Leonid Ye. Vasil'yev and A. I. Gladkov. It was mostly the new wings that accounted for the 10% improvement in the lift/drag ratio as compared to the prototype.

The shape of the vertical tail was similarly altered, with a kink at the fin/dorsal fin junction. The fin torsion box incorporated a trim tank.

On the *izdeliye* 044 demonstrator the elevons were hardly used at all to augment wing lift on take-off and landing, which was performed just like on an ordinary tailless aircraft. However, this was not good enough for the planned production version, which would have a bigger seating capacity and higher take-off and landing weights and thus would be unable to meet the stipulated field performance requirements. In order to enhance wing lift on take-off and landing the designers had the elevons droop 10° to act as flaps, leaving another ±10° of travel for roll control in these flight modes, as the most effective and most realistic option. However, this deflection created a pitch-down force which had to be negated.

The Tupolev OKB and TsAGI sought ways and means to cure this problem, undertaking a huge amount of research. The first option considered was to move the CG aft, making the aircraft statically unstable for take-off and landing. However, this option was rejected – the safety of the aircraft and its occupants would depend entirely on automatic stability augmentation systems (SAS), and the price of the system failing could be too high; SAS technologies were still too immature to allow the designers to take such a risk.

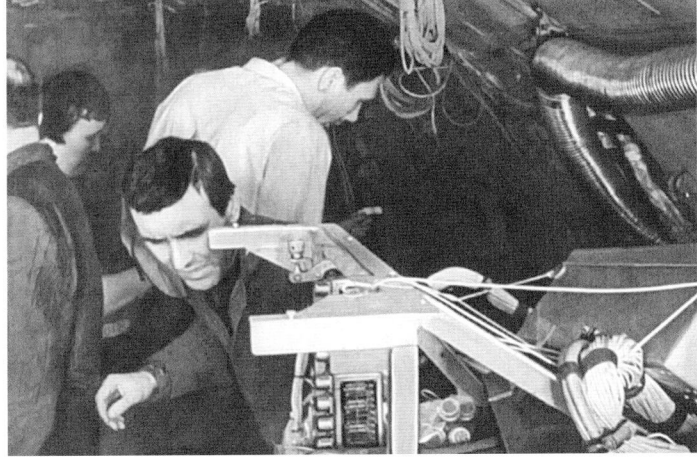

Top and above left: Tu-144 parts being manufactured.

Left: A half-finished article and a ready machined beam.

Above: The Tu-144 included 300 km (186 miles) of electric wires! Here some of the wiring bundles are being assembled.

Below: The fuselage of the first *izdeliye* 004 being assembled.

Above right: The fuselage of Tu-144 CCCP-77101 at MMZ No. 156. Note the flight deck escape hatch and the recess for the canards.

Right: A three-view of the *izdeliye* 004 from the ADP documents. Oddly, the canards are not shown at all.

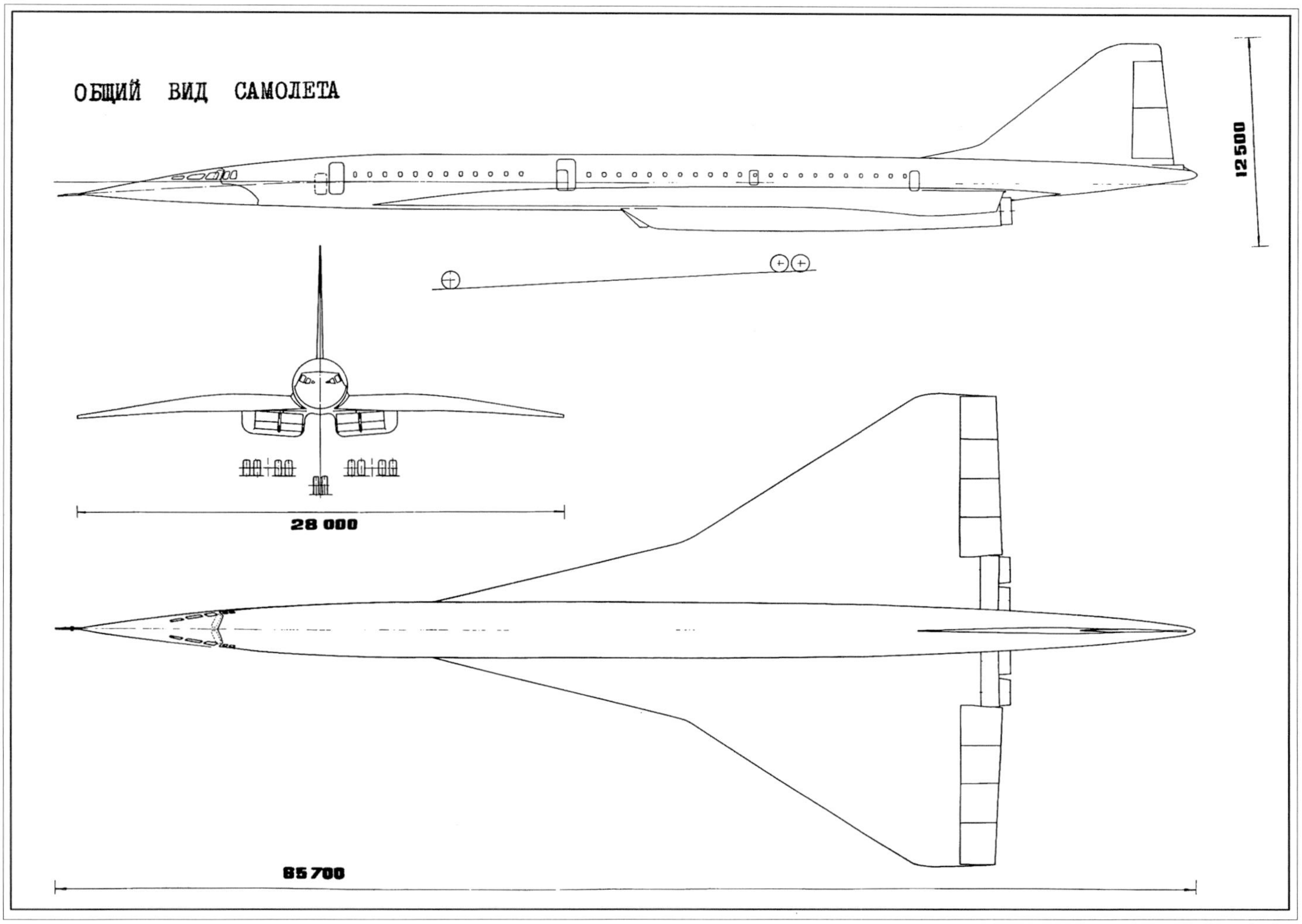

Chapter 4 - Take Two: Back to the Drawing Board

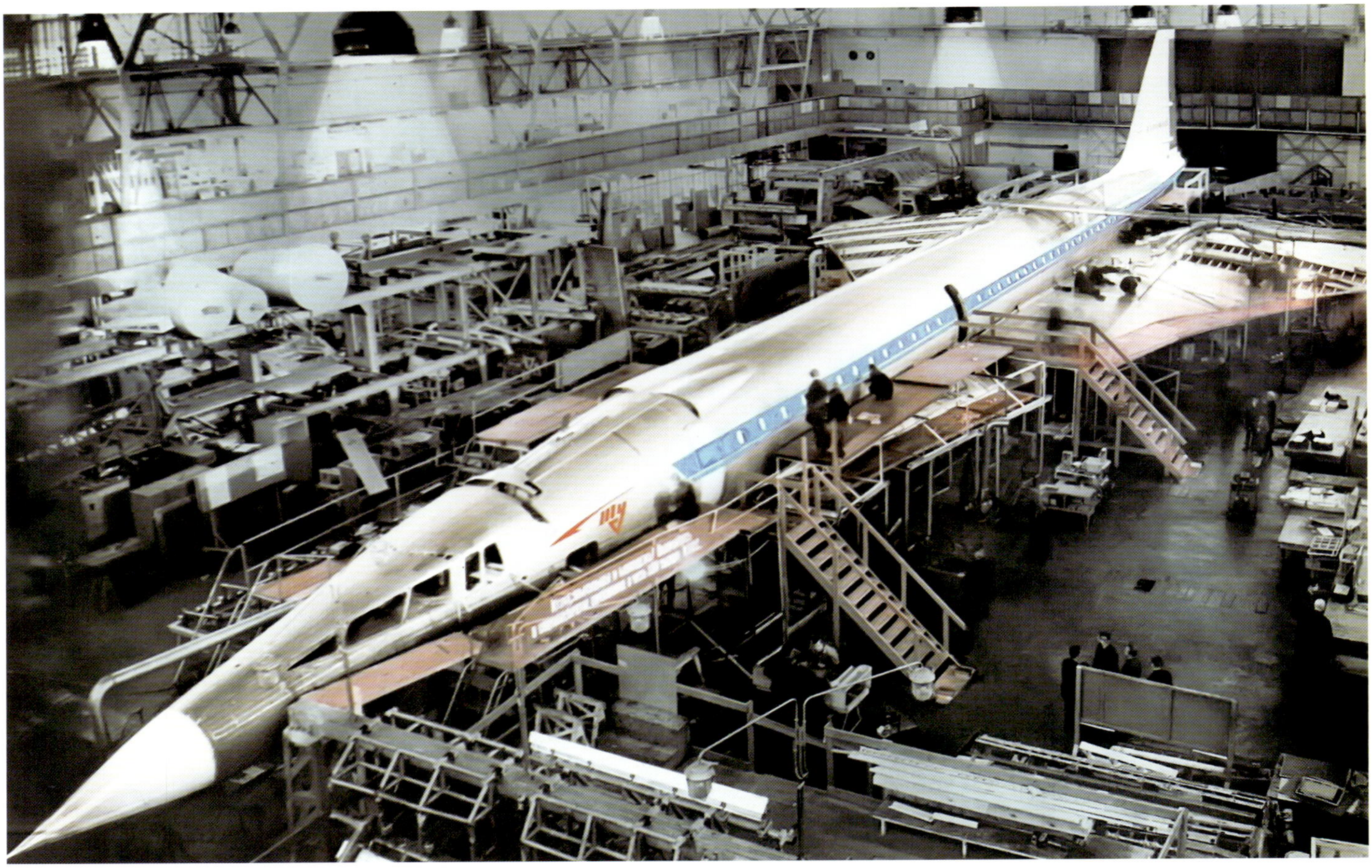

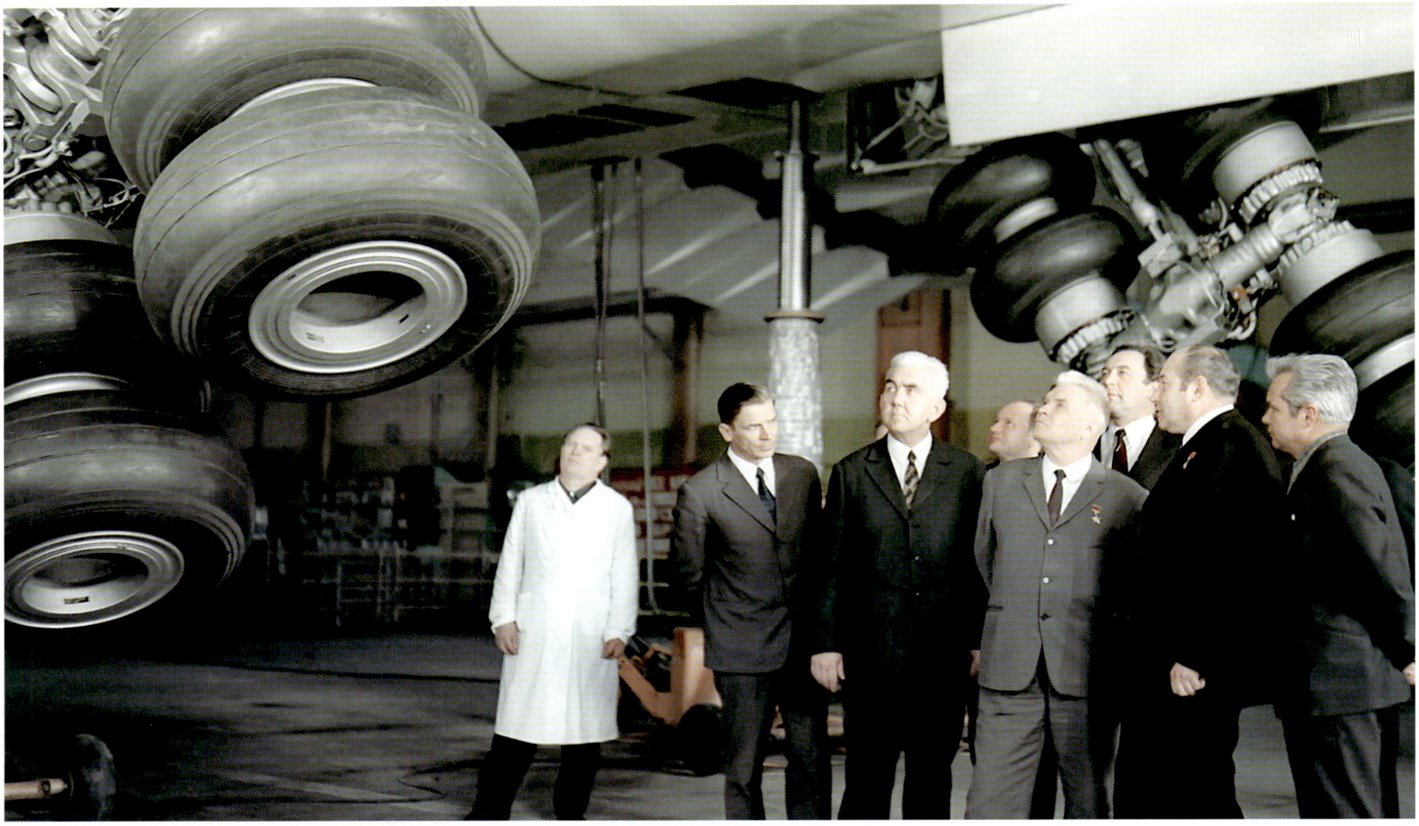

Chapter 4 - Take Two: Back to the Drawing Board

Various high-lift devices were considered next, including those which did not cause a change in pitch trim when deployed. Yet, none of the numerous proposed versions proved suitable; they did not provide a sufficient increase in lift but generated extra drag.

Eventually the designers and the scientists arrived at a unique solution – the wings were augmented by small retractable canard foreplanes whose area equalled only about 2% of the wing area. These high aspect ratio aerodynamic surfaces were shoulder-mounted just aft of the flight deck, folding aft along the forward fuselage after landing gear retraction. To maximise the canards' specific lift (per unit of area), minimise the influence of the aircraft's AOA on this lift and improve the lift/drag ratio in take-off and landing modes the canards had 15° anhedral and bristled with double-slotted (!) fixed leading-edge slats and double-slotted trailing-edge flaps; the latter deployed automatically as the canards unfolded. This feature was a world 'first'.

Left: Here CCCP-77101 is seen during final assembly at MMZ No.156. Note the detachable wing skin panels giving access to the fuel tanks.

Below left: The Tu-144 is jacked up, and (right to left) Eduard V. Yelian, Aleksey A. Tupolev, Vladimir N. Benderov, Vice-Minister of Aircraft Industry Ivan S. Silayev and other MAP officials watch as the aircraft undergoes a landing gear check. Note the position of the bogies during retraction.

Top right: Another view of Tu-144 CCCP-77101 prepared for a gear swing.

Above right: The *izdeliye* 004 static test airframe (c/n 10013) at TsAGI. Note the plugs in the inlet ducts where the engines should be and the aperture for the brake parachute container in the tailcone.

Right: Another aspect of the same airframe. The upper half of the rudder is not yet fitted.

Top left and above left: The static test airframe surrounded by a mesh of scaffolding and rods transferring the structural loads.

Left: The nose of the static test airframe with canards deployed and nose visor lowered.

Top: Another non-flying *izdeliye* 004 airframe (c/n 10014) being readied for fatigue tests at SibNIA.

Above: The static test airframe during preparations for the tests.

Chapter 4 - Take Two: Back to the Drawing Board

Right: A damage diagram for the Tu-144's repeat static tests showing specific stringers, fuselage frames, wing spars and ribs that were purposely damaged to simulate fatigue cracking.

Below right: This series of pictures shows the production-standard Tu-144's landing gear retraction sequence. Note that retraction of the main gear units is not necessarily simultaneous.

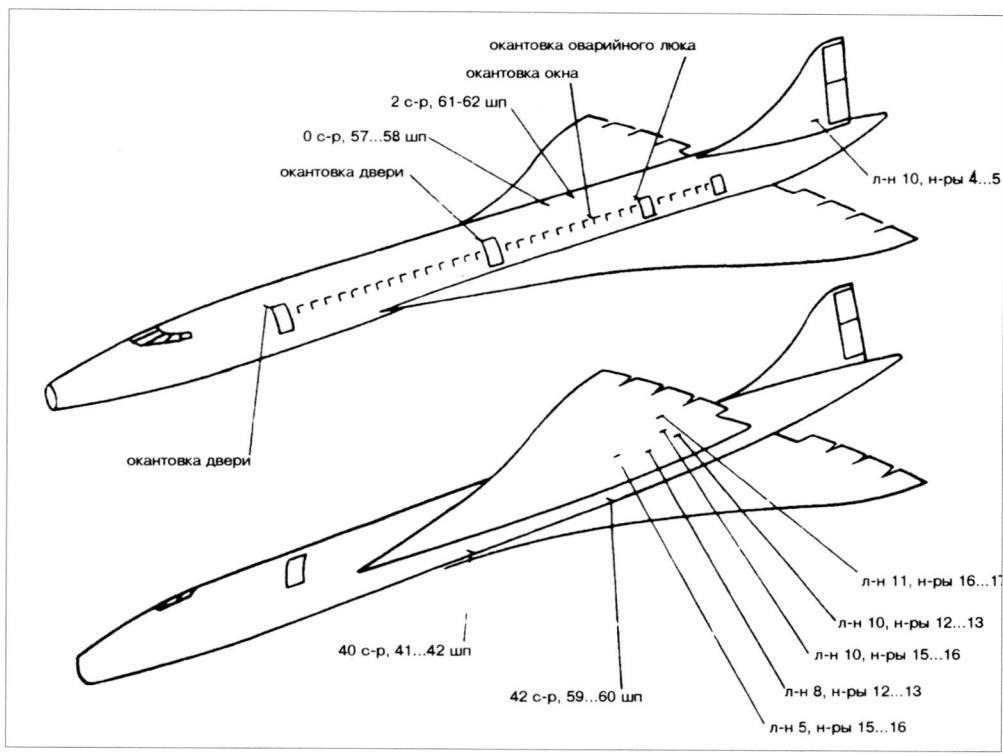

Detail design of the canards was preceded by tests of first a partial wind tunnel model designated 115MD (the forward fuselage with the canards) and then a complete model of the *izdeliye* 004 in the T-102 and T-106 wind tunnels. Jumping ahead of the story, it may be said that tests of the full-size version in TsAGI's largest wind tunnel – the T-101 – took place when the first production-standard Tu-144 had been built. The wind tunnel tests and subsequent flight tests showed that the canards affected not only longitudinal stability but also directional stability. Without the canards, the aircraft was directionally unstable at high AOAs because of the destabilising influence of the lowered nose visor. The vortices from the deployed canards disrupted the fuselage's vortex system, likewise impairing directional stability, but more than made up for this by energising the airflow across the vertical tail and enhancing rudder authority.

One of the problems associated with the canards was the effect they would have on the aircraft's critical flutter speed; it was necessary to test them for flutter resistance, even though the canards were only used at low speeds. Since the canards had a complex design with high-lift devices, the scaled-strength model used for the flutter tests was complex as well. It was designed by the Tupolev OKB but manufactured by SibNIA, which also performed the tests; the latter were supervised by L. V. Shpak.

Finding a suitable place for the canards turned out to be another problem. The designers managed to stow the retracted canards in a shallow dorsal fairing without encroaching on the pressure cabin and its load-bearing structure.

Pending availability of the more powerful RD36-51 turbojets the Tu-144 (*izdeliye* 004) was designed around the same 17,500-kgp (38,580-lbst) NK-144 afterburning turbofans. However, in order to reduce the thermal loads on the rear fuselage the designers rejected the common engine nacelle in favour of narrow nacelles housing two engines each; these were located under the wing centre section, albeit rather closer to the fuselage than on the Concorde. (It has to be said that the overheating persisted, albeit the problem was alleviated somewhat, and the *izdeliye* 004 retained the rear fuselage heat shield.)

Chapter 4 - Take Two: Back to the Drawing Board

Left: This front view of Tu-144 CCCP-77101 shows the pitch/yaw vanes on the nose pitot and the hinges of the port side escape hatch. Note that the elevons terminate level with the wingtips.

Above: CCCP-77101 takes off for its maiden flight on 1st July 1971 with a Tu-124 flying chase. Unusually, the canard remained retracted during this flight. Note the absence of 'Tu-144' nose titles.

Below: CCCP-77101 seen from the Tu-124 during the first flight. The rudder was still unpainted and there was no Soviet flag.

The new engine placement necessitated a large amount of aerodynamic research. The engine nacelles were carefully shaped to reduce the wetted area and minimise drag; so was the gap between the nacelles to prevent airflow departure, with due regard to the boundary layer spill from the air intakes. Much attention was given to such details as optimising the shape of the fairings between the pairs of nozzles to minimise boattail drag, optimising the wing/nacelle interaction etc. Also, because of the engines' position farther from the fuselage the elevons were moved outboard as well,

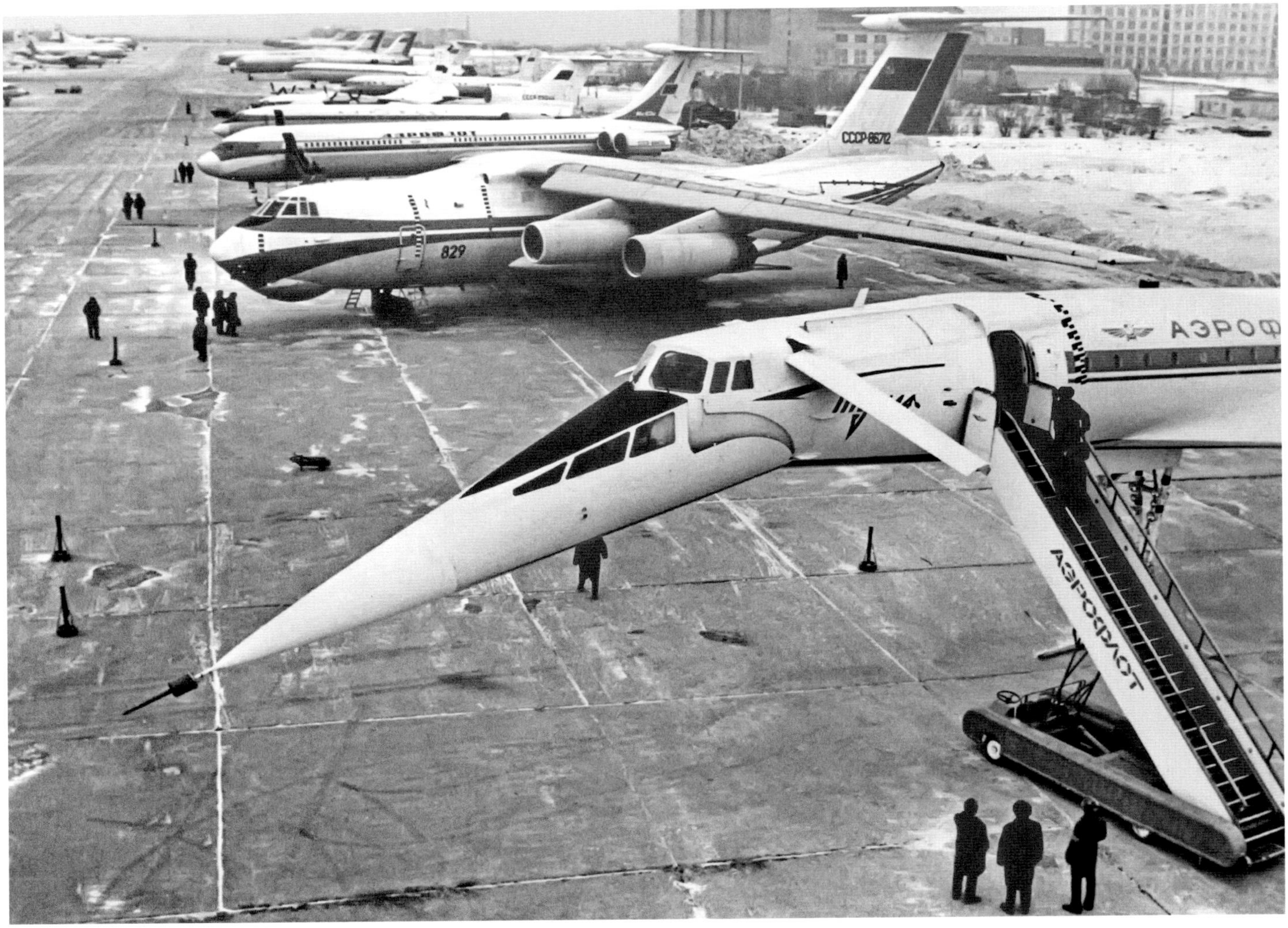
СССР-86712
829
АЭРОФ
АЭРОФЛОТ

АЭРОФЛОТ

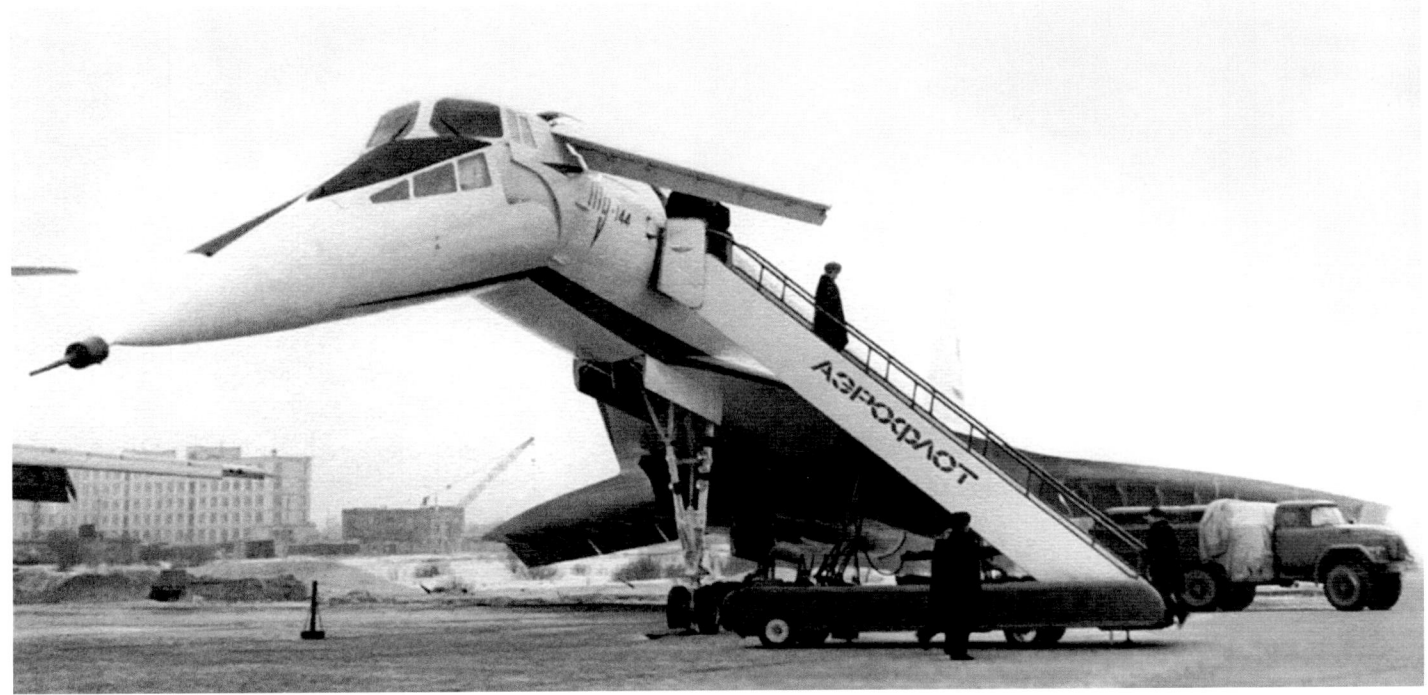

Opposite page: Tu-144 CCCP-77101 (with attendant SPT-114 gangway and APA-50M ground power unit on a ZiL-131 6x6 army lorry chassis) on the GosNII GA apron at Moscow-Sheremet'yevo during a new civil aviation hardware display in December 1973 together with the first prototype IL-76 (CCCP-86712), the IL-62M prototype (CCCP-86673 No.1) and Tu-154 *sans suffixe* CCCP-85044. Note the revised paint job and the photo calibration markings aft of the forward entry door.

This page: CCCP-77101 at Kiev-Borispol' during a demonstration flight on 4th-5th September 1974. Note the photo calibration markings near the emergency exits. Aeroflot titles and logos are carried both on the fuselage and on the fin.

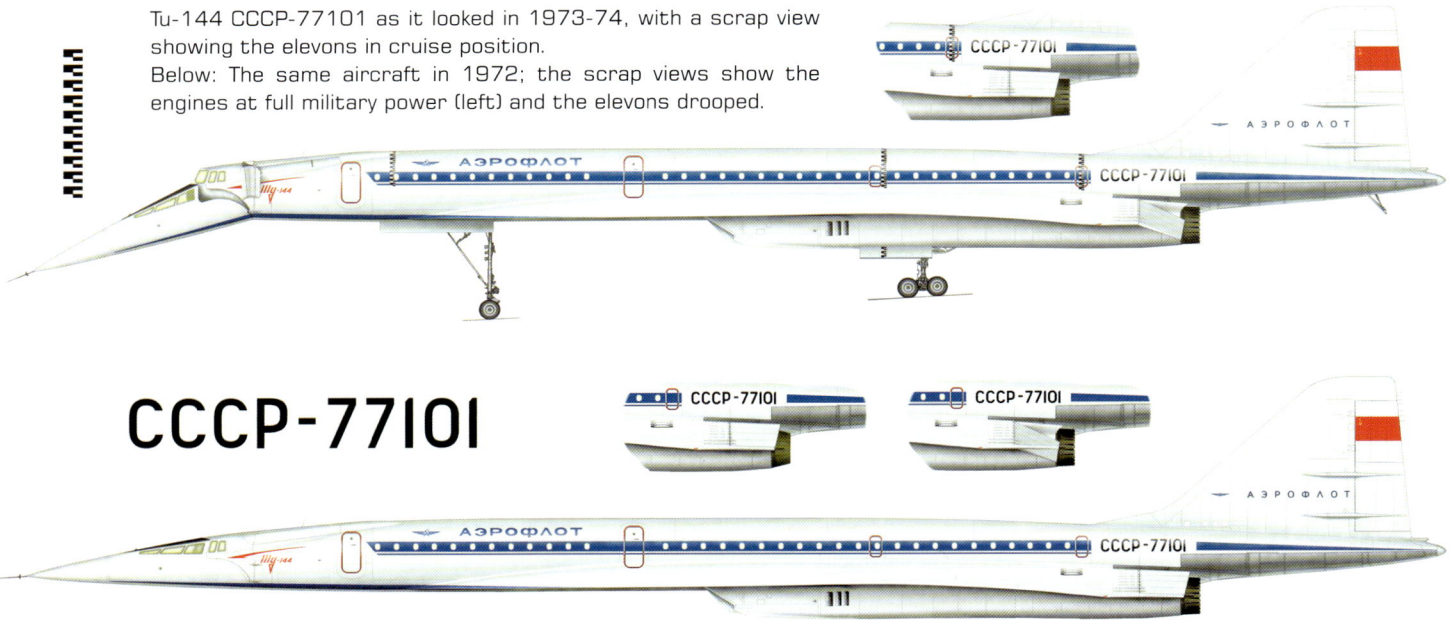

Tu-144 CCCP-77101 as it looked in 1973-74, with a scrap view showing the elevons in cruise position.
Below: The same aircraft in 1972; the scrap views show the engines at full military power (left) and the elevons drooped.

and the greater influence of wing aeroelasticity on their functioning had to be taken into account. Additionally, the APU was relocated from the rear fuselage to the starboard engine nacelle.

The air intake design received special attention. Once again, the *izdeliye* 004 had two-dimensional intakes with horizontal airflow control ramps, which were separated by vertical splitters and had a raked leading edge. The length of the inlet ducts remained unchanged at 14.5 m (47 ft $6^{55}/_{64}$ in), but the ducts themselves were reshaped, curving outward (towards the nacelle sidewalls) due to nacelle/main landing gear integration (more will be said about this later). To maximise air intake efficiency two V-shaped fairings were installed in tandem at the front of each nacelle between the wing undersurface and the inlet assembly; the first of these spilled the boundary layer separated by the intake upper lip, while the second one spilled the air sucked through the perforated front movable segment of each intake ramp. Spring-loaded blow-in doors and hydraulically actuated excess air spill doors were provided to enhance surge resistance.

As the aircraft transitioned from one flight mode to another, the air intake configuration changed as follows:

Chapter 4 - Take Two: Back to the Drawing Board

• take-off and climb/acceleration at subsonic speeds – the air intake ramps are fully retracted (in the up position), the spill doors are closed, the blow-in doors are open, closing gradually as the aircraft accelerates to 700-900 km/h (435-559 mph);

• subsonic cruise (up to Mach 0.94) – as above (the blow-in doors are closed);

• acceleration to Mach 1.3 and beyond – the air intake ramps are deployed in accordance with the ramp control algorithm, all blow-in and spill doors are closed, boundary layer bleed is in progress;

• supersonic cruise at Mach 2.0-2.2 – as above;

• deceleration/descent – the engines are throttled back to flight idle, the air intake ramps are fully deployed, all blow-in and spill doors are closed. As the aircraft decelerates, the ramps are gradually retracted and the spill doors opened, assuming subsonic cruise position at Mach 1.3.

During the development of the air intakes there were constant arguments between the aerodynamicists, who strove to maximise the lift/drag ratio, and the propulsion department. The latter needed to ensure stable operation of the engines throughout the flight envelope (and therefore sought to increase the inlet area beyond the figure calculated for the engines' design mass flow in order to create a surge resistance margin). It took a lot of effort to reconcile their conflicting requirements. As a rule, General Designer Andrey N. Tupolev sided with the propulsion department in these arguments. Anyway, the end result was that the Tu-144's large nacelles created just a little more drag than the Concorde's smaller nacelles featuring short inlet ducts.

Finally, the landing gear was completely redesigned. The twin-wheel nose unit now retracted forward, while the main units were located underneath the engine nacelles, retracting forward into a remarkably small space between the inlet ducts of each pair of engines. The number of wheels per bogie was reduced to eight (two rows of four); prior to retraction the bogies tipped up vertically, inboard ends uppermost, so that the wheels stowed vertically but at 90° to the direction of flight. A retractable tail bumper was added.

A redesign proved necessary in many other areas, including the choice of materials. For example, the Tu-144 demonstrator's fuel tanks were manufactured, using VGF-2 heat-resistant fluoride silicone sealant in the rivet joints and VGF-1 sealant elsewhere. However, when CCCP-68001 entered flight test it was quickly discovered that the hot fuel tended to wash away the low-molecular fractions of these sealants, the latter deteriorating and the tanks developing leaks as a result. After additional research the designers switched to using 51G2 fluoride rubber sealant in the rivet joints and 51G1 sealant elsewhere. Additionally, for the first time in the OKB's practice the bottom panels of the fuel tanks where condensation water might accumulate were protected against corrosion by layers of EP-0103 epoxy primer, F-5 enamel and 51G-9R sealant.

Mindful of how overweight the *izdeliye* 044 demonstrator had been, the designers devoted a lot of effort to reducing empty weight. Still, eventually the *izdeliye* 004 production version turned out to be 10 tons (22,045 lb), or 12%, over its design OEW.

To make a long story short, the combined effect of all the measures taken by the Tupolev OKB and TsAGI gave the production Tu-144 a cruise lift/drag ratio 8-10% better than the Concorde's,

Top and above: The first production Tu-144, CCCP-77102, undergoes a canards retraction check at the Voronezh aircraft factory. Note the flight deck escape door which is opened by twin hydraulic rams.

Left: CCCP-77101 already with a revised cheatline, 'Tu-144' nose titles and wing leading-edge stripes but before the addition of Aeroflot titles on the fuselage. Note the open cowling of the No. 4 engine and the deflected lower rudder section.

according to published reports. This was due in no small degree to the persistent efforts aimed at achieving a high-quality surface finish, much attention having been paid to rivet lines, skin joints, pitot heads, aerials and the like. It should be noted that the Tu-144 was unique among Soviet aircraft in this respect, meeting TsAGI's surface finish requirements in full; all other Soviet types were manufactured fairly crudely (by Western standards anyway), the drag caused by the poor surface finish exceeding the limits set by TsAGI two to three times. The excellent aerodynamics of the production Tu-144 stemmed not only from the thousands of pages of calculations but also from the results obtained with 250-plus mod-

els in wind tunnels across the nation – from Riga in the west to Novosibirsk in the east.

A joint MAP/MGA proposal for the construction of six Tu-144s with the new airframe design and updated NK-144 engines offering higher thrust and better fuel economy was accepted in 1969. This updating was seen as the first step towards achieving the required range of 4,000-4,500 km (2,480-2,795 miles). Later production versions were to be fitted with RD36-51 engines.

The design was frozen in 1969. Between October 1969 and January 1970 the Tupolev OKB issued the manufacturing drawings for *izdeliye* 004 to the Voronezh aircraft factory No.64 which had been chosen to build the Tu-144 in series. The first of the 'second-generation' Tu-144s was jointly built by plant No.64 and MMZ No.156 in Moscow, final assembly taking place at the latter plant before the aircraft was moved to flight test facility in Zhukovskiy. Actually the Tupolev OKB terms this aircraft as a pre-production machine rather than the prototype. Its take-off weight was 190,000 kg (418,880 lb).

The aircraft received the registration CCCP-77101 (c/n 01-1 – that is, Batch 01, first aircraft in the batch) and a rather different colour scheme. Among other things, the traditional round badge of the Tupolev OKB on the nose gave way to Cyrillic 'Ty-144' nose titles, and the cheatline had a pinstripe added at the bottom. Unlike CCCP-68001, whose control surfaces were natural metal for a while, here the rudder and elevons were duly painted, and the Soviet flag was applied to the rudder rather than to the fin. While the *izdeliye* 044 had been devoid of Aeroflot titles and logos, CCCP-77101 eventually carried them both on the fuselage and on the fin! All exits were heavily outlined in red. Three sets of black and white photo calibration markings were applied to the fuselage (CCCP-77101 was the only example to wear such markings).

(Speaking of construction numbers, it should be noted that Voronezh-built Tu-144s are often reported with five-digit c/ns commencing 10 (which may be an in-house product code at the factory – *izdeliye* 10), and CCCP-77101 has accordingly been reported as c/n 10011. On the actual aircraft the c/n is embossed, in the abbreviated form, in the upper right-hand corner of the data plates attached to both main gear oleos.)

Chapter 4 - Take Two: Back to the Drawing Board

Far left: A Soviet government delegation headed by Marshal Dmitriy F. Ustinov visiting the Voronezh aircraft factory descends the gangway after inspecting a production Tu-144 in the final assembly shop.

Left: Marshal Ustinov has a discussion with Tupolev OKB and factory officials in the front cabin of the Tu-144.

Below left: Continuing their inspection of plant No.64, Ustinov and Aleksey A. Tupolev lead the way, with other high-ranking military commanders in the background.

Above right: Another government delegation visiting the factory. Left to right: Soviet Air Force Commander-in-Chief Air Marshal Pavel S. Kutakhov, Minister of Aircraft Industry Pyotr V. Dement'yev, Vladimir N. Benderov (in his Major-General's uniform) and General Designer Andrey N. Tupolev.

Right: Another scene from this visit, with Andrey N. Tupolev, Pavel S. Kutakhov and Pyotr V. Dement'yev in front of a production Tu-144.

This first production batch was also the largest, comprising four aircraft (more will be said of the others later); as a rule, Tu-144 batches consisted of only two or even one aircraft. The first production version of the Tu-144 (*izdeliye* 004) is sometimes referred to as the Tu-144S (*sereeynyy* – production, used attributively), although this designation is unofficial.

On 25th June 1971 MAP's Methodical Council gave the official go-ahead for the first flight of the Tu-144. On 1st July 1977 CCCP-77101 made its maiden flight, captained by Mikhail V. Kozlov. Curiously, the canards were not deployed during this first flight; moreover, the aircraft was not even fully painted yet.

This was the first of five Tu-144s involved in the flight tests of the production version. As distinct from the *izdeliye* 044 demonstrator, the designers chose not to use ejection seats in this case;

CCCP-77101 and the next four aircraft had an escape chute with a hydraulically powered door on the port side of the flight deck for bailing out conventionally – at subsonic speeds only, of course.

In keeping with well-established practice the tests of new Soviet commercial aircraft, just like those of military aircraft, were divided into several stages. Stage 1 normally commenced with the manufacturer's flight tests; their objective was to check the aircraft's behaviour, explore its flight envelope and verify the operation of the aircraft's systems and equipment before Stage 2. The latter was known as joint state acceptance trials (in the case of civil aircraft, this means certification trials) and was held by the design bureau in close co-operation with the customer – in this instance, MGA. Less than a month after the first flight, on 18th July, the VPK issued ruling No.187 appointing the state commission that was to

Chapter 4 - Take Two: Back to the Drawing Board

Left: Aleksey A. Tupolev and the test crew (including captain Eduard V. Yelian, second from left) after a test flight in CCCP-77102.

Below left: Tu-144 CCCP-77102 seen at the moment of rotation for take-off.

Right: This view shows well the planform of the production version. Note the bulged main gear doors and the black interiors of the air intakes.

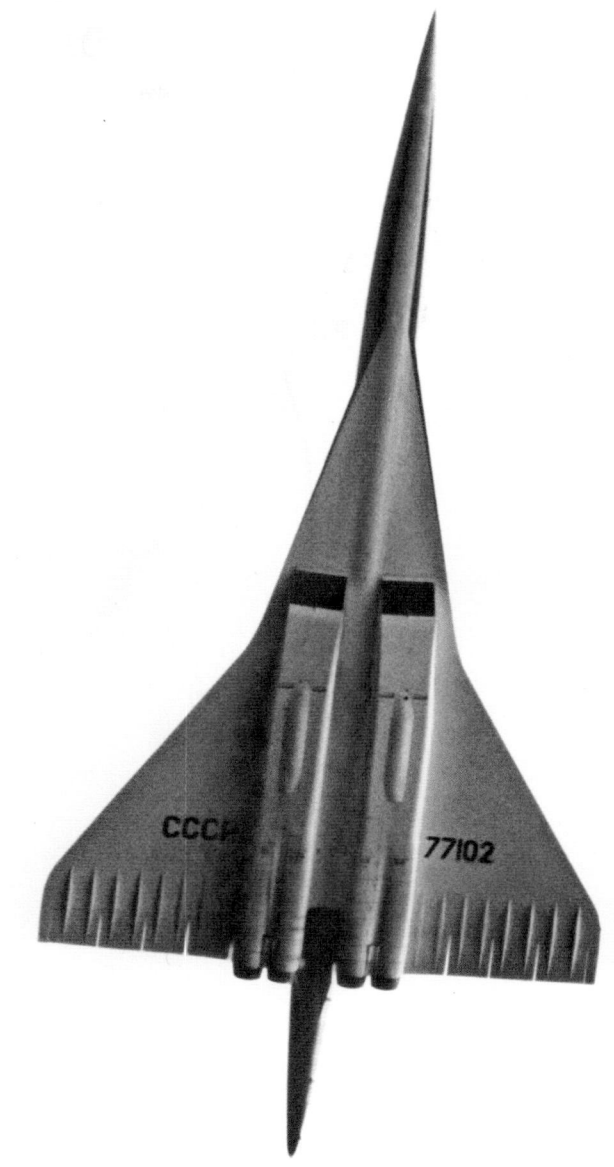

conduct the joint state acceptance trials; it was chaired by 1st Vice-Minister of Civil Aviation A. I. Semenkov. During the trials the ministry was represented by its research establishment, GosNII GA, located at Moscow-Sheremet'yevo airport.

CCCP-77101 was the only 'second-generation' Tu-144 to fly with the original NK-144 *sans suffixe* engines. Its flight tests showed that the available thrust was insufficient for attaining the performance target. Therefore the second aircraft, CCCP-77102 (c/n 10012, or 01-2 for short) – the first production Tu-144 *sans suffixe* built entirely in Voronezh – was also the first Tu-144 to be powered by improved NK-144A engines. This uprated version (*izdeliye* FA) had a take-off thrust of 20,000 kgp (49,020 lbst), a cruise thrust of 5,000 kgp (11,020 lbst) and a cruise SFC of 1.81 kg/kgp·hr at Mach 2.2. CCCP-77102 first flew from Voronezh-Pridacha (the factory airfield of plant No.64) on 29th March 1972, joining the manufacturer's flight test programme. Outwardly it differed from CCCP-77101 mainly in having small fixed wingtip fairings outboard of the elevons.

The NK-144A engine eliminated the original version's shortcoming of inadequate surge resistance. It should be noted that the engine underwent protracted bench tests which continued well into the Tu-144's flight test programme; the NK-144A's state acceptance trials report was not endorsed until 6th May 1975.

(It may as well be said here that the Kuznetsov OKB had a further improved version in the making, the NK-144V, which achieved the mass flow and SFC figures specified by the customer. The engine passed manufacturer's bench tests in 1975 with good results but was never fitted to the Tu-144, as by then the designers had made their choice in favour of the RD36-51A turbojet.)

The other two aircraft in Batch 1 were non-flying. Tu-144 c/n 10013 (or 01-3) was the static test airframe which was tested to destruction. The main part of these tests took place at TsAGI in Zhukovskiy; specifically, they were held by NIO-3, which was the static strength department. Since the preparations for full-scale fatigue tests (described below) were taking a lot of time, a decision was taken to conduct limited fatigue tests on Tu-144 c/n 10013 prior to the main static tests. This part (so-called 'cold' fatigue tests – that is, without heating/cooling cycles) envisaged 5,000 load cycles and was held under the guidance of another TsAGI department, NIO-18. The OKB and TsAGI agreed to set the Tu-144's initial designated service life at 1,000 cycles, increasing it as fatigue test data became available.

The airframe was installed in the static test rig in the NIO-3 hangar and bedecked with stress sensors – up to 10,000 in all. It was visually checked for cracks on a regular basis; NIO-18 set up a special 'bug hunter' team for this purpose, and Tupolev OKB specialists were also involved. Engineer V. A. Novikov was seconded to TsAGI as the OKB's representative at the tests. He was an unobtrusive and soft-spoken man but had considerable organising talent. Quite often there would be a discussion in the Moscow office of the OKB's structural strength department chief Vyacheslav V. Soolimenkov; a decision would be taken and Soolimenkov would phone MMZ No.156 Chief Engineer Aleksey V. Meshcheryakov, requesting that such and such work be done – only to learn that the work was already in progress because Novikov, who had arrived at the same conclusion, had given instructions. There was a lot of work to be done – in particular, skin panels had to be removed for inspection of the underlying structure. The fitters were in for a hard time: the bolts on one wing periodically worked loose and had to be tightened, while those on the other wing were so tight that they could not be unscrewed and had to be drilled out.

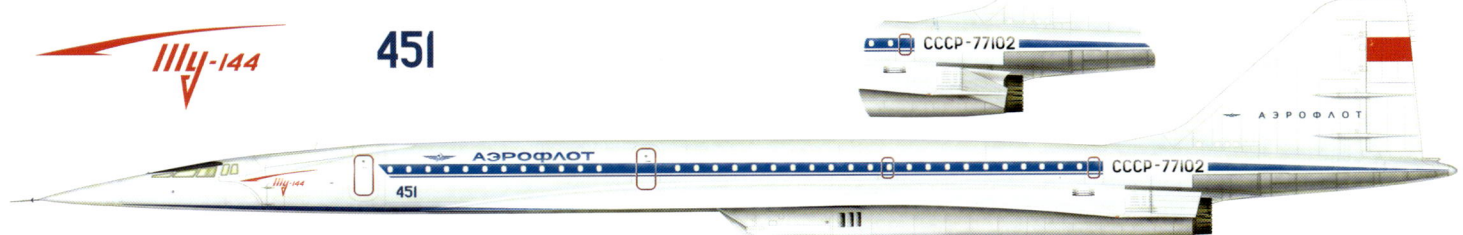

Chapter 4 - Take Two: Back to the Drawing Board

Left: Tu-144 CCCP-77102 as it appeared at the 30th Paris Air Show in 1973 with the exhibit code 451. The scrap view shows the fully drooped elevons.

Right: This photo shows the blue wing leading edge with the blue stripe continuing along the fuselage as far as the radome – a feature of the production Tu-144's early livery with the short cheatline and red nose titles. The nose visor is at the 11° take-off setting.

Above: CCCP-77102 in an early test flight with the canards deployed and the nose visor at the 17° landing setting. The aircraft maintains a high angle of attack in order to keep formation with the slow camera ship.

Left and above left: The same aircraft at rest. Note the strong spanwise camber of the wings.

Right: The new General Designer Aleksey A. Tupolev in the flight deck of CCCP-77102. Note the orange-coloured experimental control panel behind the captain's seat.

Above: Tu-144 CCCP-77102 taxies in after yet another test flight. The ZiL-131 ground support vehicle in yellow/white Aeroflot colours in the background is probably an AKZS-75M-131 oxygen charger.

Below: The same aircraft at the moment of landing, creating an unusually small puff of smoke as it touches down.

Above right: CCCP-77102 in cruise configuration.

Right: Tu-144 CCCP-77102 shares the hardstand at Zhukovskiy with sister ships CCCP-77101 (nearest) and CCCP-68001.

Below right: A fine study of CCCP-77102 in landing configuration. Note the 1973 Le Bourget exhibit code 451.

Chapter 4 - Take Two: Back to the Drawing Board

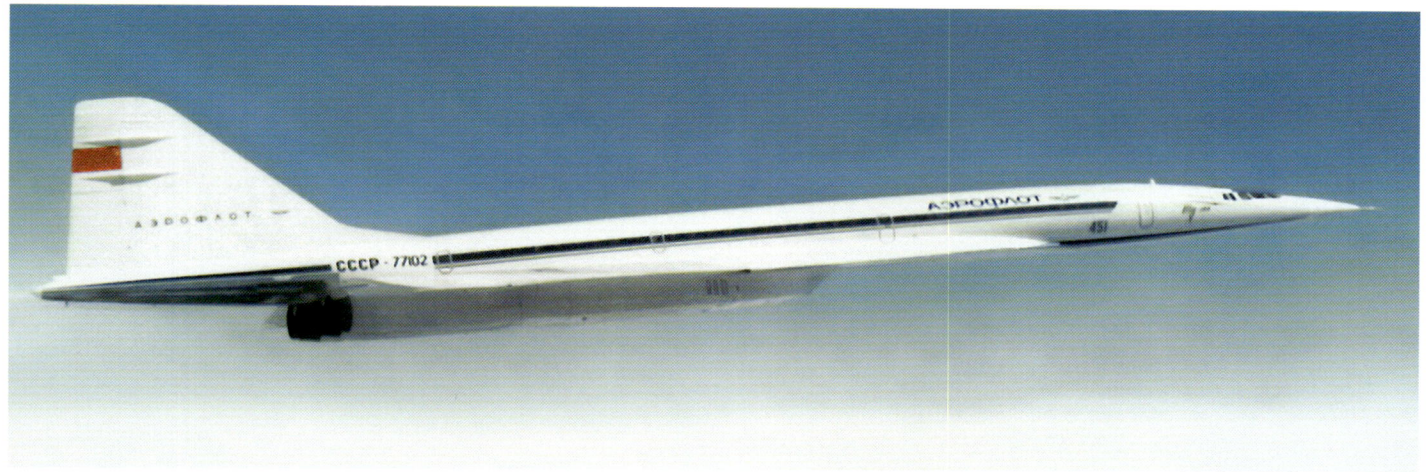

Upon completion of the 'cold' fatigue tests, which went well, the static tests began. Stage A involving maximum operational loads was cut short because the fatigue tests had furnished some of the required information. Stage B involved loading the airframe with 80% of the maximum design load but when the loads acting on the airframe at the moment of touchdown were applied, the fuselage unexpectedly broke in two at 70% of the design load. This premature failure was a rather unpleasant event, given that the Tu-144 programme was in the spotlight of the Powers That Be. The following day a large group of specialists from the OKB (notably Vyacheslav V. Soolimenkov and Igor' B. Ginko) and TsAGI (notably Vice-Director Andrey F. Selikhov) convened to assess the damage. Inspection of the airframe revealed a fatigue crack in the upper fuselage skin panel, which was subjected to considerable stress because the long slender fuselage tended to flex under the dynamic loads; the airframe's flexural centre was located near the hefty wing centre section. The crack had started at the cutout for the dorsal anti-collision light. Now the Tupolev OKB was facing the issue of fail-safe design as well.

The following day Aleksey V. Meshcheryakov chaired a meeting at the OKB and issued explicit instructions. The engineers were given one day to assess the damage to the static test airframe, two days to level the airframe, one week to issue drawings for repairing it, and the repairs were to commence straight away. In 30 days Tu-144 c/n 10013 was to be ready to resume static tests.

Later, this airframe was transported to the Tupolev OKB's own structural test lab in Moscow (at MMZ No.156) for the purpose of holding additional fatigue tests of the rear fuselage and vertical tail. Static tests at TsAGI continued with a further Tu-144 airframe, of which more will be said later.

The other non-flying airframe (c/n 10014, or 01-4) was earmarked for full-scale fatigue tests, which were performed by TsAGI and SibNIA. For the Tu-144 these tests were of special importance for three reasons. Firstly, the fatigue life of an SST was

Above: CCCP-77102 prior to a demo flight at Le Bourget, with a towed power cart connected.

Below: The same aircraft in the static park in company with IL-62M CCCP-86673, IL-76 CCCP-86711, Tu-134A CCCP-65667, Yak-40 'Salon 1st Class' CCCP-87659 and a Ka-26 helicopter.

Right: Bird's eye view of the Soviet static display at Le Bourget '73, with the Tu-144 as the centrepiece. Note the new fixed wingtip fairings which were absent on CCCP-77101.

determined not only by the usual dynamic loads but also by the thermal loads (kinetic heating) in supersonic cruise; calculating the fatigue life of structures subjected to such loads was impossible due to lack of prior experience. Secondly, while a typical subsonic aircraft's fatigue test cycles could be 'compressed' to a mere 2-8 minutes, the need to emulate the SST's heating/cooling cycles meant the test cycles had to be comparable in duration to actual flights and would require a lot of time. Thirdly, no fatigue life calculation techniques existed for the Tu-144's delta wings with their internal stresses.

All this necessitated development and construction of purpose-built 'hot' test rigs in accordance with a Council of Ministers directive and the appropriate MAP order No.345 issued on 20th November 1969. The rigs were built in Zhukovskiy (for the forward fuselage) and Novosibirsk (for the centre/rear fuselage, wings and tail unit); the SibNIA rig was called Tsikl-1S (Cycle-1S). The rigs were developed by TsAGI specialists Andrey F. Selikhov, A. Z. Vorob'yov, K. S. Shcherban' and SibNIA specialists Sergey I. Galkin, P. N. Glavanaryov, Viktor K. Grigorov, Ya. L. Dvorkin, Valeriy V. Ivliyev, V. A. Itskovich, V. Ya. Kovalyov, V. V. Kuznetsov, Aleksandr D. Lisunov, M. I. Litvak, N. M. Pestov, M. B. Polyakov, Yu. A. Rautman, V. I. Sabel'nikov, Aleksey N. Ser'yoznov, Nikolay K. Solov'yov, P. A. Solodov, V. I. Stytsiuk, Vitaliy G. Soovernev and A. G. Schmidt. Tupolev OKB specialists Aleksandr R. Bonin, Aleksey P. Gannushkin, F. A. Kocharyan, Vyacheslav V. Soolimenkov and others provided assistance.

The 'hot' fatigue test technique had its share of opponents in the OKB. During one of the meetings a heated argument began; Aleksey P. Gannushkin insisted that the kinetic heating in supersonic cruise would not have any significant effect on the fatigue life and therefore the fatigue tests might just as well be conducted at normal temperatures. Andrey N. Tupolev, who chaired the meeting, was never shy to use naughty words, and he was true to form. *'Gannushkin, would you squirm if they put your bare ass on a hot frying pan? – he said. – You would! Because your ass would be hot and your balls would be cold. In the same way the airframe structure buckles because of the temperature changes and thermal stresses; therefore it should be subjected to heating cycles in the lab, just as it would be in flight!'*

The Tsikl-1S rig was about 138 m (452 ft) long, 36 m (118 ft) wide and 47 m (154 ft) high. During the 'hot' fatigue tests the structural loads were applied by hydraulic rams governed by an automatic control system, and the cabin was pressurised by compressed air; a special safety shroud enclosed the fuselage in case the latter should suffer an explosive decompression. In addition, the entire airframe was heated and cooled from outside by a stream of air to emulate the heating/cooling cycles in actual flight. A set of blowers provided an aggregate mass flow of 1,200,000 m³/hr (42,377,600 cu ft/hr) and the air temperature ranged from –30°C to

Left: One more view of Tu-144s CCCP-77101, CCCP-77102 and the Tu-144 demonstrator (CCCP-68001) at the OKB's flight test facility.

Below left: A Tu-144 fuselage in the assembly jig at the Voronezh aircraft factory; sections F-2 (the forward fuselage) and F-3 (the centre fuselage) are being mated.

Right: Tu-144 CCCP-77103 nearing completion at plant No.64.

Below: A foreign delegation visiting plant No.64 examines the Tu-144 production line.

Overleaf: The Tu-144 SST and An-12 transport final assembly lines shared the same shop, with CCCP-77103 and CCCP 11340 nearest to the camera.

Above: The completed CCCP-77103 shows off the large and shiny heat shield. The livery is identical to the previous two aircraft.

Below: Tupolev OKB test personnel walk past CCCP-77103. Test pilot Eduard V. Yelian is second from left.

Above right: Tu-144 CCCP-77103 in cruise configuration flies above a winter landscape.

Right: Tupolev OKB engineers pose with a production Tu-144 sporting a different livery (note the blue nose titles).

АЭРОФЛОТ
СССР-77103

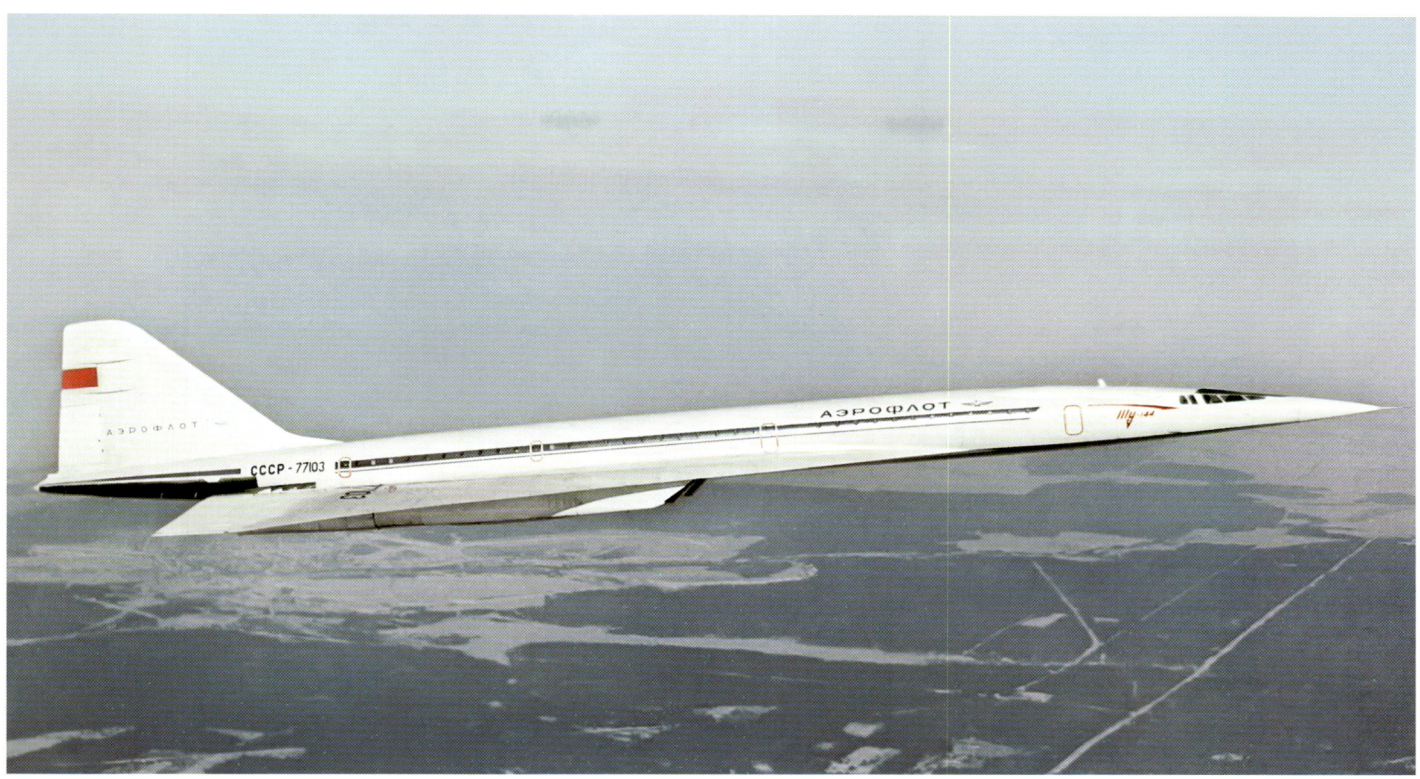

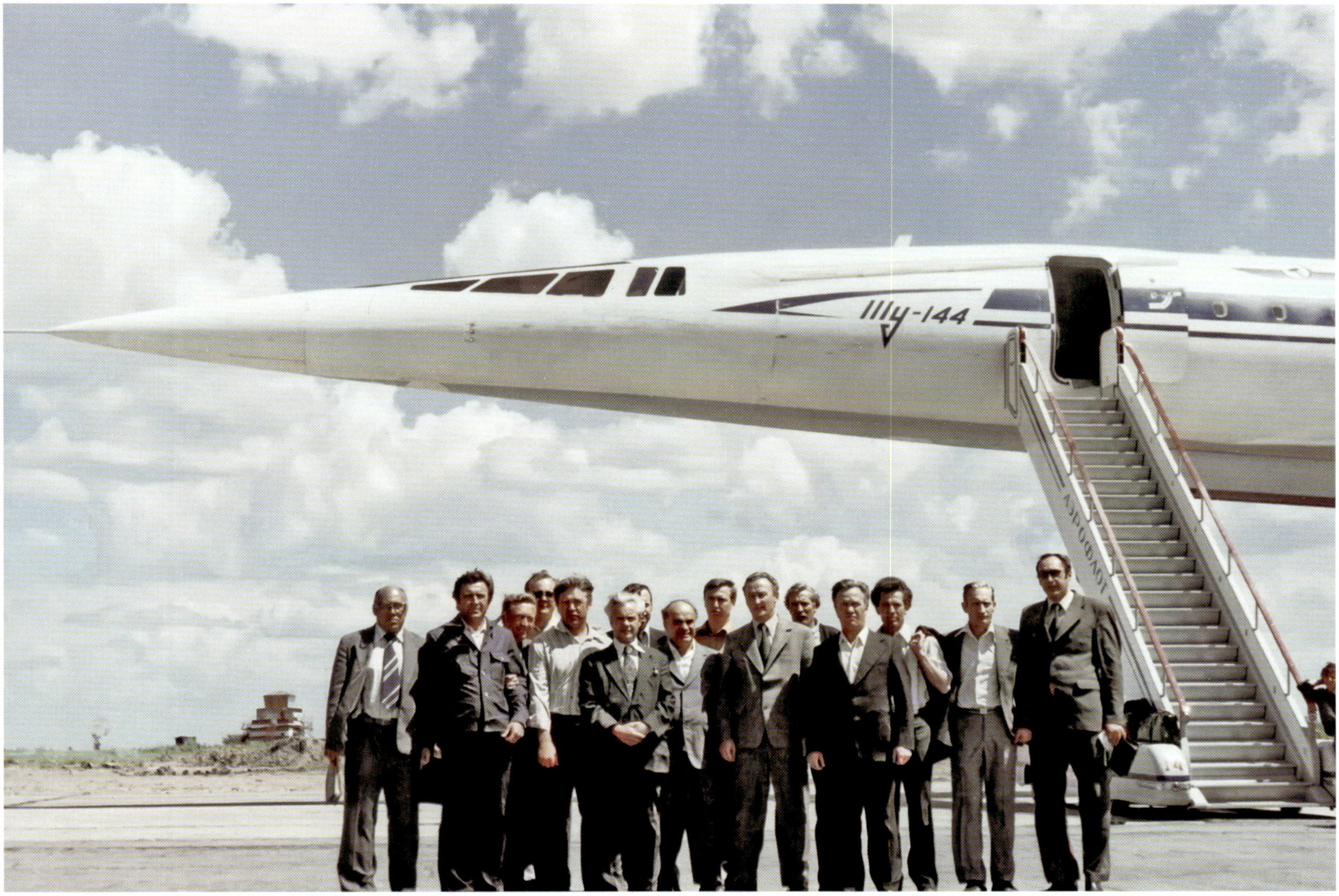
Ту-144
АЭРОФЛОТ

150°C (from –22°F to 302°F); the air was cooled in liquid/air heat exchangers, the cooling system being charged with 580 tons (1,278,660 lb) of Freon-30 chlorofluorocarbon. The insides of the air supply ducts and the walls of the working chamber were heat-insulated with thin GRP and honeycomb GRP panels respectively. A liquid nitrogen evaporation system was used for more intensive cooling. The heat from the engines was emulated by KG-220-1000 quartz lamps with a total power of 2,000 kW.

Calculations showed that if the tests were undertaken in 'real time' mode it would take nine years (!) to verify the designated service life, which was unacceptably long. In order to save time, measures were taken to reduce the length of the dynamic/thermal loading cycles. The Tsikl-1S rig made it possible to emulate the fuel load in the tanks and fuel burnoff during the flight by altering

Above left: Test pilot Vyacheslav Popov (right) pictured in 1974 at Voronezh-Pridacha airfield with the brand-new Tu-144 CCCP-77104 (still in primer finish) which he is to fly.

Left: The same aircraft seen during high-alpha tests, showing the powerful vortices generated by the wings and the canards. Note the repositioned Soviet flag on the fin.

Below: The same aircraft after receiving the new 'custom' registration CCCP-77144 and a new livery with a longer cheatline, grey undersurfaces and a repositioned registration.

Right and above right: These views of CCCP-77144 with the canards extended (taken from a Tu-134 chase plane) show that the wings again have no fixed tip fairings. Note the open APU exhaust door on the starboard wing just inboard of the registration.

Chapter 4 - Take Two: Back to the Drawing Board

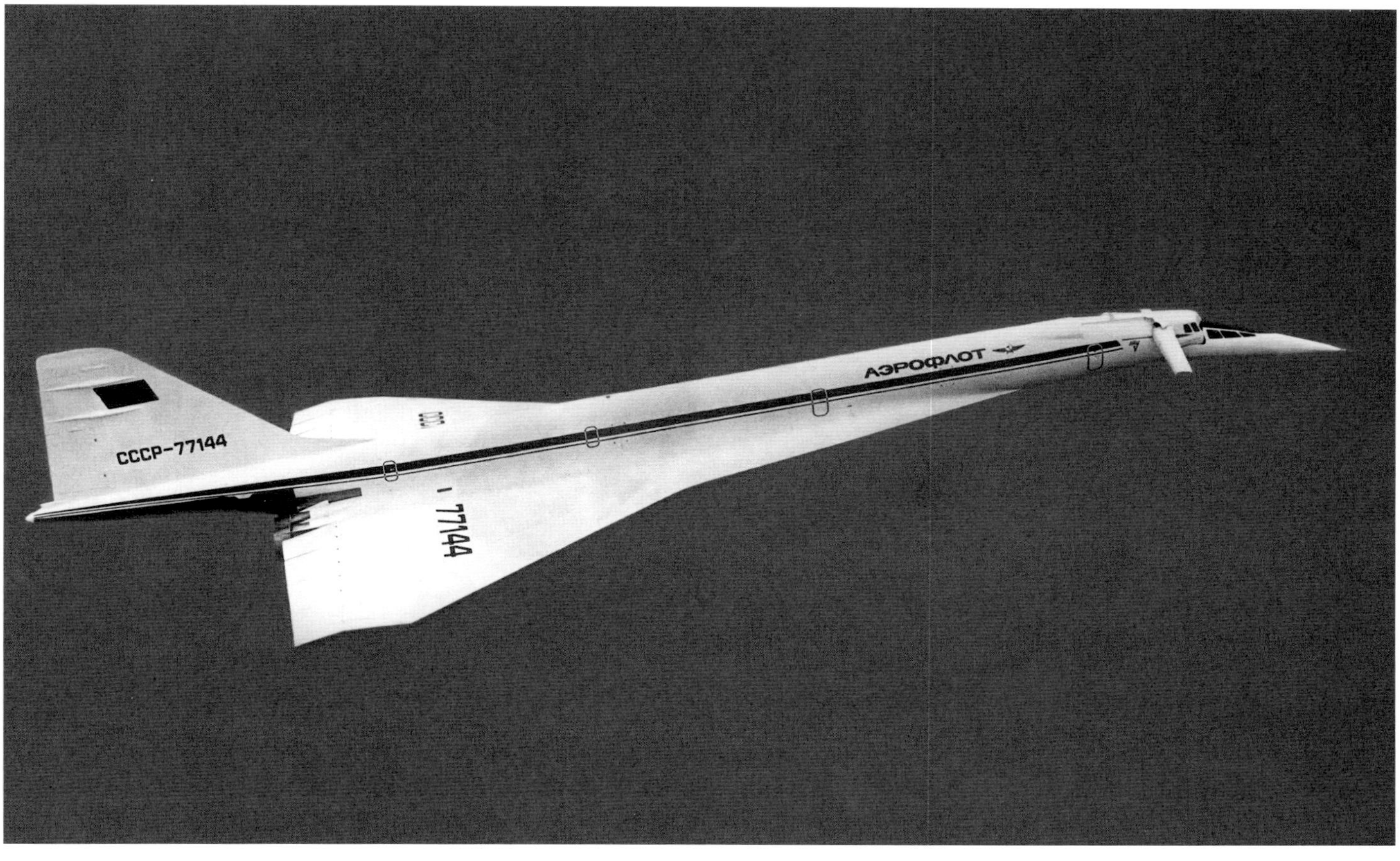

Top: CCCP-77144 'burns rubber' at the moment of touchdown.

Above: The same aircraft was used for wet runway tests at Zhukovskiy to check the risk of water ingestion by the engines.

Left: This crudely retouched photo shows CCCP-77144 fitted with a nosewheel mudguard, which gives a different spray distribution pattern from the nosewheels on a wet runway.

Top right: The tail of a Tu-144 rigged with sensors for ground tests at SibNIA.

Above right: CCCP-77144 lands on a slush-covered runway.

Right: Emergency evacuation procedures training on the Tu-144, using the inflatable escape slide at the second entry door.

the temperature of the appropriate parts of the wings; the fuel was substituted by a non-flammable liquid which was subsequently cooled in a heat exchanger. The airframe was rigged with no fewer than 10,000 strain sensors and 8,000 temperature sensors. The signals coming from the strain sensors were recorded automatically; the sensors themselves, the methods of their installation and the data processing methods were of a new generation and were specially developed under the guidance of Aleksey N. Ser'yoznov at SibNIA.

Fatigue tests of Tu-144 c/n 10014 at SibNIA began in 1975. Stage 1 involved 100 test cycles in February-November, each cycle lasting about 2.5 hours. Later, an accelerated test technique was developed by the Tupolev OKB and SibNIA; 1,314 test cycles using the new technique were performed between 18th May 1977 and 17th October 1978, lasting about 80 minutes each.

Even though Tu-144 c/n 10014 was a relatively low-time airframe, several structural failures were recorded. The most severe one occurred during the 1,315th test cycle when the rear fuselage indeed suffered an explosive decompression and was damaged beyond repair. The failure occurred during a night shift (the tests went on round the clock). The on-duty test engineer recounted: *'Some strange noise appeared (during the previous test cycle – Auth.) I waited for the next pressurisation cycle involving heating and bending loads on the fuselage, went out onto the balcony close to the rear fuselage, turned my ear towards it to get a better idea of the noise – and then the whole thing went BOOM!'*

This time, however, the design was not to blame. Analysis showed that premature fatigue cracking had been caused by the significant difference in thermal loads between a real flight and the accelerated test cycles, and also by the fact that the fin had not been heated during the tests. It was at the junction of the hot rear fuselage and the cold fin fillet that the crack started. In order to continue the tests, Tu-144 CCCP-77101, which had run out of service life in 1975, was cannibalised – its rear fuselage section was removed and mated to the rest of the fatigue test airframe; also, SibNIA revised the test cycles, reducing their duration to 70 minutes.

The rear fuselage of a Tu-144 seen at Zhukovskiy; the heat shield appears to be equipped with temperature probes.

Another failure occurred when the wing broke due to a crack near an elevon actuator which had been overlooked. A contributing factor was that during static tests the detachable skin panels were easily accessible for inspection; this was not so on the Tsikl-1S rig, forcing the test engineers to rely on the strain sensors in order to detect any change which might indicate fatigue cracking. These failures led the OKB to place the quality of the AK4-1 alloy (the Tu-144's primary structural material) under close scrutiny.

A further series of tests on the Tsikl-1S rig was performed between 28th May 1980 and 21st January 1983, comprising 1,974 test cycles. All in all, Tu-144 c/n 10014 logged 3,388 cycles on the rig. Many of the techniques used in these tests were of a groundbreaking nature. Generally the Tu-144's structural strength in all flight modes was deemed to be adequate; subsequent flight tests confirmed the validity of the results. The rig was eventually dismantled in 1984 after the closure of the Tu-144 programme.

The Tu-144's fatigue tests turned out to be a major logistical challenge. SibNIA had to build a 25,000-kW transformer station specifically to cater for the hot air blower's electric heaters, and a special railroad spur was built so that liquid nitrogen for the system's cooling part could be delivered.

The rig at TsAGI was much smaller, as the test article was also smaller; the hinged nose visor was substituted by a simulating structure. Unlike SibNIA, TsAGI did not resort to using liquid nitrogen for rapid cooling, utilising specially made refrigerating units instead. The tests of the forward fuselage involved some 15,000 loading cycles and proceeded without anything untoward.

However, let's go back in time – back to the flight tests. On 20th September 1972 the production-standard Tu-144 was demonstrated outside Moscow for the first time when CCCP-77101 made a flight from Zhukovskiy to Tashkent-Yoozhnyy ('Tashkent-South') airport and back again; the distance between the two cities was 3,200 km (1,988 miles).

On 23rd April 1973 Tu-144 CCCP-77102 made the first publicity flight, carrying members of the press, radio and TV crews from Moscow to Volgograd (Goomrak airport) and back. General Designer Aleksey A. Tupolev, Deputy Chief Designer Yuriy N. Popov, engineer in charge of the flight tests Vladimir N. Benderov and other Tupolev OKB representatives were also aboard and were interviewed during the flight, which included supersonic cruise.

All stages of the Tu-144's test programme took place at the LII airfield in Zhukovskiy with the participation of the flight and ground personnel of the Tupolev OKB's flight test facility. Early-production Tu-144s, including CCCP-77102, which was transferred to LII for test and research work, served as avionics testbeds (or rather 'dogships') for the ABSU-144 AFCS, IS-1-72 inertial navigation system, AIS astro-inertial navigation system, RTO data link system and a speed/altitude data system.

It should be noted that the success of the trials hinged to a considerable degree on the human factor. It took dedication and initiative on the part of everyone involved to develop and test an aircraft of a completely new class within a very short time span. The tests were performed by several crews, each of which was a perfectly matched team consisting of highly experienced airmen and engineers. The flights were not altogether without incident, requiring the crew to keep their heads cool and putting their skill to the test. On one occasion two of the four engines failed on the way home after a publicity flight to Hannover, forcing the crew to make an emergency landing in Sofia; to make matters worse, part of the active runway was unusable due to runway resurfacing work. The crew captained by Eduard V. Yelian and including project engineer Vladimir N. Benderov coped admirably with this emergency, preventing any further damage to the aircraft.

Other Tupolev OKB flight test personnel participating in the Tu-144 programme included flight engineers Boris A. Pervookhin and Vitaliy M. Koolesh. Vladimir N. Benderov contributed immensely to the task of organising the test programme, his unflagging enthusiasm inciting the other employees to work just as hard.

On 23rd May 1973 Tu-144 CCCP-77102 departed to Paris-Le Bourget, where it took part in the 30th Paris Air Show. The aircraft gained the exhibit code 451 for the occasion. As one might imagine, again the Tu-144 became one of the stars of the show.

Tragically, it was at this international aviation showcase that the programme suffered its first major setback. On 3rd June 1973 CCCP-77102 crashed fatally in the Parisian suburb of Goussainville during its second demonstration flight at the show; this accident is described in detail in Chapter 7. Of course the flight tests were immediately suspended while investigation of the accident was in progress.

The next Tu-144, CCCP-77103 (c/n 10021, or 02-1), first flew on 13th December 1973, landing at Zhukovskiy and joining the test programme. This aircraft's first test mission was verification of the navigation suite.

In 1973-74 the Tupolev OKB made changes to the Tu-144's structure and systems based on the findings of the Le Bourget accident investigation panel. The revised manufacturing drawings were issued to the Voronezh aircraft factory, and the complete set of changes was to take effect from Batch 5 (c/n 10051) onwards.

On 19th April 1974 the Tu-144 made its first flight to a foreign destination. Remarkably, this was not associated with any international airshow; the aircraft (CCCP-77101 or, more probably, CCCP-77103) captained by test pilot Yuriy T. Alasheyev paid a flying visit (no pun intended) to Nicosia International airport, Cyprus.

Right: Here CCCP-77144 is seen flying in landing configuration but at fairly high altitude. Note the downward deflection of the elevons.

Below: In 1975 Tu-144 CCCP-77144 was displayed at the 31st Paris Air Show with the exhibit code 361.

One more Tu-144, CCCP-77104 (c/n 10022, or 02-2), made its first flight on 16th June 1974 (some sources say 14th June). This aircraft had more pronounced camber on the outer wing panels and reverted to the original version of the wingtips with no fixed trailing-edge portions outboard of the elevons. It also introduced a revised livery that was worn by most of the subsequent examples. The cheatline was extended forward across the front pair of doors, the 'Ty-144' nose titles were abbreviated to 'Ty' and applied in blue instead of red, and the outlines of the doors and overwing emergency exits were also blue. The registration was moved from the rear fuselage to the base of the fin (where the small Aeroflot titles had been), the break in the cheatline being eliminated in so doing, and the Soviet flag was also repositioned to the fin; the large Aeroflot titles that remained on the fuselage became bolder.

The blue stripes on the wing leading edges continuing along the forward fuselage all the way to the radome were also eliminated.

Ten days later, on 26th June, the Council of Ministers issued directive No.533-186. This document tasked MAP with doing whatever it takes to put the Tu-144 into revenue service in 1975.

Meanwhile, the Tu-144 continued its series of test-cum-publicity flights around the Soviet Union. On 4th September 1974 Tu-144 CCCP-77101 flew from Moscow to Kiev's new Borispol' airport, making a demo flight there the following day before returning to Moscow. The following month the same aircraft made a multi-stop flight, going from Moscow to Baku (Bina airport) on 7th October, making a return flight to Tashkent from there on 8th October and returning to Moscow on 9th October. CCCP-77103 made one more round trip from Moscow to Tashkent on 6th February 1975.

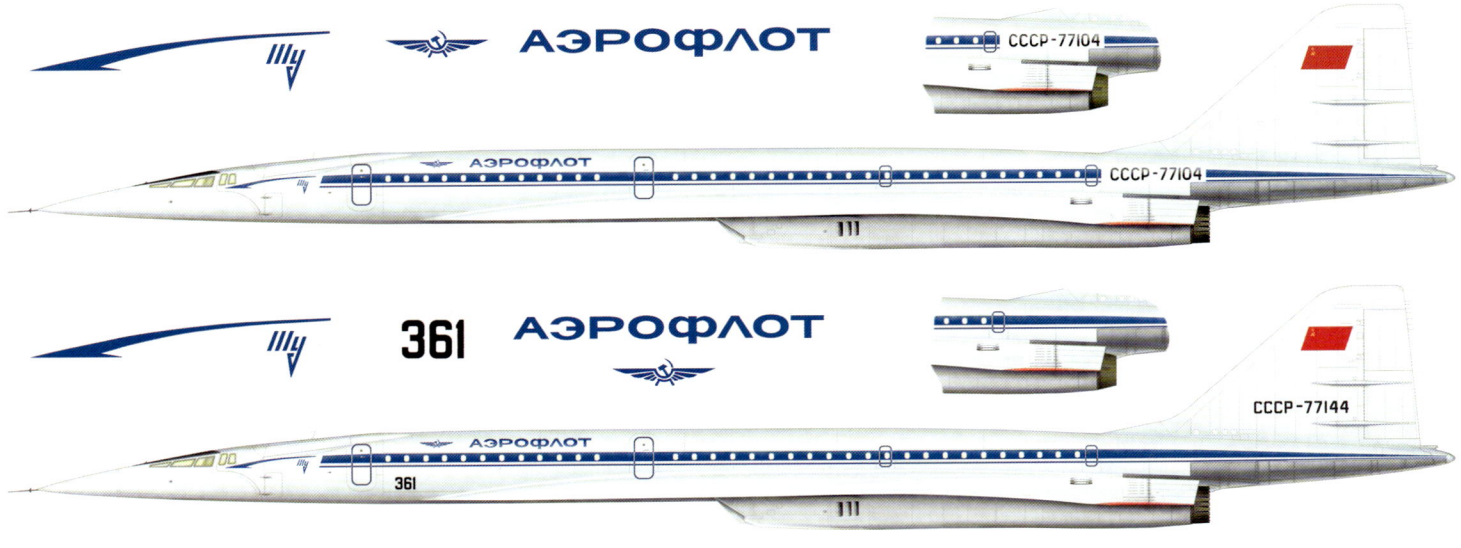

Chapter 4 - Take Two: Back to the Drawing Board

An important event took place on 28th November 1974. The MGA Council issued directive No.31 instructing the Soviet Union's Inter-Department Airworthiness Regulations Co-ordinating Commission (MVK NLGS – *Mezhvedomstvennaya komissiya [po soglasovaniyu] norm lyotnoy godnosti samolyotov*) and the State Aircraft Register (GAR – *Gosudarstvennyy aviatsionny reghistr*) to draw up airworthiness regulations for supersonic commercial aircraft (SSTs) and submit them for approval by 1st May 1975. This was to ensure timely certification of the Tu-144.

Meanwhile, production of the Tu-144 continued. The fourth production example, CCCP-77106 (c/n 10041, or 04-1) first flown on 4th March 1975, also had the old-style wingtips; it was the first *izdeliye* 004 to lack the flight deck emergency hatch. Together with the *izdeliye* 044 demonstrator, these five aircraft made a total of 462 flights at this stage of the programme. (CCCP-77105 represented a different version and is described later.)

On 28th May – 9th June 1975 the Tu-144 again appeared at Le Bourget, participating in the 31st Paris Air Show; the Soviet aviation authorities wanted to show that the programme was alive in spite of the crash. The aircraft in question was the former CCCP-77104, which had been reregistered for the occasion, receiving the 'showy' out-of-sequence registration CCCP-77144 and the exhibit code 361. Once again the aircraft was displayed both statically and in flight. One of the members of the Soviet delegation recalled that during the final demo flight the Tu-144 almost fell victim to a sabotage attempt. As the airliner took off, someone let

Top left: Tu-144 c/n 10022 with the original livery as CCCP-77104 (as flown in 1974) and in new colours as CCCP-77144 (as flown in 1975). The scrap views show the engines at full military power.

Above left: CCCP-77144 in the static park at Le Bourget in company with IL-76 CCCP-76500. Note that the nose titles read simply 'Tu' instead of 'Tu-144'.

Left: Three-quarters rear view of the aircraft at Le Bourget.

Above and right: Two shots of the Tu-144's demonstration flight at the show.

Left: The men who took the SSTs into the air for the first time. Aérospatiale chief test pilot André Turcat and Eduard V. Yelian in the cabin of Tu-144 CCCP-68001 at the 1971 Paris Air Show.

Below left: Eduard V. Yelian and BAC test pilot Brian Trubshaw, who captained Concorde 002 (G-BSST) on its first flight, in the flight deck of this aircraft at the ILA '72 airshow, Hannover, April 1972.

Above right: CCCP-77144 sits parked on the Tupolev OKB hardstand at Zhukovskiy between an older example (foreground) and a newer example illustrating the difference between the old and new liveries worn by *izdeliye* 004.

Right: One of the first three production Tu-144s parked in front of a welded steel jet blast deflector at Zhukovskiy with all four cowlings open, probably for a test run of the engines.

loose a flock of pigeons directly in its flight path, and some of them were ingested by the engines or smashed against the nose gear strut. When the Tu-144 landed, there was blood and feathers all over the place; luckily the engines suffered no serious damage.

State acceptance trials of the Tu-144 commenced in keeping with a joint MAP/MGA ruling 'On the service introduction of the Tu-144 supersonic airliner with NK-144 engines', which was endorsed by Minister of Aircraft Industry Pyotr V. Dement'yev on 31st March 1975 and by Minister of Civil Aviation Boris P. Boogayev on 7th April 1975. It contained the trials programme, the specifications of the airline-standard Tu-144 slated for service entry and a document on the introduction of special airworthiness regulations. Three days earlier, on 28th March, this ruling had been approved by the State Aircraft Register. The integrated

trials programme had been approved by the joint MAP/MGA/GAR ruling No.1339 likewise issued on 28th March; the actual trials schedule was endorsed by Vice-Minister of Aircraft Industry M. S. Mikhaïlov and Vice-Minister of Civil Aviation A. F. Aksyonov on 9th July 1975. The trials programme consisted of two stages; Stage A was intended to determine the possibility and conditions of mail and cargo carriage, while Stage B was aimed at full certification for passenger operations. The trials programme envisaged 259 flights totalling 408 hours.

Six aircraft were involved in this phase of the programme. According to the schedule CCCP-77101 was earmarked for powerplant testing and rejected take-off (RTO) tests, CCCP-77103 was to be used for verifying the NK-144 navigation suite and electric system, CCCP-77144 served for aerodynamic, structural strength and high-alpha tests, CCCP-77106 was to be used for testing the flight director landing approach mode, the automatic flight control system (AFCS) and autothrottle, while CCCP-77107 (c/n 10051, or 05-1) first flown on 12th December 1975 served for integrated evaluation of the aircraft and its systems and defining the basic type to be certified. Interestingly, the latter aircraft was built and registered later than CCCP-77108 (c/n 10042, or 04-2), which first flew on 20th August 1975 and had an out-of-sequence registration.

Here it should be noted that early-production Tu-144s *sans suffixe* were short on range. To remedy this, the Tupolev OKB increased the fuel capacity and the take-off weight, which exceeded 200 tons (440,920 lb). As already mentioned, the definitive high gross weight version powered by NK-144As entered production from Batch 5 onwards. This necessitated a new round of static tests; hence Batch 5 came to consist of three aircraft, c/n 10053 (or 05-3) being the renewed static test airframe. This aircraft is the subject of some controversy. Some sources say the airframe was delivered to TsAGI in Zhukovskiy, and the scenario of Tu-144 c/n 10013 was repeated: first, c/n 10053 was subjected to 'cold' fatigue testing, logging about 5,000 cycles, and then was tested to destruction in the spring of 1979. This time it was the wing that failed, but it failed at 105% of the design load – a very good result. Yet the designers – or maybe the certification authorities – decided this was not enough, so a new outer wing panel from Batch 6 was delivered and fitted for additional tests. In late 1980 it failed at 100% of the design load, so the Tu-144's take-off weight limit was finalised and the tests were completed. Other sources claim Tu-144 c/n 10053 was tested to destruction at SibNIA, the fuselage being delivered to Novosibirsk by a Soviet Air Force Antonov An-22 *Antey* (Antheus/NATO reporting name *Cock*) heavy transport and

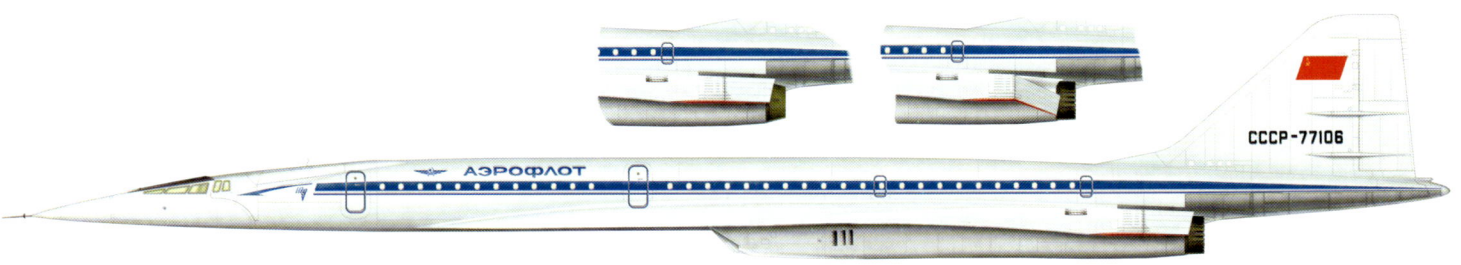

though, Minister of Aircraft Industry Pyotr V. Dement'yev and Minister of Civil Aviation Boris P. Boogayev did not endorse the trials protocol until 13th September 1977 (so much for superstition, eh?). Among other things, the document said: '*The process of developing the first indigenous supersonic airliner, the Tu-144, has made it possible to tackle a large number of hitherto unseen and complex engineering problems, evolve a number of advanced design features and technologies. It has yielded a wealth of experience in testing and refining supersonic airliners.*' On 30th September 1977 the State Aircraft Register issued Provisional Type Certificate No.02V-004 to the production Tu-144 *sans suffixe* powered by NK-144 engines (the V stood for *vremennyy* – temporary or provisional, while 004 denoted *izdeliye* 004). The proper type certificate No.03-144 for the NK-144A-powered version was issued on 29th October 1977, when the Tu-144 had completed its service evaluation programme and the appropriate protocol had been signed.

In July 1977 the Tu-144 *sans suffixe* had one last airshow appearance when CCCP-77110 was in the static park of the 32nd Paris Air Show with the exhibit code 345.

Tu-144D supersonic airliner (*izdeliye* 004D)
As mentioned earlier, back in 1964 the OKB-36 engine design bureau headed by Pyotr A. Kolesov began development of the RD36-51A non-afterburning turbojet (*izdeliye* 57) as a private venture. This engine had a take-off thrust of 20,000 kgp (44,090 lbst), a cruise thrust of 5,100 kg (11,240 lbst) and a cruise SFC of 1.26 kg/kgp·hr in supersonic cruise. The RD36-51A had a number of interesting technical features – a 14-stage compressor with a supersonic first stage increasing the engine pressure ratio, variable compressor stator vanes, a simple, lightweight and efficient variable supersonic nozzle with a translating centrebody, an accessory gearbox installed separately from the engine and driven by an extension shaft via an intermediate gearbox (this made it possible to design smaller engine nacelles and route the associated piping and wiring more rationally) and so on. Provision was made for fitting a thrust reverser and a noise attenuator ('hushkit') later on; the 'hushkit' was to utilise air jets exiting from the nozzle centrebody at right angles to the main exhaust flow to break it up.

Since the Kolesov turbojet was both more powerful and more fuel-efficient than the NK-144 turbofan, Andrey N. Tupolev succeeded in prompting the issuance of VPK ruling No.362 on 22nd October 1967 that gave the RD36-51A programme official status, stipulating the performance parameters. The reason was plain – Tupolev intended to use the new engine as a substitute for the NK-144 when it became available, developing a 'longer-legged' version of the Tu-144 that would achieve the desired range of 6,500 km (4,038 miles).

On 18th December 1968 the VPK passed a ruling titled 'On the development of an improved version of the Tu-144 aircraft with RD36-51A engines'. This was followed on 4th June 1969 by a further VPK ruling, No.131, which set the development schedule of the re-engined Tu-144 and outlined its basic performance. The aircraft was to have a range of 4,500 km (2,795 miles) at a take-off weight of 150,000 kg (330,690 lb) with 150 passengers, or 6,500 km at a take-off weight of 180,000 kg (396,825 lb) with 120 passengers. Shortly afterwards, on 25th June, the then Minister of Civil Aviation Yevgeniy F. Loginov approved more detailed specifications for the re-engined aircraft. The version with RD36-51A turbojets was designated Tu-144D, or *izdeliye* 004D (***dahl'niy*** – long-range). Boris A. Gantsevskiy was appointed the aircraft's project chief.

TsIAM, TsAGI, LII and, of course, the Tupolev OKB were actively involved in the development of the RD36-51A turbojet. The engine commenced bench testing in 1969; later, in the early 1970s, it underwent flight tests on LII's Tu-142LL engine testbed converted from the prototype of the Tu-142 *Bear-F* long-range anti-submarine warfare aircraft (c/n 4200). Meanwhile, the Tupolev OKB had to revise the air intakes, the nacelles' internal structure and the fire suppression system for the new powerplant;

Above left: Tu-144 c/n 10014 undergoing fatigue tests on the Tsikl-1S rig at SibNIA. The illuminated sign in the lower left-hand corner says: 'Attention! Danger zone!'

Left: A drawing of the Tsikl-1S rig from SibNIA materials.

Right: A Kolesov RD36-51A turbojet undergoing bench tests.

A desktop model of CCCP-77108, one of the Tu-144s involved in the type's service tests.

changes were also made to the fuel system, hydraulic system and ACS pipelines. The OKB undertook a large amount of test work at its own engine test facility at Zhukovskiy to integrate the RD36-51A with the Tu-144D's air intakes. The development engines logged a total of 577 hours in the thermovacuum chamber and on the Tu-142LL.

In 1971, at Andrey N. Tupolev's suggestion, OKB-36 developed an afterburning version of the RD36-51A to increase the available thrust in the transonic flight mode (Mach 0.95 to 1.2). However, this turned out to be a bad idea; the afterburner's burner ring obstructed the jetpipe, reducing fuel efficiency in the primary (dry thrust) mode by 3-4%. Eventually flight tests showed that the Tu-144D suffered no problems at transonic speeds, and the afterburner was deleted. Nevertheless, OKB-36 planned to increase the engine's take-off thrust to 21,000 kg (46,300 lbst) and reduce the cruise SFC to 1.23 kg/kgp·hr. Beyond that it was hoped to achieve a take-off thrust of 23,000-24,000 kgp (50,700-52,910 lbst) and a cruise thrust of 5,400 kgp (11,900 lbst).

Presently on 26th July 1974 the Council of Ministers issued directive No.533-186 requiring the aircraft industry to build the 'improved version of the Tu-144 with RD36-51A engines' and supply it to Aeroflot. The first aircraft to receive the new engines was CCCP-77105 (c/n 10031 or 03-1), the sole Batch 3 machine, which was built as a Tu-144 *sans suffixe* but converted straightaway as the Tu-144D prototype. It first flew on 30th November 1974 with Voronezh aircraft factory chief test pilot Aleksandr I. Voblikov in the captain's seat, making the ferry flight from Voronezh-Pridacha to Zhukovskiy; a Tu-134 airliner with Tupolev OKB representatives aboard flew chase. Mikhail V. Pankevich was the engineer in charge of the flight tests. Like the preceding production-standard Tu-144s, the aircraft had a port side flight deck escape hatch. CCCP-77105 sported a hybrid colour scheme – the short cheatline, red nose titles, blue wing leading edges and the placement of the registration on the rear fuselage matched the first three Tu-144s but the flag was carried on the fin, not on the rudder.

Outwardly the Tu-144D was readily identifiable by the new engine nozzles which had solid rims (without nozzle petals) and cropped conical centrebodies. The latter were translating, moving fore and aft for the purpose of adjusting the nozzle area (thus performing the same function as the nozzle petals).

The Tu-144D's flight tests proceeded with a good deal of trouble, as the new engines were in short supply. Once again, the initial production RD36-51A engines had a service life of only 50 hours; the SFC was much higher than expected, especially in the initial afterburning version (more of this later). Gradually reliability and performance improved as the bench tests continued and revisions were made; yet, debugging the engine proved to be a lengthy affair, and it was not until late 1977 that the definitive version of the RD36-51A became available. Until then, the Tu-144D prototype did not venture far from its home base in Zhukovskiy. On 5th June 1976 CCCP-77105 covered a distance of 6,200 km (3,850 miles) with a 5,000-kg (11,020-lb) payload, confirming the future prospects in continuing work on the Tu-144D.

On 28th November 1976 the VPK issued ruling No.312 requiring the Voronezh aircraft factory to build six production Tu-144Ds. In February 1977 a mock-up review commission convened to assess the changes in the Tu-144D's flight deck and systems as compared to the NK-144A-powered Tu-144 *sans suffixe*. Meanwhile, in 1976-77 the OKB was issuing manufacturing drawings for the new version and transferring them to the factory.

On 22nd-23rd February 1977 CCCP-77105 made a non-stop transcontinental flight from Moscow to Khabarovsk in the Soviet Far East and back again. The aircraft was captained by Vasiliy P. Borisov, with Sergey T. Agapov as co-pilot, Vitaliy A. Troshin as navigator, Yuriy T. Selivyorstov as flight engineer, Mikhail V. Pankevich as engineer in charge of the flight tests and Yuriy Stolyarov as his assistant. LII Director Viktor V. Ootkin and Novosti Press Agency journalist Yuriy Rost were also aboard as passengers. On the outbound leg the aircraft covered the 6,250-km (3,883-mile) distance in just 3 hours 23 minutes; the return leg lasted 3 hours 26 minutes.

Borisov recalled that *'the weather was beastly, with fog and terribly icy roads. On the way to the airfield our crew bus spun round on three occasions like a skater on ice. By the time we were scheduled to take off the ground service had cleared and thawed a [section of] runway 2.5 km [8,200 ft] long but only 30 m [100 ft] wide. Horizontal visibility was no more than 300-400 m [980-1,310 ft]. The forecast for the next day showed even worse weather in Khabarovsk, so both the bosses and the crew had to have the guts to take off in such conditions.'* The take-off weight was close to 210 tons (462,960 lb) but, in spite of this and the foul weather, the take-off went smoothly. The aircraft took an orthodromic course – a beeline from Moscow to Khabarovsk that took it almost over the Polar regions of the Soviet Union, passing 800 km (496 miles) north of Sverdlovsk (now renamed back to Yekaterinburg) and 1,500 km (931 miles) north of Novosibirsk. Cruise flight took place at 2,300 km/h (1,429 mph) and altitudes up to 20,000 m (65,620 ft). The Tu-144D's autopilot was then insufficiently reliable, and Borisov had to fly manually all the way; nevertheless, the aircraft maintained the designated speed of Mach 2.0 with an error margin of no more than 3%. As the Tu-144D passed over the northern Urals Mts. it ran into unexpectedly severe turbulence at 18,000-20,000 m (59,060-65,620 ft); the general belief had been that there were only gentle winds at those altitudes.

(It may be mentioned that Borisov had check-flown the route before this flight with a slightly different crew in Tu-144 *sans suffixe* CCCP-77109, making stops at Novosibirsk-Tolmachovo airport on the way there and back. On arrival at Khabarovsk-Novyy airport the aircraft disgorged a Tupolev OKB technical team supporting the impending flight of the Tu-144D. When taking off for the return trip, CCCP-77109 hit a pothole on the runway and suffered such a jolt that navigator Vitaliy A. Troshin was thrown out of his seat, landing on top of flight engineer Anatoliy Tararookhin; it was only the latter's habit of locking the throttles at full power during the take-off run that averted disaster. Borisov's headset cord was ripped out of his helmet, leaving him incommunicado for a while and causing alarm within the crew, which was unable to receive instructions from the captain. The Ministry of Civil Aviation was duly notified of the incident but nothing happened; it took another incident involving an Aeroflot IL-62 which hit the same pothole, dislodging several seats and injuring several passengers, to make the inert MGA take action.)

The prototype's first few long-range flights, including a transcontinental flight from Moscow to Khabarovsk in the Soviet Far East, imbued the MAP and MGA top brass with somewhat premature optimism and hopes for rapid completion of the trials. On 17th and 24th March 1977 respectively Minister of Aircraft Industry Pyotr V. Dement'yev and Minister of Civil Aviation Boris P. Boogayev endorsed the Tu-144D's test schedule. According to the plan, the prototype and the first production example were to complete the state acceptance trials in October 1978; in parallel, Aeroflot was to complete evaluation of the second and third production Tu-144Ds that same month. Also in October 1978, the RD36-51A engine was to complete its bench tests and attain a 300-hour service life. Finally, in December 1978 the Tu-144D was slated for service entry.

Yet, development problems (first and foremost with the engine) kept causing delays; the prototype made only 18 flights in 1977. It was another year after the plan was signed before the first of five production machines – CCCP-77111 (c/n 10062, or 06-2) – took to the air on 27th April 1978. (Curiously, an official Soviet document states this aircraft's manufacture date as 18th April 1978, which is unbelievable in view of the first flight date; the manufacture date always comes *after* the first flight, not *before* it!)

On 18th April – 3rd May 1978 MAP, MGA and GAR issued a joint ruling on the Tu-144D's joint state acceptance trials. In conformity with this ruling the Tupolev OKB began certification tests of the Tu-144D in parallel with the manufacturer's flight tests (the latter mostly took place in 1978-81).

The availability of a second aircraft seemed to indicate that the Tu-144D programme would now proceed at a steady pace. However, on 23rd May 1978 disaster struck again. During a routine test mission CCCP-77111 crashed fatally near Yegor'yevsk, Moscow Region, while attempting an off-field forced landing after a massive in-flight fire. This was the aircraft's sixth flight and the final pre-delivery test flight; CCCP-77111 had logged only 9 hours 02 minutes. (Again, this accident is described in Chapter 7.)

By then the Tu-144 *sans suffixe* was in Aeroflot service, and of course all scheduled Tu-144 passenger flights were immediately

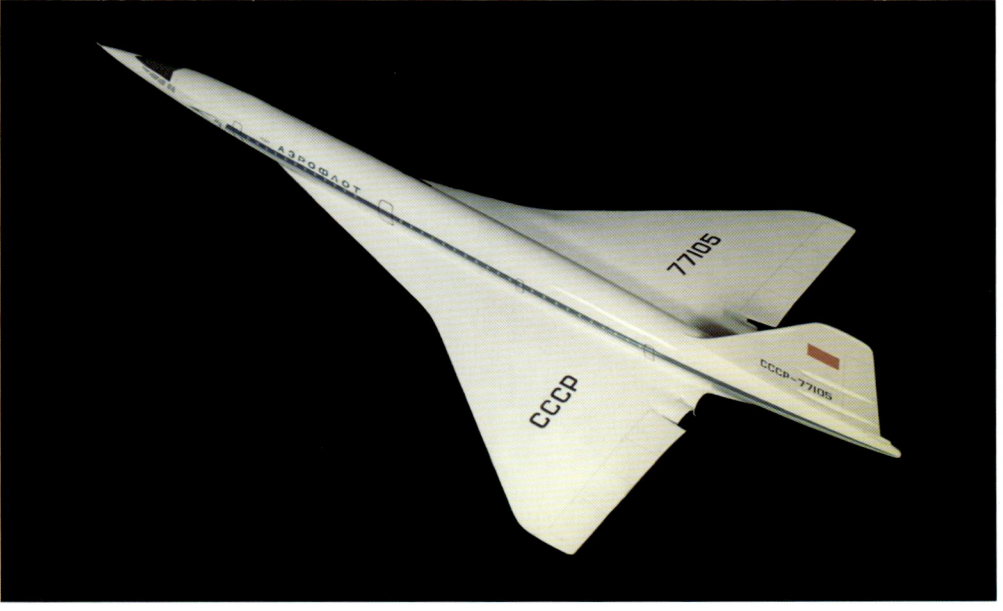

The registration CCCP-77105 identifies this display model as depicting the Tu-144D prototype, but the distinctive nozzle centrebodies are missing, suggesting NK-144A engines and hence an ordinary Tu-144 *sans suffixe*.

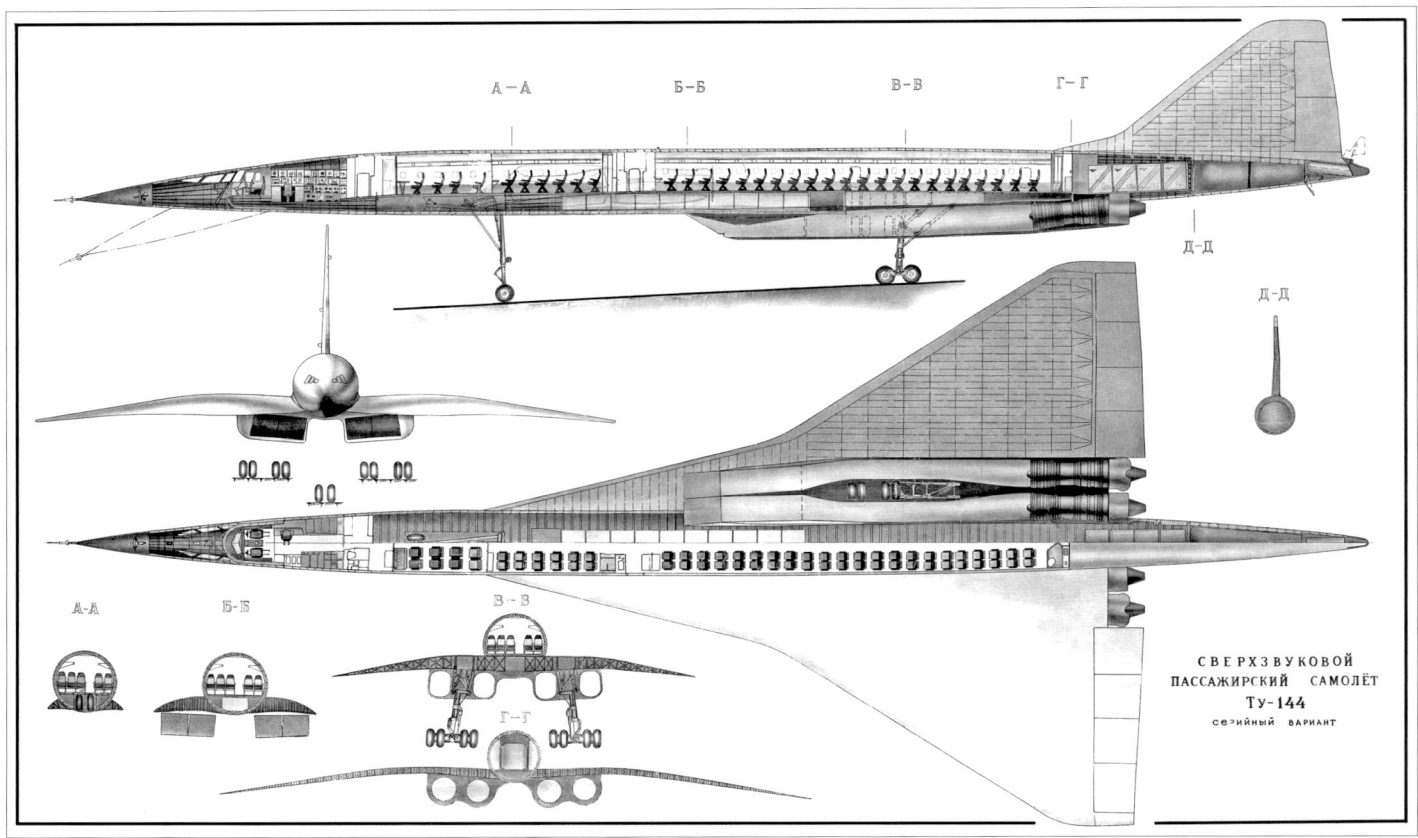

suspended pending investigation of the crash. This time the cause was traced with absolute certainty to a design flaw in the fuel system that was easy to rectify. However, the Tu-144, whose reputation had already been damaged by the 1973 Paris crash, had its share of detractors – also in the government. Now, armed with a perfectly legitimate pretext, the anti-Tu-144 lobby charged to the attack, branding the aircraft as unsafe and demanding termination of the programme.

Two more production Tu-144Ds joined the tests in 1979, considerably behind schedule; these were CCCP-77112 (c/n 10071, or 07-1) – the sole Batch 7 aircraft, which first flew on 19th February, and CCCP-77113 (c/n 10081, or 08-1) first flown on 2nd October. The delay was due to the need to modify the fuel system after the 1978 crash. (Incidentally, the last two Tu-144s *sans suffixe* were updated in the same fashion.)

The tests gave the OKB a hard time. On 5th March 1979 Tu-144D CCCP-77112 had a fuel line failure causing a massive fuel leak. As a result, a lot of aluminium alloy tubes in the fuel system were replaced with steel tubes, and the Tu-144 fleet was grounded for repairs in April-July 1979.

On 31st August 1980 Tu-144D CCCP-77113 captained by Tupolev OKB test pilot Yevgeniy A. Goryunov suffered an uncontained failure of the No.3 engine – the third turbine stage disc exploded when the aircraft was doing Mach 2.;0 at 16,000 m (52,490 ft), heading for Aktybinsk, Kazakh SSR. The failure triggered a surge of the Nos. 2 and 4 engines; a fire warning sounded and the flight deck lit up with warning lights like a Christmas tree. Reacting instantly, the flight engineer shut down the three affected engines. However, in the heat of the moment he forgot to transfer fuel to the rear trim tank and the aircraft began descending, travelling at Mach 1 and ignoring the pilot's efforts to level it off. Luckily Viktor N. Ghenov, the engineer in charge, noticed this and ran to the flight deck from his workstation in the cabin, activating the fuel transfer system in time.

Goryunov recalled afterwards: '*My thoughts were racing: had I done everything I should, had I remembered everything? Suddenly I had a flashback of a lecture on flight testing techniques at the [LII] Test Pilots School, when Mark L. Galiai told us: "When you have tried everything and still don't know how to save the situation, don't just sit there – try something unconventional, like working the control wheel erratically". Meanwhile, the aircraft was descending rapidly; soon it was down to the altitude where we had to decelerate to subsonic speed. I was stil! hauling back the control yoke all the way to my navel, but still the aircraft was slowly dropping its nose. I dared to do the impossible, even though my mind had locked my arms where they were* (that is, hauling back on the control yoke – Auth.) *So I told myself: "Let it go! And then give it a jerk!" I thrust the yoke sharply forward, then yanked it back. The sink rate increased a little, the speed was around Mach 1... Suddenly I saw the Mach meter needle move slightly, and at the same moment the [other] instruments showed that we were now subsonic and the Mach number was decreasing steadily...*'

The fire suppression system had done its job – the fire was out. The crew managed to restart the No.2 engine at 8,000 m (26,250 ft) and make a safe emergency landing on two engines at Engels-2 airbase (a strategic bomber base) at a weight well above the maximum permitted landing weight – dumping the fuel was out of the question. It transpired that the fragments of the turbine disc had torn large holes in the nacelle but mercifully had not punctured the fuselage, causing decompression. Moreover, one large fragment had passed squarely between a fuel line and an oil line; had it hit either of them, the consequences would have been grave. Thus, a combination of excellent airmanship and luck had saved the day. CCCP-77113 was repaired on site and flown back to Zhukovskiy. Of course, these incidents did not speak in favour of the Tu-144 either.

On 30th December 1980 MAP, MGA and GAR approved the integrated programme of the Tu-144D's state acceptance trials. On 20th February 1981 LII filed a report stating that the Tu-144D conformed to the VNLGSS airworthiness regulations. Yet another production machine, CCCP-77114 (c/n 10082, or 08-2), joined the fleet on 13th April that year.

Meanwhile, OKB-36 embarked on a series of measures aimed at improving the engine's reliability. The work continued until May 1981, whereupon the Tu-144D was submitted for state acceptance trials and formally accepted for these by MGA on 11th May. The greater part of the trials programme had been completed by the end of that year. On 9th June 1981 the Tu-144D received provisional type certificate No.11V-144D.

Still, engine reliability problems persisted – albeit not necessarily with disastrous consequences. On 5th October 1981 CCCP-77112 (using the ATC callsign CCCP-77339) made a precautionary landing at Alma-Ata airport due to a false fire warning in the No.4 engine. On 12th November that year an RD36-51A engine failed during check-up bench tests, causing the fleet to be temporarily grounded. The engine's SFC was some 3.4% higher than expected – 1.27 kg/kgp·hr instead of 1.23 kg/kgp·hr. Also, the Rybinsk aero-engine factory No.36 was late in delivering production RD36-51A turbojets, with the result that the already completed Tu-144D airframes sat engineless for a long time. As a

Left: A cut away drawing of the Tu-144D from the ADP documents.

Right and below: Another case of mistaken identity – this model portrays CCCP-77106 as a Tu-144D (note the nozzle shape), and with a red cheatline into the bargain for some reason.

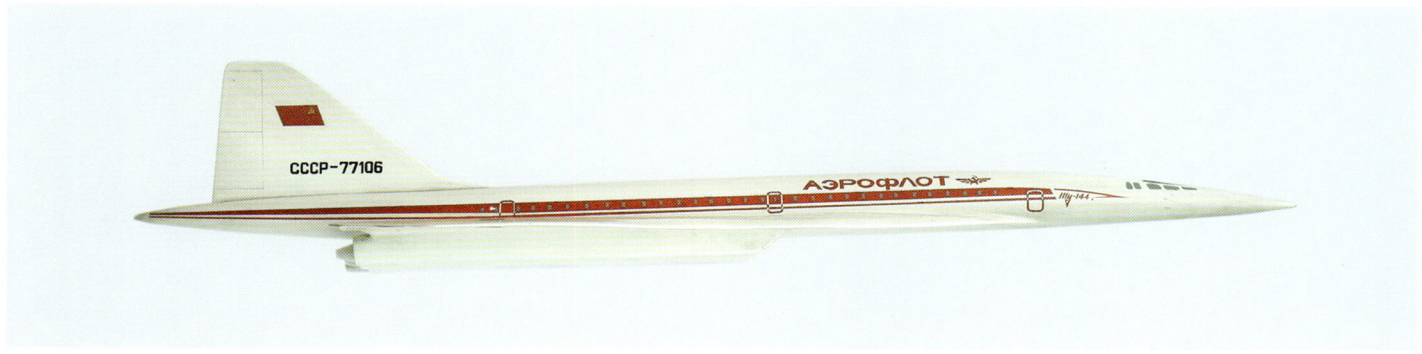

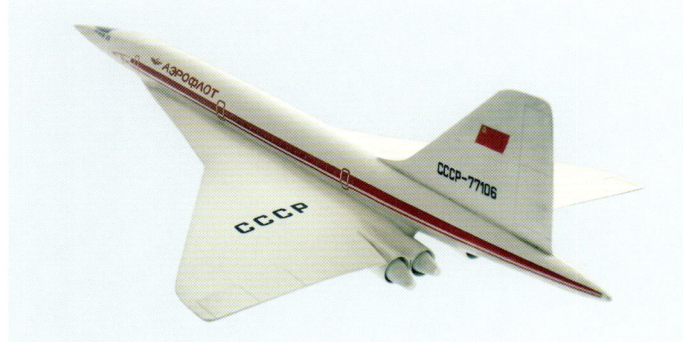

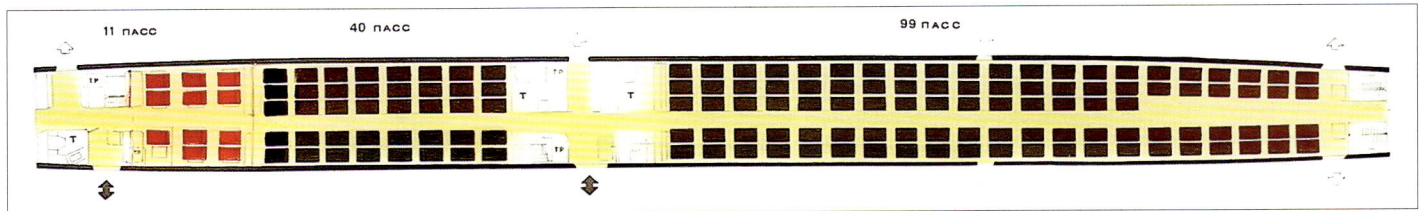

Top: CCCP-77105, the Tu-144D prototype, was the only one to combine the old version of the livery with the Soviet flag painted on the fin (rather than on the rudder), as in the new livery.
Above: The cabin layout of the Tu-144D's 150-seat version

Below: CCCP-77105 on the apron at Khabarovsk-Novyy during trials in company with Tu-154 *sans suffixe* CCCP-85032 (a Tupolev OKB support aircraft), a TZ-22 fuel bowser and an ATs-40(375)-Ts1A fire engine.

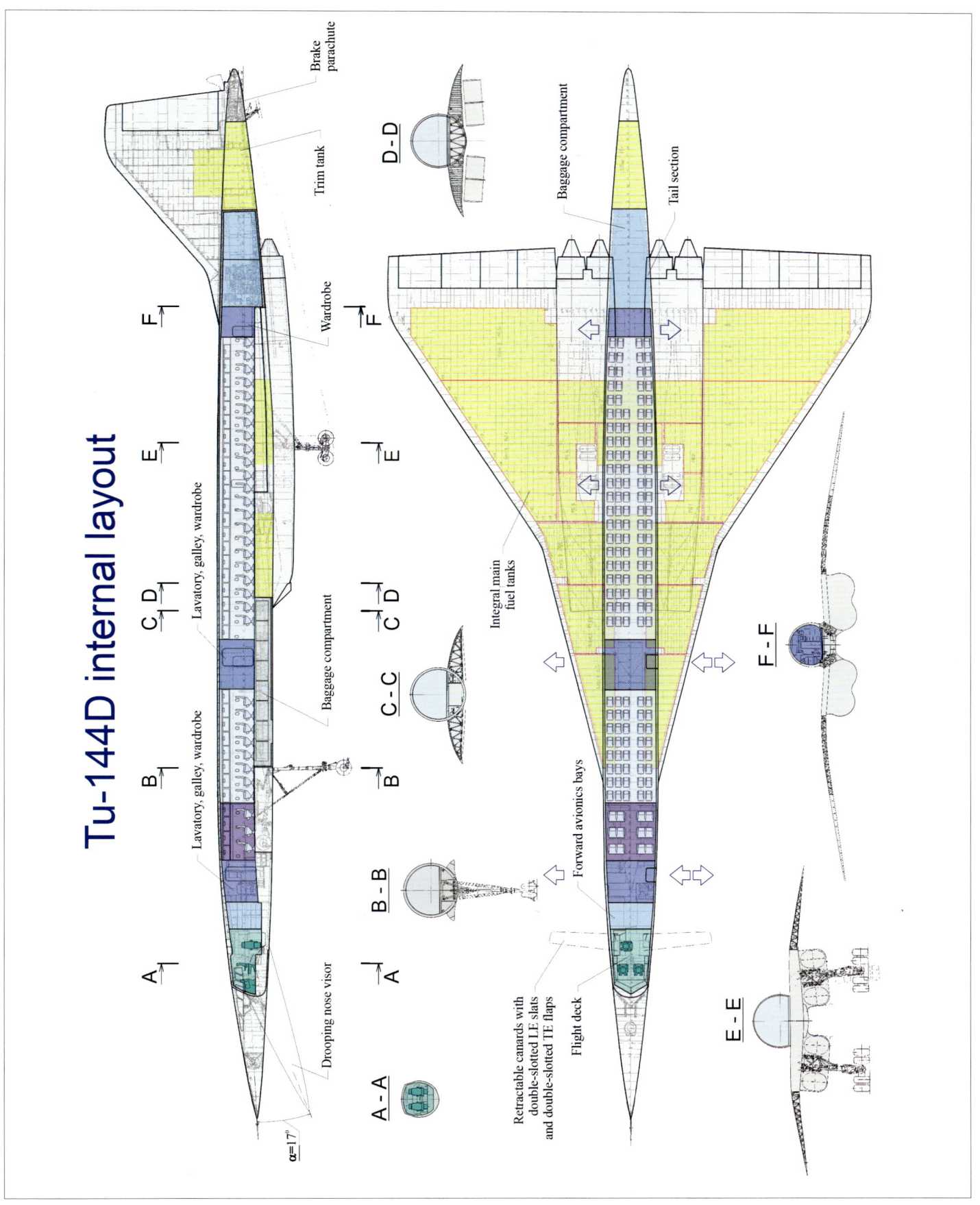

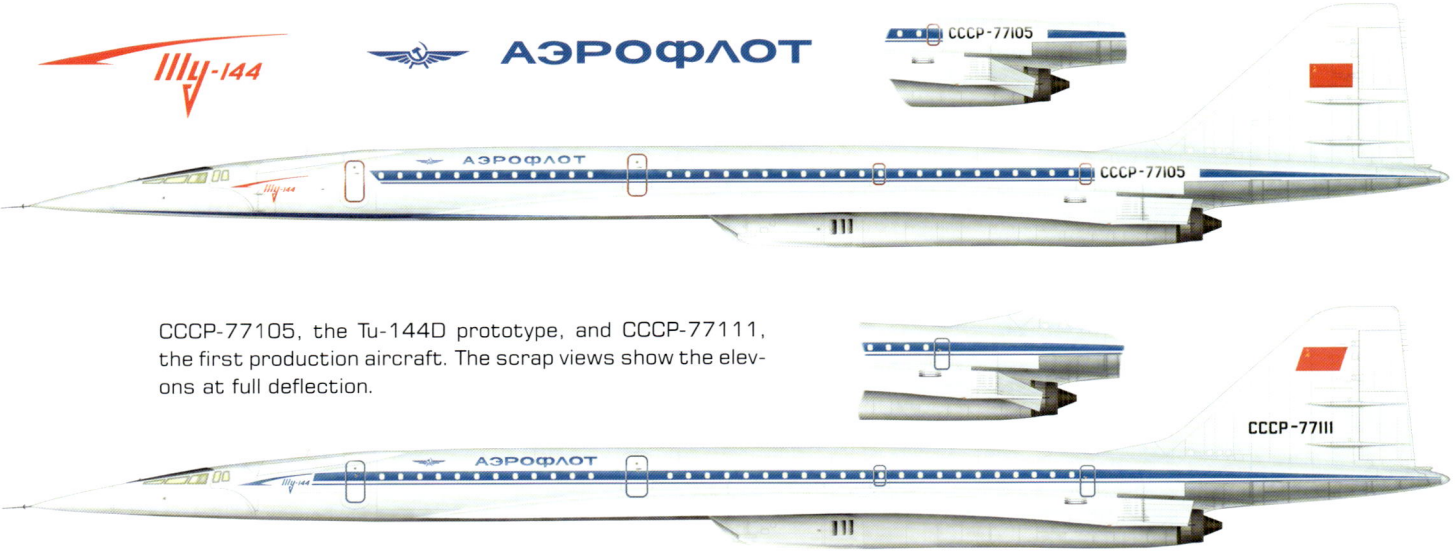

CCCP-77105, the Tu-144D prototype, and CCCP-77111, the first production aircraft. The scrap views show the elevons at full deflection.

result, the test fleet made only 110 flights by the end of 1980 instead of the planned 230.

State acceptance trials of the Tu-144D took place during July-November 1981. In the course of the trials the Tu-144Ds performed a total of 411 flights, logging 764 flight hours. The participating airmen were test pilots Vyacheslav D. Popov, N. I. Yoorskov (both representing GosNII GA), Sergey T. Agapov, Yevgeniy A. Goryunov (both representing the Tupolev OKB) and Anatoliy S. Levchenko (representing LII), flight engineers Viktor V. Solomatin, O. N. Kochetkov (both representing the Tupolev OKB) and M. P. Isayev (GosNII GA), navigators V. A. Kachalov (GosNII GA) and Vitaliy A. Troshin (Tupolev OKB). The engineers in charge were V. A. Isayev (GosNII GA), Sergey P. Avakimov and V. N. Ghenov (both representing the Tupolev OKB). The trials report was endorsed by the new Minister of Aircraft Industry Ivan S. Silayev and Minister of Civil Aviation Boris P. Boogayev as late as 19th April 1982; its concluding part stated that the Tu-144D could be cleared for operational evaluation, providing the reliability of the engines was improved and this was confirmed by additional bench tests.

Chapter 4 - Take Two: Back to the Drawing Board

Above: Tu-144D CCCP-77112 with a pair of TZ-22s, an APA-50M and an SPO-15 'cherry picker' on a Ural-375D chassis in attendance.

Below left: The same aircraft caught at the moment of touchdown; note the brake parachutes beginning to deploy.

Below: CCCP-77112 also made several flights to Khabarovsk-Novyy in the course of the trials.

Left: Tupolev OKB ground personnel pose with Tu-144D CCCP-77114.

Below: Tu-144D CCCP-77113 pictured at Zhukovskiy in 1996. The aircraft is already dead and engineless, awaiting disposal (it was scrapped in 2001).

Right: A drawing showing the temperature fields on the Tu-144's airframe.

Still, the Tu-144D was never put into service and the programme was gradually run down – officially due to the protracted development of the RD36-51A engines. On 27th January 1982 the Minister of Aircraft Industry issued instruction No.S24/464 cancelling further production of the Tu-144D; c/n 10092 was to be the last one built. On 1st July 1983 the Council of Ministers ultimately pulled the plug on the programme, issuing directive No.461-169 which cancelled all further work on the Tu-144 and relegated the surviving examples to the testbed role.

Tu-144D CCCP-77115 (c/n 10091, or 09-1) was the last to fly, making its first flight on 4th October 1984. The last example built, CCCP-77116 (c/n 10092, or 09-2), was not completed and sat on the factory apron at Voronezh-Pridacha until the 1990s when it was broken up. The others were retained by the OKB and used for test and research purposes.

Back in 1980, CCCP-77105 was to serve as a testbed for the *izdeliye* 61 turbojet – a derivative of the RD36-51A with a thrust reverser, a take-off thrust of 21,000 kgp (46,300 lbst) and a cruise SFC reduced to 1.23 kg/kgp·hr. Development of this engine began pursuant to MAP order No.265 dated 7th August 1978 but was hampered by lack of resources at OKB-36. The first prototype engine ran in late 1978, and six engines had been built by the end of 1980. One of them, a flight-cleared example, was fitted to Tu-144D CCCP-77105 but never flew in this aircraft because defects were discovered; the engine was removed and returned to OKB-36.

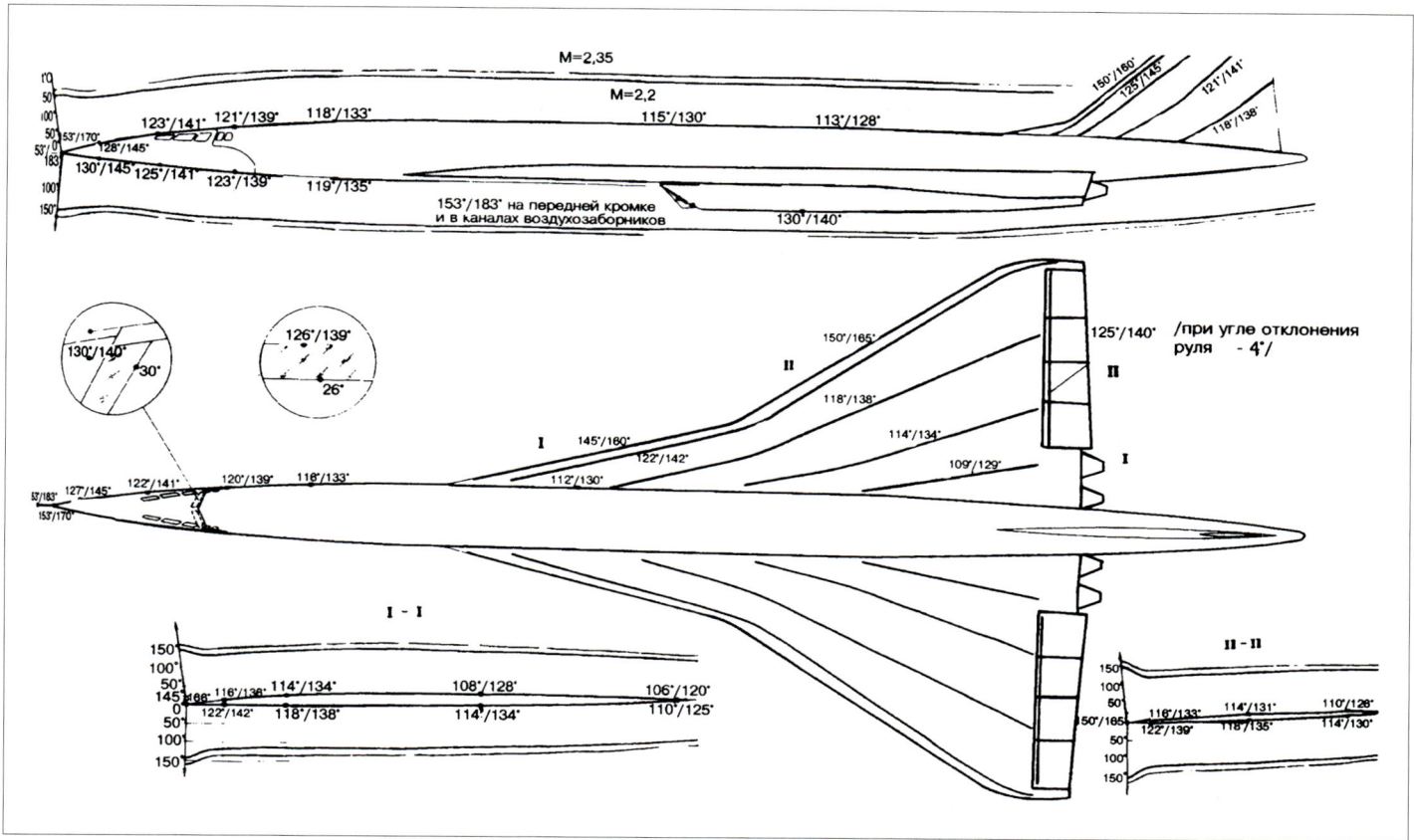

CCCP-77113 was used for atmospheric ozone research, helping to fight ozone layer depletion. The first round of modifications in the interests of the Institute of Medico-Biological Problems (installation of scientific equipment) was in 1986; in 1987-88 the aircraft made a series of research flights from Moscow to Ishim (Tyumen' Region, Russia) and back and to Kazakhstan along the Moscow – Ural'sk – Goor'yev – Shevchenko – Moscow route. Additional equipment was installed in 1988-89, but the second series of the experiments never took place as the financing was cut off. The aircraft made its last flight on 27th February 1990.

CCCP-77115 was used for training the future pilots of the Soviet space shuttle Buran (Blizzard, pronounced *boorahn*) in 1986-88. To this end the cabin was equipped with rapid depressurisation valves at the overwing emergency exits in case of an emergency descent. Eventually, however, the Buran never did actually fly in piloted mode.

'Aircraft 101' (Tu-144D) record-breaking aircraft

In July 1983 Tu-144D CCCP-77114 flown by a Tupolev OKB crew including captain Sergey T. Agapov and co-pilot Boris I. Veremey set 14 world speed and altitude records. On 13th July, defying

Tu-144D test flights in 1979-80			
Registration	1979	1980	Planned flights
CCCP-77112	54 flights, 131 hrs	None	120 flights, 280 hrs
CCCP-77113	14 flights, 35 hrs	42 flights, 76 hrs	70 flights, 160 hrs
CCCP-77114	None	None	40 flights, 100 hrs
Total	68 flights, 166 hrs	42 flights, 76 hrs	230 flights, 540 hrs

The Tu-144D's utilisation in the trials		
Registration	Flights	Flight hours
CCCP-77105	212	314
CCCP-77111	6	9
CCCP-77112	81	199
CCCP-77113	103	223
CCCP-77114	9	21
Total	411	764

Basic performance of the Tu-144D	
Cruising speed	Mach 2.0
Effective range (ISA, no wind, 10-ton/ 22,045-lb fuel reserves):	
with an 11 to 13-ton (24,250 to 28,660-lb) payload	5,700-5,500 km (3,540-3,416 miles)
with a 15-ton (33,070-lb) payload	5,330 km (3,310 miles)
with a 7-ton (15,430-lb) payload	6,250 km (3,880 miles)
Service ceiling	16,000-18,000 m (52,490-59,055 ft)
Maximum take-off weight	207,000 kg (456,350 lb)
Maximum landing weight	125,000 kg (275,570 lb)
Minimum unstick speed	360 km/h (223 mph)
Minimum approach speed	290 km/h (180 mph)

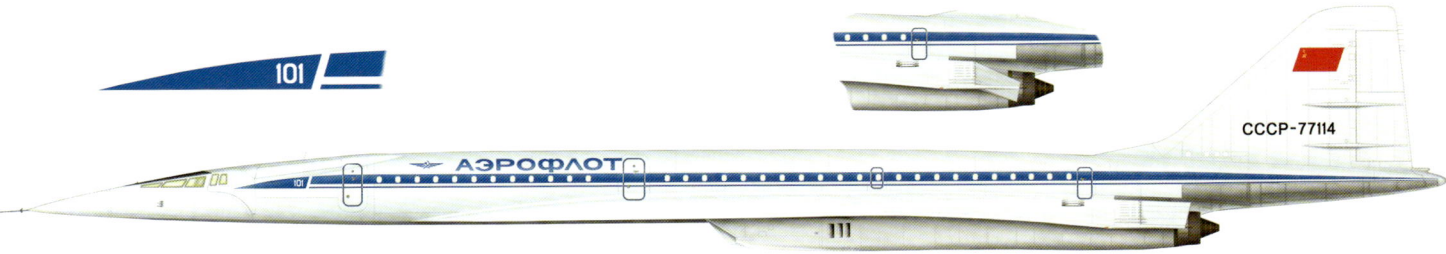

superstition, the crew established four speed records on a 1,000-km (621-mile) closed circuit when the Tu-144D attained a speed of 2,031.55 km/h (1,262.35 mph) with payloads of 5, 10, 20 and 30 tons (11,020; 22,045; 44,090; and 66,140 lb). A week later, on 20th July, the aircraft set five speed records on a 2,000-km (1,242-mile) closed circuit with payloads of 0, 5, 10, 20 and 30 tons, plus five payload-to-altitude records, taking payloads of 10, 15, 20, 25 and 30 tons (22,045, 33,070; 44,090; 55,115; and 66,140 lb) to an altitude of 18,200 m (59,711 ft).

It was not uncommon for the Soviet aviation authorities to use bogus designations for the aircraft and its engine(s) in the documents submitted to the World Air Sports Federation (FAI – *Fédération Aéronautique Internationale*) when claiming world records. This was also the case in this instance; the Tu-144D was notified to the FAI as the '101' and its RD36-51A engines were listed as 'R-105 turbojets'. In fact, CCCP-77114 had a slightly amended livery for the occasion, wearing '101' nose titles instead of the normal 'Tu-144' titles. This deception was justified when the record-setting aircraft were military – for example, the Mikoyan MiG-25PU *Foxbat-C* combat trainer used for setting world speed records in 1975 and 1977-78 was entered as the Ye-133. Similarly, the much-modified Sukhoi Su-27 *Flanker-B* fighter used for establishing a

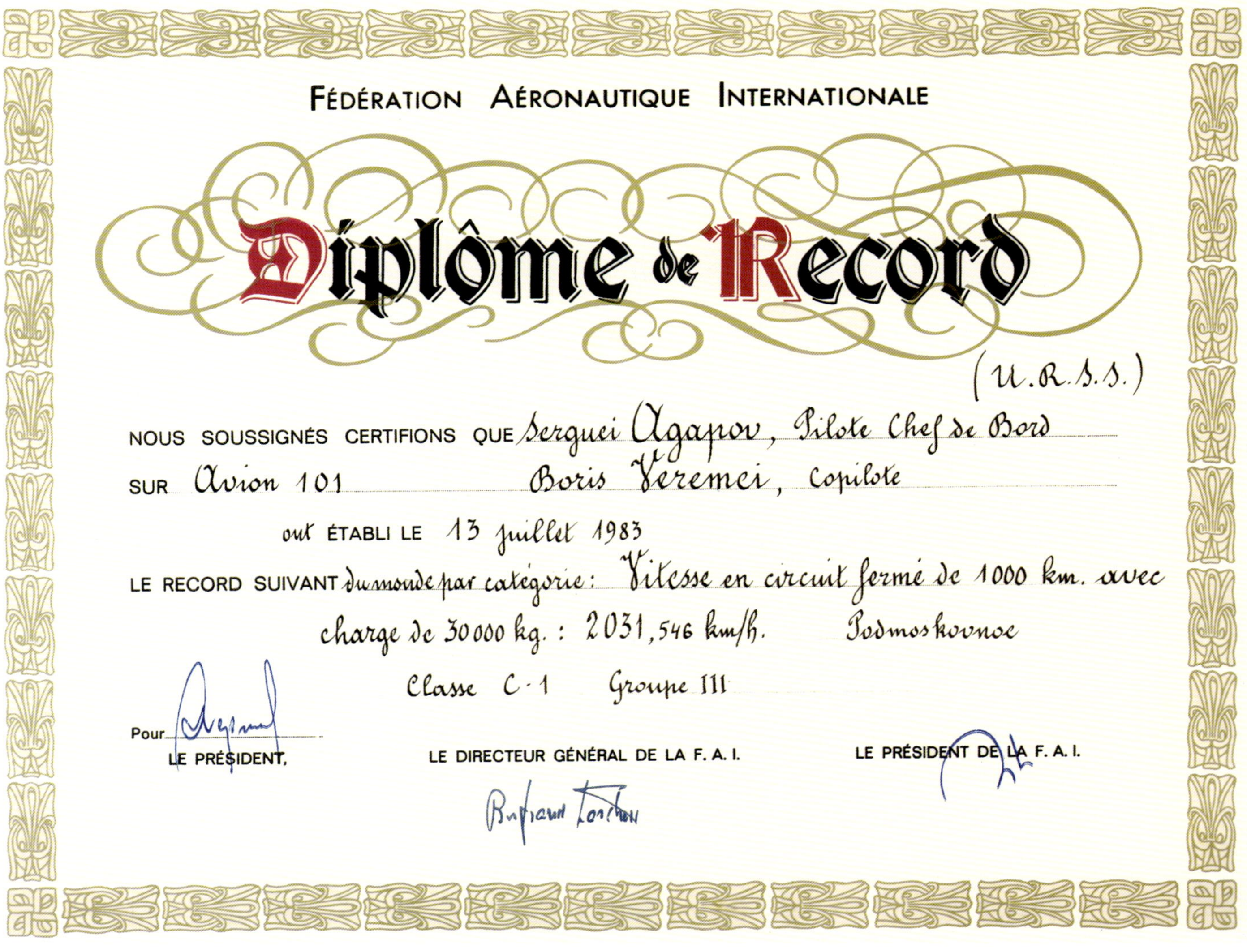
FÉDÉRATION AÉRONAUTIQUE INTERNATIONALE

Diplôme de Record

(U.R.S.S.)

NOUS SOUSSIGNÉS CERTIFIONS QUE Serguei Agapov, Pilote Chef de Bord

SUR Avion 101 Boris Veremei, Copilote

ont ÉTABLI LE 13 juillet 1983

LE RECORD SUIVANT du monde par catégorie: Vitesse en circuit fermé de 1000 km. avec charge de 30000 kg. : 2031,546 km/h. Podmoskovnoe

Classe C-1 Groupe III

Pour LE PRÉSIDENT,

LE DIRECTEUR GÉNÉRAL DE LA F. A. I.

LE PRÉSIDENT DE LA F. A. I.

Left: Tu-144D CCCP-77114 with the nose titles amended to '101' for the record-setting flights in 1983.

Right: Here CCCP-77114 is seen at Kipelovo AB from where the records were established in October 1983.

Below: A cut away drawing of the projected Tu-144M from the ADP drawings showing the shorter engine nacelles and the new 12-wheel main gear bogies stowing with the wheels horizontal. The drawing does not show where the APU has been moved to.

number of time-to-height and altitude records in 1986-88 was designated P-42, while its Lyul'ka AL-31F afterburning turbofans were referred to as 'R-32 engines'. In this case, however, the bogus designations appear illogical, considering that the Tu-144D was a commercial aircraft – and a highly publicised one at that.

Tu-144DA supersonic airliner (project)
The 1970s saw new projects to update the Tu-144, the Tu-144D having proved that it could meet range requirements and had the potential for future development. Changes to the airframe, systems and equipment would allow greater fuel capacity. This new project was designated Tu-144DA.

Early studies indicated that, with a take-off weight of 235 tons (518,080 lb), the fuel load could be increased to 125 tons (275,570 lb) as opposed to 90-95 tons (198,410-209,435 lb) on the Tu-144D. The wing area was increased from 507 m² (5,451 sq ft) to 544 m² (5,849 sq ft), and RKBM 'izdeliye 61' turbojets were envisaged. The seating capacity was increased to 130-160 in all-economy

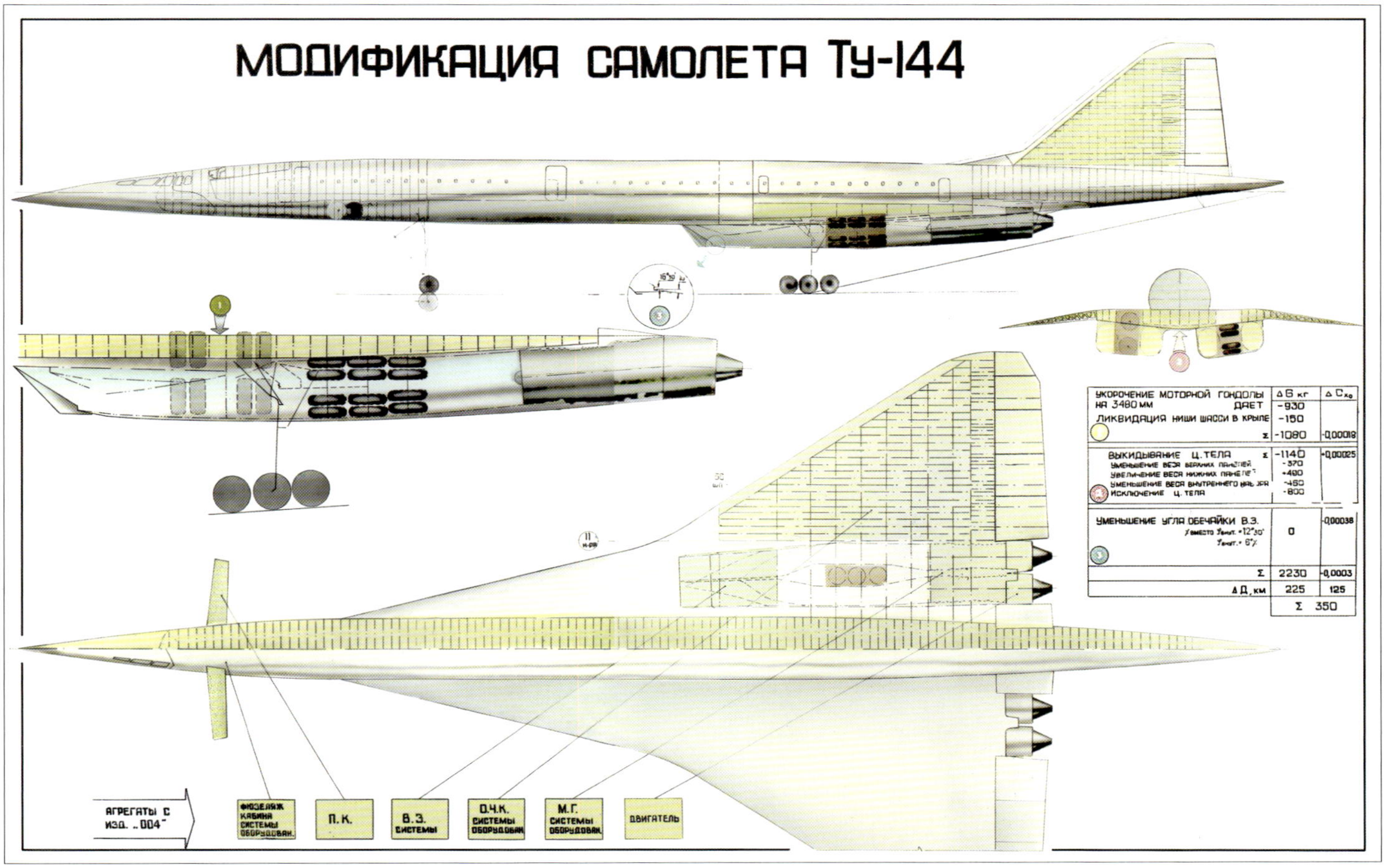

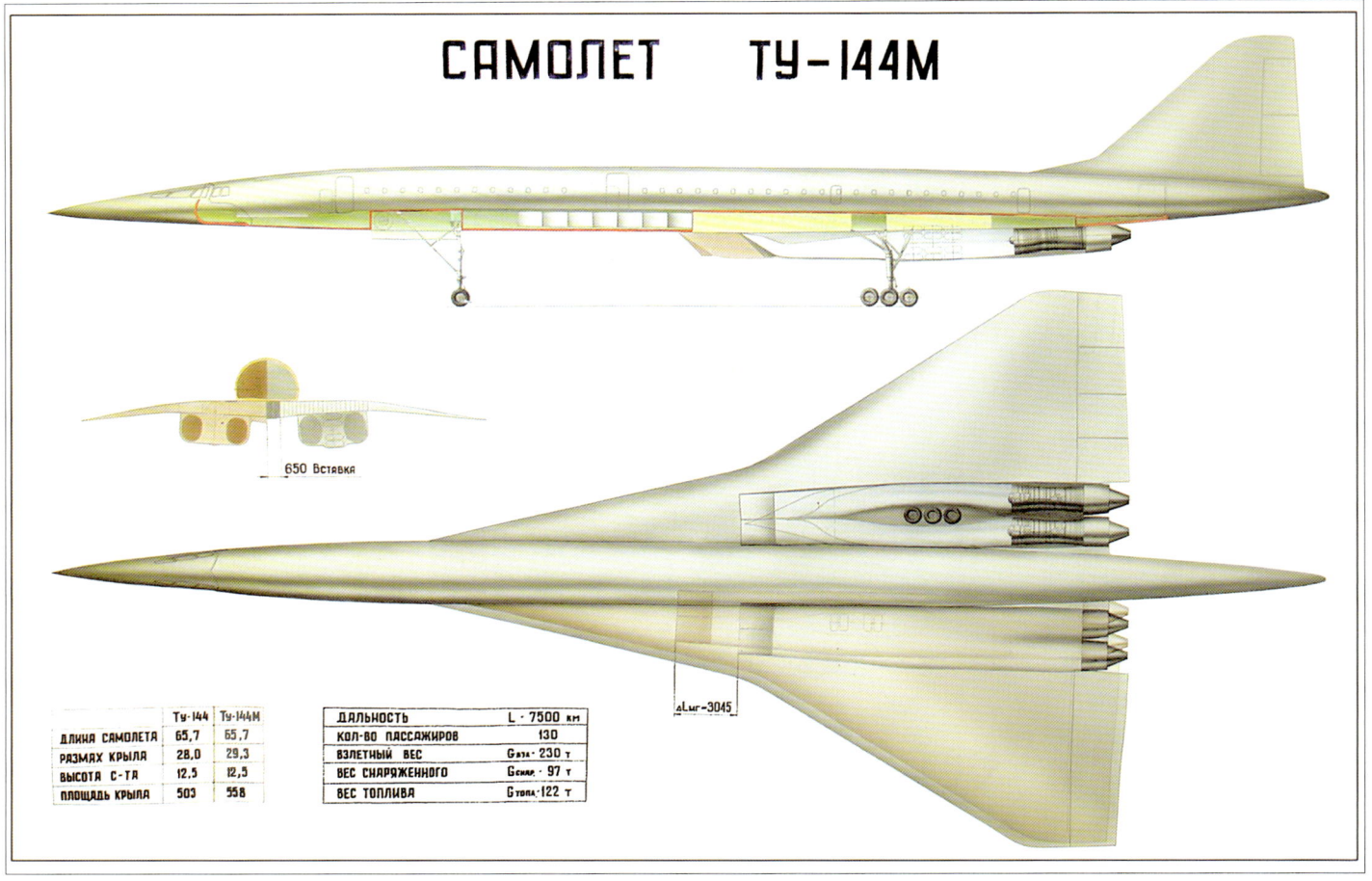

A drawing of the Tu-144M from the project documents showing the increase in wing span and the shorter engine nacelles (the silhouettes of the standard Tu-144 in pale brown are superimposed for comparison).

configuration, and range with a normal payload was extended to 7,000-7,500 km (4,350-4,660 miles).

No further work was done on the Tu-144DA due to the closure of the Tu-144 programme, but the project work was drawn upon during early research on the SST-2 (Tu-244). However, the latter lies outside the scope of this book.

Tu-144M supersonic airliner (project)

In 1981 the Tupolev OKB made yet another attempt to update the Tu-144D, the new version being designated Tu-144M (*modifitseerovannyy* – modified). The most important (albeit not the most obvious) change to the airframe was the new wings of 1.3 m (4 ft 3³/₁₆ in) greater span, which was 29.3 m (96 ft 1³⁵/₆₄ in) versus 28.0 m (91 ft 10²³/₆₄ in) as per project documents. This increase was entirely in the wing centre section; thus, the engine nacelles were moved outward 0.65 m (2 ft 1¹⁹/₃₂ in), increasing the distance between the engine nozzles and the rear fuselage and thereby reducing the thermal load on the latter. The wing sweep remained unchanged both on the LERXes and on the outer wings; thus, the greater span led to a broader chord across the entire span, and wing area was increased from 503 to 558 m² (from 5,414 to 6,006 sq ft) as per project documents. The overall length and the height on ground were identical to those of the Tu-144D – 65.7 m (215 ft 6³⁹/₆₄ in) and 12.5 m (41 ft 0¹/₈ in) respectively. (The length is given as per project documents; some sources give different length, span and wing area figures for the Tu-144D – *Auth*.)

The engine nacelles were not only moved outward – they (and hence the inlet ducts) were shortened by 3.045 m (9 ft 11⁷/₈ in). The main gear units were redesigned to retract aft instead of forward, retaining the 'knee-action' struts. The bogies were now similar to those of the *izdeliye* 044 demonstrator aircraft, featuring 12 wheels in three rows. They still tilted into vertical position (inboard ends up) during retraction but stowed with the wheel axles vertical, not horizontal, involving an even more complex retraction sequence than hitherto; the bogies were narrower than the Tu-144D's and thus were stowed entirely within the nacelles, not encroaching on the wing torsion box. The redesign of the main gear units necessitated relocation of the APU because there was no room for it in the starboard nacelle; unfortunately the available project drawings give no idea of the APU's new location.

According to the project the Tu-144M was to have an operating empty weight of 97,000 kg (213,850 lb), a take-off weight of 230,000 kg (507,060 lb) and a fuel load of 122,000 kg (268,960 lb). The aircraft was to carry 130 passengers over a range of 7,500 km (4,660 miles). The project was not proceeded with.

Chapter 5

The Production Versions in Detail

The following description applies to the production-standard Tu-144/Tu-144D.

Type: Four-engined medium/long-haul supersonic airliner of tailless-delta layout designed for operation on domestic and international services. The aircraft was designed with due regard to international requirements applying to contemporary airliners as regards operational reliability, flight safety and economic efficiency. The Tu-144's aerodynamic layout ensures a lift/drag ratio in excess of 8.0 at a cruising speed of Mach 2.2.

The airframe is of all-metal construction embodying the fail-safe design principle; aluminium alloys are the primary structural material, with titanium in certain hot areas, and flush riveting is used throughout. In common with the *izdeliye* 044 prototype the production-standard *izdeliye0* 004/004D makes large-scale use of panels with integral lengthwise and transverse stiffeners, chemi-

A cut away drawing of the Tu-144 (*izdeliye* 004) from a 1970s aviation magazine. The artist has made a couple of errors, depicting the aircraft with 12-wheel main gear bogies and showing the fuel tanks in the wrong place (leaving no room for the mainwheel wells).

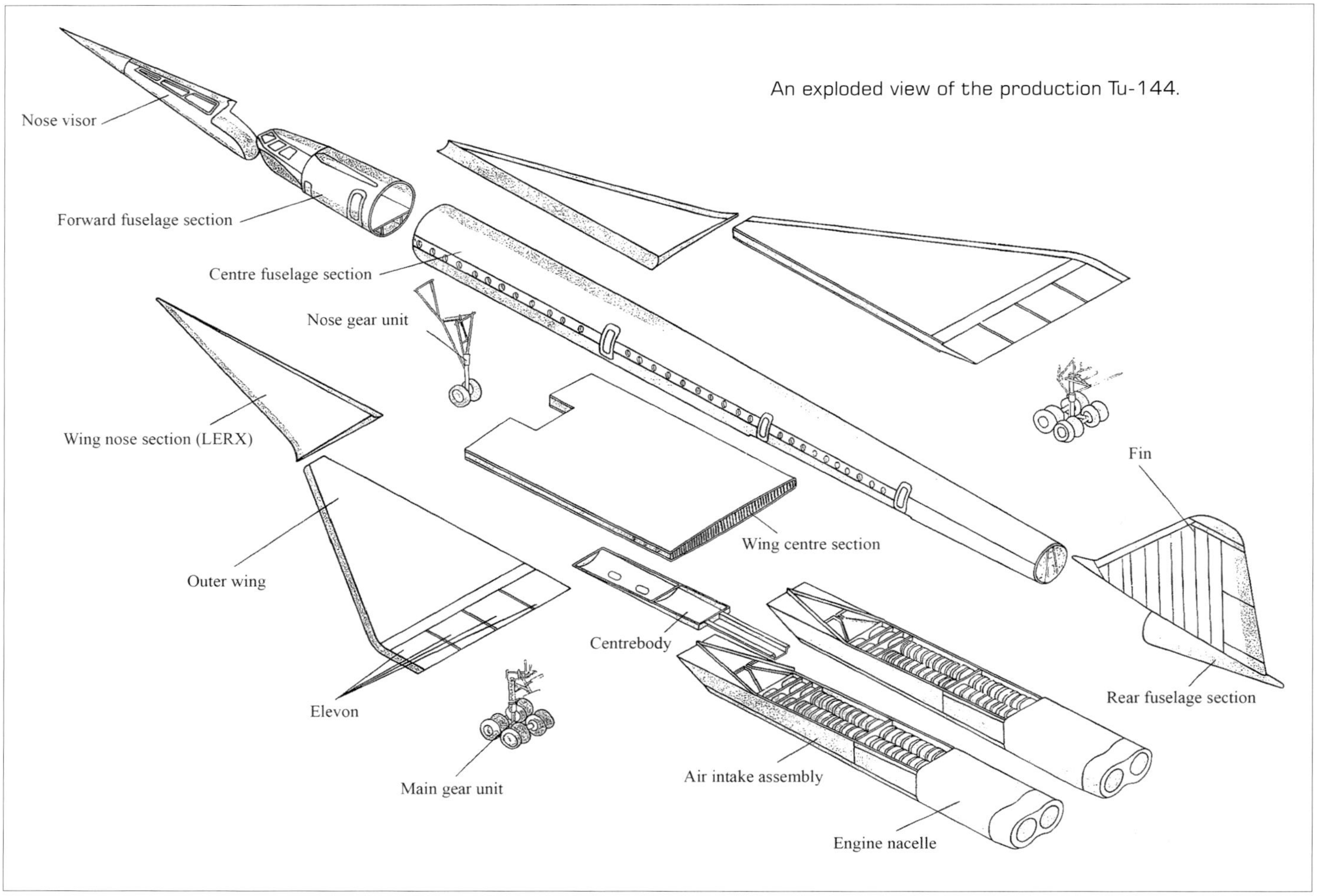

An exploded view of the production Tu-144.

cally milled skin panels and flexible fittings reducing the stress caused by cyclic expansion/contraction due to kinetic heating.

Fuselage: Semi-monocoque riveted stressed-skin structure with a high fineness ratio; the skin is supported by frames and extruded stringers. The fuselage has a basically circular cross-section (except for the area aft of the flight deck where the retractable canard foreplanes are located), with a maximum diameter of 3.3 m (10 ft $9^{59}/_{64}$ in) and a fineness ratio of 19.55, and its contours and dimensions differ considerably from the *izdeliye* 044 prototype's.

Structurally the fuselage is divided into four sections: the movable nose visor (Section F-1), the forward fuselage (Section

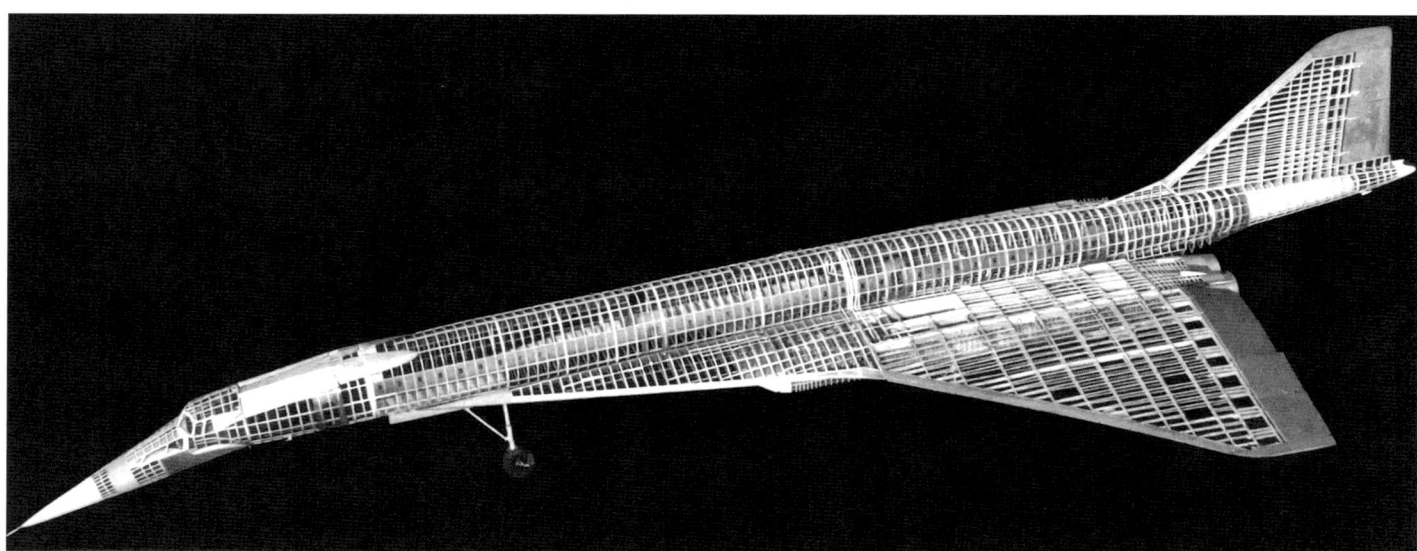

Chapter 5 - The Production Versions in Detail

Top: The nose visor of the production Tu-144 in cruise position. The Plexiglas of the visor windows has become yellow and opaque due to ageing, while the other side windows have remained clear. Note the pitots on and aft of the radome.

Top right: The nose visor in take-off position (lowered 11°). Interestingly, the black anti-glare panel on top has been omitted.

Above left and right: The fully deployed canards, showing the fixed double-slotted LE slats (inboard) and retractable double-slotted flaps. Note the mechanically linked 'dog ear' covers over the canards' pivots.

Right: The deployed canards show their 15° anhedral.

Below left: A model reproducing the internal structure of the production Tu-144's airframe.

Below: The interior layout of the Tu-144 (*izdeliye* 004) in a 98-seat two-class version (F11 + CY18 + CY69).

F-2), the centre fuselage (Section F-3) and the rear fuselage (Section F-4). The unpressurised *nose visor* hinged to the bottom of the forward fuselage's frame 13 incorporates three narrow windows on each side made of E-2 Plexiglas providing a measure of forward view in cruise flight; it terminates in a conical GRP radome tipped with a pitot. The visor is lowered 11° for take-off and 17° for landing. It is actuated by a duplicated electrically-driven screwjack, with hydropneumatic lowering in an emergency; the controls for

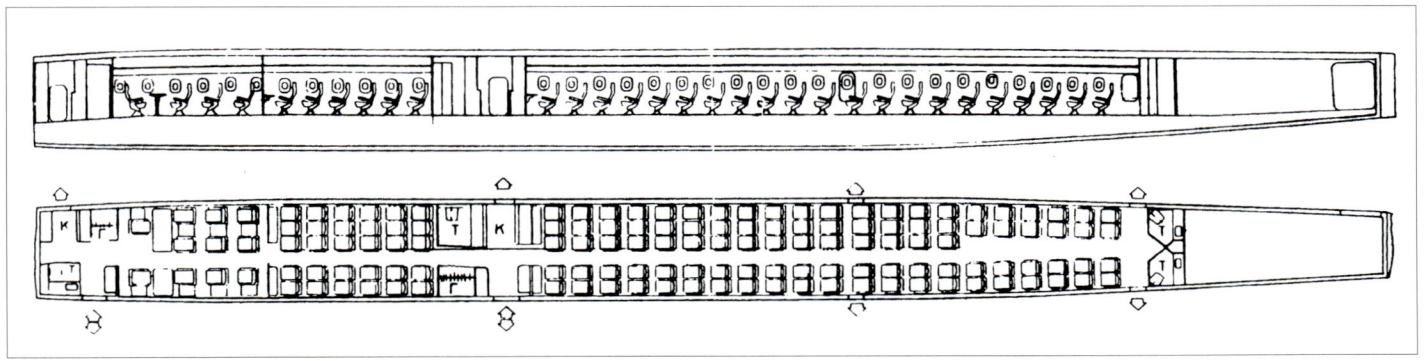

 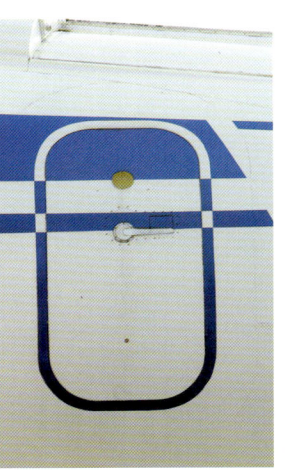 

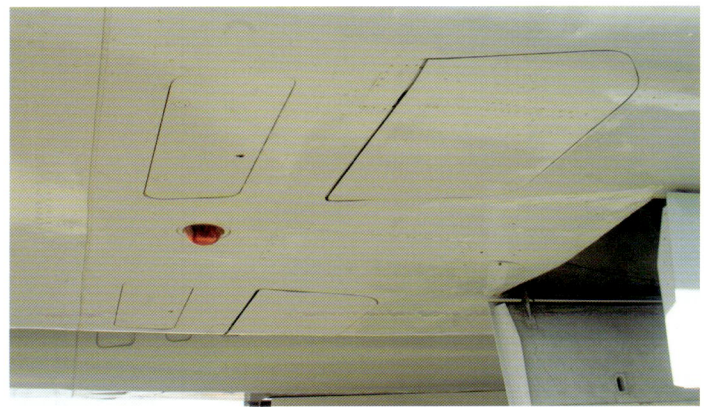 

Top left: The starboard overwing emergency exit amidships. On this aircraft (Tu-144D CCCP-77115) the window is blanked off because the exit mounts a cabin depressurisation valve. The vertically positioned external handle is barely visible ahead of the window.

Top right: The forward service door on the starboard side, with a tiny window to admit some light into the forward galley (again, the Perspex has become yellow with age.

Centre: The tunnel between the Tu-144D's engine nacelles. Note the unpainted titanium skin.

Above: The spill doors (right) and the rearmost ventral blow-in doors of the port nacelle, with the lower anti-collision light between them.

Top: The door of the rear baggage compartment on the starboard side encroaches on the wing/fuselage fairing and is partially skinned in titanium, like the surrounding rear fuselage structure.

Centre: The GRP tailcone is hinged at the top, acting as the cover of the brake parachute container.

Above: The extended tail bumper and its actuator/shock absorber.

The photos on the right show the interior of a Tu-144D. Top row: the forward vestibule/forward galley and forward lavatory; centre row: the second galley amidships and emergency equipment stowage near the second entry door; bottom row: an open overhead baggage bin and the passenger service unit for seats 4C/D/E.

Chapter 5 - The Production Versions in Detail

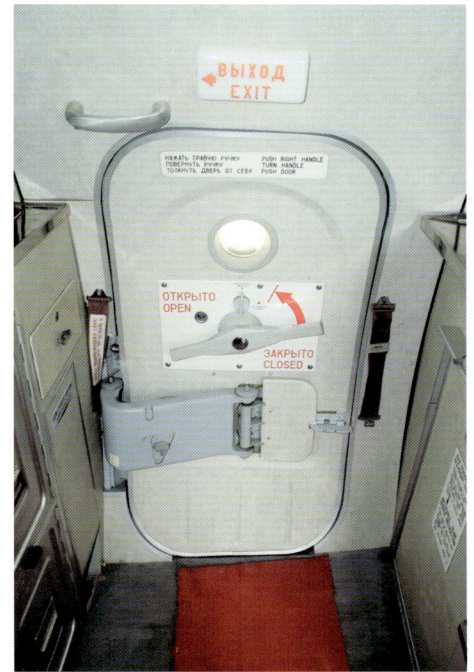

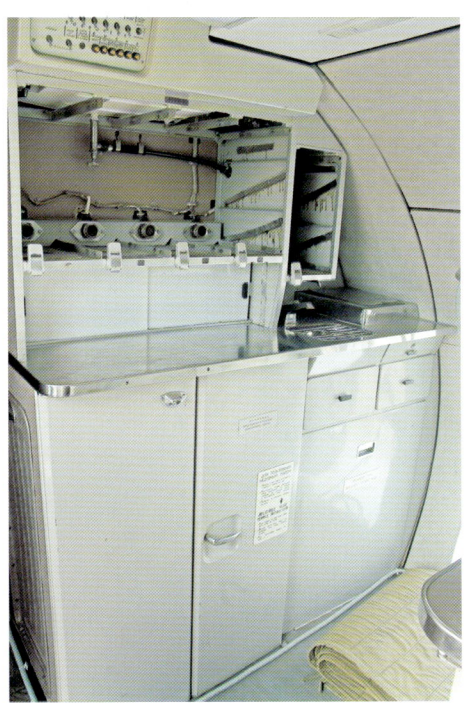
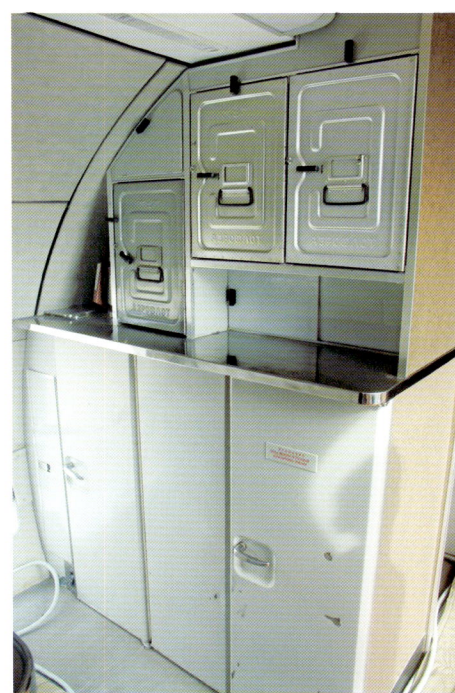
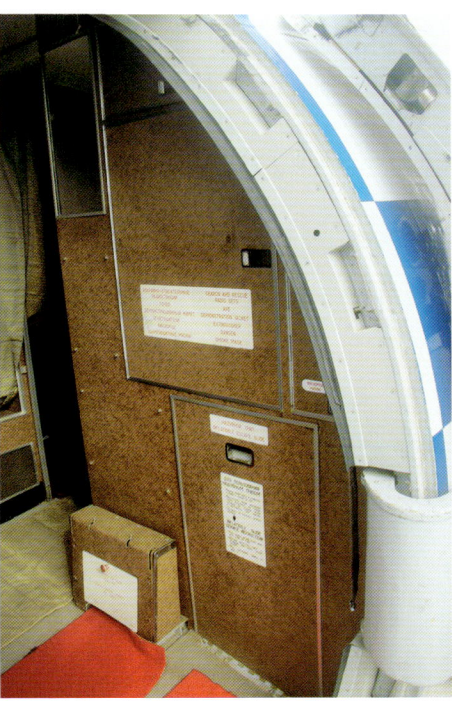

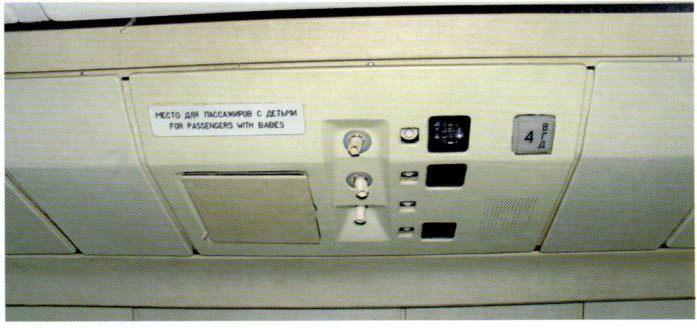

This page, left row, top to bottom: The foremost (first class) cabin of Tu-144 *sans suffixe* CCCP-77106 at the Central Russian Air Force Museum, Monino, after restoration of the interior; the No. 2 and No. 3 cabins of Tu-144 *sans suffixe* CCCP-77110 at the Civil Air Fleet Museum in Ul'yanovsk.

Right-hand row: The No. 3, No. 2 and No. 1 cabins of CCCP-77110.

Opposite page, left: The stark empty rear cabin of Tu-144D CCCP-77115 as it was in August 2007, looking towards the tail; note the seat tracks, with the aisle offset to port, and the emergency depressurisation valves on the inside of both emergency exits.

Opposite page, right: The toilets at the end of the No. 3 cabin of CCCP-77110. They are missing on Tu-144D CCCP-77115; instead, there is a centreline door leading to the rear baggage compartment.

Chapter 5 - The Production Versions in Detail

normal and emergency actuation are located on the central control pedestal and the flight engineer's instrument panel respectively.

The *forward fuselage* (frames 2-19) commences with the forward pressure dome to which the nose visor actuator is attached. It accommodates the three-man flight deck, with the flight engineer sitting aft of the first officer, facing starboard. The flight deck glazing comprises a birdproof triplex glass windscreen of shallow V shape (exposed when the nose visor is lowered) and two side windows on each side, with Plexiglas glazing; the rear pair are aft-sliding direct vision windows. The windshield is provided with wipers. On pre-production examples used in the flight test programme a rectangular escape hatch with external hinges is located on the port side just aft of the flight deck windows; in an emergency the hatch cover opens forward by means of twin hydraulic rams to act as a slipstream deflector, allowing the crew to bail out.

Avionics racks enclosed by easily detachable panels are located aft of the flight deck on both sides. Further aft is the forward vestibule with a rectangular entry door on the port side and a service door opposite. These are of similar design to the doors of *izdeliye* 044, swinging outward on L-shaped arms, but move aft as they open, not forward. A toilet is located on the starboard side, with a wardrobe opposite; aft of these, the front and rear walls of the forward vestibule are occupied by the forward galley, with storage lockers, food heaters and a water boiler. A shallow dorsal fairing with two recesses is located in this area, accommodating the canard foreplanes when these are stowed (see Wings).

The *centre fuselage* (frames 19-110) terminating in the rear pressure dome forms a common pressure cabin together with the forward fuselage; it has a cylindrical shape but curves slightly upward at the rear end to lessen the drag at the wing/fuselage junction. The greater part of Section F-3 is occupied by the passenger cabins, with the centre vestibule in between; the latter features a second pair of entry/service doors, more galley equipment, a second toilet to starboard and wardrobes on both sides. Two rectangular plug-type overwing emergency exits are located halfway down the length of the rear cabin (frames 71-72); behind it is the rear vestibule with two more toilets (Tu-144 *sans suffixe*) and two rectangular plug-type overwing emergency exits or larger doors which open inward and slide aft. The cabins have 34 oval windows with triple glazing made of E-2 Plexiglas on each side.

The nosewheel well is located between frames 20-31. Immediately aft of it is the forward baggage compartment (frames 31-66) with a capacity of 9.7 m³ (342.5 cu ft) located under the cabin floor; it is designed for carrying containerised baggage and accessed via a ventral door between frames 34-36. Further aft is the No.1 avionics/equipment bay (frames 66-70) accessible from inside the cabin via removable panels in the cabin floor. The rear baggage compartment with a capacity of 11.4 m³ (402.5 cu ft) located between frames 96-110 is intended for bulk baggage; its front end is flanked by the two halves of the No.2 avionics/equipment bay (frames 96-98). A rectangular baggage loading door is located on the starboard side immediately aft of the engine nozzles, but the rear baggage compartment is also accessible via a door in the rear vestibule on the Tu-144D.

Along most of its length the centre fuselage is mated to the wing centre section forming the cabins' pressure floor. Again, a large load-bearing subassembly (the so-called centrebody) made up of monolithic milled panels with integral stiffeners encloses the wing/fuselage joint from below. Its forward portion forms part of the integral fuel tank structure, while the unpressurised rear portion houses hydraulic equipment and control system components; the rear wing/fuselage fairings flanking the centrebody accommodate the air conditioning system.

The unpressurised *rear fuselage* (frames 110-128) carries the tail unit. It accommodates an integral fuel tank, a retractable tail bumper and the brake parachute container enclosed by an upward-hinged tailcone. The rear fuselage underside features a full-length wraparound heat shield made of titanium.

Wings: Cantilever low-wing monoplane with low aspect ratio compound-delta wings featuring large LERXes and a cranked leading edge (the kink is in line with fuselage frame 66). Leading-

Top: The port LERX and outer wing, showing the shape of the leading edge; the curvature of the wing trailing edge illustrates the spanwise camber.

Above: A different perspective of the port wing; the downward curvature towards the tip is even more evident in this view.

Below: The rear end of Tu-144D CCCP-77115, showing the titanium heat shield on the rear fuselage and the two-section rudder with port side actuators on the lower half.

Top: The port wingtip of a Tu-144D, showing the faired navigation light; note the elevon actuator fairings on the wing underside.

Above: The outermost portion of the trailing edge is fixed on both the Tu-144D and most Tu-144s *sans suffixe*. The elevons 'bleed' down to maximum deflection after engine shutdown.

Below: Starboard side view of the rear fuselage and tail, showing the actuators of the rudder's upper half.

edge sweep 76° inboard of the kink and 57° outboard, trailing edge sweepback 0°; aspect ratio 1.636 if the LERXes are included or 1.895 disregarding the LERXes; wing taper 10.575 or 7.09 respectively. The wings feature spanwise and chordwise camber. The wing planform minimises the shift of the wings' pressure centre as the aircraft slips through the sound barrier. The shape/camber of the wing centre section is optimised for ensuring good longitudinal trim and maximising the lift/drag ratio in supersonic cruise mode. The wing shape was chosen in such a way as to provide the optimum (required) wing deformation of the wing centre section at Mach 2.2 with due regard to the wing flexure.

The basic delta portion of the wings (less LERXes) utilises the TsAGI P-109S high-speed airfoil with a thickness/chord ratio of 2.4%. Inboard of the leading-edge kink (on the LERXes) the airfoil gradually changes to TsAGI P-53S with a thickness/chord ratio of 2.8% at the roots. Thanks to the low thickness/chord ratio, the sharp leading edge on the outer wings and the relatively blunt leading edge of the LERXes this set of airfoils offers minimum drag in both subsonic and supersonic flight. The rational spanwise distribution of the thickness/chord ratios also accounts for the Tu-144's low wave drag.

The wings are stressed-skin multi-spar structures. Structurally they are built in seven pieces: the nose sections of the LERXes (port and starboard), the forward sections of the LERXes (port and starboard), the centre section (which is the main load-bearing component) and two detachable outer wing panels.

The *nose sections* (attached to the fuselage between frames 23-47) and the *forward sections* (frames 47-66) are joined together to form single airframe subassemblies before they are mated to the fuselage and the wing centre section. The portions between frames 31-66 are 'wet', housing integral tanks separated by a bulkhead at frame 47.

The *centre section* is attached to the fuselage between frames 66-96, forming the pressure floor of the rear cabin. It carries the engine nacelles and houses six fuel tanks, including four service tanks from which the engines are fed. The structure includes eleven spars and 23 ribs (No.1 is the centreline rib).

The detachable *outer wings* (ribs 11-36 on each side) are joined to the centre section by flanges at ribs 11L/11R. Each outer wing section has eleven spars, ribs (mostly girder-type), ten detachable upper skin panels and ten lower skin panels. The outer wings incorporate two integral tanks each. The spar webs and rib webs (on the 'solid' ribs) are corrugated to compensate for the cyclic expansion/contraction. The torsion boxes carry the trailing-edge sections, detachable leading edge sections and tip fairings. To save weight the spars and ribs are manufactured with a variable cross-section, using CNC milling machines.

The trailing edge of the outer wing sections is entirely (or almost entirely) occupied by four-section elevons whose welded structure is made entirely of titanium alloy. Each section is suspended on two hinges and has twin ventral actuator fairings; again, the gaps between the sections widen towards the trailing edge. The outermost portions of the trailing edge are fixed on late-production Tu-144s *sans suffixe* and Tu-144Ds.

The Tu-144's aerodynamic layout ensures good field performance and take-off/landing behaviour. The vortices generated by the LERXes energise the airflow over the wings, giving a 15% increase in lift. At extremely low altitude the wing lift increases by 50% thanks to the ground effect created by the large cambered wings. Lowering the elevons symmetrically 10° in flap mode for take-off and landing provides a further 40% increase in lift but creates a pitch-down force. To neutralise the latter, shoulder-mounted unswept canard foreplanes of relatively small area and high aspect ratio are mounted aft of the flight deck, retracting aft into a special fairing when not in use. The foreplane pivots are located between fuselage frames 6-7 and closed by doors mechanically linked to the foreplanes. When deployed, the canards have 15° anhedral. For maximum efficiency they are equipped with fixed double-slotted leading-edge slats on the inboard portions and two-section hinged double-slotted trailing-edge flaps. The foreplanes are actuated by an IUS-3PTV electric drive mechanism via reduction gear and VP-7 screwjacks (*vintovoy podyomnik*), the flaps deploying automatically by means of mechanical linkages as the canards swing into position; during retraction the flaps' rear segments fold downward through nearly 180° so that their trailing edges face outward when retracted.

Tail unit: Vertical tail only, comprising a large fin and an inset rudder. The fin is a one-piece subassembly built integrally with the rear fuselage and has a trapezoidal planform with a kinked leading edge and a large root fillet terminating ahead of the wing trailing edge. Leading-edge sweep 50°, no trailing-edge sweepback; aspect ratio 0.9, taper 3.88 (less the fin fillet in both cases. The vertical tail utilises a TsAGI P-109S symmetrical airfoil; the thickness/chord ratio is 3.5% at the root and 3% at the tip.

The fin structure comprises a torsion box with 12 spars (Nos. 4-12 are integrated into the rear fuselage structure), regular and reinforced ribs, a leading-edge false spar, milled and extruded skin panels, leading-edge and tip fairings (the tip fairing houses a radio antenna), a trailing-edge section and the root fillet. The fin houses an integral fuel tank used for longitudinal trim in supersonic cruise. The two-section rudder is similar to the elevons, being made of titanium alloy; the twin actuator fairings are located to port on the lower half and to starboard on the upper half.

Landing gear: Hydraulically retractable tricycle type; all three units retract forward. All units have two-chamber oleo-pneumatic shock absorbers and scissor links.

The semi-levered-suspension nose unit attached to fuselage frame 31 has an inverted-A shaped strut carrying the shock absorber and a forward-mounted breaker strut with a locking mechanism. It is fitted with twin 960 x 300 mm (37.79 x 11.81 in) non-braking wheels rotating together with the axle and a three-piece mud/snow/slush guard with lateral and rear sections. The nose unit features an aft-mounted steering mechanism/shimmy damper and is remote-controlled via the rudder pedals.

The main units are located underneath the engine nacelles, retracting into narrow wheel wells located between the inlet ducts of each pair of engines. Each unit has a 'knee-action' oleo strut with an N-shaped upper segment, an aft-mounted retraction strut and a wide-track eight-wheel bogie fitted with 950 x 400 mm (37.40 x 15.74 in) wheels in two rows of four, with tubeless tyres.

The mainwheels are equipped with multi-disc brakes and built-in electric fans that keep the brakes from overheating. Auto-brake and anti-skid units are provided; the anti-skid unit monitors each wheel separately and its tacho-generators are integrated with the brake cooling fans.

The main gear bogies are attached to the oleo struts via universal joints allowing them to rock both fore-and-aft and sideways. During retraction they are tilted through 90° by separate actuation rams/rocking dampers on the inboard side so that the axles are disposed vertically (with the inboard ends uppermost) before the struts swing forward; thus, the wheels remain vertical but at 90° to the direction of flight.

The nosewheel well is closed by two pairs of doors. Each main unit has two large main doors and a small rear segment linked to the oleo strut. All doors remain open when the gear is down.

A retractable tail bumper is built into the rear fuselage to protect it in the event of overrotation or a tailstrike. For emergencies or wet/icy runway operations the Tu-144 is equipped with twin brake parachutes housed in the tailcone.

Powerplant: The Tu-144 *sans suffixe* is powered by four Kuznetsov NK-144A afterburning turbofans – an uprated version of the NK-144 (see Chapter 3) delivering 20,000 kgp (49,020 lbst) in full afterburner for take-off, 5,000 kgp (11,020 lbst) in minimum-afterburner cruise mode at 18,000 m (59,055 ft) and 2,350 km/h (1,460 mph) and 3,000 kgp (6,610 lbst) in non-afterburning cruise mode at 11,000 m (36,090 ft) and 1,000 km/h (621 mph).

Bypass ratio 0.6; overall EPR at sea level 14.75; mass flow at take-off power 236 kg/sec (520 lb/sec). Turbine temperature 1,390°K. SFC 1.65 kg/kgp·hr at take-off, 1.81 kg/kgp·hr in minimum-afterburner cruise and 0.92 kg/kgp·hr in non-afterburning cruise. The dimensions are identical to those of the NK-144 *sans suffixe*.

Engine operation is monitored by means of ITE-2T tachometers, EMI-3FTIS multi-function engine indicators, UV-33 throttle lever position indicators, UP-21 nozzle position indicators, the IA-7A-950 exhaust gas temperature measurement kit with sensors located ahead of the LP turbine, and the IV-144 vibration monitoring kit (*izmeritel' vibrahtsiï*). The engines have a surge prevention system and an SG-9 afterburner control/indication system.

The Tu-144D is powered by four Kolesov RD36-51A axial-flow non-afterburning turbojets rated at 20,000 kgp for take-off, 5,000 kgp in maximum cruise mode and 3,000 kgp in minimum cruise mode at the same speeds and altitudes.

The RD36-51A is a single-shaft turbojet with a fixed-area air intake featuring adjustable inlet guide vanes, a 14-stage compressor featuring a supersonic first stage and anti-vibration snubbers on the first three stages, plus adjustable stator vanes on stages 1-5 and 9-13, an annular combustion chamber with 16 burners, a three-stage turbine featuring air-cooled blades on the first stage and a variable nozzle. Nozzle area is adjusted by a cropped conical centrebody which translates in accordance with the throttle setting by means of a hydraulic ram. The centrebody is perforated and compressed air is forced into the exhaust jet through the perforations for noise attenuation purposes.

Construction is mostly of titanium. The air intake assembly has a fixed parabolic spinner and seven angled struts with hot-air de-icing. To minimise the space required for the engine the accessory gearbox is installed separately (on the airframe) and driven by an extension shaft via an intermediate gearbox off the engine shaft or the air turbine starter. The latter is powered by compressed air separately from the engine.

EPR at sea level 15.8. Turbine temperature 1,355°K. SFC 0.882 kg/kgp·hr at take-off power, 1.23 kg/kgp·hr at maximum cruise rating and 0.94 kg/kgp·hr at minimum cruise rating. Length overall 5.976 m (19 ft 7^{9}⁄$_{32}$ in). Inlet diameter 1.486 m (4 ft 10½ in). Dry weight 3,900 kg (8,600 lb).

The engine is started, using compressed air from the APU, ground supply or cross-feed from the other engines. Engine starting is automatic, once the sequence has been initiated.

On both versions the engines are housed in pairs in nacelles located under the wing centre section close to the fuselage. Each pair of engines breathes through two-dimensional supersonic air intakes divided into individual inlet ducts by a vertical splitter and featuring three-segment horizontal airflow control ramps. Each engine's air intake is 1.345 m (4 ft 4^{61}⁄$_{64}$ in) wide and 1.003 m (3 ft 3^{31}⁄$_{64}$ in) high. The inlet ducts are 14.5 m (47 ft 6^{55}⁄$_{64}$ in) long and are built in three sections, which are attached to the wing structure by steel brackets and rods; the telescopic joints of the duct sections are sealed by rubber tubes. The rectangular-section forward section of the duct is 5.4 m (17 ft 8^{19}⁄$_{32}$ in) long and is made of titanium alloy; the skin panels are reinforced by corrugated panels on the reverse side, while the movable airflow control ramp segments have skins reinforced by longitudinal and transverse beams. The centre section is made of heat-resistant aluminium alloys; it features four spring-loaded auxiliary blow-in doors (thee lateral and one ventral) plus a hydraulically powered spill door for each engine, each door having a rubber perimeter seal. The skins are attached to the duct frames, which are common for each pair of ducts, mostly by rivets via rubber grommets (press riveting is used to preclude the risk of rivet heads becoming detached and ingested by the engines); captive screws are used in the area of the blow-in and spill doors. The rear section is likewise made of heat-resistant aluminium alloys; the skin is reinforced by riveted transverse channel-section pro-

---

Opposite page, top row: The inboard (left) and outboard sides of the starboard main landing gear unit, showing the torque link on the outside and the rocking damper/tilting actuator on the inside. Note the apertures for the integral brake cooling fans in the wheel hubs, which are arranged in the shape of a pentastar.

Centre row, left to right: Front view of the nose gear unit, showing the four landing lights (upper/lower pairs) and the pair of taxi lights between them; a look into the nosewheel well, showing ta bulkhead with a cutout for the strut and two recesses for the nosewheels; and a side view of the nose gear unit, showing the breaker strut/downlock, the aft-mounted shimmy damper/steering mechanism and the mudguard.

Bottom row: The double-hinged main gear strut design (left) and a front view of the starboard bogie showing the wheel brake housings.

Chapter 5 - The Production Versions in Detail

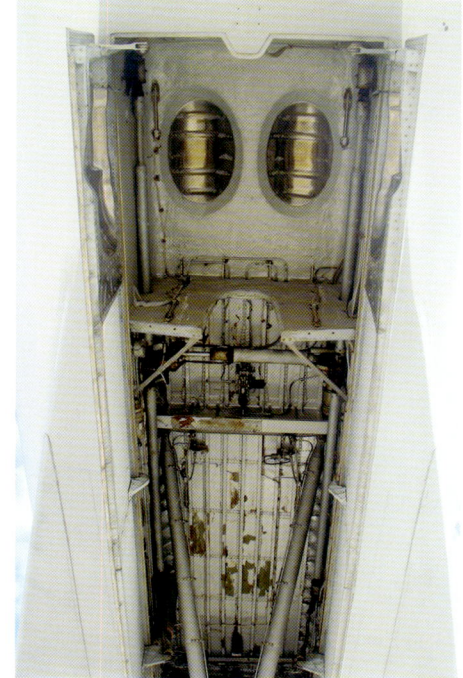

189

Left: The Kolesov RD36-51A turbojet, showing the inlet with seven fixed angled struts and variable inlet guide vanes immediately downstream of them, as well as the accessory gearbox driven via an extension shaft.

Below left: The air intakes of a rather neglected Tu-144, showing the front segments of the airflow control ramps (and an intake blank or two thrown in). Note the fully open spill doors just ahead of the mainwheel wells.

Below: This view shows how the intake splitters protrude beyond the lower and lateral intake lips. Note the boundary layer spill gap and the lateral blow-in doors of the No. 3 engine.

Bottom left: The distinctive nozzles of the RD36-51A engines of a Tu-144D, with the centrebodies in the fully forward position.

files. The duct skin and the nacelle skin are not attached to each other, being attached to the wing structure independently.

To prevent boundary layer ingestion the intakes are set apart from the wing undersurface so that their upper lips act as a boundary layer splitter plates, with two consecutive V-shaped fairings spilling the boundary layer; additionally, the front segments of the airflow control ramps are perforated for boundary layer suction. The first fairing spills the boundary layer separated by the intake's upper lip, the second fairing spills the air sucked through the perforated ramp segment. The inlet ducts curve around the mainwheel well located between them ahead of the engines and have an oval section in this area (with the larger axis vertical); further downstream the ducts' cross-section changes to circular at the compressor face. The engine bays are separated from each other by titanium firewalls and are air-cooled.

Chapter 5 - The Production Versions in Detail

The air intake assembly for each pair of engines is manufactured as a single unit made of titanium and heat-resistant aluminium alloys; the air intake leading edge incorporates a de-icer. Each inlet duct features four spring-loaded auxiliary blow-in doors (three lateral ones and one ventral) used at low speeds and a single spill door which opens in cruise flight to spill excess air. The airflow control ramps and the spill door are controlled by an automatic air intake control system. This comprises an SU39-4 ramp and spill door automatic control system, an SIOD-3 pressure ratio measurement system (*sistema izmereniya otnosheniya davleniya*), a system feeding inputs from the pitots and static ports to the pressure sensors of the SU39-4 and SIOD-3, and the hydraulic actuators.

A Stoopino Machinery Design Bureau TA-6F APU is installed in the starboard engine nacelle aft of the mainwheel well for self-contained engine starting, ground AC/DC power supply and air conditioning. The air intake is located ventrally and the exhaust on the wing upper surface; both are closed by rectangular doors. The APU can be used as an emergency source of electric power and compressed air (notably for the turbine-driven hydraulic pumps) in flight at up to 3,000 m (9,840 ft). The APU control panel is on the flight engineer's left-hand control console.

Control system: The combined electrohydraulic control system provides for the following control modes:
• manual control throughout the flight;
• automatic climbout from the point of origin, flight along the designated route, descent and circuit flight at the destination airfield, using inputs from the NK-144 navigation suite;
• landing approach and go-around in automatic or flight director mode in ICAO Cat II weather minima (decision altitude 30 m/100 ft, horizontal visibility 400 m/1,300 ft);
• automatic stabilisation of barometric altitude, pitch, heading, indicated airspeed, Mach number and total temperature;
• alteration of pitch, heading, indicated airspeed and Mach number and execution of co-ordinated turns;
• automatic stabilisation and control of the aircraft in turbulence;
• presentation of flight and navigation data.

The control system includes a hydromechanical control system for the elevons and rudder, the ABSU-144 automatic flight control system and the canard foreplane control system. The hydromechanical control system with irreversible hydraulic actuators in all three control channels deflects the elevons and rudder, using control inputs from the pilots, the AFCS and the SAB-4 automatic longitudinal trim system (*sistema avtomaticheskoy balansirovki*). It incorporates an artificial-feel feature providing adequate control column and pedal forces, regardless of the aerodynamic loads acting on the control surfaces. The actuators are powered by four separate hydraulic systems for maximum reliability and are connected to the control columns and rudder pedals by conventional mechanical linkages (push-pull rods and bellcranks) passing under the floor.

Pitch and roll control is provided by elevons the outer wings divided into four sections for greater reliability and ease of handling at different speeds. Directional control is provided by a two-section rudder.

As already mentioned, the canard foreplanes are actuated by an electromechanical drive; the control handle is located on the central control pedestal.

The ABSU-144 is an integrated automatic flight control system comprising the SUU-144 stability and control system, the SAU-144 automatic control system, the STU-75 approach/landing system, the AT-6 autothrottle and the SVK-144 built-in test equipment. Working in concert with other systems and equipment, the ABSU-144 enhances stability and handling in manual control mode, enables automatic control as directed by the NK-144 navigation suite, landing approach and go-around in automatic or flight director mode and automatic or manual longitudinal trim. It also automatically stabilises the principal flight parameters and allows them to be altered, using the AFCS control panel. Flight and navigation data are displayed on the PKP-72-2 flight director (*peelotazhno-komahndnyy pribor*), the PNP-72-5M artificial horizon (*plahnovyy navigatsionnyy pribor*) and the US-I airspeed indicator (*ookazahtel' skorosti*).

Fuel system: The wings, fuselage and fin house a total of 14 integral fuel tanks (seven main tanks, four service tanks and three trim tanks). The total fuel load is 98,000 kg (216,050 lb). In addition to its primary purpose, the fuel system maintains the required CG position throughout the flight and cools various systems components. The triangular No.1 trim tank and trapezoidal No.2 trim tank (each divided into port and starboard halves) are located in the LERXes between fuselage frames 31-47; the No.3 main tank contained by frames 47-66 is made up of three sections located in the LERXes and the centre fuselage. Aft of it is the No.6 main tank of almost square shape flanked by two pairs of L-shaped service tanks – Nos. 2 and 1 (in that order) outboard of the port mainwheel well and Nos. 3 and 4 outboard of the starboard mainwheel well; the numbers of the service tanks match the engines they cater for. Further aft is the rectangular No.7 main tank extending all the way to the centre section/outer wing joints. The outer wing torsion boxes house the Nos. 4L/4R trapezoidal main tanks, with the almost rectangular Nos. 5L/5R main tanks (stopping short of the wingtips) aft of these. The No.8 trim tank in the rear fuselage has a complex shape resembling a fragment of a submarine – a conical main portion with a concave front end to match the rear pressure dome and an angular 'superstructure' fitting inside the fin torsion box.

Even though each engine has its own service tank and associated group of main tanks, a cross-feed system enables each engine to draw fuel from any service tank. Each tank features three transfer pumps (two electric pumps and one jet pump). The refuelling, fuel transfer and fuel usage sequence is observed automatically; manual control is also possible. The fuel flow and the fuel status for each tank are monitored by means of RT-31 flow meters (*raskhodomer toplivnyy*) and the SUIT1-3 fuel management/metering system (*sistema oopravleniya i indikahtsiï topliva*). The latter, together with the SU12-2 fuel status indicator, also serves for controlling the refuelling, fuel transfer and fuel usage sequence and calculating the aircraft's CG position.

The rivet joints in the fuel tanks are sealed with 51G2 heat-resistant fluoride rubber sealant during assembly, whereupon the insides of the tanks are sprayed with a thin coat of 51G1 sealant

(some sources state 51G22R and 51G9R respectively). The lower skin panels forming the bottoms of the tanks are additionally protected against moisture by coats of EP-0103 primer and F-5 enamel. The fuel tanks are pressurised via the vent system connected to the cabin's dynamic cooling system. Fuel jettison valves are provided in each service tank.

The Tu-144 has two standard pressure refuelling connectors in each mainwheel well. Filling a full fuel load takes no more than 20 minutes. Nitrogenated fuel is used; additionally, a supply of gaseous nitrogen is stored in 14 spherical 10-litre (2.2 Imp gal) bottles charged to 150 kg/cm² (2,133 psi) for pressurising the fuel tanks during descent from cruise altitude to 10,000 m (32,810 ft) because the dissolved nitrogen does not emanate too readily in these conditions.

Hydraulics: Four separate hydraulic systems, each with its own reservoir, for maximum reliability. Hydraulic power is provided by eight NP-103 variable-delivery plunger-type pumps (two on each engine), each system including two pumps driven by different engines, and by two TNU back-up pumps driven by air turbines using APU bleed air (*toorbonasosnaya oostanovka*). All systems have a nominal pressure of 210 kg/cm² (3,000 psi).

The No.1 system (powered by pumps driven by the Nos. 1 and 2 engines) operates the wheel brakes, control surface actuators and the back-up supply of the port engines' intake ramp actuators. The No.2 system (powered by the other pumps driven by the same two engines) operates the control surface actuators, the primary supply of the port engines' intake ramp actuators, the landing gear retraction rams, the longitudinal trim system's fuel transfer pumps and the wheel brakes. The No.3 system (powered by pumps driven by the Nos. 3 and 4 engines) operates the control surface actuators, the primary supply of the starboard engines' intake ramp actuators, the nosewheel steering mechanism and the longitudinal trim system's fuel transfer pumps. Finally, the No.4 system (powered by the other pumps driven by the same two engines) operates the control surface actuators and the back-up supply of the starboard engines' intake ramp actuators. The two TNU turbine pump units cater for the Nos. 2 and 4 hydraulic systems if all four engines fail.

Electrics: Three electric systems The primary system uses 200 V/400 Hz and 115 V/400 Hz three-phase stable-frequency AC supplied by four 60-kVA brushless generators, one for each engine, driven via hydromechanical CSDs. The primary system is split into port and starboard halves powered by Nos. 1/2 and Nos. 3/4 generators respec-

Chapter 5 - The Production Versions in Detail

Left: The flight deck of a very early-production Tu-144 *sans suffixe*. The large keypads mounted on the control wheels were a trademark feature of the type. Note that all four throttle levers on the central control pedestal are of different length.

Below left: The same flight deck seen from a point farther aft to include the flight engineer's workstation featuring a second bank of throttles.

Right: The very similar flight deck of Tu-144 CCCP-77106 at Monino shows subtle differences in the location of the instruments. The rear portion of the overhead panel looks a bit bare. Note the lurid turquoise colour of the panels typical of Soviet aircraft (it was supposed to reduce crew fatigue), the rubber-bladed cooling fans and the closed window blind on the captain's side. One control panel on the first officer's side console is missing.

Right: Here, for comparison, is the flight deck of Tu-144 *sans suffixe* CCCP-77110 featuring considerably altered instrument panels. The radar display is relocated, there are a lot more circuit breakers and what-not on the overhead panel; even the instrument panel shroud is shaped differently, featuring two strings of warning lights instead of the centrally located TS-4 master warning panel.

tively; each generator works independently and the pairs of generators may work in parallel. The generators are provided with appropriate voltage regulators and overload protection devices which disable a malfunctioning generator to prevent damage to the system. The APU features a 40-kVA AC generator providing back-up power for the primary system.

Any two engine-driven generators provide enough power to cater for all of the aircraft's equipment, except for the cabin lighting and galley equipment. For overload protection the primary electric system circuitry incorporates quick-action fuses.

Secondary 36 V/400 Hz three-phase AC is provided by two step-down transformers (main and stand-by), with a 500-VA AC converter fed by the DC batteries as a back-up. 27 V DC power is supplied by four 6-kW rectifiers, a 12-kW DC starter/generator driven by the APU; back-up power is provided by lead-acid batteries. A ShRAP-500K DC ground power receptacle (*shtekernyy raz'yom aerodromnovo pitahniya*) and a ShRAP-400-3F AC ground power receptacle are on the underside of the starboard engine nacelle.

Exterior lighting equipment includes navigation lights at the wingtips and above the tailcone, four landing lights and two taxi

The flight deck of CCCP-77110 seen from the first officer's seat. The transparent box aft of the throttles was added after the aircraft became a museum exhibit.

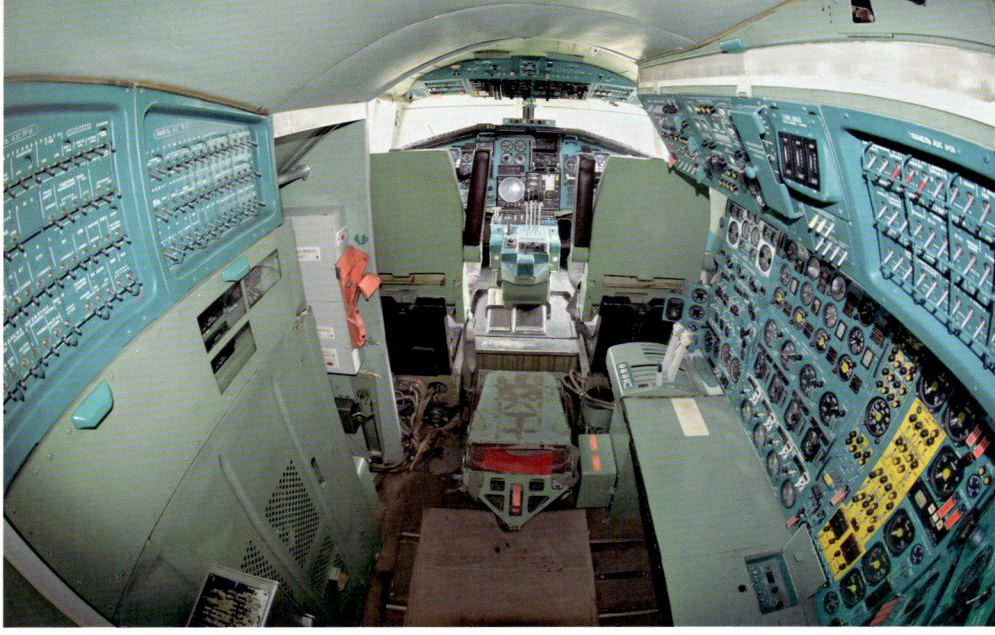

The flight engineer's workstation of CCCP-77110, with lots of circuit breakers on both sides of the passage. The flight engineer's seat is missing.

lights on the nose gear strut and two red anti-collision strobe lights on the upper centre fuselage (ahead of the emergency exits) and under the port engine nacelle.

Oxygen system: The Tu-144 has a permanently installed oxygen system using high-pressure gaseous oxygen for the flight crew (used for fighting fatigue or in the event of decompression) and a stationary oxygen system using low-pressure gaseous oxygen and featuring KP-67 breathing apparatus for the cabin crew. Portable breathing apparatus is provided for the passengers. Additionally, during the flight test phase the crew wore VKK-6 pressure suits and GSh-6 pressure helmets allowing them to bail out safely at high altitude.

Pneumatic system: The pneumatic (nitrogen) system is an ancillary system of the powerplant, controlling the fuel jettison valves and the engine bay cooling control flaps; it also pressurises the fuel tanks. The charging connectors also serve the nitrogen bottles used for emergency lowering of the nose visor, hydraulic system pressurisation and brake parachute deployment/release.

Air conditioning and pressurisation system: The forward and centre fuselage form a single pressure cabin pressurised and ventilated by engine bleed air. The air conditioning system ensures comfortable conditions for the crew and passengers in all flight modes and on the ground. It is adjusted by the flight engineer to maintain the cabin temperature anywhere between 20° and 30°C

(68-86°F). The ACS is split into independent port and starboard halves, each with its own cooling turbine; they draw air from the port and starboard pairs of engines respectively. On the ground, air for the ACS is supplied by the APU or a mobile air handling unit plugged into a ventral connector. The ACS components are housed in the wing/fuselage fairing.

Cabin ventilation is performed by a decentralised air ejection system mixing the cabin air with fresh air. The air ejected from the cabin serves for cooling various systems and equipment components.

In addition to the usual heat- and soundproofing mats, the Tu-144 utilises a dynamic heat insulation system used during supersonic flight. Air is forced between the cabin wall lining and the fuselage structure, protecting the cabin against the kinetic heating at high Mach numbers. Supersonic flight can be continued if one of the cooling turbines fails.

The pressurisation system automatically maintains the prescribed pressure depending on the flight altitude. The maximum pressure differential in cruise flight is 0.72 kg/cm² (10.28 psi). At cruise altitude the cabin pressure equals 2,400 m (7,870 ft) above sea level.

De-icing system: Electric (AC) de-icing on the engine air intake leading edges, pitot heads, static ports and flight deck windshield. The air intake de-icers have a cyclic operating algorithm and a power consumption of some 30 kVA. The integral windshield de-icers consume another 20 kVA; the heated panes are provided with a temperature regulator to prevent cracking. The de-icers are activated by the flight engineer. Additionally, the windshield is equipped with wipers which can be operated at speeds up to 500 km/h (310 mph). No de-icers on the wing and fin leading edges.

Fire suppression system: Nine 8-litre (1.76 Imp gal) UBSh-8-1 fire extinguisher bottles (*oonifitseerovannyy ballon sharovoy* – standardised spherical [fire extinguisher] bottle) charged with $114V_2$ grade CFC are fitted for fighting fires in the engine nacelles and in the APU bay. A separate system featuring three 1-litre (0.22 Imp gal) UBSh-1-1 bottles fights fires inside the engines proper. Both systems have a three-stage operating algorithm. The first shot is triggered automatically by flame sensors, the second and third shots are fired manually at the discretion of the crew and activated by the flight engineer. Impact sensors are provided to trigger all nine UBSh-8-1 fire extinguishers automatically in a wheels-up landing, pre-empting a possible fire. Additionally, portable fire extinguishers are provided in the cabin and flight deck.

An SSP-2A fire warning system (*sistema signalizahtsii pozhara*) with DS-1 flame sensors provides audio and visual warnings of fires in the engine nacelles and in the APU bay. The engines feature a separate SSP-11 fire warning system.

The design embodies features intended to lessen the risk of a fire or to stop the propagation of the fire, should it break out. The engine nacelles incorporate firewalls and heat shields; hydraulic and fuel lines and crucial control system components located in 'hot' areas are made of heat-resistant steel. Non-flammable or low-combustible materials are used for the cabin structures (such as partitions or baggage bins), trim and fittings.

Avionics and equipment: The Tu-144 is fully equipped for poor-weather day/night operation in all regions of the world, including automatic flight along pre-programmed routes and landing in ICAO Cat II weather minima.

a) navigation and piloting equipment: The Tu-144 has an NK-144 navigation suite enabling domestic and international flights in any geographical conditions, including flights over large stretches of water. The suite is automatic, obviating the need for a navigator. Together with the AFCS the NK-144 enables the aircraft to follow a pre-programmed route; to this end, airway layouts and the coordinates of waypoints, airfields and radio beacons are entered into the navigation computer. The system automatically calculates the aircraft's position, using inputs from autonomous navigation equipment – the Roomb-II (Compass Point) inertial navigation system and DISS-7 Doppler speed/drift sensor system (***dop**lerovskiy **iz**meritel' **s**korosti **i s**nosa*) – and makes course corrections, using the RSBN-8S short-range radio navigation system (***rah**diotekh**nich**eskaya sis**tem**a **bli**zhney na**vigah**tsiï – SHORAN), the Koors-MP2 (Heading) compass system and the SDK-67 distance measuring equipment (DME). The crew can enter the aircraft's coordinates and wind parameters manually (such as making corrections for an unexpected headwind). All navigation parameters are displayed by the onboard instrumentation.

The NK-144 comprises the following components:
• a TsVM10-TS-144 digital computer (*tsifrovaya vychislitel'naya mashina*);
• a VPNK-154 flight/navigation processor (*vychislitel' pilotazhno-navigatsionnovo kompleksa*);
• a Roomb-II INS;
• a DISS-7 Doppler speed/drift sensor system complete with a V-144V processor and an I-144 display;
• a duplicated SVS-P-72-3-1 air data system with an altitude comparator module;
• a duplicated RSBN-8S SHORAN;
• a duplicated Koors-MP2 compass system;
• an SDK-67 DME kit;
• a K12 gyro;
• a PINO-12 navigation moving-map display (*proyektsionnyy indi**kah**tor navigatsionnoy ob**sta**novki* – 'navigation situation projection display');
• a UUT-144 pitch angle indicator (*ookazahtel' oogla tangazha*);
• an IVR climb/descent indicator (*indikahtor vertikahl'nykh rezheemov* – 'vertical modes indicator');
• an ARK-15 automatic direction finder (*avtomaticheskiy rahdiokompas*);
• control panels.

The NK-144 suite is linked to the ABSU-144 AFCS, the SOM-64 and SOM-70 ATC transponders (*samolyotnyy otvetchik mezhdunarodnyy* – international [traffic] airborne responder), the SUIT1-3 fuel management system and the VK-90 correction switch (*vyklyuchatel' korrektsii*).

Additionally, the Tu-144 is fitted with the following autonomous navigation equipment and flight instrumentation: an

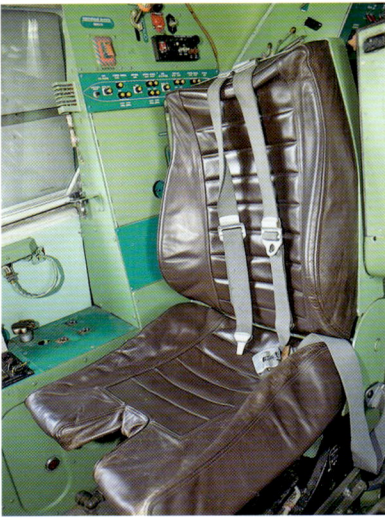

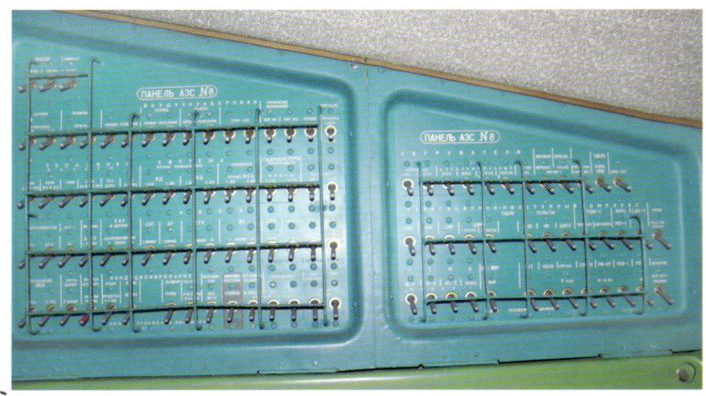

Left: The flight deck of CCCP-77107 (the first Tu-144 *sans suffixe* with the new instrument panel) at the Kazan' Aviation Institute. The box on top of the instrument panel is smaller than on CCCP-77110, with room for only two dials.

Above: The first officer's seat of CCCP-77110. The oblong panel beside it shows if all doors and hatches are closed and secured.

Left: The flight deck of Tu-144D CCCP-77115 as seen in 2007.

Below left: The overhead panel of CCCP-77115 with communications radio controls and other switches.

Below: The port circuit breaker panel at the flight engineer's station of CCCP-77115 catering for the intakes, ACS, fuel system, avionics and so on.

Opposite page: More views from the flight deck of CCCP-77115.

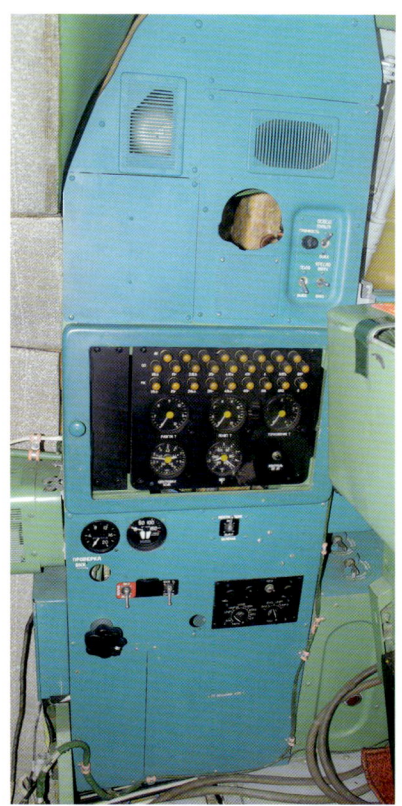

AGR-72 artificial horizon with a VK-90 correction switch, an AUASP-21KR automatic AOA/speed/G load limiter (*avtomaht oogla atahki, skorosti i peregroozki*), a VKR-S dangerous flight mode computer (*vychislitel' kriticheskikh rezheemov*), VAR-30 and VAR-75 vertical speed indicators (the latter is used during emergency descent only; VAR = *variometr* – VSI), VT-25 and VTF-8000 altimeters (the latter calibrated in feet), a duplicated RV-5 radio altimeter (*rahdiovysotomer*), US-1600 and UNSM-I airspeed indicators, a PZVE flight level setting panel (*panel' zadahtchika vysoty elektricheskaya*) and a TS-4 master warning/caution light panel (*tablo signalizahtsiï*). These are installed on the pilots' and flight engineer's instrument panels.

A Groza-144A weather radar is installed in the drooping nose visor. It is capable of detecting ground objects at a maximum range of 350 km (217 miles).

b) communications equipment: The Tu-144 has a Mikron HF communications/command link radio, a Landysh-20 (Lily of the valley) UHF radio and an SPGS-1 speakerphone intercom (*samolyotnaya peregovornaya gromkogovoryashchaya sistema*). An RI-65B automatic voice annunciator (*rechevoy informahtor*) warns the crew of critical failures and dangerous flight modes.

c) IFF system: SRO-2M Khrom IFF transponder (*samolyotnyy rahdiolokatsionnyy otvetchik* – aircraft-mounted radar [IFF] responder). The aircraft also features SOM-64-144 and SO-70-144

Specifications of the Tu-144 (izdeliye 004)	
Length overall (including pitot)	67.05 m (219 ft 11^{49}⁄$_{64}$ in) *
Fuselage length	64.45 m (211 ft 5^{13}⁄$_{32}$ in)
Fuselage diameter	3.5 m (11 ft 5¾ in)
Fuselage cross-section area	8.54 m² (91.92 sq ft)
Wing span: †	
at rest	27.65 m (90 ft 8^{37}⁄$_{64}$ in)
at maximum wing flexure in flight	28.8 m (94 ft 5^{55}⁄$_{64}$ in)
Height on ground	12.5 m (41 ft 0⅛ in)
Wing MAC	23.301 m (76 ft 5^{23}⁄$_{64}$ in)
Wing area:	
with LERXes	507.0 m² (5,457.3 sq ft)
less LERXes	437.65 m² (4,710.83 sq ft) ‡
Aggregate elevon area	42.78 m² (460.48 sq ft)
Vertical tail height above fuselage	6.65 m (21 ft 9^{13}⁄$_{16}$ in)
Vertical tail area:	
with dorsal fin	55.0 m² (592.02 sq ft)
less dorsal fin	49.24 m² (530.01 sq ft) ‡
Rudder area	11.397 m² (122.676 sq ft)
Vertical tail MAC (less dorsal fin)	8.264 m (27 ft 1^{3}⁄$_{64}$ in)
Engine nacelle length	20.355 m (66 ft 9⅜ in)
Engine nacelle cross-section area	2 x 5.915 m² (2 x 63.668 sq ft)
Air intake cross-section area	4 x 1.35 m² (4 x 14.53 sq ft)
Landing gear track	6.05 m (19 ft 10^{3}⁄$_{16}$ in)
Landing gear wheelbase	19.63 m (64 ft 4^{27}⁄$_{32}$ in)
Cabin cross-section	3.03 x 1.95 m (9 ft 11^{19}⁄$_{64}$ in x 6 ft 4^{49}⁄$_{64}$ in)
Cabin volume (total)	185 m³ (6,533 cu ft)
Flight deck volume	10.1 m³ (356 cu ft)
Baggage compartment volume (total)	21.1 m³ (745 cu ft)
Empty weight	91,800 kg (202,380 lb)
Operating empty weight	92,700 kg (204,365 lb)
Equipment weight	900 kg (1,980 lb)
Normal TOW	180,000 kg (396,825 lb)
Maximum TOW	195,000 kg (429,900 lb)
Maximum landing weight	120,000 kg (264,550 lb)
Fuel load	98,000 kg (216,050 lb)
Payload	13,000-15,000 kg (28,660-33,070 lb)
Seating capacity	150
Cruising speed:	
supersonic cruise	2,000-2,350 km/h (1,242-1,459 mph)
subsonic cruise	950 km/h (590 mph)
Normal cruise altitude:	
supersonic cruise	16,000-18,000 m (52,490-59,050 ft)
subsonic cruise	8,000-10,000 m (26,250-32,080 ft)
Average fuel consumption:	
supersonic cruise	18 kg/km (63.8 lb/mile)
subsonic cruise	16 kg/km (56.7 lb/mile)
Average fuel consumption:	
supersonic cruise	39 tons/hr (85,980 lb/hr)
subsonic cruise	15.2 tons (33,510 lb/hr)

* Some sources give the overall length as 65.7 m (215 ft 6^{19}⁄$_{64}$ in).

† Some sources give the wing span as 28.0 m (91 ft 10^{23}⁄$_{64}$ in).

‡ Some sources give the wing area less LERXes as 433 m² (4,656 sq ft).

Note: The stated flight performance figures were recorded on an NK-144A powered Tu-144 *sans suffixe* in 1975.

The Tu-144's performance with a 195,000-kg TOW, a 14,000-kg (30,860-lb) payload and 10,000 kg (22,045 lb) of fuel reserves		
	Supersonic cruise	Subsonic cruise
Range, km:		
overall	3,240 (2,012)	760 (472)
acceleration/climb phase	2,100 (1,304)	380 (236)
cruise phase	4,300 (2,670.8)	170 (105.6)
deceleration/descent phase	4,000 (2,484.4)	130 (80.75)
Fuel burn, kg (lb)	78,300 (172,620)	78,300 (172,620)
Endurance	2 hrs 12 min	4 hrs 55 min
Required runway length		
at sea level, ISA, m (ft)	n.a.	3,050 (10,000)

ATC transponders, which transmit the aircraft's registration, speed and altitude for presentation on ATC radar displays and may operate in 'Mayday' mode.

d) data recording equipment: MSRP-12-96 flight data recorder and MS-61B cockpit voice recorder. The FDR captures 12 parameters, including barometric altitude, indicated airspeed, roll rates, vertical and lateral G forces, control surface deflection and throttle settings, as well as gear/flap transition and so on.

Accommodation and cabin equipment: The flight deck is configured for a crew of three – two pilots and a flight engineer. The cabin crew comprises four flight attendants.

In the 150-seat mixed-class configuration the Tu-144 has two cabins separated by the centre vestibule. The forward cabin is divided by a partition into a first-class section seating 16 four-abreast and a tourist-class section seating 30 five-abreast (2+3); the rear cabin offers tourist-class accommodation for 104 passengers. The first-class cabin has four-abreast seating at 102 cm (40^{5}⁄$_{32}$ in) pitch. The seat backs can recline up to 45° and feature built-in meal trays; folding tables on the cabin bulkhead are provided for the first row of seats in each cabin. The tourist-class cabins have five-abreast seating at 87 cm (34¼ in) pitch with an aisle offset to port. All cabins feature enclosed overhead baggage bins and passenger service units with individual lighting, ventilation nozzles and stewardess call buttons. Several seats in the forward cabin are optimised for passengers travelling with babies.

The forward and centre vestibules house the two galleys, as well as coat racks and toilets; they also provide accommodation for the cabin crew on dual jump seats. One more toilet is located at the end of the rear cabin; each of the three toilets has its own water supply system and septic tank. The cabin, vestibule and toilet walls are upholstered in non-flammable synthetic materials and the floor is covered with a synthetic carpet having a foam rubber base.

Passenger evacuation in an emergency takes place via the overwing emergency exits and the entry and service doors. All doors except the rearmost pair feature inflatable escape slides; the onboard emergency kit includes escape ropes and axes for chopping through the fuselage skin if the regular exits are unusable. For overwater flights the aircraft is provided with five inflatable rafts equipped with survival kits and SOS radio beacons, as well as with life vests for all occupants.

Chapter 6

The Tu-144 in Aeroflot Service

As already mentioned, the joint MAP/MGA ruling 'On the service introduction of the Tu-144 supersonic airliner with NK-144 engines' was endorsed on 31st March and 7th April 1975. In keeping with established practice Aeroflot was required to evaluate the aircraft before declaring it suitable for passenger operations – the Tu-144 would perform route proving flights, carrying freight and mail. On 10th December 1975 Minister of Aircraft Industry Pyotr V. Dement'yev and Minister of Civil Aviation Boris P. Boogayev endorsed a document titled 'On the commencement of operational flights of the Tu-144 aircraft and their order'. The actual operational trials programme was approved by MAP, MGA and the State Aircraft Register between 19th August and 7th September 1976.

The evaluation proceeded in two stages; the first of these was the so-called operational flights, which began pursuant to the joint MAP/MGA ruling dated 10th December 1975 when the joint state acceptance trials were still in progress. On 26th December 1975 Tu-144 CCCP-77106 made the first flight on the route linking Moscow (Domodedovo airport) and Alma-Ata (now called Almaty), the capital of the Kazakh SSR, carrying an urgent cargo of spares for some agricultural machinery. The aircraft was flown by captain Ivan K. Vedernikov (Tupolev OKB), first officer Vyacheslav D. Popov (GosNII GA), flight engineer Anatoliy V. Tararookhin (Tupolev OKB), back-up flight engineer Vyacheslav L. Venediktov (GosNII GA) and navigator Vitaliy. A. Troshin; I. S. Maïboroda and Sergey P. Avakimov were also aboard as engineers in charge of the tests.

On this first flight CCCP-77106 carried a number of journalists and news reporters – V. V. Belikov (the *Izvestiya* daily newspaper),

Tu-144 CCCP-77109 parked in front of a special jet blast deflector at Alma-Ata airport, with the purpose-built gangway on a MAZ-500A chassis at the forward entry door and Antonov An-2R agricultural biplanes parked in the background.

Left: Aeroflot pilot Boris F. Kuznetsov reports to Minister of Civil Aviation Boris P. Boogayev (just visible, second from left) on 1st November 1977 that Tu-144 CCCP-77109 is ready for the first revenue flight.

Below: General Designer Aleksey A. Tupolev with OKB and MGA specialists during the Tu-144's evaluation.

Opposite page: CCCP-77109 on the apron at Moscow-Domodedovo, with CCCP-77110 visible in the lower photo.

Boris A. Korzin (the TASS News Agency), V. R. Mikhaïlenko (the All-Union Radio Company), R. R. Carmen (Central Television) and V. V. Zaïtsev (a publication from Sverdlovsk). The next day all Soviet media carried emotionally worded reports on this event that brought Mach 2 passenger transportation one step closer. This extensive media coverage – which was benevolent at the time – was a great moral boost for the participants of the tests.

Tu-144 CCCP-77106 bore the brunt of this stage of the evaluation. The flights were made once a week, the aircraft departing Moscow each Wednesday at 0830 hrs and Alma-Ata at 1400 hrs; dispatch reliability was very high. In addition to cargo and mail, a maintenance crew numbering up to ten was carried on each flight (these were not exactly passengers). At the concluding phase of this stage a second aircraft, CCCP-77108, joined in; together the two of them logged 739 hours in 395 flights, including 430-plus hours supersonic.

All flights were performed by mixed Tupolev OKB/Aeroflot crews, which took an appropriate three-month training course; Tupolev OKB test pilots Eduard V. Yelian and Vasiliy P. Borisov were among the instructors. The crews included test pilots Sergey T. Agapov, Ivan K. Vedernikov, Vyacheslav D. Popov and Mikhail S. Kuznetsov, flight engineers Anatoliy V. Tararookhin, Yuriy T.

Chapter 6 - The Tu-144 in Aeroflot Service

Above and left: CCCP-77109 shortly after arriving at Alma-Ata on 1st November 1977, with support vehicles around it. A meeting has been staged for the occasion, with an *ad hoc* grandstand, slogans, portraits of Soviet statesmen and a PAZ-672 bus outfitted as an 'agitmobile' with amplifiers and loudspeakers. Note that the nose visor is raised – the aircraft looks better that way!

Below: CCCP-77109 is readied for the return flight to Moscow, with the Trans-Ili Alatau mountains as a backdrop. An ATs-40(375)-Ts1A fire engine based on a Ural-375D 6x6 army lorry stands by.

Chapter 6 - The Tu-144 in Aeroflot Service

Selivyorstov, V. L. Venediktov and A. S. Troyepol'skiy, navigators V. A. Troshin and Nikolay I. Tolmachov. Engineers V. M. Koolesh, I. S. Maïboroda, V. A. Isayev, Sergey P. Avakimov, Ye. A. Fedoolov and Mikhail V. Pankevich supervised the flight operations.

Besides familiarisation, these flights were meant to check the aircraft for compatibility with Aeroflot's existing ground support systems and logistics schemes. Special hardstands provided with all necessary ground support equipment, including fuel nitrogenation equipment, were set aside at Moscow-Domodedovo and Alma-Ata airport. Routine maintenance was performed by mixed ground crews composed of Tupolev OKB flight test facility staff and the personnel of the respective airports who were undergoing on-the-job training. A stock of spares was maintained at Alma-Ata airport. Tupolev OKB engineering and production teams maintained a full-time duty at both locations, keeping in touch with the head office to resolve any technical issues.

It should be noted that the Tu-144 had its share of opponents in high places, especially after the 1973 Paris accident. Thus, some high-ranking persons in the civil aviation system – first and foremost Minister of Civil Aviation Boris P. Boogayev himself – thoroughly resented the SST and sought to delay its service entry if at all possible by ensnaring the matter in red tape. There is no other plausible explanation why the document titled 'On the order of the Tu-144 aircraft's operational evaluation on the MGA's routes' was endorsed by MAP, MGA and the State Aircraft Register as late as 19th August 1977 – a full year after the trials programme had been approved.

Stage 2, which began shortly afterwards pursuant to MAP/MGA order No.149-223 on the operational evaluation of the NK-144 powered Tu-144 dated 13th September 1977, was characterised by greater involvement of Aeroflot's resources. This document continued a clause appointing the two ministries' joint commission that would supervise the tests; it was chaired by Vice-Minister of Civil Aviation Boris D. Groobiy. This commission assigned four crews to the operational tests, a decision later formally approved by a further MAP/MGA order signed on 30th September and 5th October 1977. The first crew comprised pilots Boris F. Kuznetsov from the Moscow Transport Civil Aviation Directorate (MTU GA – *Moskovskoye **trahns**portnoye oopravleniye grazh**dahn**skoy aviahtsii*) and Sergey T. Agapov from the Tupolev OKB, navigator S. P. Khramov (MTU GA), flight engineers Yu. N. Avayev (MTU GA) and Yuriy T. Selivyorstov (Tupolev OKB), and engineer in charge Sergey P. Avakimov (Tupolev OKB). The second crew comprised pilots Valentin P. Voronin (MTU GA) and Ivan K. Vedernikov (Tupolev OKB), navigator A. A. Senyuk (MTU GA), flight engineers Ye. A. Trebuntsov (MTU GA) and Viktor V. Solomatin (Tupolev OKB), and engineer in charge V. V. Isayev (GosNII GA). The third crew comprised pilots Mikhail S. Kuznetsov (GosNII GA) and Ghennadiy V. Voronchenko (Tupolev OKB), navigator V. V. Vyazigin (GosNII GA), flight engineers M. P. Isayev (MTU GA) and, again, Viktor V. Solomatin, and engineer in charge V. N. Poklad (Tupolev OKB). Finally, the fourth crew comprised pilots Nikolay I. Yoorskov (GosNII GA) and Vladimir A. Sevan'kayev (Tupolev OKB), navigator Yu. A. Vasil'yev (GosNII GA), flight engineer V. L. Venediktov (GosNII GA) and engineer in charge I. S. Maïboroda (GosNII GA).

Before the evaluation the OKB had undertaken a large amount of test work and submitted the results to the MGA in the hope that these results would be taken into account. Yet, the ministry would not give up the fight so easily; it insisted that the operational evaluation programme drafted by GosNII GA back in 1975 under the guidance of project engineer A. M. Teteryukov be implemented by all means. This meant another 750 flights and 1,200 hours of tests on Aeroflot's routes which would be a pointless repetition of the work already done.

Unfortunately the argument between the OKB and the ministry dragged on for so long without any result that Boris A. Gantsevskiy, the Tu-144's project chief, finally grew tired of it and agreed to the GosNII GA programme. Taking advantage of this error in judgement, the Tu-144's opponents at the ministry wasted no time in getting this programme endorsed in as-was condition by Vasiliy A. Kazakov, who was then Vice-Minister of Aircraft Industry, and Vice-Minister of Civil Aviation I. S. Razumovskiy on 19th August 1976. However, this would have stretched the OKB's resources too far – the OKB was simply not in a position to perform this huge work.

This led the parties involved, including the State Aircraft Register, to rethink their approach. Now the question was not whether the Tu-144 met the requirements of MGA as the customer, but rather whether it conformed to the VNLGSS airworthiness regulations as a state standard. In the latter case the scope of the operational evaluation was reduced to 50 flights and 96 hours. Hence the state commission reconsidered its previous decision and issued ruling No.004-20-77 on 19th August 1977 concerning operational evaluation. The evaluation flight schedule was approved on 23rd September, envisaging 12 return flights on the Moscow – Alma-Ata route, two route proving flights with passengers aboard and 14 closed-circuit flights from Moscow-Domodedovo via Aktyubinsk which were equivalent in length to the Moscow – Alma-Ata route.

Stage 2 of the operational evaluation took place between 24th September and 22nd (some sources say 23rd) October 1977, involving the abovementioned 50 flights with a total time of 96 hours, including 46 hours at supersonic speeds. All in all, the Tu-144 made 445 flights under the operational evaluation programme, logging a total of 835 hours (including 475 hours at supersonic speeds) and making 128 return flights on the Moscow – Alma-Ata route. The commission's report on the evaluation results was endorsed by the two ministers on 25th October.

From a technical standpoint Stage 2 did not cause any major headaches – the flights proceeded on schedule and without major defects. Some of the flights were purposely made with diversions to Tashkent-Yoozhnyy airport in Uzbekistan and Frunze-Manas airport (now Bishkek-Manas) in Kirghizia, which were designated as the alternate airports on the Moscow – Alma-Ata service. The engineering and tech staff evaluated the Tu-144's cabin equipment (galleys, lavatories and the like) in anticipation of the actual passenger flights. Aeroflot's flight attendants and GosNII GA specialists joined in at this stage, practicing the operational procedures. A so-called 'dry run' was made on 16th October 1977 – the personnel acted out the complete flight procedure, from passenger/baggage

Left: Sweet dreams are made of this. The map shows the Tu-144D's envisaged routes – from Moscow to Khabarovsk, Yakutsk, Tashkent, Delhi, Ulaanbaatar, Havana (via Azores), from Paris to Tokyo via Novosibirsk (!) and from Paris to New York (!).

Below left: A still from the Soviet comedy **Mimino** ('falcon' in Georgian) filmed in 1977 where the lead character (an Aeroflot pilot) prepares to fly Tu-144 CCCP-77106.

Below: Tu-144D CCCP-77112 shares the apron at Khabarovsk-Novyy with the resident IL-62s *sans suffixe* and Tu-154s of the Far East Civil Aviation Directorate's 202nd Flight and 198th Flight respectively.

check-in and boarding through a simulated full-length flight to disembarkation and baggage reclaim at the destination airport. The abovementioned two route proving flights with passengers, which took place on 20th and 21st October 1977, were a big hit, with the best employees of the Tupolev OKB's head office and flight test facility, GosNII GA and other organisations involved in the trials competing for seats on the flights. There is no sarcasm here – the passengers on these two flights were people who had been directly involved in the development and testing of the Tu-144, not some self-important officials. The catering on these flights was top-

Chapter 6 - The Tu-144 in Aeroflot Service

Top: Tu-144D CCCP-77112 taxies out for take-off during the evaluation; the nose visor is at the 11° take-off setting but the canards are still retracted.

Above and right: Tu-144 *sans suffixe* CCCP-77110 retained its 1977 Le Bourget exhibit code 345 throughout its brief operations on Aeroflot's Moscow – Alma-Ata service.

Left: Bird's eye view of Tu-144D CCCP-77114 (still in record-setting guise with '101' nose titles) at Zhukovskiy in the 1990s.

Below: Gleaming with fresh paint, Tu-144D CCCP-77115 is seen here at Zhukovskiy after restoration to static exhibit condition for the MAKS-2007 airshow. Note that the registration across the wings is omitted, as is the anti-glare panel, and that the Aeroflot logo is applied in a not entirely correct type face – compare the rendering of the letter F (Ф) on the two aircraft.

Below right: Another bird's eye view of the same aircraft. The rudder is fully deflected to starboard.

notch, as the menu was to first-class air travel standards, and the passengers were happy as can be. Not only because of the food – they were given the opportunity to experience firsthand the results of their own work, and the atmosphere aboard on these flights was that of pride and high hopes for the aircraft's future.

Presently MAP and MGA decided that scheduled passenger services could be launched. On 25th October 1977 the new Minister of Aircraft Industry Vasiliy A. Kazakov and Minister of Civil Aviation Boris P. Boogayev endorsed the report on the Tu-144's evaluation with positive results. Four days later the Tu-144 *sans suffixe* received its type certificate. On 31st October the two ministers signed an appropriate joint order (No.173-269) clearing the Tu-144 for commercial operations on Aeroflot's Moscow – Alma-Ata service.

It deserves mention that the said order contained the following provisos. Scheduled flights were still to be performed by mixed MAP/MGA aircrews and the aircraft were to be serviced by MAP tech staff with the participation of MGA staff. The aircraft themselves remained MAP property and were not formally handed over to Aeroflot; operations were to proceed in accordance with Tupolev OKB manuals endorsed by the General Designer. Operations were limited to daytime, with the following weather minima: cloudbase 100 m (330 ft), horizontal visibility 1,000 m (3,280 ft), coefficient of friction higher than 0.3 on dry or wet runways.

The first revenue flight of a Tu-144 took place the following day, on 1st November 1977; it was performed by CCCP-77109, the first Tu-144 built to full airline standard, with a mixed MGA/MAP crew at the controls. This was one of only two Tu-144s ever to see commercial service; the other was CCCP-77110, the last Tu-144 *sans suffixe*.

So great was the significance of the event that General Designer Aleksey A. Tupolev and the top brass of MAP and MGA came flocking to Moscow's Domodedovo airport to witness it. The crew on the inaugural service was captain Boris F. Kuznetsov (Civil Aviation Pilot 1st Class), first officer Sergey T. Agapov, navigator S. P. Khramov and flight engineers Yu. N. Avayev and Viktor V. Solomatin. When the 80 passengers had taken their seats, Kuznetsov reported to Boogayev that the aircraft and the crew were ready to fly. However, Murphy's Law worketh, and if anything can go wrong in the presence of the big brass, it will. An experimental self-propelled gangway based on the MAZ-500A 8-ton (71.42-cwt) diesel-engined cabover lorry was used for boarding; the boarding steps featured a built-in escalator (!) and lighting, which was a good thing, as it was pretty dark at 8 AM in November. The vehicle was

Left: Tu-144 CCCP-77101 on the flight line at Olen'ya AB during the abortive snow-covered runway tests in 1975. A wheeled maintenance platform was used for boarding/deplaning for want of suitable airstairs.

Below left: A Tupolev OKB representative and high-ranking Naval Aviation officers pose for a photo with CCCP-77101, which is being refuelled by two TZ-22 fuel bowsers (KrAZ-258B1 6x4 tractor units with 22,000-litre semitrailers).

Bottom left: Another view of Tu-144 CCCP-77101 parked at Olen'ya AB. The Tu-134A in pre-1973 standard blue-tailed Aeroflot livery in the background is almost certainly a Tupolev OKB support aircraft.

Right: CCCP-77101 touches down at Olen'ya AB. The tests were unsuccessful – there was simply not enough snow; the aircraft made one flight from Olen'ya and returned to Zhukovskiy.

a brand-new model, and the personnel had not yet learned how to operate it properly. When it was time to remove the gangway, it turned out that the escalator and lighting had sapped the lorry's DC battery; as a result, the engine could not be started and the hydraulic supports stabilising the vehicle could not be raised. Attempts to move the immobilised gangway with a tractor proved futile – the thing would not budge, and the steel hawsers snapped like threads. Not until a hydraulic vent was opened to reduce the pressure, spilling part of the fluid on the apron, did the ground crew succeed in towing the gangway. By then, however, the two ministers had run out of patience and left without waiting for the take-off (which says a thing or two about their attitude towards the Tu-144). Vice-Minister of Civil Aviation Col.-Gen. Yuriy G. Mamsoorov was fit to be tied – it was he who had suggested using the experimental gangway (despite the objections of the OKB team) and thus had screwed up in front of his boss. Although he had worked his own misery, this incident rankled, making him an enemy of the Tu-144.

As a result, CCCP-77109 took off 40 minutes late, becoming airborne at 0903 hrs Moscow time. Exactly two hours later the airliner touched down at Alma-Ata airport; the landing was not without incident, too – the aircraft burst one of the mainwheel tyres, starting a small fire which was quickly put out. The return flight departed Alma-Ata at 1328 hrs and touched down at Moscow-Domodedovo at 1531 hrs. Again, there was an incident – the aircraft lost a piece of skin on the lower rudder half in cruise flight (fortunately without grave consequences).

As for the abovementioned experimental gangway, only two were ever built; the enraged MAP top brass gave orders to *'throw these (expletive deleted) things away and make sure they never appear near the Tu-144 again!'* During scheduled flights the Tu-144 was serviced by much simpler and lighter SPT-114 electrically-powered gangways (*samokhodnyy passazheerskiy trahp* – self-propelled gangway). As the designation implies, they had been designed for the Tu-114 four-turboprop long-haul airliner with its tall landing gear, being a taller version of the SPT-104 designed for the Tu-104; thus, the SPT-114s, which had found themselves unwanted when the Tu-114 was withdrawn from Aeroflot service, briefly got a new lease of life.

There have been caustic comments that the inauguration of passenger operations with the Tu-144 was timed to the anniversary of the October Revolution (or, as it was referred to in Soviet times, the Great October Socialist Revolution), which was celebrated on 7th November. (Here it should be explained that on 26th January 1918, three months after the revolution, Soviet Russia switched from the outdated Julian calendar to the Gregorian calendar; thus, 25th October – the 'old-style' date of the revolution – equals 7th November according to the current calendar.) This was one of the most important public holidays in the Soviet Union, especially considering that in 1977 it was the 60th anniversary. Well, the claims were very probably true; ostensibly timing major achievements to public holidays and other important events (such as a Communist Party congress or the birthday of Vladimir I. Lenin, the founder of the Soviet state) was common practice in Soviet times. In keeping with another time-honoured Soviet tradition, at the end of the year a large group of MAP and MGA employees received state awards for the service introduction of the Tu-144 supersonic airliner.

It should be mentioned that the Tupolev OKB offered military derivatives of the Tu-144 to the Naval Aviation (these projects are dealt with in Chapter 8). As a run-up to possible military uses, in 1977 Tu-114 CCCP-77110 – still with the Le Bourget exhibit code 345 on the fuselage – made a promotional visit to Severomorsk-1 airbase in the Murmansk Region of north-western Russia, which hosted the North Fleet air arm's 967th ODRAP (*otdel'nyy dahl'niy razvedyvatel'nyy aviapolk* – Independent [= direct reporting] Maritime Reconnaissance Air Regiment) equipped with Tu-16RM-1 *Badger-D* reconnaissance aircraft. An SPT-104 gangway was brought to the base for the occasion; the Tupolev OKB's Tu-134A CCCP-65667 acted as a support aircraft.

Two years earlier, in 1975, Tu-144 CCCP-77101 captained by Eduard V. Yelian made a similar visit to Olen'ya AB (Olenegorsk, Murmansk Region), which was home to the North Fleet air arm's 924th MRAP (*morskoy raketonosnyy aviapolk* – Maritime Missile Strike Air Regiment), likewise operating Tu-16s at the time. However, this deployment had nothing to do with the military – the objective was to test the Tu-144 on a snow-covered runway. The plan was foiled by the weather – there was not enough snow. The aircraft was struck off charge and scrapped later that year.

As early as 17th February 1978 the two ministries held a joint conference on the Tu-144's flight operations. The general assessment of the airliner was favourable, but there were lots of specific problem areas to be addressed. The conference worked out measures aimed at improving the type's operational parameters; plans to increase the operating frequency during the summer high season and launch Tu-144 flights to other destinations were also discussed. Unfortunately, these plans never came to fruition.

Day-to-day operation of the Tu-144s was performed by MAP staff assisted by Aeroflot staff; the idea was that the Aeroflot personnel would gradually take over as experience was built up and more personnel were trained by the MTU GA's training detachment. Vice-Minister of Civil Aviation Yuriy G. Mamsoorov did not hesitate to call at the Tu-144's hardstand at Domodedovo at 6 AM or 7 AM, monitoring the entire pre-flight procedure – apparently in the hope of finding faults. Yet, even he had to give the devil his due, mentioning in his publications that *'the specialists servicing the Tu-144 showed a high degree of responsibility which made it possible to preclude in-flight hardware failures almost completely'*.

It should be mentioned that the MGA top bosses' attitude towards the Tu-144 was by no means universal in the Aeroflot

Chapter 6 - The Tu-144 in Aeroflot Service

system; many people, especially at the middle and lower levels, were extremely supportive. These included Vice-Minister of Civil Aviation I. S. Razumovskiy, Chairman of the State Aircraft Register Ivan K. Moolkidjanov and his Vice-Chairman Rudolf A. Teymurazov, MTU GA Deputy Chief Engineer A. A. Yemtsov, director of Moscow-Domodedovo's aircraft maintenance base N. A. Nebosya, chief engineer of the Alma-Ata airport's maintenance base R. A. Iofis and many others who did their job professionally, helping to find the optimum solutions to the Tu-144's operational problems.

New entries reading 'Flight 499 Moscow – Alma-Ata, departure 08:30' and 'Flight 500 Alma-Ata – Moscow, departure 15:30' appeared in the timetable at Moscow-Domodedovo. Again, these flights covering a distance of 3,260 km (2,024 miles) at an altitude of 16,000-17,000 m (52,490-55,770 ft) and a speed of 2,000 km/h (1,240 mph) took place once a week. On average the Tu-144 covered the distance in 2 hours 5 minutes (the shortest time en route was 1 hour 58 minutes); in contrast, the subsonic IL-62 needed more than four hours to fly the same route.

It should be noted that the Tu-144 was popular with the passengers and the flights were almost fully booked, despite the higher-than-average fare. A ticket to Alma-Ata for the Tu-144 cost 68 roubles versus 48 roubles for a ticket to the same destination for the subsonic IL-62; to put these figures into perspective, it should be noted that the average Soviet office clerk's salary in those days was 130 roubles. There were foreign nationals on virtually every single flight; makes you wonder if perhaps they bought the tickets specifically for the purpose of sampling the 'Concordski' and experiencing supersonic air travel at a fraction of the cost of 'the real McCoy'!

Questionnaires distributed among the passengers showed that most of the passengers were quite happy with the cabin, rating it as comfortable. Yet there was a deal of criticism as well; one Lady Whose Girth Defies Measurement complained that the seats were too narrow and uncomfortable, suggesting that wider seats be installed for portly passengers. Many female passengers were displeased with that fact that the meals served on the flight included a 33-cl (11.15 fl. oz.) bottle of dry wine; this allegedly created a queue to the loo and deprived them of the chance to powder their noses before deplaning in Moscow! Still, every airline probably has an issue with such never-happy passengers who don't know a good thing when they see it.

There was a case when the primary air conditioning system failed in supersonic cruise at 18,000 m (59,055 ft) and the back-up ACS took over. To be on the safe side, captain Ivan K. Vedernikov decelerated to subsonic speed, descended to 11,000 m (36,090 ft) and continued in this mode to Alma-Ata. Fortunately the time en route increased only a little and the passengers were not alarmed.

Top left: Tu-144 CCCP-77110 parked at Severomorsk-1 AB during the brief visit in 1977. An SPT-104 gangway was used, and the people had to use the port rear emergency exit and walk all the way along the port wing!

Above left: The same scene, showing the recently repainted Tu-134A CCCP-65667 support aircraft and a UGZS.M-A nitrogen charger vehicle on a ZiL-131 6x6 army lorry chassis.

Far left: This view shows the Tu-144's open brake parachute container.

Left: CCCP-77110 is refuelled by two TZ-22s at Severomorsk-1 AB.

Below left: CCCP-77110 touches down at Severomorsk-1.

Top: Final approach to Severomorsk.

Right: CCCP-77109 at Domodedovo.

Left: Tu-144 CCCP-77106 in the open-air display of the Central Russian Air Force Museum in Monino, with the MiG-21I/2 Analog proof-of-concept vehicle just visible beyond.

Below left: CCCP-77107 pokes its nose over the fence of the Kazan' Aviation Institute (KAI) compound where it serves as a teaching aid.

Right and above right: If you think the Kazan' example is weathered, check this out! CCCP-77108, a ground instructional airframe at the Samara State Aviation University (SGAU), has had the blue and red paint washed away completely by the elements.

Below right: In contrast, CCCP-77110 residing in the Civil Air Fleet Museum at Ulyanovsk-Baratayevka looks pristine after receiving a new coat of paint in August-September 2008. As of now, it is the most complete and well-kept Tu-144 *sans suffixe*.

Tu-144 flights continued on schedule until mid-May 1978. The next flight, which was scheduled for 30th May, was cancelled at the orders of General Designer Aleksey A. Tupolev in the wake of the crash of Tu-114D CCCP-77111 on 23rd May. Almost immediately it became apparent that the crash had been caused by a fuel system defect. Now, the fuel systems of the Tu-144 *sans suffixe* and the Tu-144D differed substantially; therefore, the failure that caused the crash of the Kolesov-powered CCCP-77111 could not possibly occur on the Kuznetsov-powered operational version, and therefore the decision to terminate passenger services seemed rather illogical. Immediately after the crash MGA demanded an inspection and ground checks of the two Tu-144s in airline service (CCCP-77109 and CCCP-77110). The checks did not turn up anything untoward, and protocols to this effect were duly filed to Aleksey A. Tupolev, who approved them. Still, on 29th May the MGA top brass demanded a special document authorising further operations. Such authorisation was given, but… We'll let the Tu-144's deputy project chief Yuriy N. Popov, who was responsible for supporting the type's operations, tell the story:

'The ruling "On the continued operation of Tu-144s c/ns 05-2 and 06-1 with NK-144 engines" was endorsed by the General Designer and the MAP bosses. In the afternoon Aleksey A. Tupolev and I drove to MGA to have this ruling endorsed by Vice-Minister of Civil Aviation Yuriy G. Mamsoorov, who was in charge of aircraft operations. Our mood was sombre as we drove. Everyone [in the business] knew that Mamsoorov and Minister of Civil Aviation

Chapter 6 - The Tu-144 in Aeroflot Service

Left: Tu-144D CCCP-77112 is seen here going past the Kremlin on a barge which took it up the Moskva River from Zhukovskiy en route to a new home in Germany.

Below: Reassembled and repainted (albeit minus Aeroflot titles), the aircraft is seen here on display at the Auto- und Technik-Museum Sinsheim; the interior is accessible to the visitors.

Right and below right: 'Aircraft 101' CCCP-77114 in the static park at the MAKS-93 airshow in company with the Tu-54 agricultural aircraft mock-up and a Tu-22M3 bomber.

Boris P. Boogayev were opposed to the Tu-144; they had done a lot to stop the Tu-144 from entering service and subsequently to have its operation discontinued. At [MGA] conferences and in his memoranda Yuriy G. Mamsoorov had always denounced the aircraft in particular and the work of the General Designer in general. This meeting was no exception to the rule. We had a long and difficult discussion but eventually succeeded in convincing Mamsoorov; therefore – or possibly for some other reason – he endorsed the ruling authorising further operations. On leaving his study we congratulated each other on this success and left for our respective homes at around 10 PM on 29th May. The next flight was due to take place on 30th May, and at 0730 hrs I arrived at the hardstand where the aircraft was prepared for the flight, as usual. To my surprise there was none of the usual hustle and bustle associated with pre-flight procedures. I was accosted by V. A. Gortsepayev, the deputy chief of the technical team. He told me that at 7 AM he had received a phone call from Aleksey A. Tupolev, who told him to cancel the scheduled Tu-144 flight to Alma-Ata; he had already forwarded these instructions to the management of Domodedovo airport, and an IL-62 was being readied to fly the day's Moscow – Alma-Ata service. I had no idea what could have happened during these past nine hours – what events, thoughts or even outside advice could have led Aleksey A. Tupolev to change his mind on the continuation of Tu-144 operations. When I finally

Chapter 6 - The Tu-144 in Aeroflot Service

managed to get Tupolev on the phone, his reply was succinct: "We have to do it!" To this day, the reason for this decision of the General Designer remains a mystery for me. Still, that same day Aleksey A. Tupolev endorsed a document called "Additional work plan for [modifications of] the fuel system of Tu-144s c/ns 05-2 and 06-1" and sent it to me for implementation; possibly these two events were related.

Anyway, the cancellation of this particular flight led to the cessation of Tu-144 operations on MGA's routes. The General Designer's indecision allowed the Tu-144's enemies to act at will. The times when national interests meant more than safeguarding a specific official's position were past; a new style was emerging that eventually was the Soviet Union's undoing – nobody was fired for failing to make relevant decisions, but initiative was mercilessly punished. MGA's leaders were happy about the cancellation of the [Tu-144's] flights – they were never interested in introducing new hardware, and now they were free of the burden of supersonic aviation which required constant attention on their part, necessitated development of ground support services and incurred costs. Now, all they had to do was to find a pretext to kill off the Tu-144, and they quickly invented one. Yuriy G. Mamsoorov claimed that the aircraft was unreliable. Yet the Tu-144's in-flight failure statistics and operational experience with the type showed otherwise; during scheduled flights there had been no critical failures compromising flight safety. Other MGA officials became economically conscious all of a sudden. However, the Tu-144's operating economics had been known for more than four years; providing large-scale operations were organised, it was possible to make them economically viable (discounting the development costs), the way it was done with the Concorde. From then on, political struggle began between MAP and MGA; both parties pursued one goal – not to be held responsible for failing to fulfil the government's directives.' (Here it should be mentioned that launching SST operations during the 9th Five-Year Economic Development

Plan was one of the tasks posed by the 24th Communist Party Congress, and such assignments were, for all practical purposes, equivalent to laws for the Soviet industry.)

At the time it seemed this would be just a temporary suspension of service until the cause of the crash had been found and remedial action taken. Yet, as Russian folk wisdom goes, 'there's nothing more permanent than something temporary'.

The investigation of the accident and the ensuing modification of the Tu-144D took a long time. More than a year later, on 24th August 1978, the new Minister of Aircraft Industry Vasiliy A. Kazakov signed order No.329 'On the coordination of the procedure for resuming Tu-144 operations on MGA's Moscow – Alma-Ata service with MAP and the Air Force'. On 2nd-14th September that year MAP, MGA, the State Aircraft Register and the military worked out a set of measures necessary for resuming scheduled passenger flights on Tu-144s CCCP-77109 and CCCP-77110 (that is, modifications to the fuel system based on the investigation board's findings). Yet, it took inordinately long – from 7th October 1978 to 17th March 1979 – to get the joint MAP/MGA/Air Force ruling No.004-20-78 dealing with the upgrading of these two aircraft and resuming their operation approved. On 10th February 1981 MAP issued order No.81 appointing a special commission to implement the upgrades. Finally, on 12th March 1981 this commission signed the protocol formally clearing the NK-144A engines and the modified fuel systems of CCCP-77109 and CCCP-77110 for service during commercial operations.

In spite of all this, scheduled flights of the Tu-144 never resumed. Now MGA came up with another argument – let's drop the Tu-144 *sans suffixe* with the old Kuznetsov engines and concentrate on the more promising Tu-144D with the more fuel-efficient Kolesov engines. The two aircraft remained in storage at Domodedovo for a long time before finally returning to Zhukovskiy.

Meanwhile, the ministry masterminded a smear campaign in the media, with all manner of scare stories to undermine public trust in it. As the 'cherry on the cake', in 1980 Minister of Civil Aviation Boris P. Boogayev filed a report to the government. The name of the report spoke for itself: 'On the operations of the Tu-144 aircraft'. Considering that there had been no Tu-144 operations since May 1978, it is easy to guess the tone and the purpose of the report. The minister went to great lengths to dig up every bit of incriminating evidence against the Tu-144; inevitably, the conclusion he arrived at was that, in spite of all efforts made by MGA, the aircraft was unsafe and, moreover, uneconomical to operate in comparison with subsonic airliners. The VPK spent several months assessing this report, concluding that its main 'selling points' were unfounded.

In 1980 MAP made another attempt to resume scheduled services with the Tu-144 *sans suffixe* – this time on Aeroflot's Moscow-Novosibirsk service. Once again, an agreement in principle was reached; preparations were made at Moscow-Domodedovo and Novosibirsk-Tolmachovo, and alternate airfields were assigned. The final step was to make a route proving flight, which was planned for 17th February 1981; however, this had to be authorised by the Tu-144's nemesis, Boris P. Boogayev, who – predictably – refused to do it. Once again, MGA started the same old yarn – 'resuming operation of the Tu-144 *sans suffixe* is inexpedient, let's complete the trials of the Tu-144D, blah-blah-blah'. Unfortunately General Designer Aleksey A. Tupolev and MAP supported this idea.

The official explanation as to why Tu-144 operations were terminated so early – just seven months after inauguration – is that Aleksey A. Tupolev decided to play safe. The unofficial explanation is that the anti-Tu-144 lobby had won. Tu-144 operations required runways and ground equipment/services to be upgraded; this was a costly and messy process, and the inert MGA would have no part of it. Added to this, there was personal animosity between the MGA top brass and Aleksey A. Tupolev. In spite of the hounding he was subjected to by MGA's leaders, it has to be said that he had done all he could for the Tu-144 programme. Also, consider that in 1974 a new important military programme – the Tu-160 missile carrier – came on the scene, and many of the Tupolev OKB specialists developing the Tu-144 were reassigned to this high-priority project.

The Tu-144D fared even worse. Stage 1 of its evaluation programme began in 1979 in order to accumulate operational statistics in flights according to a typical mission profile (and hopefully make the anti-Tu-144 lobby shut up). Between 21st May and 26th December 1979 the Tu-144Ds made 51 such flights, logging a total of 127 hours, including more than 90 hours at supersonic speeds. Most of these were closed-circuit flights from Zhukovskiy, although at least one was made on the Moscow-Khabarovsk route. On the latter occasion CCCP-77112 was captained by Sergey T. Agapov and carried a number of passengers, including Vice-Minister of Aircraft Industry Anufriy V. Bolbot, Vice-Minister of Civil Aviation I. S. Razumovskiy, General Designer Aleksey A. Tupolev and OKB-36 Chief Designer Pyotr A. Kolesov. The flights showed that on the latter route the Tu-144D could carry a 7,000-kg (15,430-lb) payload – some 70 passengers and their baggage – in any weather.

Stage 1 was performed by Tupolev OKB test pilots Sergey T. Agapov, Boris I. Veremey, Ivan K. Vedernikov, Ghennadiy V. Voronchenko, Yevgeniy A. Goryunov, Vladimir A. Sevan'kayev

Some of the Tu-144D's operational evaluation flights (Stage 1)						
Date	25-5-1979	2-6-1979	8-6-1979	12-6-1979	16-6-1979	23-6-1979
Route	CC*	CC	CC	CC	CC	DME-KHV*
Range, km (miles)	6,050 (3,757)	6,370 (3,956)	7,050 (4,378)	6,300 (3,913)	5,800 (3,602)	6,185 (3,841)
Mach number	2.0	2.01	2.03	2.01	1.97	1.97
Max altitude, m (ft)	18,100 (59,380)	17,900 (58,730)	18,330 (60,140)	17,800 (58,400)	18,000 (59,055)	18,100 (59,380)
Duration	3 hrs 15 min	3 hrs 25 min	3 hrs 43 min	3 hrs 25 min	3 hrs 05 min	3 hrs 21 min

* CC = closed circuit; DME = Moscow-Domodedovo; KHV = Khabarovsk-Novyy

Chapter 6 - The Tu-144 in Aeroflot Service

Right: Tu-144D CCCP-77115 (with an SPT-114 bearing the Tupolev JSC logo) on display at the MAKS-2011 – as far away from the main entrance to the airshow as you could get.

Right: Three-quarters rear view of CCCP-77115 soaking up the August morning sunshine shows well the nozzles of the mighty RD36-51A engines.

Below right: A head-on aspect of the Tu-144D showing the aircraft's impressive lines. Note the support placed under the tail – just in case.

and LII test pilot Vladimir I. Kryzhanovskiy, navigators V. A. Troshin and Nikolay I. Tolmachov, flight engineer Viktor V. Solomatin and engineers in charge of the tests Sergey P. Avakimov, Viktor N. Ghenov and Oleg A. Kooptsov. The test data obtained at this stage made it possible to receive the Tu-144D's provisional type certificate.

Kazakov's ministerial tenure was rather brief, and on 27th May 1981 the recently appointed new Minister of Aircraft Industry Ivan S. Silayev endorsed the joint MAP/MGA ruling 'On the service introduction of the Tu-144D supersonic airliner with RD36-51A engines'; Minister of Civil Aviation Boris P. Boogayev followed suit on 2nd June. This ruling set out a schedule of measures for the type's service entry. On 17th-20th July 1981 MAP, MGA and the State Aircraft Register approved the Tu-144D's operational trials programme. On 22nd July the joint MAP/MGA order No.139-181 on the operational evaluation of the Tu-144D was issued and a joint commission that would supervise the tests – again chaired by Boris D. Groobiy – was appointed; some sources name a different Vice-Minister (I. F. Vasin) as the chairman. The long-range version was to be tried out on a different Aeroflot service connecting Moscow-Domodedovo and Krasnoyarsk-Yemel'yanovo airport.

Finally, on 28th July 1981 MAP issued a further order (No.178) requiring Tu-144Ds CCCP-77112 and CCCP-77114 to redeploy from Zhukovskiy to Domodedovo for the purpose of commencing route proving flights to Krasnoyarsk. These aircraft had received the latest upgrades and conformed to the type certificate.

The route proving programme comprised 80 flights, 60 of which (totalling 200 hours) would be performed by CCCP-77112 and the remaining 20 (totalling 50 hours) by CCCP-77114. This stage was to be completed by 25th October 1981. Once again, mixed MAP/MGA crews would fly the aircraft, while maintenance would be the responsibility of a Tupolev OKB team in Moscow and a Voronezh aircraft factory team in Krasnoyarsk.

By November 1981 the preparations were basically completed. Yet, Murphy's Law interfered again. On 12th November, two days before the planned beginning of the tests, an RD36-51A engine failed catastrophically during bench tests, and all Tu-144Ds were immediately grounded. The investigation panel demanded that 18 RD36-51A engines be modified and two of them be subjected to 300-hour check-up tests; this meant operational evaluation would be postponed indefinitely.

Eventually the Tu-144D was to be introduced on the Moscow-Khabarovsk service. Yet, passenger operations never started. After the engine failure during bench tests the MGA top brass (Boris P. Boogayev, Yuriy G. Mamsoorov and I. F. Vasin) stepped up their attacks against the Tu-144, bombarding the government with memos and reports. *Carthaginem esse delendam*. Presently their efforts bore fruit; on 27th January 1982 MAP ordered Tu-144 production stopped, and on 1st June 1983 the Council of Ministers ran out of patience and cancelled all further work on the programme.

During the Soviet SST's all-too-brief career with Aeroflot it logged 181 hours 3 minutes in 102 flights, including 55 passenger flights in which 3,170 passengers were carried (some sources say 3,194 or 3,284); the average load factor was 80%. All in all, including the test programme, the small Tu-144/Tu-144D fleet made 2,556 flights and logged 4,110 hours.

Four Tu-144s *sans suffixe* and three Tu-144Ds survive to this day. CCCP-77106 was donated to the Soviet Air Force Museum in Monino south of Moscow, being flown to Monino airfield by a Tupolev OKB crew captained by Ghennadiy V. Voronchenko on 29th February 1980; in so doing the aircraft made the Tu-144's one and only landing on an unpaved runway. CCCP-77107 became a ground instructional airframe at the Kazan' Aviation Institute (KAI), while CCCP-77108 served the same purpose at the Kuibyshev Aviation Institute (KuAI; now called the Samara State Aerospace University, SGAU – *Samarskiy gosudarstvennyy aviatsionnyy ooniversitet*). CCCP-77110 was flown to Ul'yanovsk-Baratayevka airfield on 1st July 1984, becoming an exhibit of the Civil Air Fleet Museum in 1990. After sitting idle at Zhukovskiy for several years Tu-144D CCCP-77112 was sold to the Auto- und Technik Museum in Sinsheim, Germany, in 2000 and delivered there by barge (via the Moskva River, the Baltic Sea, the North Sea, the Rhine and the Neckar) and then by road. Sister ship CCCP-77114 was converted to the Tu-144LL research aircraft for the SST-2 programme (see Chapter 10). CCCP-77115 still sits at Zhukovskiy and is a candidate for preservation, although it was in danger of being scrapped for a while. This aircraft was displayed statically at four consecutive Moscow airshows – MAKS-2007 (21st-26th August), MAKS-2009 (18th-23rd August), MAKS-2011 (16th-21st August) and MAKS-2013 (27th August – 1st September). The others (apart from the two crashed aircraft) have been scrapped.

Lessons learned

Thus, the development and operation of the Tu-144 was not merely the creation of just another new airliner (or, God forbid, merely a 'can-do' exercise of expensive showmanship) – it truly marked a new lap in the development of aviation science and technology, yielding new structural materials and so on. The whole of the Soviet Union's scientific and technological potential associated with aircraft technology was brought into play and the following objectives were completed:

Knowledge was obtained and theoretical and practical methods were evolved of creating aerodynamic layouts offering a high lift/drag ratio at supersonic speeds. At Mach 2.2 the Tu-144 had a lift/drag ratio close to 8.0; by comparison, the production Tu-22 supersonic bomber had an L/D ratio no better than 4.4 at Mach 2.0, while the projected Tu-135 bomber was expected to achieve 6.4.

The development and refining of the Tu-144 was by far the largest and most complex programme the Soviet aircraft industry had tackled until then. The result was a world-class aircraft.

The Soviet engineers evolved methods of calculating stable and gradient temperatures of aircraft structures and methods of designing airframe structures able to withstand temperatures of 100-120°C (212-247°F). Typical airframe structures able to withstand kinetic heating cycles and the methods of their calculation were devised; manufacturing technologies and equipment for producing heat-resistant airframe structures (including those made of titanium) were developed. The foundations were laid for large-scale use of titanium in airframe structures.

Methods of creating heat-resistant structural materials, lubricants, sealants and so on were devised. As part of a joint effort with Western companies, the Tu-144LL research aircraft was created.

The ecological aspects of operating an SST (the emission of large amounts of exhaust gases at high altitude and the impact on the ozone layer) were explored. The effects of the SST's engine noise and sonic boom on people, animals and buildings were explored, as was the effect of solar radiation on the occupants of the aircraft during prolonged flight at high altitude.

A new air conditioning system ensuring passenger comfort during prolonged flight in kinetic heating conditions at up to 20,000 m (65,620 ft) was created. New devices and systems enabling automatic flight control, accurate navigation during prolonged supersonic cruise and automatic landing were created.

The creation of the Tu-144 boosted the development of the Tupolev OKB's other heavy supersonic aircraft. Many of the Tu-144's aerodynamic and structural features, as well as its systems design philosophy, were used for the Tu-22M *Backfire* multi-mode heavy bomber and Tu-160 *Blackjack* multi-mode strategic bomber.

Chapter 7

The Accidents

Episode One: The Le Bourget mystery
On 4th June 1973 all of the Soviet Union's leading newspapers with nationwide distribution ran a news item reading as follows: *'The Communist Party Central Committee and the Soviet Council of Ministers inform with deep regret that Merited Test Pilot M. V. Kozlov (Hero of the Soviet Union), test pilot V. M. Molchanov, aircraft navigator G. N. Bazhenov, deputy chief project engineer Engineer-Major-General V. N. Benderov, engineer in charge B. A. Pervookhin and flight engineer A. I. Dralin have lost their lives during a demonstration flight of the Soviet Tu-144 aircraft near Le Bourget airfield in the vicinity of Paris on 3rd June 1973, and extend their condolences to the families and relatives of the deceased'*. Such official obituaries were fairly common in the Soviet press when a statesman or some other notable person passed away. However, in this case it was, in effect, an advance obituary for the Tu-144 – from this point its fortunes suffered a dramatic downturn.

As mentioned earlier, Tu-144 CCCP-77102 arrived at Le Bourget for the 30th Paris Air Show on 23rd May 1973. The aircraft remained in the static display for the trade days, but two demonstration flights were scheduled for the weekend, when the show was open to the general public.

In accordance with the officially approved demonstration flight profile, after taking off from runway 03 – the longest of the three runways at Le Bourget – with an unstick speed of 360 km/h (223 mph) the Tu-144 was to initiate a left turn with 35° bank,

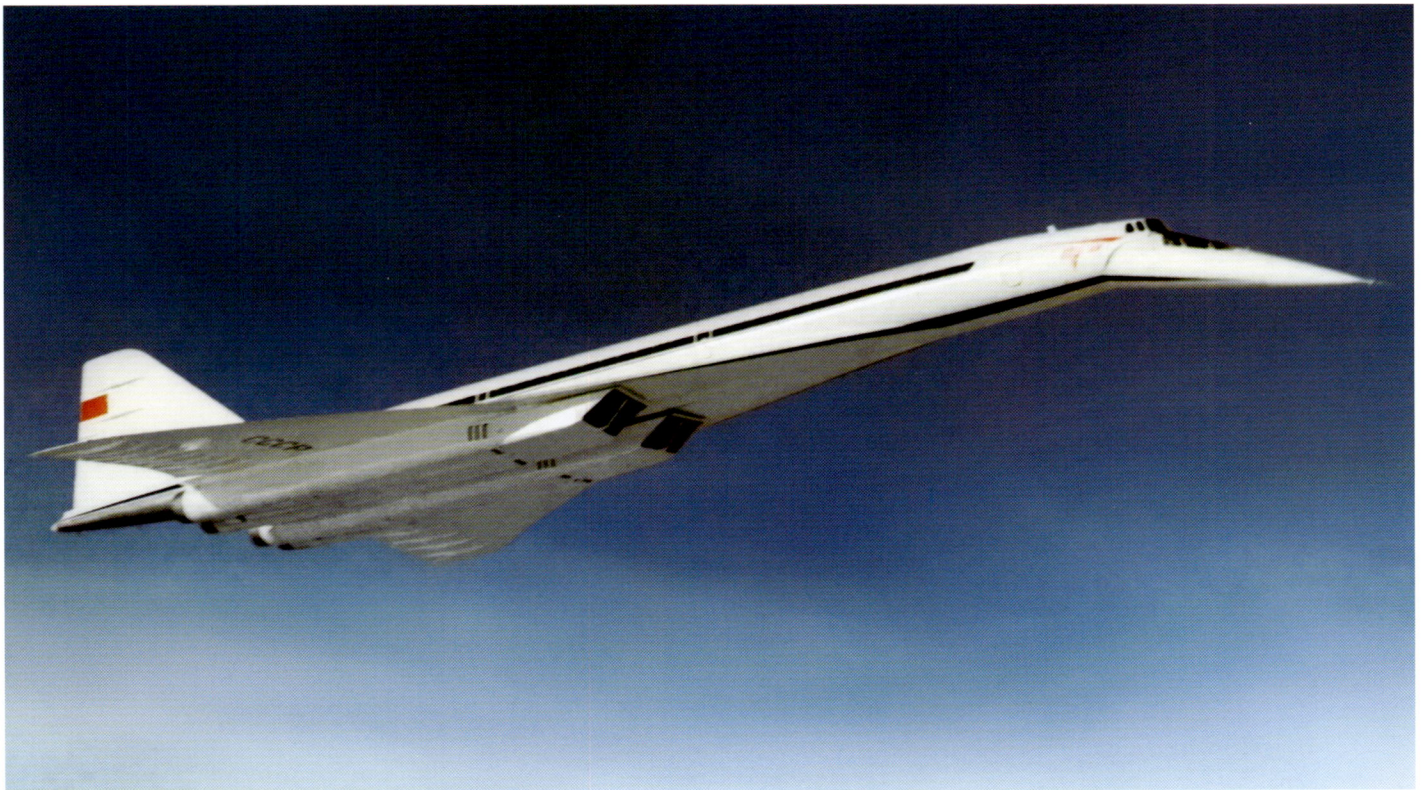

CCCP-77102, the ill-fated Tu-144 that would be lost at the 1973 Paris Air Show, in an early test flight. The aircraft is in intermediate configuration – the landing gear and canards are retracted but the nose visor is still at maximum deflection.

Standoff at Le Bourget – the Tu-144 taxies in after the demo flight on 2nd June 1973 while Concorde 001 F-WTSS begins its display routine with a steep climb.

Left: The Tu-144 rotates for take-off from Le Bourget's runway 03.

Below left: CCCP-77102 produces an impressive puff of smoke as its 16 mainwheels touch the runway on 2nd June. Little did anyone know that this would be its last landing...

Above right: Tu-144 CCCP-77102 depicted during one of its 'low and slow' passes over runway 03/21 as part of its display routine.

Right: CCCP-77102 makes a steep climbing turn during its last take-off on 3rd June 1973.

accelerating to 400 km/h (248 mph), 'clean up', then make a right turn with 35-40° bank onto a reciprocal heading and accelerate to pass over runway 21 at 550 km/h (341 mph) with the nose in cruise configuration. Maintaining this speed, it would then make a U-turn to the right with 45° bank, decelerate to 450 km/h (279 mph) at the end of the downwind leg, make another U-turn, lower the nose visor, extend the landing gear and canards, and pass over the runway in approach configuration at 350 km/h (217 mph). Next, the Tu-144 would make a right turn with 32° bank and break left to land, with an approach speed of 350-300 km/h (217-186 mph). The entire routine lasted 10 minutes 48 seconds.

During the first demo flight on 2nd June the crew of CCCP-77102 stuck unfailingly to this flight profile. But the chief competitor – Concorde 001 (the first prototype, registered F-WTSS) – was also there, and of course it was also in the flying display; interestingly, its exhibit code 154 was the reverse of the Tu-144's exhibit code, 451. The Concorde wowed the crowds at Le Bourget with its demonstration flight; immediately after take-off it pulled up into an extremely steep climb, which was followed by a series of spectacular tight turns at low altitude. The 'cherry on the cake' was the efficient deceleration by reverse thrust when the aircraft came to a halt in the middle of the runway, then applied full thrust and took off again.

Of course, the Soviet delegation at the show saw this; the officials heading the delegation decided that 'we have to do better than that' and that the Tu-144's demo flight the next day had to overshadow the Concorde by all means. And overshadow it did...

On 3rd June, the closing day of the show, the Tu-144 made its second demo flight. Almost as soon as it became airborne at 1519 hrs local time, the pilots of the other Soviet machines at the show sensed something was wrong; the Tu-144 crew was trying to emulate the Concorde's flight profile. After a series of very tight turns CCCP-77102 made a 'low and slow' pass instead of touching down, then engaged full afterburner at approximately 190 m (620 ft) and pulled up into a 45-50° climb about 1 km (3,280 ft) from the runway's end, retracting the landing gear and the canards. Seconds later, the Tu-144 levelled off at approximately 1,200 m (3,940 ft), then inexplicably entered a steep dive and broke up in mid-air when trying to recover from it, the port wing failing at the root and separating from the rest of the airframe. A pall of kero-

sene mist enveloped the falling aircraft for a second before it burst into flames, crashing in the Parisian suburb of Goussainville (aka Le Vieux Village), 6.5 km (4 miles) from the end of runway 03. The time was 1529 hrs.

The entire crew – captain Mikhail V. Kozlov, co-pilot Valeriy M. Molchanov, flight engineer Anatoliy I. Dralin, navigator Gheorgiy N. Bazhenov, engineer in charge Boris A. Pervookhin and deputy chief designer Vladimir N. Benderov – died on the spot. There was also collateral damage – 15 houses were destroyed or damaged, and eight residents of Goussainville, including three children, lost their lives.

Edgar F. Krupyanskiy, a former Tupolev OKB engineer who was then assigned as maintenance team chief to another Soviet aircraft at the show (Tu-154 *sans suffixe* CCCP-85012, exhibit code 452) and assisted with the maintenance of the Tu-144, recalls these events as follows:

'In early 1973 we started preparing the Tu-144 for the 30th Paris Air Show. This involved flying along air routes with navigation beacons; the flight plan envisaged supersonic cruise until the West German border and subsonic flight from there to Paris. The crew included Aeroflot navigator Gheorgiy Nikolayevich Bazhenov and our (Tupolev OKB – Auth.) first officer Valeriy Mikhaïlovich Molchanov, both of whom [had been picked because they] spoke English. [...]

After the first flying display day we took a long stroll around night Paris, just to say goodbye to the city because the airshow would be closing after the flying display on 3rd June. On returning to the hotel I found that my suite was locked (I shared a suite with E. V. Yelian) (the captain of Tu-154 CCCP-85012 – Auth.). As I walked past V. N. Benderov's suite I overheard a lively discussion inside. When I entered, the entire flight crew [of the Tu-144] was there, as was E. V. Yelian. On seeing me they fell silent abruptly; I realised they were discussing something that I was not supposed to know. I took the key [from Yelian] and walked off, intending to go to bed.

Early in the morning we drove off to the airfield in order to prepare the jets for the day's flying. Once the pre-flight maintenance on the Tu-144 was completed, I climbed the gangway and entered the aircraft to report to the crew that the aircraft was ready to fly. They had a visitor – the [Soviet] cosmonaut [Vladimir A.] Shatalov, who was having a lively conversation with the crew. Yuriy G. Yefimov, who was also aboard, suggested that I should ask M. V. Kozlov for permission for us to fly with him. I declined on the pretext that we had yet to prepare the Tu-154 for flight. Together with Shatalov and his retinue we left the aircraft, only the flight crew remaining aboard. [...] The Tu-144's planned flight profile was the same as the other day. We watched the flight from the Tu-154's hardstand, which was well away from the runway.

The Tu-144 executed the two planned passes over the runway perfectly. Then, instead of coming in to land, it began a third fly-by, which was not on the flight plan. I expected the Soviet representative on the control tower, the chief of MAP's flight operations department Oleg Ivanovich Belostotskiy, to cancel this unscheduled pass and order the crew to land, but this was not done. The

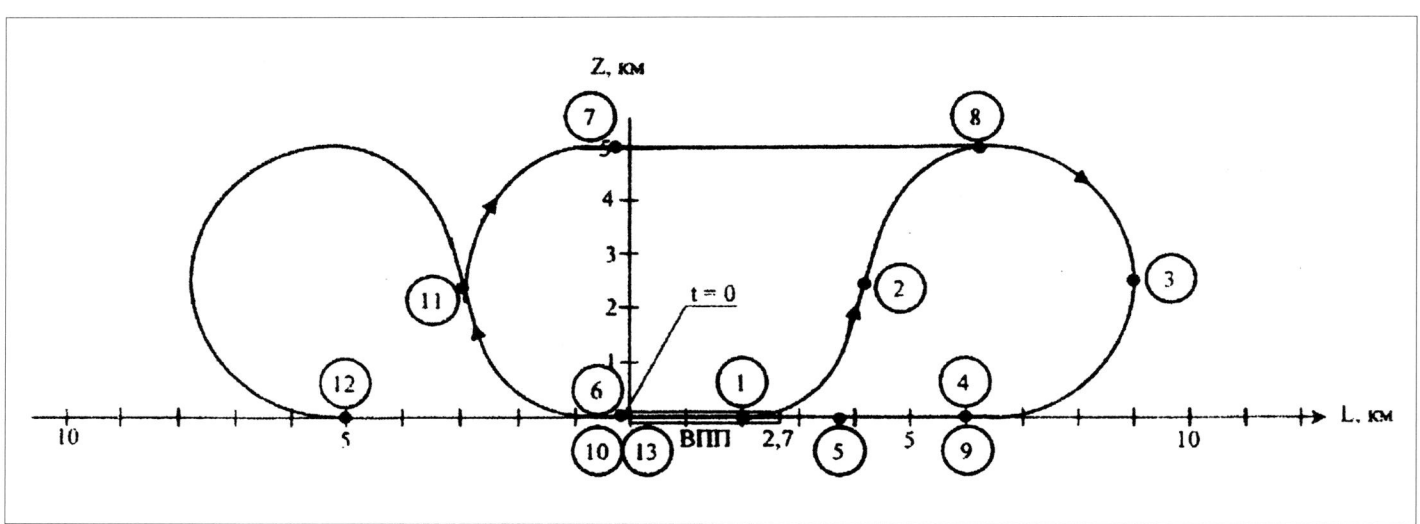

A diagram of the Tu-144's officially approved demonstration flight profile at Le Bourget on 2nd/3rd June 1973. The coordinate lines show the distance from the spot where the aircraft began its take-off run. The numbers in circles are decoded as follows:

0-1. Take-off run, acceleration to 360 km/h (223 mph) – executed in 36 seconds (mission time 00:36).
1-2. Left turn at 400 km/h (248 mph), 35° bank – 36 sec (01:12).
2-3. Right turn at 400 km/h, 35° bank – 72 sec (02:24).
3-4. Right turn at 450 km/h (279 mph), 40° bank – 30 sec (02:54).
4-5. Acceleration to 550 km/h (341 mph) – 18 sec (03:12).
5-6. Flypast over the runway at 550 km/h – 30 sec (03:42).
6-7. U-turn at 550 km/h, 45° bank – 54 sec (04:36).
7-8. Flypast and deceleration to 450 km/h, wings level – 30 sec (05:06).
8-9. U-turn, gear extension, nose visor lowering – 72 sec (06:18).
9-10. Flypast at 350 km/h (217 mph) – 48 sec (07:06).
10-11. Right turn at 350 km/h, 32° bank – 42 sec (07:48).
11-12. 270° turn (break to land) at 350 km/h, 32° bank – 120 sec (09:48).
12-13. Final approach and landing at 350-300 km/h (217-186 mph) – 60 sec (10:48).

Thus, the entire demo flight lasted just under 11 minutes.

Chapter 7 - The Accidents

aircraft continued the fly-by. I told Nikolay Tolmachov (a well-known test navigator – Auth.), who was standing next to me, that a departure from the flight plan was bound to cause trouble... Of course, I never even imagined what sort of tragedy it would cause; I was merely thinking that after the flight our pilots would get a dressing-down from flight ops for these unauthorised manoeuvres. But what happened was that the aircraft pulled up into a very steep climb when it was about halfway down the runway. We could clearly see the deployed canards. I even had the impression it was going to flip over on its back. Then the aircraft abruptly started descending – almost diving, and as it levelled out abruptly at 400-500 m [1,310-1,640 ft], the aircraft came apart in mid-air before our very eyes.

It took a while for the tragedy to sink in. Exclaiming "What have they done, what have they done!", E. V. Yelian jumped into a car that was standing on ready alert beside the hardstand and sped off to somewhere, leaving the rest of us beside the Tu-154. We stood there in sullen silence, mulling over the tragedy that had just occurred. A while later a coach carrying several OKB employees drove up and we were told to lock up the aircraft because our demo flight had been cancelled – although we could see that the flying display was going on as if nothing had happened. We boarded the coach and drove to the crash site in the town of Goussainville, about 7 km (4.35 miles) from the airfield. We were not allowed to leave the bus because rescue work was in progress and the locals were incensed by the fatalities in their town.'

A joint Franco-Soviet accident investigation board was formed on 4th June to determine the cause of the tragedy. It was chaired by Engineer-General Forestier and included Engineer-General Carour (Vice-Chairman), engineers de Batz and Dumas, and pilots Maj. Bolliet and Maj. Dudal of the French Air Force. In keeping with an agreement between the Soviet Minister of Aircraft Industry Pyotr V. Dement'yev and the French Minister of National Defence Robert Galley, the Soviet Union was represented by Vice-Minister of Aircraft Industry Vasiliy A. Kazakov (head of the Soviet expert team), Vice-Minister of Civil Aviation A. A. Aksyonov, Engineer-Colonel-General Mikhail N. Mishuk (Deputy C-in-C of the Soviet Air Force), General Designer Aleksey A. Tupolev, TsAGI Director Gheorgiy P. Svishchev and LII Director Vasiliy V. Ootkin. Additionally, Tupolev OKB specialists and test pilots – Yuriy V. Lyubimov, Gheorgiy A. Cheryomukhin, Valentin I. Bliznyuk, Aleksandr L. Pookhov, Yuriy N. Popov, Eduard V. Yelian, Donat A. Kozhevnikov and V. V. Tishchenko – were called upon to assist with the investigation.

The painstaking work of collecting bits and pieces of wreckage from the crash site for examination and studying photos and cine/video footage of the Tu-144's last flight began. The pictorial evidence was of special importance, since (according to the official story) the cockpit voice recorder had been switched off during the last flight, while the test equipment recorders and the flight data recorder (FDR) were so badly damaged they could not be deciphered. The French government even promised a reward for photo/video materials that would shed light on the causes of the crash. Much of the incoming material had to be rejected as it had been filmed on 2nd June, but footage shot by French television and amateur cine footage filmed from Goussainville proved helpful.

CCCP-77102 caught by the camera of the French Mirage IIIR as it strays to the right from the extended centreline of runway 03/21 and begins its terminal dive. The canards are beginning to deploy.

Here we will let Edgar F. Krupyanskiy, who was one of the 'tin kickers', tell the story again. *'We spent the rest of the day* (3rd June – *Auth.*) *at the hotel, discussing possible causes of the accident. In the morning we were divided into teams, each team member receiving a personal assignment, and were driven to Goussainville. R. Kvitsiniya, N. Mironov and I were tasked first with taking samples of fuel, hydraulic fluid and engine oil if possible, then joining the team of Yu. I. Bol'shakov, Yu. G. Yefimov and V. F. Molchanov searching for the FDR. First, however, we were taken to the flight deck section's resting place to help with identifying the bodies of our comrades. There were four of them there – V. N. Benderov, V. M. Molchanov, M. V. Kozlov and G. N. Bazhenov; the bodies were badly mutilated and hard to identify. [...] The other two crew members – A. I. Dralin and [B. A.] Pervookhin – had been thrown clear of the aircraft as it disintegrated; their bodies were later found in the streets of Goussainville. Next, each team received one or two French policemen as escort and set off to do their respective jobs. [...] Soon enough we found the fuel, oil and hydraulic system filters and obtained the required samples.*

At the end of the first day [of the investigation] I joined the team looking for the 'black box', but we found nothing that day. The following day, however, we noticed a round dent in the wall of one of the small houses in Goussainville (the MSRP-12 FDR had a spherical casing) and decided we should check out the adjoining

grounds. The police officer escorting us made arrangements with the proprietor, and we were allowed on the grounds. [...] To our disappointment we found a piece of the FDR's tape tract; this meant that the recorder had disintegrated on impact, and the chances of finding the tape were close to nil. (By the way, the other teams turned up many fragments of magnetic tape, but these were of a different type and came from the test equipment recorders, of which there were about ten.) Just when our hope was lowest we noted a trash can which the proprietor, who was cleaning the grounds, was carrying. It contained a badly damaged object which resembled the FDR tape cassette we were after; a close look confirmed that we had hit the jackpot. Mindful of the test engineer's circuit breaker panel (which they had found on the first day and which had strange switch settings; more about this later – *Auth*.), *now we had to get this cassette to our bosses without attracting the French officer's attention.* (Apparently Krupyanskiy implies there were apprehensions that the French side might attempt to conceal

Top left: A still from an amateur cine film shot from outside Le Bourget airfield, showing the burning Tu-144 plunging earthwards over the rooftops of Goussainville.

Above: The Tu-144's wreckage mingled with the debris of a house. One of the engines is clearly visible in the foreground.

Above left: French fire-fighters at work at the scene of the crash.

Left: An armed French policeman guards a large piece of wreckage – clearly a fragment of one of the Tu-144's LERXes – lying in one of the streets of Goussainville.

Right: An aerial view of the crash site showing the devastation in the part of Goussainville where the main wreckage came down.

Below right: Another large piece of wreckage – apparently again a fragment of the Tu-144's wing. The cylindrical object in the foreground is probably not part of the aircraft.

Bottom: One more view of the LERX fragment resting on the damaged fence of a private house.

Bottom right: A fireman looks at a house in Goussainville demolished by the falling wreckage of the aircraft.

relevant information or otherwise hinder the investigation – *Auth*.) *The French had set aside a place in the town square where the aircraft's wreckage was accumulated in two large heaps – parts that were of interest for the accident investigation board and parts that were irrelevant. Of course, it was the Russian specialists who did the sorting, being familiar with the aircraft's design. So what we did was throw the cassette in the 'irrelevant' heap along with other minor fragments. Later, one of the designers (Donat Andreyevich Kozhevnikov, if memory serves) was asked to retrieve the cassette from the heap and urgently take it to Moscow, which is what he did. Officially the FDR tape was listed as "not found".*

At the Soviet Air Force's Aviation Hardware Operation & Repair Research Institute (NII ERAT VVS – *Naoochno-issledovatel'skiy institoot ekspluatahtsii i remonta aviatsionnoy tekhniki Voyenno-vozdooshnykh seel*) *the tape was deciphered under the auspices of a high-ranking KGB general. The four of us who had found the tape had to give a written pledge not to divulge anything about the tape, because it was classified information.'* (It should be noted that Vadim M. Razumikhin, a control systems specialist of the Tupolev OKB, casts doubt on this part of the story, stating that the FDR tape was indeed not found and that Kozhevnikov carried the CVR tape, which turned out to be blank. Krupyanskiy's memoirs were written 20 years after the event in question, and the man might be forgetting things – or inventing things, said Razumikhin.)

The wreckage was initially stored in a hangar at Le Bourget. Later several quasi-civil Soviet Air Force An-22s carried it to Zhukovskiy, where a wooden mock-up of the Tu-144 had been built, and the bits and pieces were matched to it for reconstruction of the airframe. The parts of the aircraft's control system were laid out separately alongside.

Eventually the accident investigation board found no technical fault with the Tu-144, ascribing the accident to several human causes. One of these was the presence of an unsecured crew member in the flight deck holding a cine camera, which might have been dropped, becoming wedged against the control column, impairing pitch control. Fact is, before the second demo flight the French TV channel RTF approached the Soviet delegation at the show, requesting permission for a cameraman to fly aboard the Tu-144 and film the crew at work. Given that the Tu-144's flight deck was rather cramped and there was no room for any extra persons, the request was turned down; however, as the next-best thing, Vladimir N. Benderov offered to act as the cameraman. The offer was gladly accepted, and during the 3rd June flight Benderov went aboard armed with an 8-mm Bell & Howell hand-held cine camera lent to him by the French TV crew.

The other was the presence of a Dassault Mirage IIIR photo reconnaissance aircraft from the French Air Force's ER 3/33 'Moselle' reconnaissance squadron which had taken off from Entzheim AB near Strasbourg to film a panorama of the airshow. Unbeknownst to the Tu-144's crew, it was passing over Le Bourget's runway 03/21 at high altitude at the exact time of the airliner's flight – according to one theory, specifically for the purpose of filming the Soviet SST and its famous canards. The theory was that the fighter came too close to the Tu-144 and the latter's pilots took violent evasive action on seeing it, overstressing the aircraft. We will come back to these theories a little later.

After analysing the wreckage and studying other available evidence the accident investigation board concluded that there had been no engine failures, no stall caused by exceeding AOA limits, no sabotage, no explosion or fire prior to the aircraft's disintegration, no incapacitation of the crew members; the flight control system was fully functional until the moment of the aircraft's disintegration, which was caused by the aircraft exceeding its G limits during recovery from the dive. The official conclusion ran as follows:

'1.1. No abnormalities in the functioning of the aircraft and its systems that might suggest the cause of the accident have been detected.

1.2. One hypothetical explanation of the cause of the accident has been suggested, proceeding from the following four factors:
- *the probable presence of Monsieur Benderov in the flight deck;*
- *the presence of a Bell & Howell cine camera in the flight deck;*
- *the presence of a Mirage IIIR aircraft close to the Tu-144 aircraft;*
- *the presence of a recess at the base of the Tu-144's control column.*

1.3. However, this hypothesis does not take account of all available facts [relating to the crash], and there is no material evidence to prove or disprove it.

That said, the cause of the accident cannot be determined.

Executed on 6th February 1974 in Paris.' (signed by the members of the investigation board and the experts)

Proceeding from the above, the following official statement was made and circulated in the Soviet press:

'Statement on the investigation of the crash of the Tu-144 aircraft at the airshow in France on 3rd June 1973.

The French panel investigating the crash of the Tu-144 has completed the conclusive research of all materials and circumstances relating to the accident. The panel received all possible assistance from a group of Soviet experts; it was also assisted by competent organisations researching the case in the Soviet Union.

The French and Soviet experts are unanimous in their conclusion that there were no abnormalities in the aircraft's design, nor in the functioning of the aircraft and its systems. Therefore, the human factor is the most likely cause.

The most often cited hypothesis is based on two facts. On the one hand, a Mirage IIIR aircraft was flying close to the Tu-144

aircraft. Even though investigation has shown that there was no real danger of a mid-air collision, the Soviet pilot may have been startled [by the appearance of the Mirage] and may have made a sudden evasive manoeuvre.

On the other hand, a crew member (the person in charge of the flight tests) was in the Tu-144's flight deck without being strapped in. The final manoeuvres of the aircraft may have caused this crew member (probably holding a cine camera) to fall, temporarily impairing the pilot's actions.

However, this hypothesis does not take account of all available facts [relating to the crash], and there is no material evidence to prove or disprove it. Therefore, the investigation panel and the Soviet experts have agreed that the cause of the accident cannot be determined and the case should be closed.'

The aviation community was disgusted by such a conclusion, and the aviation experts were seriously miffed by this attempt to put the blame on the crew. Yet, there was no point in discussing the matter because all materials related to the crash were immediately stamped 'Secret' (air accident investigation materials were generally classified in the Soviet Union until the mid-1980s). Also, such a conclusion suited the Soviet and French governments just fine – especially since the Soviet Union agreed to pay for the collateral damage. The Soviet and French governments agreed to keep the investigation results secret. High-level politics were involved; the Soviet government regarded France as a privileged partner and did not want anything to cloud the Franco-Soviet relations – like suggestions that maybe France was to blame for the crash or whatever.

The true cause of the accident remained a mystery. Not surprisingly, given the lack of readily accessible true information, this crash became a popular subject for unscrupulous persons seeking political dividends and all manner of conspirologists accusing the West of *'sabotaging our Tu-144 in order to eliminate the competitor to their Concorde'.*

Coming back to the abovementioned theories: the idea that the dive was an evasive manoeuvre in order to avoid a collision with the Mirage IIIR was seriously considered by the Soviet specialists for a while. This was about apportioning blame: if the Soviets managed to prove that the Mirage pilot was at fault, then the French could be persuaded to split the compensation for the collateral damage 50/50. During the investigation the Soviet team

Left: The wreckage of Tu-144 CCCP-77102 pieced together in a hangar at Zhukovskiy during the investigation.

Above: The crew of CCCP-77102. Left to right: Mikhail V. Kozlov, Gheorgiy N. Bazhenov, Vladimir N. Benderov, Boris A. Pervookin, Anatoliy I. Dralin and Valeriy M. Molchanov.

Right: The grave of the Tu-144 crew at the Novodevich'ye Cemetery in Moscow.

would gather each afternoon at the Soviet embassy to report on progress to Vasiliy A. Kazakov. One evening LII Director Vasiliy V. Ootkin turned up late at such a meeting; apologising for this, he told that he had had a talk with the French pilots and received photo materials from the pilot of that very Mirage. Aleksandr L. Pookhov recalled: *'[Ootkin] produced three photos. the first of these showed the Tu-144 below and to the right [of the Mirage], seen from behind and climbing vigorously; the second showed the Tu-144 quite close and to the right, and the third was a picture of Goussainville with explosions where the Tu-144 had fallen. Since I had by then plotted several flight paths of the Mirage and the Tu-144 with respect to each other, I addressed Kazakov and Tupolev, speaking loud and clear: "These photos let us prove beyond doubt that the Mirage interfered with the Tu-144's flight". In the ensuing silence Kazakov said: "If we are able to prove it, that will put us in a much better position..."*

Claims that the Mirage pilot had (albeit unintentionally) provoked the crash by creating the danger of collision persisted for a while; for example, test pilot Eduard V. Yelian commented in the 1990s that *'this accident was a bitter reminder of how a number of what at first seem trivial acts of carelessness – in this instance by the French flight control – can have tragic consequences'*. Even in 1997, one Yuriy Kovalenko – a staff writer for the Russian daily *Izvestiya* – stuck to this point of view in his newspaper feature.

Yet the 'Mirage theory' can hardly be considered viable – for two reasons. Firstly, the fighter was directly above the airliner – that was the prerequisite for photographing a good plan view of it. With the nose visor raised, the way it was immediately before the crash, the Tu-144's pilots had an extremely limited field of view – mostly to the sides and, to a lesser extent, forward – and would have been unable to see an aircraft flying above them. Secondly, people in the trade who knew Mikhail V. Kozlov characterised him as a highly professional pilot, saying he would not have made such a dangerous manoeuvre intentionally, initiating a steep dive at such low altitude – even as an evasive manoeuvre; he would more likely have made a horizontal manoeuvre. Thus, the dive must have been caused by reasons outside the pilots' control, coming as a complete surprise for them.

The theory that Vladimir N. Benderov dropped the camera, which blocked the control column, was disproved in the course of experiments following the crash. For one thing, the FDR readouts do not support this theory; for another, when the Tu-144 entered the dive Benderov, who was not strapped in, would be lifted to the flight deck ceiling together with the camera. Finally, attempts to replicate the situation on the 'iron bird' control system test rig/simulator in Moscow failed – the dummy camera would not block the controls, no matter how it was tossed. 'Success' came only when the aperture in the floor at the base of the control column was enlarged. This goes to show that some of the investigators were more interested in finding evidence to support a politically convenient conclusion than in establishing the true facts.

That said, it can be stated that neither the Mirage IIIR nor the cine camera were contributing factors to the accident.

The underlying reason of the Le Bourget disaster was simple. Driven by the political and technological rivalry between the East and the West, the bosses of the Soviet delegation decided that the Tu-144 had to excel the Concorde by all means. Therefore, after lengthy discussions, in the evening of 2nd June the flight crew received off-the-record instructions to depart from the officially approved flight profile and 'show them'. This explains why Mikhail V. Kozlov performed that extra pass and climb; being a disciplined and sober-minded pilot, he would not have performed such antics spontaneously. (Kozlov was opposed to this plan and took a lot of persuading before he agreed; eyewitnesses said after-

The charred wreckage of Tu-144D CCCP-77111 in a field near Yegor'yevsk on 23rd May 1978. The aircraft was almost completely consumed by the post-crash fire. Only the No. 1 engine remains in place, the other three having broken off on impact.

Chapter 7 - The Accidents

wards he looked worried before the flight.) It also explains why Oleg I. Belostotskiy did not intervene – he obviously knew about this 'contingency plan', which had been approved by his boss, Minister of Aircraft Industry Pyotr V. Dement'yev. Finally, it explains why the air traffic controller gave the Tu-144 crew another five minutes for the 3rd June display routine.

However, it does not explain why the aircraft made such abrupt manoeuvres. Test pilots who flew the type said that with the control system operating normally it was impossible to generate such extreme G loads which overstressed the airframe of CCCP-77102. And here the explanation is different: in the last flight the control system was *not* operating normally. The aircraft's ABSU-144 AFCS included a stability and control augmentation system (SCAS) which was to generate additional control inputs in the pitch and roll channels. One of the two types of signals generated by the SCAS deflected the rudder in concert with the elevons when the latter were used for roll control; this mode had been tested on Tu-144 CCCP-77101 in 1971-72. The other type of signals was for pitch control/trim and had not been tested yet; importantly, it was generated only when the canards were retracted.

Here, two facts deserve special mention. Firstly, since the SCAS was experimental and there was not enough time to test it properly before the 1973 airshow, a decision was taken to disable the system before the show. Yet, according to Vadim M. Razumikhin (one of the system's designers), the wiring for the system's sensors, which had been purposely disconnected, was mistakenly reconnected when the aircraft was being serviced for the show. The SCAS was activated by two circuit breakers on the AFCS's gearing ratio control panel at the test engineer's workstation which allowed the control surface gearing ratio to be altered (it was this panel Krupyanskiy was referring to).

Secondly, during the demo flights this control panel was supposed to be closed by a hinged cover with a lead seal; yet, examination of the wreckage showed that the cover was open and this was *not* a result of the impact. Moreover, of the 20 switches on this panel only the two SCAS circuit breakers were set to 'on'.

So, what happened on 3rd June? It is known that one of the SCAS channels – the roll channel – had been activated during the flight on 2nd June (which went normally). Accordingly on 3rd July one of the crew members – it is hard to say who, but probably Boris A. Pervookhin – had wanted to repeat this procedure and accidentally switched on both channels of the SCAS, and with maximum gearing ratio at that; this proved fatal.

When CCCP-77102 pulled up into that last climb at 30°, the canards were deployed. At about 800 m (2,620 ft) the crew initiated retraction of the canards (which takes about 20 seconds) in order to ease the planned transition to level flight before the break to land. Ten seconds after the transition at 1,200 m (3,940 ft) the canards locked into retracted position – and the SCAS was thus activated, generating a control input that instantly deflected the elevons 10° down. At a speed of 500 km/h (310 mph), the aircraft immediately tipped over into a dive, pulling –1.5Gs; the pitch rate was about 8°/sec and the dive angle eventually reached 38°. The Tu-144 descended with a sink rate of 100 m/sec (19,680 ft/min), accelerating to 650 km/h (403 mph); the pilots hauled back on the control columns but were unable to override the additional artificial-feel unit which kicked in concurrently with retraction of the canards. Seven seconds into the dive, realising what had provoked it, Kozlov gave orders to deploy the canards again. As the canards started deploying, this artificial-feel unit was deactivated and the elevons moved to maximum upward deflection. As a result, the aircraft pulled +4 Gs, overstressing the wings as it started to recover from the dive with a 5°/sec pitch rate; had the wing structure been stronger, the recovery would have been successful at 100-150 m (330-490 ft) and 4.2 Gs. Five seconds after recovery initiation the port wing failed at 280 m (920 ft), the aircraft rolled to port and the fuselage broke as well. The maximum speed in the dive reached 780 km/h (464 mph).

It has to be said that measures were taken immediately after the cause of the accident became known. In August 1973 the Tupolev OKB, TsAGI and LII joined forces to modify the ABSU-144 AFCS. Elevon travel commanded by the servos was reduced from 10° to 5°, the additional control inputs generated by the SCAS were eliminated, leaving this system with only damping functions, a pitch trim function dependent on the canards' position was added and so on. Additionally, structural revisions were made. All these changes were introduced fleetwide in 1974-75.

Another consequence of the Le Bourget accident was that Tu-144 CCCP-77101 underwent a special high-alpha test programme a few months after the crash, with Yevgeniy A. Goryunov as project test pilot. For safety's sake the high-alpha test runs were made at 6,000 m (19,685 ft) to provide ample room for recovery in the event of a stall or spin. The canards were in the deployed position, as they had been during the last flight of CCCP-77102. The pilot was to haul back on the control yoke until the aircraft reached an AOA of 15-17° and then push the control yoke fully forward. The aircraft's reaction to this latter control input was slow at first, and the rate at which the nose would drop depended on the flight speed. The most dangerous behaviour was recorded at 340 km/h (211 mph). Goryunov recalled: *'It was a most uncomfortable feeling, sitting in the flight deck during those tests. The nose dipped very gently at first, and only when the canards started giving negative lift – apparently it was the canards that were to blame – the nose would suddenly drop, sharply and treacherously. And then you had to pull the aircraft out of the dive, slowly and carefully...'*

During the dive and recovery the Tu-144 would lose at least 1,300 m (4,260 ft) of altitude; in contrast, with the canards retracted the altitude loss in these circumstances was 200-300 m (660-980 ft). It should be noted that by then CCCP-77101 had been retrofitted with a G limiter which CCCP-77102 lacked.

Episode Two: In-flight fire

The launch of scheduled services with the type seemed to indicate that the Tu-144 programme would now proceed at a steady pace. However, exactly five years after the ill-fated Tu-144's arrival at Le Bourget disaster struck again. On 23rd May 1978 CCCP-77111, the first production Tu-144D, was flying a routine test mission from Zhukovskiy; the crew comprised captain Vyacheslav. D. Popov (GosNII GA), co-pilot Eduard V. Yelian (Tupolev OKB), navigator V. V. Vyazigin (GosNII GA), flight engineers Oleg A. Nikolayev (Tupolev OKB) and Vyacheslav L. Venediktov (GosNII GA), engineers in charge of the tests Vitaliy. M. Koolesh (Tupolev

OKB), V. A. Isayev and V. N. Stolpovskiy (GosNII GA; Stolpovskiy was responsible for the powerplant).

After the customary pre-flight checks CCCP-77111 took off at 1730 hrs Moscow time. The main part of the day's flight assignment – Mach 2 cruise flight – was performed without anything untoward. As the aircraft headed back to Zhukovskiy, the crew discovered that the fuel usage rate was abnormally high, which suggested a leak had developed. There was a discrepancy of as much as 4.7 tons (10,360 lb) between the readings of the SUIT1-3 fuel metering system and the RT-32 fuel flow gauge. Here it should be noted that the aircraft was brand-new (this was its sixth flight) and the fuel system had not been calibrated, and the crew didn't know what instrument to believe. Notwithstanding this, at 1845 hrs Vitaliy M. Koolesh decided to perform one of the last items of the mission and start up the TA-6F APU in flight. By then the Tu-144D had changed course and was heading away from Zhukovskiy, towards the flight test airspace zone.

The first attempt was made when the aircraft had descended to 3,000 m (9,840 ft) and decelerated to 480 km/h (298 mph) – unsuccessfully: the APU hot-started, with a turbine temperature of 600°C (1,112°F). Increasing the speed to 500 km/h (310 mph), the crew tried again. As the APU started up, the visual and audible fire warnings went off in the flight deck, indicating a fire in the starboard engine nacelle, and the first shot of the fire suppression system was activated automatically. Almost immediately, black smoke poured into the cabin and flight deck through the air conditioning system; someone shouted orders to turn off the ACS but it is not certain if this was actually done.

Flight engineer Nikolayev, whose workstation was in the forward cabin, shut down the No.3 engine and activated the remaining two shots of the fire suppression system. The pilots made a U-turn and set course for Zhukovskiy, requesting an emergency landing with a straight-in approach (without the usual circuit of the field) and asking that crash rescue teams stand by. The No.4 engine was shut down next. Nevertheless, the fire continued.

Then the No.2 engine quit on its own, and the influx of smoke got worse. Realising they were not going to make it back to base on one engine, the pilots opted for an off-field emergency landing near the town of Yegor'yevsk, Moscow Region. A suitable field was found next to Il'yinskiy Pogost village, but as the aircraft came in for a wheels-up landing on a heading of 240°, the crew lowered the nose visor all the way – 17° – instead of the 11° position prescribed by the flight manual for such an emergency. Trying to avoid a whiplash effect at the moment of touchdown that might injure the crew, V. D. Popov reduced the angle of attack to a minimum, flaring out at 3-5 m (10-16 ft); the aircraft clipped a few treetops with the starboard wing but did not roll over. The touchdown was indeed fairly smooth, the aircraft being almost parallel to the ground, but when the nose visor dug into the soft earth it broke away, folded aft and punctured the fuselage exactly where the flight engineers sat.

As the aircraft came to rest after ploughing a 600-m (1,970-ft) furrow and shedding the engines, the fire flared up as kerosene spilled from the ruptured tanks. The pilots and the navigator evacuated through the sliding windows in the flight deck, using the escape ropes, while the rest of the crew used the forward entry door. Unfortunately not all of them were able to leave the burning aircraft. Oleg A. Nikolayev was trapped at his workstation when his instrument rack was dislodged by the impact; Vyacheslav L. Venediktov stayed behind, trying to extract him (some accounts of the crash state that he was trapped as well), and both men lost their lives, succumbing to carbon monoxide poisoning. Realising that the flight engineers were missing, V. M. Koolesh and V. D. Popov attempted to rescue them, climbing in through the flight deck window, but unsuccessfully. Also, Yelian was badly injured in the accident. The emergency had lasted six minutes. The post-crash fire destroyed the aircraft completely, only the forward fuselage section remaining relatively intact. By then CCCP-77111 had logged only 9 hours 02 minutes total time since new.

The crash was a sore blow to the Tupolev OKB – not only due to the loss of the aircraft and the death of two experienced flight engineers (Nikolayev and Venediktov were both aged 42 and were highly professional testers). The entire Tu-144 programme was now hanging in the balance; the Paris disaster was still fresh in everyone's memory. Everyone was aware that the latest accident would play into the hands of the Tu-144's opponents and could be the last straw that might lead to the termination of the programme.

As part of the accident investigation, the Tupolev OKB had to build special rigs featuring the APU, part of the fuel system and venting systems and so on in order to simulate the circumstances of the accident; it was necessary to establish how the fuel had ended up in the APU bay. After lengthy experiments, investigation showed that a fuel line had failed due to fatigue cracking near an experimental temperature sensor inside the wing centre section, causing a massive leak at a rate of approximately 220 litres (48.4 Imp gal) per minute. The cause of the failure was fuel pressure fluctuations at a rate quite unlike anything seen hitherto – the pulsation frequency was as high as 1,500 Hz versus the expected 100 Hz. Also, the lines had been subjected to hydraulic shocks when the fuel cocks were operated. Added to this, a similar technique involving a pulsing flow had been used for cleaning the fuel lines; together, these factors had 'eaten up' more than 50% of the fuel lines' service life, leading to fatigue failure at such an early stage. Nothing of the sort had been encountered on the NK-144A-powered Tu-144 *sans suffixe*. This led the OKB to redesign the fuel system – in particular, aluminium alloy pipelines were substituted with steel.

The failure of the fuel line occurred presumably at 1818 hrs (about half an hour before the crash), causing more than 8,000 kg (17,640 lb) of fuel to leak out into the surrounding wing structure, including a bay immediately above the APU. Some of it entered the APU bay via the exhaust duct; when the APU was started up it ignited the fuel vapours, and a massive fire ensued.

A few words need to be said about why the crew did not react to the perceived fuel leak. The flight was the final one in the aircraft's pre-delivery tests. As mentioned earlier, the fuel system had not yet been calibrated, and such discrepancies in the readings of the fuel management system and the fuel flow gauge (and the actual fuel amount measured on the ground!) had been seen in the previous five flights. Therefore the crew chose to trust the fuel flow gauge, which was working normally, not the fuel management system. Also, consider that the crew was under pressure to complete the pre-delivery tests and, having successfully completed most of the programme, did not want to postpone the APU check.

Chapter 8

The Tu-144 in Uniform? (Projected Military Versions)

Since the project of the Tu-144 SST that held promise of outstanding flight performance was making steady progress, the Tupolev OKB began contemplating possible military uses for this aircraft. Almost from the inception of the programme, while the Tu-144 was in the throes of its gestation period and then enjoyed its brief production life, the Tupolev OKB had several military versions on the drawing boards. For a while the Soviet military also regarded the Tu-144 as a possible platform for various missions. It should be noted that the Ministry of Defence kept an eye on the SST programme from an early stage; the Council of Ministers' Secretary on Defence Matters Marshal Dmitriy F. Ustinov (he was appointed Minister of Defence in 1976) and the Soviet Air Force Commander-in-Chief Air Marshal Pavel S. Kutakhov both frequently visited MMZ No.156 in Moscow, the OKB's flight test facility in Zhukovskiy and aircraft factory No.64 in Voronezh producing the Tu-144. The Soviet Naval Aviation (AVMF – *Aviahtsiya Voyenno-morskovo flota*), too, showed an interest in the aircraft. The reason was that at the end of the 1960s neither the Air Force nor the Navy had a reconnaissance/strike aircraft capable of penetrating the potential adversary's (read: NATO's) advanced air defence system after covering large distances in supersonic flight. At that time the Myasishchev OKB and the Sukhoi OKB were working on such aircraft – the M-70 project and the T-4 (*izdeliye* 100) respectively; yet it was the Tupolev OKB that enjoyed the strongest position in the Soviet Union as a developer of strategic strike and reconnaissance aircraft. Since the Tu-144 incorporated quite a few cutting-edge technologies and design features, military aviation would surely benefit from these as well.

When exploring possible military uses for the Tu-144, the OKB worked in two directions at once. One envisaged maximum commonality between the future combat aircraft and the commercial Tu-144 (and subsequently Tu-144D); the other envisaged an aircraft that would differ in overall dimensions and aerodynamic layout, albeit retaining the tailless-delta layout and many of the SST's design features. The following is a brief description of the military aircraft projects related to the Tu-144 that were developed in the late 1960s and in the 1970s.

Liquid hydrogen-fuelled reconnaissance aircraft

Back in 1967, when the Tu-144 powered by NK-144 afterburning turbofans did not even exist in hardware form, the OKB developed a spyplane version of the airliner. This, in itself, would be nothing out of the ordinary, had it not been for one thing – the aircraft's engines were to run on liquid hydrogen (LH_2)! The project got as far as the ADP review stage but was abandoned when the Ministry of Defence refused to finance it.

In passing, it should be noted that there were several projected versions of the Tu-144 as an airliner utilising cryogenic fuels – LH_2 and liquefied natural gas (LNG). The cryogenic tanks were to be housed in the fuselage, with an attendant reduction in seating capacity and payload. Estimates showed that, while the conversion would lead to a 10% reduction in the cruise lift/drag ratio, a hydrogen-fuelled version of the Tu-144 would have a 25-30% lower take-off weight. Of particular importance was the fact that the fuel burn of the cryogenic version would be reduced by more than 65% thanks to the higher calorific value of the cryogenic fuels.

Tu-144R missile strike system

In the early 1970s the production-standard Tu-144 *sans suffixe* powered by NK-144A engines served as the basis for a projected stand-off missile strike system. Designated Tu-144R (*raketonosets* – missile carrier), the aircraft was to carry up to three air-launched intercontinental ballistic missiles (ICBMs) with solid-propellant rocket motors carried internally in a weapons bay occupying the entire fuselage between the nosewheel well and the wing trailing edge. The designers used an ingenious weapons stowage arrangement. Since the missiles would be launched one at a time anyway, the weapons bay doors located between the engine nacelles were just a little longer than the missile, stretching from the intake lips to the main gear fulcrums. The three missiles were suspended in tandem on an overhead monorail transporter running the full length of the weapons bay, the No.2 missile being attached to a launcher that would be lowered by a pantographic mechanism into a semi-recessed position before the missile was released. When the first missile had been launched, the launcher would be raised and the next missile would slide into position.

The launch was to take place over Soviet territory, the aircraft accelerating to 2,300-2,500 km/h (1,428-1,552 mph) before releasing the missile. A number of Tu-144Rs were to stand on quick-reaction alert at airbases around the country, ready to mount a missile attack at any time; to minimise reaction time the crew would sit in a special cabin on the aircraft, waiting for the 'action

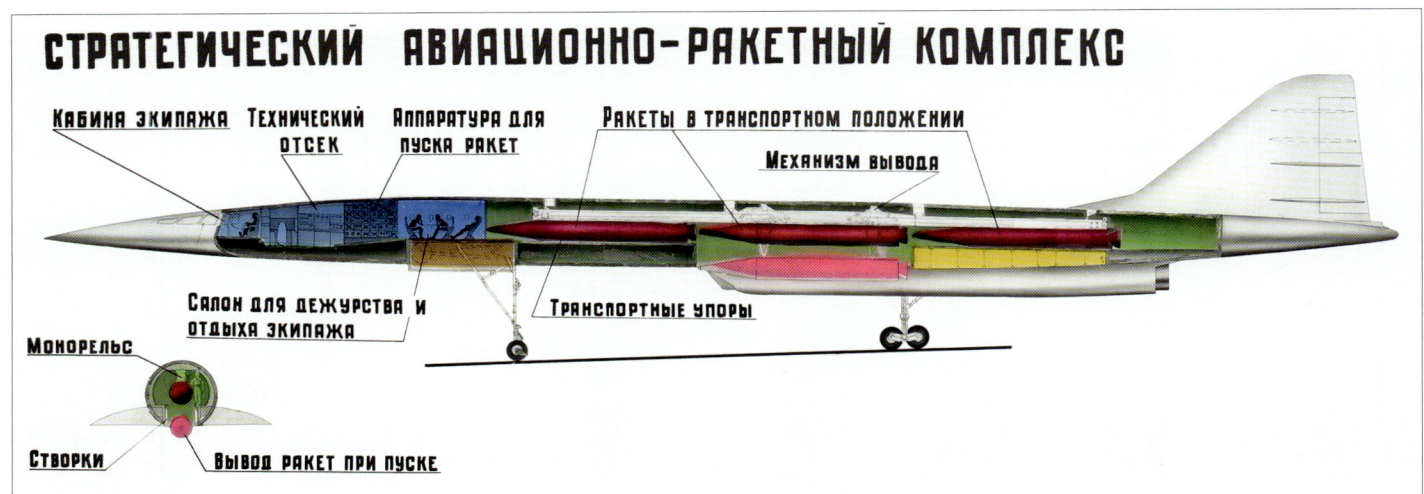

stations' command and ready to scramble within a few minutes when the order came.

This combination of round-the-clock readiness and the missile platform's high supersonic speed significantly improved the air-launched missile system's reaction time, which matched that of ground- and sea-launched ballistic missiles, and significantly reduced the system's deployment costs thanks to the relatively cheap ground components. Such a two-stage system made it possible to add the relatively short supersonic range of the aircraft to the missile's long range. The missile platform's high mobility, and the fact that the launch was to take place over 'friendly' territory where the aircraft was immune against enemy air defences, improved the system's survivability. Also, unlike ground-launched ICBMs, in the event the alarm turned out to be false the attack could be aborted within the first hour after the order to attack had been given.

The flight performance of the Tu-144R was similar to that of the airliner version. The maximum launch radius was set at 2,500 km (1,552 miles) from the base, which gave the missile system an overall range of 7,000-9,000 km (4,350-5,590 miles).

Shortly afterwards a similar weapons system based on the longer-range Tu-144D was devised. The aircraft was to have an increased fuel capacity as compared to the airliner version and be armed with much smaller and lighter missiles having a range of 3,000-5,000 km (1,860-3,100 miles), again with solid-propellant rocket motors. In order to save fuel the aircraft would proceed to the launch point mostly in subsonic cruise mode, accelerating to supersonic speed immediately before the launch. Depending on the ordnance load, the system's operational range would be 9,000-11,000 km (5,590-6,830 miles) with one missile and a flight range of some 6,000 km (3,730 miles); 8,500-10,000 km (5,280-6,210 miles) with two missiles and a flight range of some 4,500 km (2,795 miles); and 8,000-9,500 km (4,970-5,900 miles) with three missiles and a flight range of some 3,500 km (2,170 miles).

Other missile strike versions of the Tu-144 which did not proceed past the preliminary design stage included versions armed with long-range air-launched cruise missiles – rather similar to the weapon which was later carried by the Tu-95MS *Bear-H* and Tu-160 as the Kh-55 (NATO codename AS-15 *Kent*). Interestingly, the programme included studies of a powerplant in which the engines ran on kerosene while their afterburners used LH_2; such an installation based on the NK-144A passed bench tests.

Air Marshal (Retd.) Vasiliy V. Reshetnikov, who was Commander of the Soviet Air Force's long-range bomber arm (DA – **Dahl'**nyaya aviahtsiya) in the 1970s in the rank of Colonel-General, commented thus on this project:

'As we took our seats in a small conference room and examined the drawings and diagrams attached to a display stand, I was surprised to see the familiar lines of the Tu-144 supersonic airliner. Could it actually be the same aircraft? The Tu-144 fell short of its performance target, was beset by reliability problems, fuel-thirsty and difficult to operate. The civil aviation would have no part of it... [...]

Aleksey Andreyevich [Tupolev] was not quite his usual self as he approached the stand, pointer in hand. His proposal boiled down to providing weapons bays for the bombs and missiles in the space between the engine packs occupying the fuselage undersurface. There is no need to relate Tupolev's discourse that followed; it was obvious that, weighed down by the offensive and defensive armament, this unsuccessful airliner-turned-bomber would be robbed of whatever structural strength reserves it had and all performance characteristics would drop.

About five or ten minutes later I rose and, cutting the lecture short, stated that we were not going to consider the project any longer because, even in revamped condition, an aircraft originally designed for carrying passengers would have some inherent properties which were absolutely unnecessary for a combat aircraft while still not meeting the demands applying to a strategic bomber.

Apparently Aleksey Andreyevich was prepared for this outcome. Without saying a word he turned towards the largest diagram pinned in the middle of the stand, grasped it and tore it down with a jerk. The sharp crack of heavy paper being rent asunder resounded in the complete silence. Then he faced me again and apologised, adding that he would invite us again when a new PD project would be ready.'

Tu-160M strategic multi-role aircraft
Development of new-generation multi-role/multi-mode supersonic strategic strike aircraft began at several Soviet aircraft

Chapter 8 - The Tu-144 in Uniform? (Projected Military Versions)

design bureaux in the late 1960s ('multi-mode' refers to subsonic and supersonic cruise or attack modes). The Tupolev OKB brought out one of the first PD projects of such an aircraft in 1969; the aircraft had a blended wing/body (BWB) layout – a novel feature at the time – and variable-geometry (VG) wings. It was the latter feature that killed the project; preliminary calculations showed that the wing pivots and the heavy-duty beam connecting them imposed an unacceptable weight penalty, reducing the payload/weight ratio to such an extent that the required performance could not be achieved. Therefore, General Designer Andrey N. Tupolev took the decision to use the Tu-144 SST as a basis for further work on the multi-mode supersonic strategic aircraft.

In 1970 the Tupolev OKB prepared two further projects of such an aircraft which drew heavily on the Tu-144's design and were designated Tu-160M (to be precise, Tu-160M-1 and Tu-160M-2); the M apparently stood for *mnogotselevoy* – multi-role. Two roles were envisaged: a missile strike aircraft armed with various types of air-to-surface missiles for various missions and a strategic reconnaissance aircraft. The reconnaissance version was to be capable of carrying *Voron* (Raven) Mach 3 reconnaissance drones for reconnoitring heavily defended areas too dangerous for manned aircraft; the Voron was a version of the Lockheed D-21 drone reverse-engineered by the Tupolev OKB.

Several versions of the Tu-160M project differing in aerodynamic details and structural design were considered. Calculations showed that the most promising one was a tailless-delta aircraft utilising the BWB layout. The aircraft was shorter than the Tu-144 but had a much longer wingspan – 35.2 m (115 ft $5^{53}/_{64}$ in) versus 27.65 m (90 ft $8^{37}/_{64}$ in); wing area was 516.7 m² (5,561.71 sq ft) less LERXes or 650 m² (6,996.54 sq ft) including LERXes, and overall area in plan view was 667 m² (7,179.53 sq ft). At a glance the wings appeared to have a similar double-delta planform with clipped tips; however, the LERXes ran the full length of the forward fuselage (or rather lifting body), which had a shallow quasi-rhomboid cross-section with sharp chines beginning almost immediately aft of the nose pitot in similar manner to the Lockheed SR-71 Blackbird (as opposed to the conventionally designed Tu-144 with a circular-section fuselage and the LERXes beginning well aft). The

Opposite page: A drawing from the Tupolev OKB project documents showing an air-launched ballistic missile system based on the Tu-144R. The legend reads: 'Flight deck; Avionics/equipment bay; Missile launch equipment; Missiles in transport (en route) position; Pre-launch lowering mechanism; Crew ready room/rest area; Missile transport position restraints; Monorail transporter; Weapons bay doors; Missile lowered into pre-launch position'.

Above right and right: Front and rear views of a model depicting the Tu-160M bomber, showing the rhomboid fuselage cross-section and the wider-spaced, canted engine nacelles.

Below: A side view of the same model illustrating the slender silhouette.

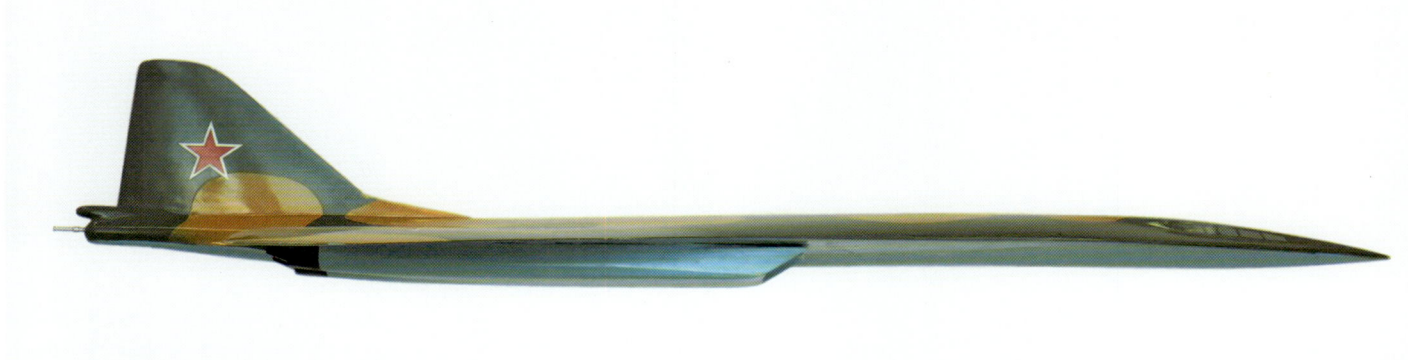

Above: This aspect of the Tu-160M model illustrates the blended wing/body layout and the sharp chines running all the way to the tip of the nose.

Left: As this view suggests, the Tu-160M was to be powered by RD36-51A turbojets. Note the tail cannon installation.

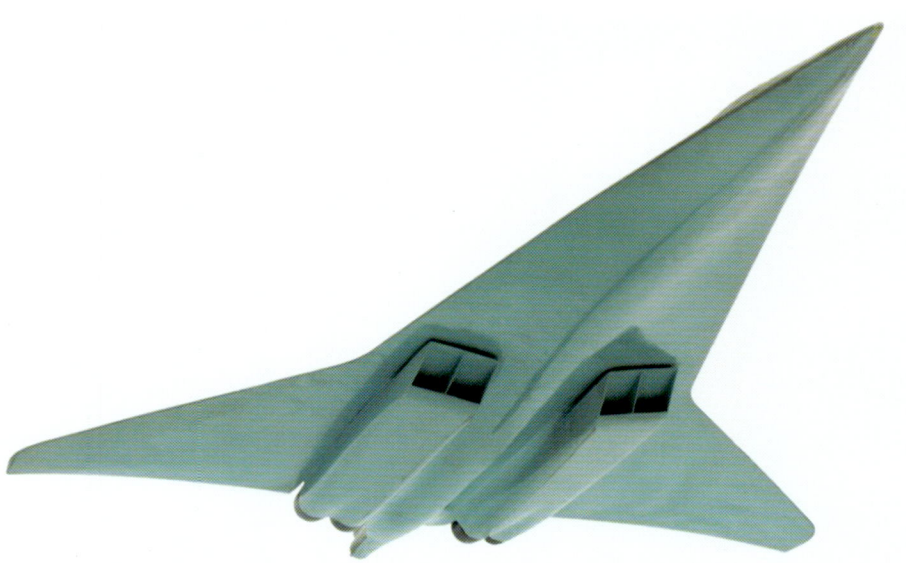

Below left: This lower view illustrates the convex fuselage underside between the engine nacelles (in the area of the weapons bay).

Right: A three-view of the Tu-160M with a side view of the Tu-144D to the same scale (the registration is deliberately non-existent). The widely spaced engine nacelles resulted from the wide weapons bay accommodating two K-45 missiles side by side.

Chapter 8 - The Tu-144 in Uniform? (Projected Military Versions)

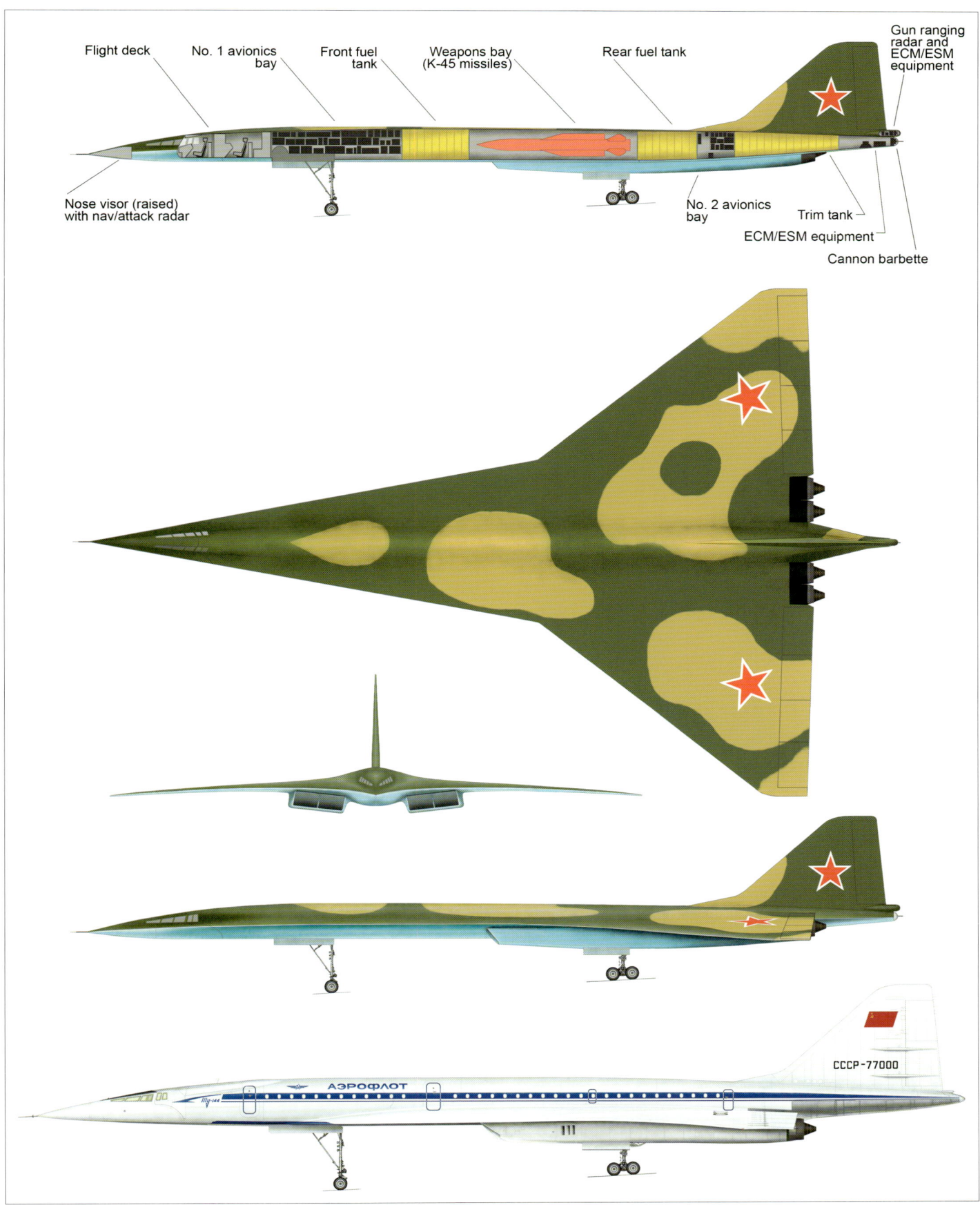

235

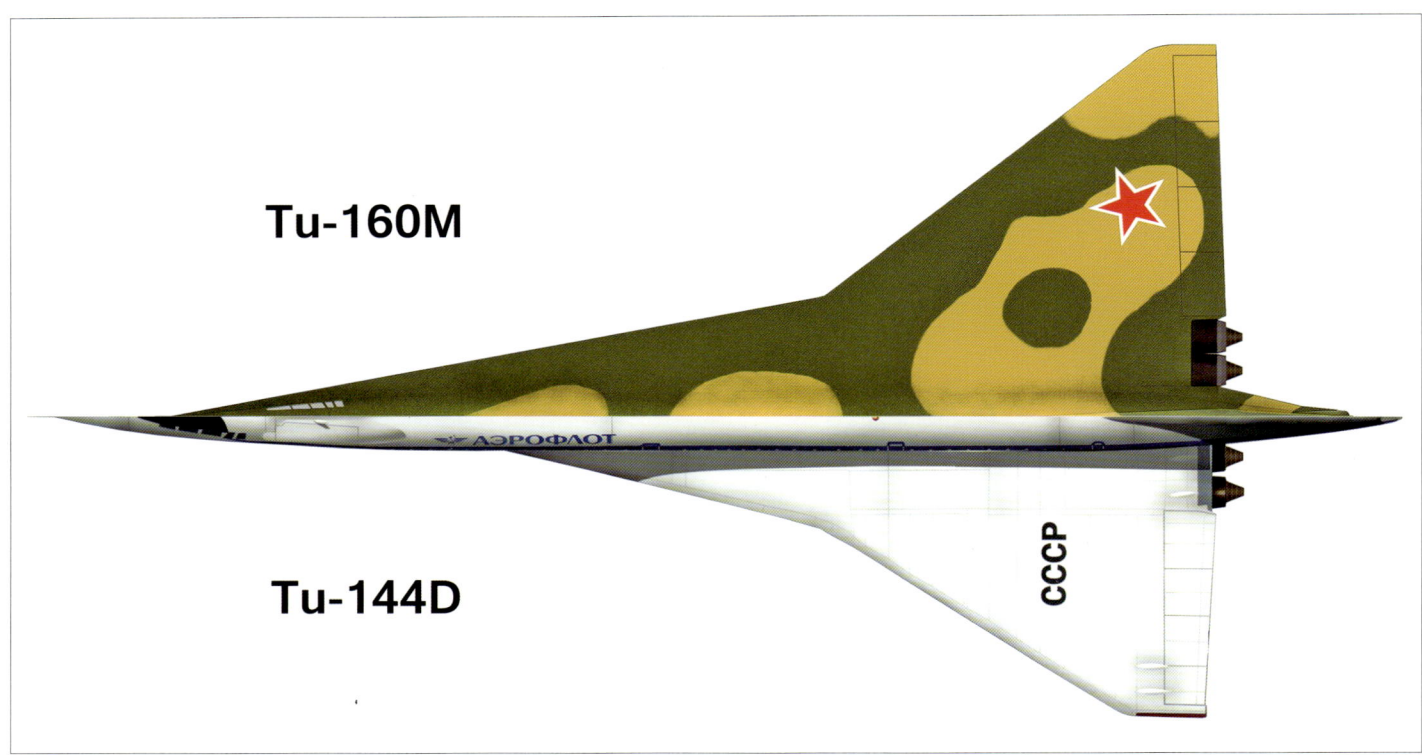

leading-edge sweep angles were also different – 78° onboard of the kink and 50° outboard versus 76° and 57° respectively for the Tu-144. The trailing edge was occupied almost entirely by four-section elevons with a total area of 50.5 m² (543.58 sq ft), which had a travel limit of ±22°30'. The vertical tail was similar in appearance to that of the Tu-144, having the same leading-edge sweep of 50° and a two-section rudder; the latter had a travel limit of ±24°30'. The fin rose 6.32 m (20 ft 8¹⁄₆₄ in) above the fuselage; vertical tail area was 44.5 m² (478.99 sq ft), including 10.27 m² (110.55 sq ft) for the rudder. By comparison, the corresponding figures for the Tu-144 were 6.65 m (21 ft 9¹³⁄₁₆ in), 55.0 m² (592.02 sq ft) and 11.397 m² (122.676 sq ft).

Similarly to the Tu-144, the forward fuselage incorporated a drooping nose visor ahead of the flight deck – even the glazing shape was the same, and this visor incorporated a large radome. The four-man flight deck was followed by the large forward avionics bay with the nosewheel well underneath it. Further aft was the No.1 fuselage fuel tank, followed by the weapons bay, the No.2 fuselage tank, a small rear avionics bay and the No.3 fuselage tank situated below the base of the fin which was the trim tank. The weapons bay was unusually wide and accommodated two K-45 air-to-surface missiles side by side; this allowed the length of the bay to be minimised, leaving more internal volume available for fuel. The missiles were separated by a longitudinal bulkhead which doubled as a centreline keel beam, increasing the stiffness of the centre fuselage structure. The rear fuselage appeared shorter than on the airliner; instead of a brake parachute bay it terminated in a remote-controlled defensive cannon barbette, with a gun ranging radar in a cigar-shaped fairing above it.

The engine nacelles were very similar to those of the Tu-144D, the project drawings and desktop models showing the distinctive nozzles of the RD36-51A turbojets, but the nacelles were moved outward because of the weapons bay. The landing gear was taken virtually wholesale from the airliner, with a forward-retracting twin-wheel nose unit and eight-wheel main bogies retracting forward into the nacelles – except that all wheels were of the same size and slightly larger than the airliner's (1,000 x 450 mm, or 39.37 x 17.71 in). The Tu-160M had a wheelbase of 17.8 m (58 ft 4²⁵⁄₃₂ in) and a wheel track of 8.5 m (27 ft 10⁴¹⁄₆₄ in) versus 19.63 m (64 ft 4²⁷⁄₃₂ in) and 6.05 m (19 ft 10³⁄₁₆ in) respectively for the Tu-144.

The projected K-45 *Molniya* (Lightning) hypersonic air-to-surface missile had been developed by MKB Raduga ('Rainbow' Machinery Design Bureau) in Moscow. It utilised a conventional layout with low aspect ratio cruciform wings and aft-mounted cruciform rudders; it featured inertial mid-course guidance and an active radar seeker for terminal guidance. The missile was to have a launch weight of 4,500 kg (9,920 lb), a 600-km (372-mile) range and a cruising speed of 7,000 km/h (4,347 mph). Depending on the type of warhead (nuclear or conventional shaped-charge/high-explosive), the warhead weight varied between 500 and 1,000 kg (1,102-2,204 lb).

Another version of the Tu-160M was very similar but had wings of even greater span and area. The elevons terminated well inboard of the wingtips, which were hinged and could be lowered hydraulically in similar manner to the North American XB-70 Valkyrie; apparently this feature served the same purpose as on the American bomber, being used for longitudinal trim at high speed.

The airframe structure made maximum possible use of the design features and manufacturing technologies developed for the Tu-144. The Tu-160M had a design operating empty weight of 83,300 kg (183,650 lb); the maximum take-off weight was 230,000 kg (507,060 lb).

Chapter 8 - The Tu-144 in Uniform? (Projected Military Versions)

The Tu-160M's intended mission profile was as follows. The aircraft would cruise towards the target at medium altitude in subsonic mode. After approaching within a certain range of the target it would either go supersonic at high altitude or descend to ultra-low altitude for air defence penetration, minimising detection and intercept time. As the aircraft approached the target, the defensive avionics (electronic countermeasures/electronic support measures) suite would be activated, operating ever more intensively as the Tu-160M penetrated deeper into the air defence zone. In the event of a concerted attack by several such aircraft the formation would create a strong ECM environment, reducing the risk of engagement by the enemy air defence assets.

Left: This view provides a plan view comparison of the Tu-144D and the Tu-160M, illustrating the latter's shorter fuselage and larger wings.

The photos on this page show a slightly different model representing a version of the Tu-160M with drooping wingtips in the manner of the XB-70 Valkyrie. Actually the model gives a false impression – the wingtips were to be angled down, not vertical.

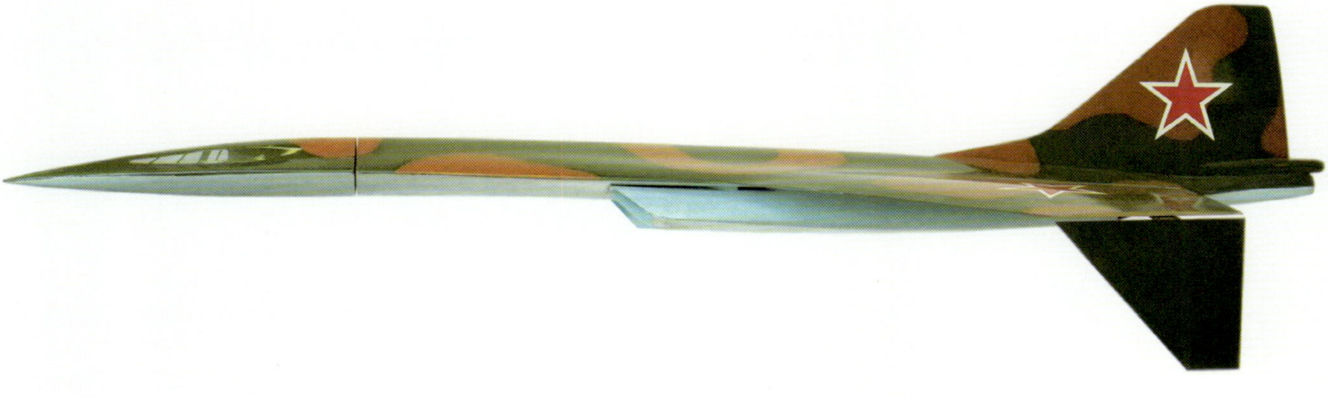

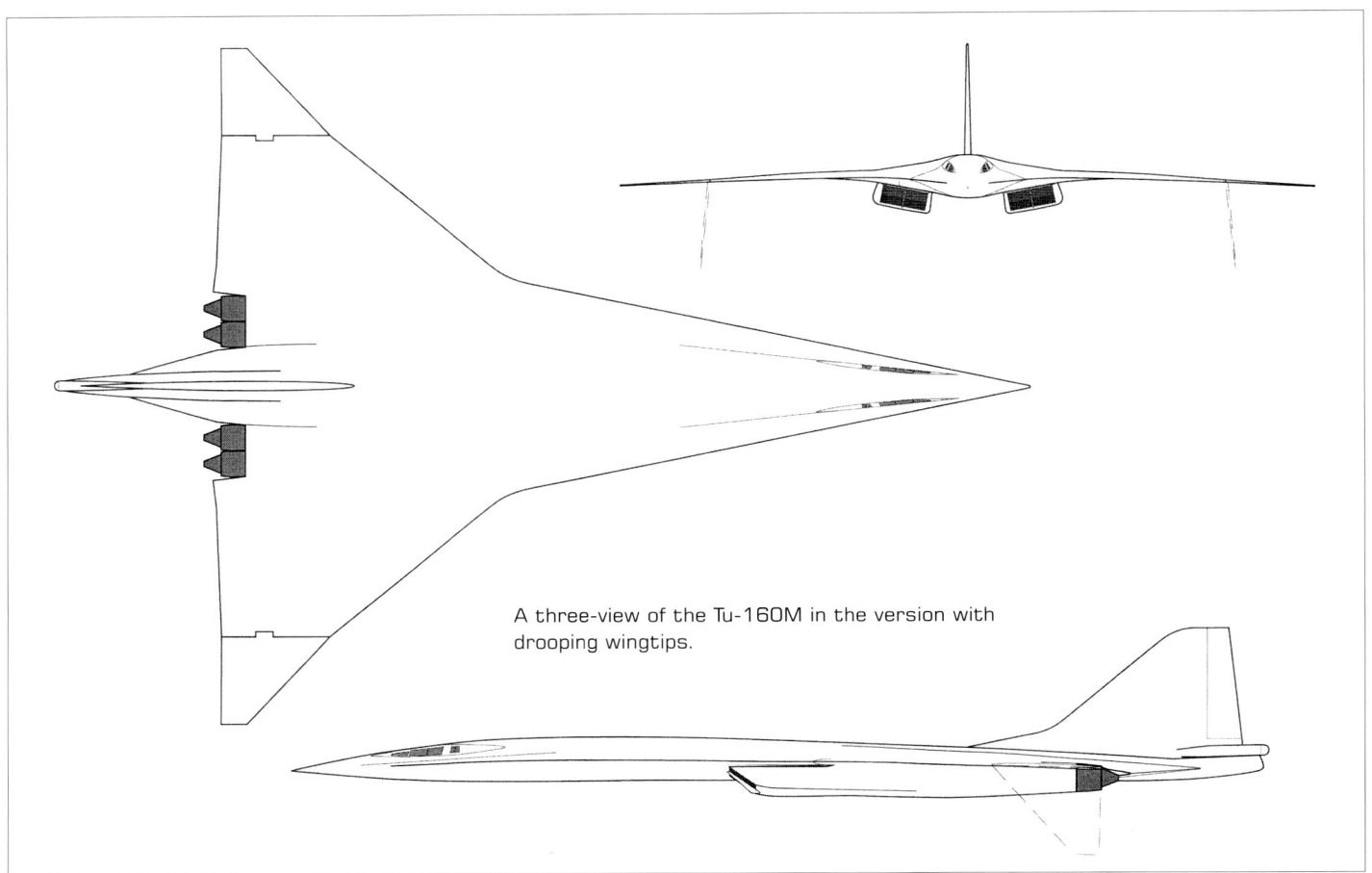

A three-view of the Tu-160M in the version with drooping wingtips.

The shape and design of the BWB/tailless-delta version were a logical continuation of the ideas that went into the Tu-144. The chosen wing shape based on TsAGI's recommendations ensured the Tu-160M its intended multi-mode capability (subsonic cruise, low-level air defence penetration and high-altitude supersonic cruise).

Another version of the Tu-160M project reverted to VG wings, bearing a certain similarity to the aircraft that eventually flew as the Tu-160. It shared the tailless-delta version's BWB design and such features as the drooping nose visor, the engine nacelle design with horizontal air intake ramps, and the landing gear design (the main bogies still retracted into the nacelles). However, the aircraft had a much more slender fuselage, conventional tail surfaces with unusually large stabilisers and two-section inset elevators, and a shorter wheelbase. Wing leading-edge sweep was 72° on the fixed inner wings (wing gloves) and on the outer wings at maximum sweepback for high-speed cruise; in take-off and landing mode the outer wings had a leading-edge sweep of 14°. The armament was the same as on the previous version; however, because of the narrow fuselage the two K-45 missiles were carried in separate weapons bays fore and aft of the wing carry-through box. This aircraft was hardly related to the Tu-144 any more, but it was this project version that evolved into the present-day *Blackjack*.

Tu-144 long-range naval escort aircraft version
In 1975 the OKB contemplated a version of the Tu-144 *sans suffixe* powered by NK-144A engines which was intended for escorting long-range missile strike aircraft of the AVMF. Unfortunately no details are known, but it can be surmised that the aircraft was to provide electronic countermeasures (ECM) support.

DP-1 long-range heavy interceptor
In the late 1970s the above project apparently evolved into a heavy interceptor based on the Tu-144D and designated DP-1 (***dah**l'niy* ***per**ekhvaht**chik*** – long-range interceptor). Actually it was more than just an interceptor; its mission was to escort 'friendly' strike aircraft on long-range missions, protecting them from enemy fighters, provide air defence of key areas within a large radius from its base and disrupt the enemy's air supply routes, seeking and destroying enemy transport aircraft.

Tu-144PP long-range heavy interceptor/ECM aircraft
The DP-1 project was developed further into a multi-role aircraft for the AVMF designated Tu-144PP (*posta**nov**shchik [po**mekh**]/ per**ekhvaht**chik* – ECM aircraft/interceptor) – again powered by RD36-51A turbojets. As the suffix letters indicate, it had the additional role of providing ECM cover for 'friendly' strike aircraft formations and facilitating their task of penetrating the enemy's air defences. A desktop model of the Tu-144PP shows large conformal ECM pods (presumably detachable) low on the outer sides of the engine nacelles and an aft-looking ECM antenna in a bullet fairing above the rudder. Moreover, the model features long-range air-to-air missiles carried in tandem pairs on ejector racks under

Chapter 8 - The Tu-144 in Uniform? (Projected Military Versions)

the outer wings; these AAMs resemble the K-33 which eventually became the R-33 (AA-9 *Amos*) – the primary weapon of the Mikoyan MiG-31 *Foxhound* interceptor.

Tu-144PR long-range reconnaissance/ECM aircraft
In 1980 (some sources say the late 1970s) the Tupolev OKB started project studies on a further derivative of the Tu-144D designated Tu-144PR (*posta**novsh**chik [po**mekh**]/razved**chik*** – ECM/reconnaissance aircraft). The aircraft was intended for theatre-strategic reconnaissance and suppression of enemy air defence radars. The Tu-144PR was conceived as a multi-role aircraft capable of operating in the interests of the Long-Range Aviation (DA) and the Air Defence Force (PVO – **Pr**otivovoz**dooshnaya oborona**) by reconnoitring air targets and guiding other interceptors to them or providing target data for surface-to-air missile systems. The aircraft was to have defensive armament and a defensive ECM suite.

Tu-144K missile strike aircraft
In the early 1980s the OKB made one more attempt to develop a missile strike derivative of the Tu-144D for the Navy. The aircraft was designated Tu-144K, the suffix denoting ***kompleks** [vo'oruzheniya]* – weapons system, as was the case with several other Tupolev missile carriers; cf. Tu-16K-10 *Badger-C*, Tu-95K *Bear-B*, Tu-22K *Blinder-B* and so on. No details have been reported.

Tu-144KP air defence suppression aircraft
A further development of the Tu-144K was the Tu-144KP designed in parallel. Again, no details have been reported; however, it stands to reason that the Tu-144KP was a suppression of enemy air defences (SEAD) version armed with passive radar homing anti-radar missiles, by analogy with the Tu-22KP *Blinder-B* – hence the P for *pa**ssiv**noye* **s**amo**nave**deniye – passive [radar] homing.

Tu-144MR long-range maritime reconnaissance/strike aircraft
One of the last attempts to 'sell' the Tu-144 to the military was a project of a long-range reconnaissance aircraft for the AVMF. Designated Tu-144MR, it was again based on the Tu-144D and intended for providing target information to the Navy's offensive components (surface ships and submarines) on sea and oceanic

Right, above right and top right: This model demonstrates the two project versions (with and without drooping wingtips) of the Tu-160M rolled into one; of course the aircraft was not meant to fly in such a lop-sided configuration!

Top and above: A model of the Tu-144PP 'swing-role' interceptor/ECM aircraft. Actually it shows both the detachable ventral ECM packs and the K-33 missiles (albeit under one wing only); in reality only one option would have been carried. The bullet fairing above the rudder likewise housed ECM gear. The model was probably converted from a model showing a stock civil Tu-144, hence the colour scheme.

Above right: A three-view of the Tu-144MR reconnaissance/strike aircraft from the ADP documents. Note the four-cannon barbette.

Right: A cut away drawing of the Tu-144MR from the project documents.

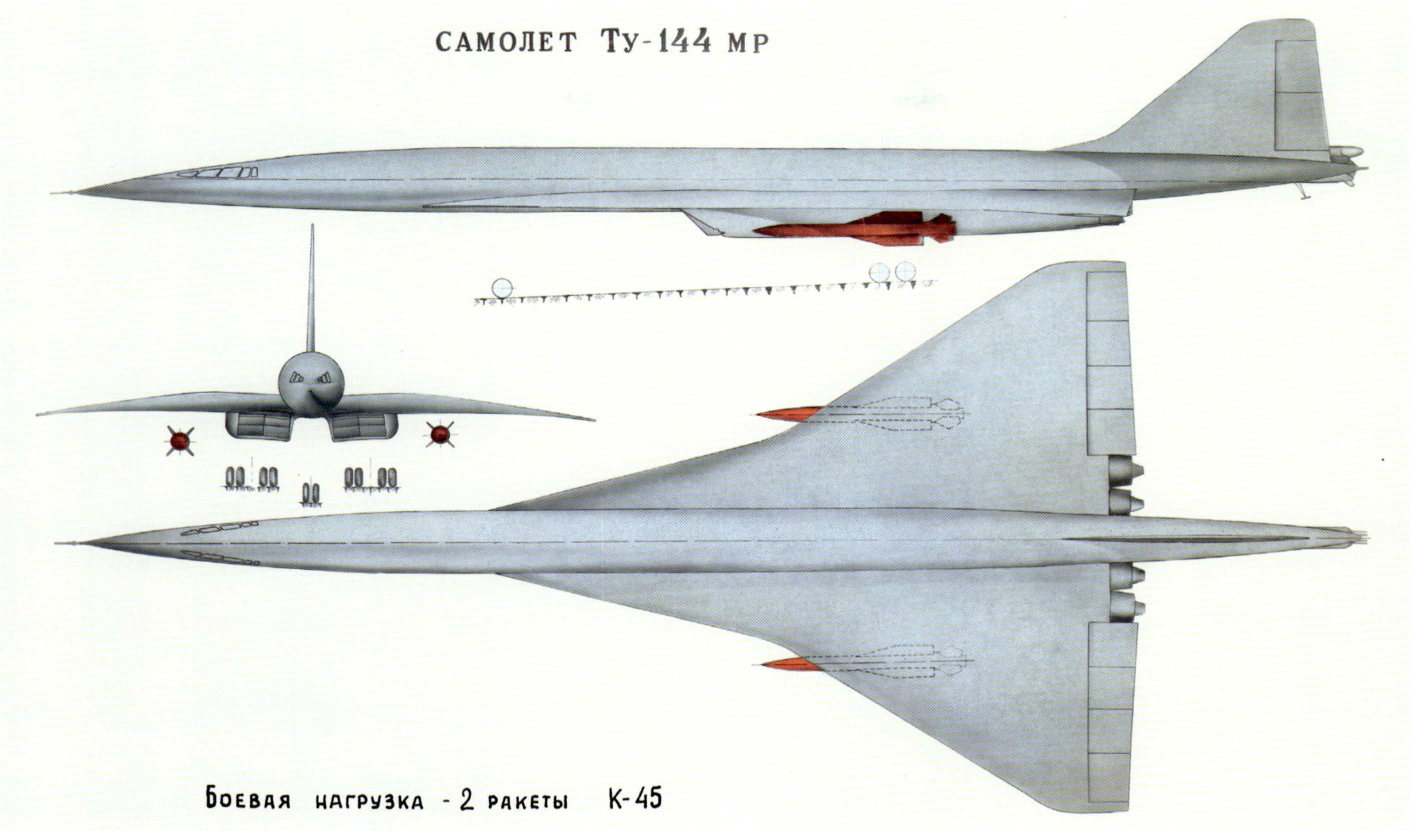

Chapter 8 - The Tu-144 in Uniform? (Projected Military Versions)

САМОЛЕТ Ту-144 МР

Боевая нагрузка - 2 ракеты К-45

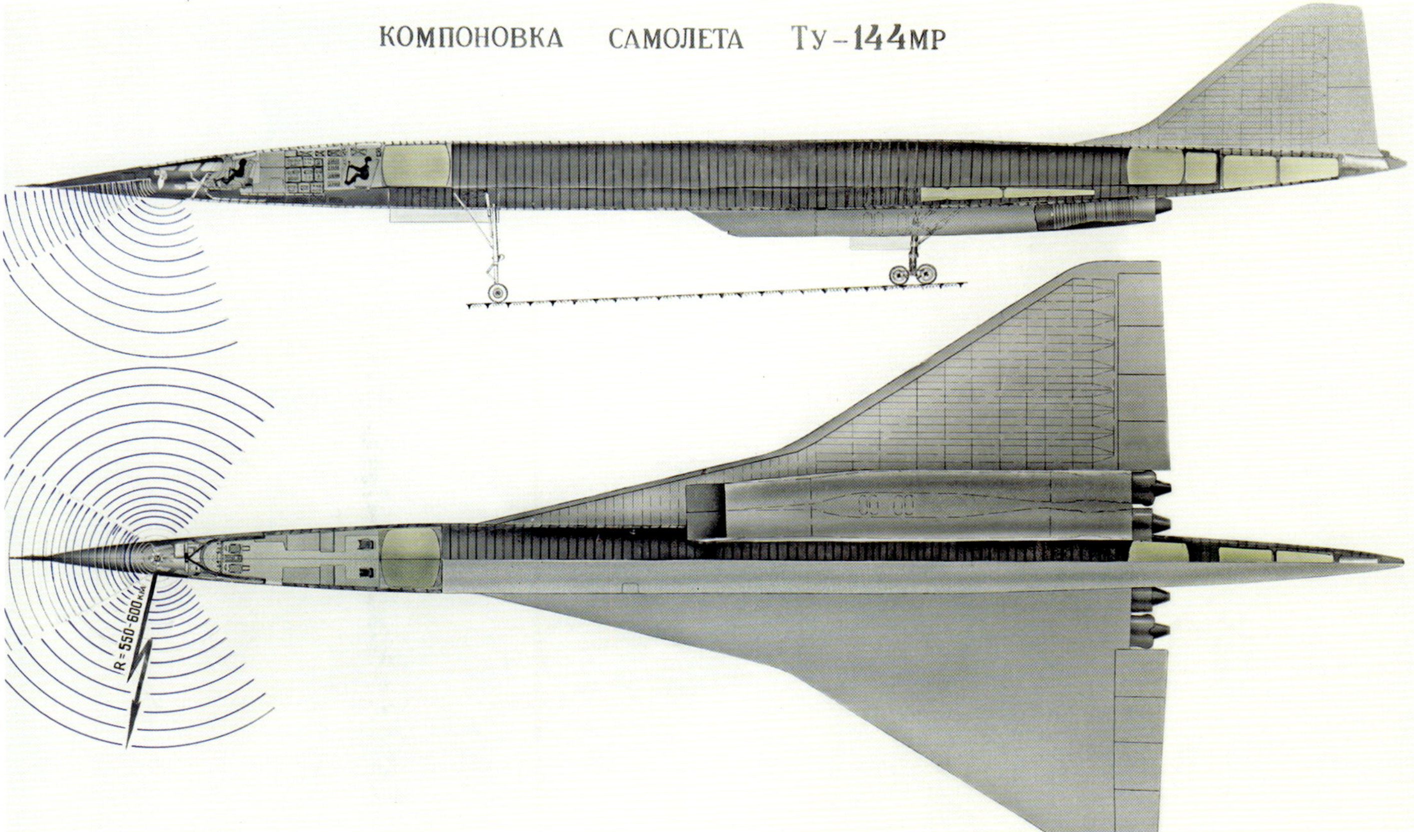

КОМПОНОВКА САМОЛЕТА Ту-144МР

241

theatres of operations. The meaning of the designation suffix is not entirely clear; it has been deciphered both as *morskoy razvedchik* (maritime reconnaissance aircraft) and as **mno**gotse*levoy razved*chik (multi-role reconnaissance aircraft).

The aircraft had a crew of four, and the crew section was similar to that of the Tu-144/*izdeliye* 044 prototype (and the Tu-22M *Backfire* bomber, for that matter): the forward-facing flight engineer and electronic warfare officer (EWO) sat some way aft of the pilots, with the entry vestibule and avionics racks in between. Considering the aircraft's military role, it stands to reason that the crew was provided with ejection seats. The rear pressure bulkhead was immediately aft of the crew section, with a fuel tank aft of it; more fuel tanks were located where the rear baggage compartment had been, but the former cabins remained unused. The three antennas of the radar suite were housed in the drooping nose visor, providing radar imagery within a radius of 550-600 km (341-372 miles); in side-looking mode the suite was to have a resolution of 15-30 m (49-98 ft) at a range of 100-150 km (62-93 miles).

Two configurations were envisaged. In daytime configuration the Tu-144MR carried a comprehensive photo reconnaissance (PHOTINT), electronic intelligence (ELINT) and radiation reconnaissance (RINT) suite. It included an Alpha RINT system capable of measuring radiation levels of 5-500 R/h, a Temp (Tempo, or Pace) thermal imager with a resolution of 2-3°C covering a swath whose width was equal to the flight altitude, Koob-3M (Cube), Koob-4 and *Virazh* (Banked turn) general-purpose signals intelligence (SIGINT) sets with a wavelength range of 2.95-32.4 m, 30-300 m and 0.8-300 m respectively (*sic* – as per project documents). The Koob-3M (*izdeliye* 3M) and Virazh SIGINT sets were identical to those used on the Mikoyan MiG-25RBV *Foxbat-D* reconnaissance aircraft. The daylight camera suite comprised AFA-70/M (**a**ero**fo**to**app**a**raht** – aerial camera), AT-10, 2AT-20, PA-1, AFA-54/50 and Shpil' (Spire) cameras. The first three models covered a strip whose width was 4.6 times the flight altitude and whose length was 3,000 km (1,863 miles), the resolution being 0.4-0.6 m (1 ft 3¾ in to 1 ft 11⅝ in) for the AFA-70/M and 5-7 m (16 ft 4⁵⁵⁄₆₄ in to 22 ft 11¹⁹⁄₃₂ in) for the AT-10 and 2AT-20. The PA-1 covered a 120-km (74.5-mile) strip whose width was ten times the flight altitude, with a resolution of 0.3-0.6 m (11¹³⁄₁₆ in to 1 ft 11⅝ in). The AFA-54/50 could photograph a 12 x 30 km (7.46 x 18.6 miles) area with a resolution of 1-2 m (3 ft 3⅜ in to 6 ft 6⁴⁷⁄₆₄ in). Finally, the Shpil' camera covered a 1,000-km (621-mile) strip whose width was three times the flight altitude, with a resolution of 0.4m (1 ft 3¾ in)

The night reconnaissance configuration differed only in the camera fit comprising the Shpil' and 2NA-100 cameras, the latter having a film capacity of 30 exposures. Both versions were equipped with an OPB-17 optical bomb sight (*opticheskiy pritsel bombardirovochnyy*) used for aiming the cameras, with a field of view of ±30° (left/right), 88° forward and 15° aft from the vertical.

To expand the Tu-144MR's capabilities, the OKB suggested developing and fielding a reconnaissance/strike version armed with two K-45 missiles alongside the pure reconnaissance variant. The latter was to have a range of 10,000 km (6,210 miles), a top speed of 2,500 km/h (1,552 mph) and a typical flight altitude of 20,000 m (65,620 ft); the take-off weight was specified as 185,000 kg (407,850 lb), which was nearly 10% less than the passenger version's. The missiles were just a little too bulky to be carried internally; hence they were to be carried on ejector racks outboard of the nacelles.

The designers hoped that the Tu-144MR would be convertible from day recce to night recce configuration, or from recce to strike configuration, in service conditions within a few hours. However the K-45 never actually materialised because its intended missile platforms either remained in prototype form (the Sukhoi T-4) or never left the drawing board (the Myasishchev M-70 and Tupolev Tu-144MR).

As mentioned in Chapter 6, during the operational evaluation period preceding the Tu-144's service entry the AVMF command assessed the possibility of using the Tu-144 as a long-range maritime reconnaissance aircraft in practice. To this end Tu-144 *sans suffixe* CCCP-77110 visited Severomorsk-1 AB where high-ranking AVMF officers had the opportunity to examine the aircraft at close range and assess its performance in high latitudes. Here it is worth quoting DA Commander Vasiliy V. Reshetnikov again:

'*Aleksey Andreyevich [Tupolev] was not to blame. The development and construction of the supersonic airliner, the future Tu-144, was included in the five-year economic development plan and was under the auspices of the influential D. F. Ustinov who regarded this mission as a personal responsibility – not so much to his country and people but rather to "dear Leonid Il'yich"* (Brezhnev, the head of state – *Auth.) whom he literally worshipped – sometimes to the point of adulation...*

Yet the supersonic passenger jet was apparently not making headway and, to the dismay of its curator, it looked like Brezhnev might be disappointed. It was then that Dmitriy Fyodorovich jumped at someone's bright idea to foist Aeroflot's "bride in search of a wedding" on the military. After it had been rejected in bomber guise, Ustinov used the VPK to promote the aircraft to the Long-Range Aviation as a reconnaissance or ECM platform – or both. It was clear to me that these aircraft could not possibly work in concert with any bomber or missile carrier formations; likewise, I could not imagine them operating solo as "Flying Dutchmen" in a war scenario, therefore I resolutely turned down the offer.

Naval Aviation Commander Aleksandr Alekseyevich Mironenko, with whom I had always worked in close co-operation, did the same.

Nothin' doin' – Ustinov would not be put off that easily. He managed to persuade the Navy C-in-C [Admiral] S[ergey] G. Gorshkov, who agreed to accept the Tu-144 for Naval Aviation service as a long-range maritime reconnaissance aircraft without consulting anyone on the matter. Mironenko rebelled against this decision, but the Commander-in-Chief wouldn't hear or heed – the issue is decided, period. On learning of this I was extremely alarmed: if Mironenko had taken the Tu-144, this meant I was going to be next. I made a phone call to Aleksandr Alekseyevich, urging him to take radical measures; I needn't have called because even without my urging Mironenko was giving his C-in-C a hard time. Finally Ustinov got wind of the mutiny and summoned Mironenko to his office. They had a long and heated discussion but eventually Mironenko succeeded in proving that Ustinov's ideas were unfounded. That was the last we heard of the Tu-144.'

Chapter 9

East vs. West, or 'Concordski' vs. Concorde: the Two SSTs Compared

The Tu-144 story would be incomplete without at least a brief comparison with its Anglo-French counterpart, the BAC-Aérospatiale Concorde. Development of this aircraft began in 1954 when the first British committee was formed to look into the feasibility of developing an SST. Early studies based on existing wing designs led to the conclusion that the idea was not feasible. Shortly afterwards, however, a British team of aerodynamicists led by the German-born Dietrich Küchemann began exploring the so-called 'slender delta' concept – that is, delta wings of very low aspect ratio with a very broad root chord; such wings generated vortices dramatically enhancing wing lift at high AOAs. By 1956 this research had generated enough official interest to warrant the creation of the Supersonic Transport Aircraft Committee (STAC) on 1st October 1956 under whose auspices the SST was developed. One of the companies that took on the SST programme was the Bristol Aeroplane Co., where several projects were developed in parallel under the guidance of aerospace engineer Archibald Russell. He concluded that the SST had to have transatlantic range – at shorter ranges the reduction in flight time would not justify the extra cost and complexity. Early projects included several versions under the generic designation Type 198 – a 150-seat eight-engined (!) high-wing aircraft designed to cruise at Mach 2 and, later, a smaller 136-seat low-wing aircraft cruising at Mach 1.8, as well as a higher-speed aircraft designated Type 213. The latter was to have an air-

Two models to the same scale showing the Tu-144 (*izdeliye* 044) and the Concorde 001 with the early-style flight deck glazing.

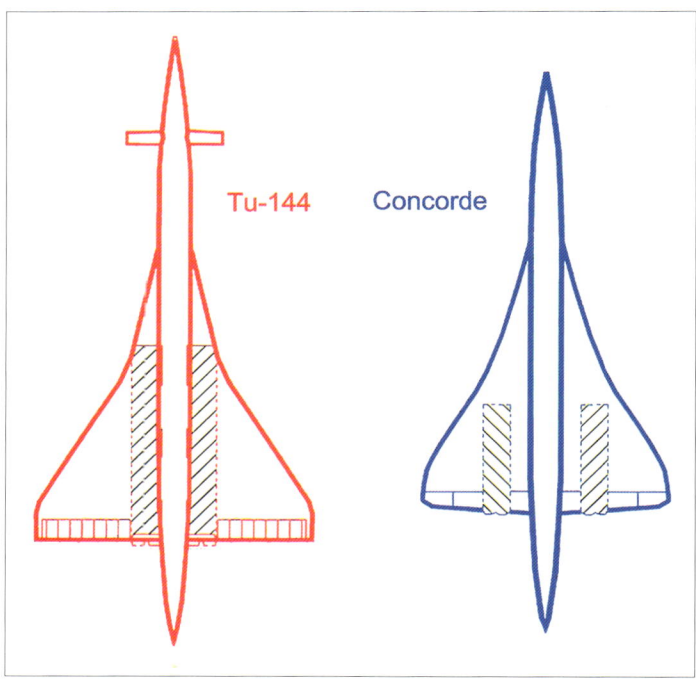

This drawing gives a comparison of the production Tu-144 and the Concorde; the shaded areas are the engine nacelles.

frame made of heat-resistant stainless steel; however, the cost of using this material proved prohibitive, and Russell concentrated on aircraft cruising at Mach 2.2 or less, which would permit use of aluminium alloys. An aluminium alloy airframe would be cheaper and easier to build.

In March 1959 STAC recommended that the UK should build two SST designs – a long-range 150-seat Mach 2 aircraft for use on the London-New York route and a shorter-range Mach 1.2 aircraft for use in Europe. That year Bristol, which became part of the British Aircraft Corporation (BAC) on 1st January 1960, and Hawker Siddeley Aircraft were awarded study contracts for PD projects of SSTs using Küchemann's 'slender delta' wings. The Bristol Type 198 proved superior to the competing Hawker Siddeley HSA.1000 and was selected for further development. However, Archibald Russell soon had second thoughts about the 150-seat version and began development of a smaller 110-seat design known as the Bristol Type 223, a four-engine low-wing aircraft similar to the Type 198 (some accounts say development of the Type 223 began in 1961 after the creation of BAC).

After considering three basic wing shapes – the classic delta, the so-called 'gothic delta' resembling a gothic arch, and ogival wings featuring a compound-curvature S-shaped leading edge – the design team selected the latter option. The reason for this choice was that ogival wings provided the optimum position of the CG relative to the wings' centre of pressure, or 'lift point'. It deserves mention that the Type 223 originally featured canards – although these were later deleted in favour of a tailless configuration.

Since development costs were going to be high, initially both Bristol and Hawker Siddeley sought risk-sharing partnerships with US aircraft manufacturers (which were working on SST programmes of their own), but the latter showed a singular lack of interest. This was probably due to the belief that the US government would be funding the programme and would frown upon such a partnership for fear of 'giving away the US technological lead'. Conversely, France, which was also pursuing its own SST programme, proved much more open to co-operation. Sud Aviation, the winner of the French contest, offered the Super Caravelle intended to replace the earlier and very successful SE 210 Caravelle short-haul airliner. This project, which was unveiled at the 1961 Paris Air Show, was remarkably similar to the Type 223 with its ogival wings but was a much smaller, 70-seat design optimised for routes 2,000-3,000 km (1,200-1,900 miles) long to avoid competition with the larger transatlantic SSTs. This similarity was no matter of chance; it was later revealed that the original STAC report had been leaked to the French in order to win political favour.

The British and French design teams had meetings throughout 1961, discussing possible joint development of the SST. Eventually, after consultations with prospective customers, the smaller design was dropped and the teams focused on a single transatlantic version, a four-engined aircraft similar to the Type 223. Negotiations between the British and French governments about forming a consortium to share development and production costs went on throughout 1962; finally, an agreement was signed on 29th November 1962 and the Concorde project was formally launched. The principal designer for the project was Pierre Satre, with Archibald Russell as his deputy.

Like the Tu-144 programme, the Concorde programme was largely motivated by political expediency. For one thing, the UK was then pressing for admission to the European Common Market, a move which was being blocked by Charles de Gaulle because of the UK's strong ties with the USA; the British Cabinet of Ministers felt that a joint SST programme might help resolve this issue. For another, the UK Committee on Civil Scientific Research and Development, which assessed the project in 1962, supported it for the simple reason that everyone else was developing SSTs and the UK would be locked out of future markets if it didn't follow suit.

Construction of two prototypes by the Aérospatiale consortium and BAC began in February 1965. The French-built first prototype, Concorde 001 (registered F-WTSS for *Transport Supersonique*), first flew at Toulouse-Blagnac on 2nd March 1969, just over two months after the Tu-144's maiden flight, and first went supersonic on 1st October that year. The British-built Concorde 002, no less eloquently registered G-BSST, first flew at Bristol-Filton on 9th April 1969. On 7th-8th June 1969 the Concorde made its public debut when both prototypes were presented at the 28th Paris Air Show. On 4th September 1971 the first prototype made the Concorde's first transatlantic crossing.

Now if we compare the Concorde to the Tu-144, there are some obvious differences between the two. While both aircraft shared the tailless-delta layout, the wing shape was rather different. Like the Bristol Type 223 project from which it was derived, the Concorde had ogival wings with a continuously curved leading edge; there were none of the straight leading-edge portions seen on the Tu-144 (*izdeliye* 044) demonstrator, to say nothing of the production version. Also, the aspect ratio was somewhat lower than the Tu-144's. The leading-edge sweep varied from 76° to 58° on the Concorde prototypes; on the production aircraft it was reduced to

Chapter 9 - East vs. West, or 'Concordski' vs. Concorde: the Two SSTs Compared

55° on the outer wing portions. The Concorde's vertical tail was rather smaller than that of the Soviet aircraft, and again it had an almost ogival form.

The Concorde had a fuselage of elliptical cross-section measuring 3.3 m (10 ft 10 in) high and 2.87 m (9 ft 5 in) wide, as compared to the production Tu-144's circular-section fuselage with a maximum diameter of 3.5 m (11 ft 5¾ in). Hence the Concorde's cabin was somewhat narrower, permitting only four-abreast seating versus five-abreast on the Soviet airliner, and the seating capacity was also smaller – 92 to 120 passengers (128 in high-density layout) versus a maximum of 150 on the Tu-144. On the other hand, thanks to its sophisticated navigation suite the Anglo-French airliner could be flown by a crew of three (captain, first officer and flight engineer); in contrast, the Tu-144 required a crew of four which included a navigator.

A feature the two aircraft had in common was the hinged nose ahead of the flight deck that could be drooped to give the pilots an acceptable field of view on take-off and landing. Yet, again there was a difference. The Concorde's drooping nose section did not obscure the windshield completely when raised. Moreover, it incorporated a large curved transparency – the so-called visor – which could be slid upward and aft, level with the flight deck roof, after the nose was raised; this made for a smooth nose contour in supersonic cruise while affording the pilots a much better view

Right: The two SSTs together again: Tu-144D CCCP-77112 and Concorde 101 F-BVFB mounted on the roof of Auto- und Technik-Museum Sinsheim.

Below: Another angle on the two SSTs at Sinsheim. Placing them together like this was a good idea, giving the visitors a clear illustration of the two types' similarity and differences.

245

forward than on the Soviet aircraft. The droop angles were smaller than the Tu-144's – 5° and 12°30' versus 11° and 17°.

As compared to the Tu-144, the Concorde's landing gear was just as tall (this was necessary to provide the required rotation angle on take-off) but had a much simpler design, the inward-retracting main units being equipped with four-wheel bogies; it also had a noticeably wider track. It should be noted that, despite this simplicity, the landing gear turned out to be one of the aircraft's problem areas because of the high loads it was subjected to.

Another major difference from the Soviet SST was the powerplant. The Concorde was powered by four Rolls-Royce/SNECMA Olympus 593 two-spool afterburning turbojets. Since the aircraft was designed for intercontinental flights in order to be economically viable, powerplant efficiency was a key factor, and turbofan engines were rejected due to their larger cross-section producing excessive drag. The Olympus 593 was a purpose-built Anglo-French derivative of the RR Olympus 320 powering the ill-starred BAC TSR.2 supersonic reconnaissance/strike aircraft, itself a derivative of the non-afterburning Bristol (later Rolls-Royce) Olympus developed for the Avro Vulcan bomber.

The Olympus 593 had a thrust-by-wire engine control system – the precursor of today's full authority digital engine control (FADEC) systems – as opposed to the conventional hydromechanical controls of the NK-144 and RD36-51A engines powering the Soviet SST. All four engines had thrust reversers which proved to be highly effective; together with carbon disc brakes, they ensured efficient deceleration from the Concorde's high landing speed. Conversely, the Tu-144 never got the envisaged thrust reversers, making do with brake parachutes. In order to reduce the noise footprint the Concorde's engines had built-in noise attenuators; the Tu-144 had none, and noise abatement procedures were limited to throttling back the engines – both on take-off and on final approach. (According to Tupolev OKB sources, the Tu-144D was quieter than the Tu-144 *sans suffixe* – and the Concorde.)

A comparison of the engines powering the two SSTs shows that the Olympus 593 afterburning turbojet was more fuel-efficient than the NK-144, albeit heavier and marginally less powerful. The Soviet engine designers ran out of time before they had a chance to create a hushkitted version of the RD36-51 (known as *izdeliye* 61) having an SFC on a par the Olympus; with two or three more years' time available, this engine could have flown on the Tu-144.

As compared to the Tu-144, the Concorde's engine nacelles were placed a lot farther away from the fuselage, reducing the thermal load on the latter, so that the innermost of the three elevon sections on each side was between the nacelle and the fuselage. The nacelles were also a lot shorter, the length of the inlet ducts being only four times their diameter at the engine compressor face versus ten times for the Soviet jet. Both aircraft utilised two-dimensional external/internal compression air intakes with horizontal airflow control ramps; yet the Concorde's intakes were more sophisticated, featuring digital Air Intake Control Units and a higher overall pressure ratio at a similar mass flow. The air intakes were programmed in such a way that in the event of an engine failure in supersonic flight the forward intake ramp segment was lowered all the way and an auxiliary spill door on the underside of the nacelle opened, directing most of the air past the failed engine and reducing drag. The aircraft could fly at Mach 2 with both engines on the same side shut down without experiencing control problems; in fact, Concorde pilots were routinely trained to handle double engine failure.

A major difference between the two aircraft was that the Tu-144 used afterburner mode throughout supersonic cruise, whereas the Concorde used afterburners only for take-off and for passing the sound barrier and accelerating to supersonic speeds (between Mach 0.95 and Mach 1.7). Cruise flight took place in dry thrust mode (this is known as supercruise).

The Soviet and British/French engineers took different approaches to protecting the airframe (and, first and foremost, the cabin) against kinetic heating. As mentioned earlier, the Tu-144 utilised a unique active heat insulation system in which cooling air was forced between the outer skin and the cabin wall liners (a system described by some sources as excessively noisy). On the Concorde, fuel was used as a heat sink. Additionally, the airframe, which was entirely made of Hiduminium R.R.58 low-creep aluminium alloy, was coated with a specially formulated reflective white paint as a means of thermal protection.

The Concorde was the first airliner to have a fly-by-wire flight-control system (in this case, analogue FBW controls); in contrast, the Tu-144 had conventional mechanical control runs. Likewise, the Concorde had the distinction of being the first commercial aircraft to employ hybrid integrated circuits (HICs) in its avionics; the Tu-144's avionics used traditional components of the day.

Basic performance of the engines powering the first-generation SSTs				
	NK-144	**NK-144A**	**RD36-51A**	**Olympus 593 Mk 610**
Application	Tu-144 (*izdeliye* 044)	Tu-144 (*izdeliye* 004)	Tu-144D (*izdeliye* 004D)	Concorde
Take-off thrust, kgp (lbst)	17,500 (38,580)	20,000 (49,020)	20,000 (49,020)	14,900/17,260 (32,850/38,050)
Maximum cruise thrust, kgp (lbst)	5,000 (11,020)	5,000 (11,020) *	5,000 (11,020) * †	4,550 (10,030)
SFC at max cruise thrust, kg/kgp·hr	1.58 ‡	1.81 ‡	1.22	1.19
Dry weight, kg (lb)	3,540 (7,800)	3,540 (7,800)	3,900 (8,600)	3,175 (7,000)
Thrust/weight ratio	4.94:1	5.64:1	5.128:1	5.4:1
Service life, hours	n.a.	500	300	n.a.

* At 18,000 m (59,055 ft) and Mach 2.2 † Also quoted as 4,600 kgp (10,140 lbst) ‡ At 16,100 m (59,055 ft) and Mach 2.0

Chapter 9 - East vs. West, or 'Concordski' vs. Concorde: the Two SSTs Compared

Both aircraft had a common feature in their fuel systems – the tanks in the LERXes (and between them, on the Concorde) and in the rear fuselage were used for pitch trim to maintain the CG position at various stages of the flight. However, the Anglo-French airliner used ordinary Jet A-1 fuel, not special grade kerosene which was nitrogenated into the bargain. This was probably due to the Concorde's lower cruising speed and hence less severe kinetic heating.

In service

Now, if we compare the two types' operational histories, the Concorde definitively emerges as the winner. Its production run totalled 20 aircraft – that is, airworthy examples (discounting the static/fatigue test airframes) – and was distributed equally between BAC and Aérospatiale. Of these, six aircraft were retained by the manufacturers as development aircraft and 14 were delivered to customers; thus, the share of Concordes in airline service was 70%. In contrast (again discounting the very different *izdeliye* 044 demonstrator, the static/fatigue test and unfinished airframes), 15 Tu-144s – nine Tu-144s *sans suffixe* and six Tu-144Ds – were built. Of this total, only two aircraft were ever in airline service, which equals 13.3333…%! Also, as mentioned earlier, the two aircraft were never even formally taken on charge by Aeroflot; attempts to attract orders for the Tu-144 in other Eastern Bloc countries failed.

Yet, 20 aircraft built and 14 in service was definitely not the result that the creators of the Concorde had aimed at. When the type was first shown at Le Bourget, the consortium secured orders (or rather options) for over 100 aircraft from 19 major airlines of the day. These were the British and French flag carriers – British Overseas Airways Corp. (BOAC) and Air France, six US carriers – Pan Am, American Airlines, Continental Airlines, United Airlines, Braniff International Airways and TWA, as well as Air Canada, Lufthansa, Olympic Airways (the Greek flag carrier), Air India, Qantas, Japan Airlines, Panair do Brasil, Singapore Airlines, Iran Air, Middle East Airlines (the Lebanese carrier) and – of all things – CAAC, the state airline of Communist China!

Soon enough, however, most of the customers backed out of the programme. There were several reasons for this. For one thing, development costs (and hence the airliner's price tag) had risen dramatically since the programme was launched; for another, the crash of the Tu-144 at Le Bourget in 1973 had 'tripped up' the Concorde by frightening potential customers; thirdly, environmentalists were becoming increasingly vocal, instilling the public against SSTs with sonic boom take-off-noise and pollution issues. Also, the 1973 Oil Crisis (the Arab nations' embargo on oil exports in retaliation for American support of Israel in the Yom Kippur War of 6th-25th October 1973) took its toll on the airline market – with soaring fuel prices, airlines were not prepared to operate such a thirsty bird as the Concorde. Finally, the advent of new efficient wide-body airliners offered the airlines a low-risk alternative to SSTs. As a result, development of the Concorde was a substantial economic loss.

Thus, initially the type entered service with only Air France and British Airways (BOAC's successor), who took delivery of seven each (the French and British versions were designated Concorde 101 and Concorde 102 respectively). The aircraft entered service on 21st January 1976 after a good deal of testing and refining (including changes to the wing camber and shape).

The first Concorde services were London – Bahrain and Paris – Rio de Janeiro (via Dakar), followed by Paris – Caracas (via Azores) and other destinations. New York-John F. Kennedy International and Washington-Dulles were popular destinations; the Concorde covered the distance to these airports from London-Heathrow and Paris-Charles de Gaulle in just under 3.5 hours – less than half the time of other airliners, using specially designated high-altitude airways or 'tracks'. However, this only became possible in late 1977 after a legal battle against a ban imposed by the US authorities; first, the US Congress banned Concorde landings in the US – ostensibly due to sonic boom-related complaints, and then, when the nationwide ban had been repealed, New York imposed a local ban. There are reasons to believe that the bans were acts of protectionism – the Boeing 2707 SST project had been cancelled in 1971, and now, having no competitor to the Concorde, the US government was trying to throw a spanner in the works. India, and Malaysia, too, banned Concorde supersonic flights over the noise issue.

Two other carriers operated the Concorde briefly. In 1977 Singapore Airlines briefly wet-leased a British Airways machine, using it on the London – Singapore International (Paya Lebar) service via Bahrain, but dropped the idea after only three flights. In 1978-80 Braniff International Airways did in fact operate no fewer than ten Concordes leased from British Airways and Air France. This was an extraordinary joint operation, as the airliners flew subsonic from Dallas-Fort Worth to Washington-Dulles with Braniff aircrews, then BA and Air France crews took over and flew the aircraft in supersonic mode to London and Paris respectively. The flights were discontinued as unprofitable, with load factors less than 50%

Until 2000 the type had an unblemished safety record. On 25th July 2000, however, Concorde 101 F-BTSC suffered a catastrophic fire just as the aircraft was becoming airborne from Paris-CDG, bound for New York. The stricken airliner attempted to return to the airport, but when the Nos. 1 and 2 engines quit the airliner pitched up, rolled left and crashed in the Parisian suburb of Gonesse, killing all 109 aboard and four on the ground. Investigation showed that a tyre on the port main gear bogie had exploded, sending a 5-kg (11-lb) tyre fragment through the lower wing skin next to the engines, and the resulting massive fuel leak caused the fire.

After a period while the Concorde fleet was grounded for investigation and modifications, operations resumed on 7th November 2001. Yet, the Concorde was retired in 2003 due to a general downturn in the aviation industry after the 11th September 2001 ('9/11') terrorist attacks in the USA and a decision by Airbus Industrie, the successor firm of Aérospatiale and BAC, to discontinue maintenance support. Air France's final commercial Concorde flight took place on 30th May 2003; British Airways retired its Concorde fleet on 24th October 2003, ending 27 years of commercial flights with the type.

Over the years the Concorde established a string of records on the transatlantic routes. The fastest transatlantic airliner flight was on 7 February 1996 when British Airways Concorde 102 G-BOAD flew from New York to London in 2 hours 52 minutes 59 seconds from take-off to touchdown.

Basic specifications of the first-generation SSTs				
	Tu-144 (*izdeliye* 044)	Tu-144 (*izdeliye* 004)	Tu-144D	Concorde
Length overall (including pitot)	59.422 m (194 ft 11²⁹⁄₆₄ in)	67.05 m (219 ft 11⁴⁹⁄₆₄ in) [1]	67.05 m (219 ft 11⁴⁹⁄₆₄ in) [1]	61.66 m (202 ft 4 in)
Height on ground	12.25 m (40 ft 2³⁄₃₂ in)	12.5 m (41 ft 0⅛ in)	12.5 m (41 ft 0⅛ in)	12.2 m (40 ft 0 in)
Wing span [2]	27.65 m (90 ft 8³⁷⁄₆₄ in)	28.0 m (91 ft 10²³⁄₆₄ in)	28.8 m (94 ft 5⁵⁵⁄₆₄ in)	25.6 m (84 ft 0 in)
Wing area, m² (sq ft)	470 (5,059) [3]	503.0 (5,414.25)	507.0 (5,457.3)	358.25 (3,856)
Vertical tail area, m² (sq ft)	51.625 (555.676)	55.0 (592.02)	55.0 (592.02)	33.9 (364.9)
Overall cross-section area, m² (sq ft)	n.a.	20.75 (223.35)	20.75 (223.35)	18.5 (199.13)
Wetted area, m² (sq ft)	n.a.	1,518 (16,339)	1,518 (16,339)	1,248 (13,433)
Landing gear track	n.a.	6.05 m (19 ft 10³⁄₁₆ in)	6.05 m (19 ft 10³⁄₁₆ in)	7.7 m (25 ft 4 in)
Take-off thrust/weight ratio	n.a.	0.406	0.406	0.373
Maximum L/D ratio:				
subsonic cruise	n.a.	n.a.	12.25 at Mach 0.92	13.2 at Mach 0.94
supersonic cruise	7.0	n.a.	8.1 at Mach 2.1	7.14 at Mach 2.04
Empty weight, kg (lb)	84,000 (185,185)	92,700 (204,365)	98,000 (21,605)	78,700 (173,500)
airframe	n.a.	n.a.	21.45%	21%
powerplant	n.a.	n.a.	15.5%	12.9%
systems & equipment	n.a.	n.a.	63.05%	66.1%
TOW, kg (lb):				
normal	n.a.	180,000 (396,825)	n.a.	n.a.
maximum	180,000 (396,825)	195,000 (429,900)	207,000 (456,350)	185,000 (407,850)
Maximum landing weight, kg (lb)	n.a.	120,000 (264,550)	125,000 (275,570)	111,000 (244,710)
Payload, kg (lb)	12,000 (26,455)	13,000-15,000 (28,660-33,070)	15,000 (33,070)	13,380 (29,500)
Fuel load, kg (lb)	70,000 (154,320)	98,000 (216,050)	98,000 (216,050)	95,680 (210,930)
Maximum speed, km/h (mph)	2,443 (1,518) Mach 2.35	2,500 (1,552)	2,285 (1,419)	2,179 (1,354) Mach 2.04
Cruising speed, km/h (mph)	2,300 (1,428)	2,200 (1,366) [4]	2,120 (1,316)	2,158 (1,340) Mach 2.02
Landing speed, km/h (mph)	270 (167)	270 (167)	270 (167)	295 (183)
Range, km (miles):				
maximum	n.a.	n.a.	n.a.	7,222 (4,488)
with full payload	2,920 (1,813)	3,080 (1,913)	5,330 (3,310)	6,470 (4,018)
Service ceiling, m (ft)	n.a.	n.a.	20,000 (65,620)	18,300 (60,060)
Cruise altitude, m (ft):				
supersonic cruise	n.a.	16,000-18,000 (52,490-59,050)	n.a.	18,000 (59,050)
subsonic cruise	n.a.	8,000-10,000 (26,250-32,080)	n.a.	n.a.
Average fuel consumption, kg/km (lb/mile)	n.a.	18/16 (63.8/56.7) [6]	n.a.	13.2 (46.85) [7]
Take-off run, m (ft)	n.a.	n.a.	2,930	n.a.
Landing run, m (ft)	n.a.	n.a.	2,570	n.a.
Cabin length	n.a.	36.6	36.6	35.2
Cabin width	n.a.	3.03 m (9 ft 11¹⁹⁄₆₄ in)	3.03 m (9 ft 11¹⁹⁄₆₄ in)	2.62 m (8 ft 7 in)
Cabin height	n.a.	1.95 m (6 ft 4⁹⁄₆₄ in)	1.95 m (6 ft 4⁹⁄₆₄ in)	1.96 m (6 ft 5 in)
Cabin volume, m³ (cu ft)	n.a.	n.a.	185 (6,533)	164.3 (5,802)
Baggage compartment volume (total), m³ (cu ft)	n.a.	21.1 (745)	21.1 (745) [5]	20 (706.29)
Passengers	–	80	Up to 150	92-128
Crew	4	4	4	3

1 Some sources give the overall length as 65.7 m (215 ft 6³⁄₆₄ in).   2 At maximum wing flexure in flight.   3 Also reported as 438 m² (4,714.59 sq ft).
4 Also reported as 2,000-2,350 km/h (1,242-1,459 mph) in supersonic cruise and 950 km/h (590 mph) in subsonic cruise.
5 Also reported as 178.1 m³ (6,289 cu ft).   6 Supersonic/subsonic.   7 Operating for maximum range.

Chapter 10

A New Lease of Life: the Tu-144LL Testbed

The beginning of actual co-operation between Russia and the Western world in the field of aviation technology dates back all the way to the days of the First World War, when Russian factories produced several types of French combat aircraft under licence. These aircraft were flown in combat against a common enemy, Kaiser Wilhelm II's Germany and Austro-Hungary, by Imperial Russian Air Fleet pilots.

When the Bol'sheviks seized power in October 1917, they continued purchasing Western aircraft in sizeable numbers for a while. These aircraft were operated by the Red Army Air Force and the Civil Air Fleet (Aeroflot and its subsidiaries) and were carefully examined by the Soviet aircraft designers wishing to learn from their Western colleagues. As the Soviet Union proceeded with its first five-year economic development plans, manufacturing licences were obtained for French (Renault and Gnôme-Rhône), American (Wright and Ford), British (Bristol) and German (BMW) aero engines which powered Soviet-designed aircraft for many years and laid the foundation for the national aero engine design practice. During the Second World War thousands of American and British warplanes delivered under the Lend-Lease Agreement fought alongside indigenous designs to defeat Nazi Germany's war machine in the skies of the Soviet Union and Eastern Europe. In the immediate post-war years, the delivery of Rolls-Royce Nene I and Nene II turbojets and their subsequent production in the USSR as the RD-45F and Klimov VK-1 made it possible to create such outstanding combat aircraft

An artist's impression from the project documents faithfully reproducing the Tu-144LL's colour scheme, including the Russian inscription 'Moskva' (Moscow) which took a while to appear on the actual aircraft.

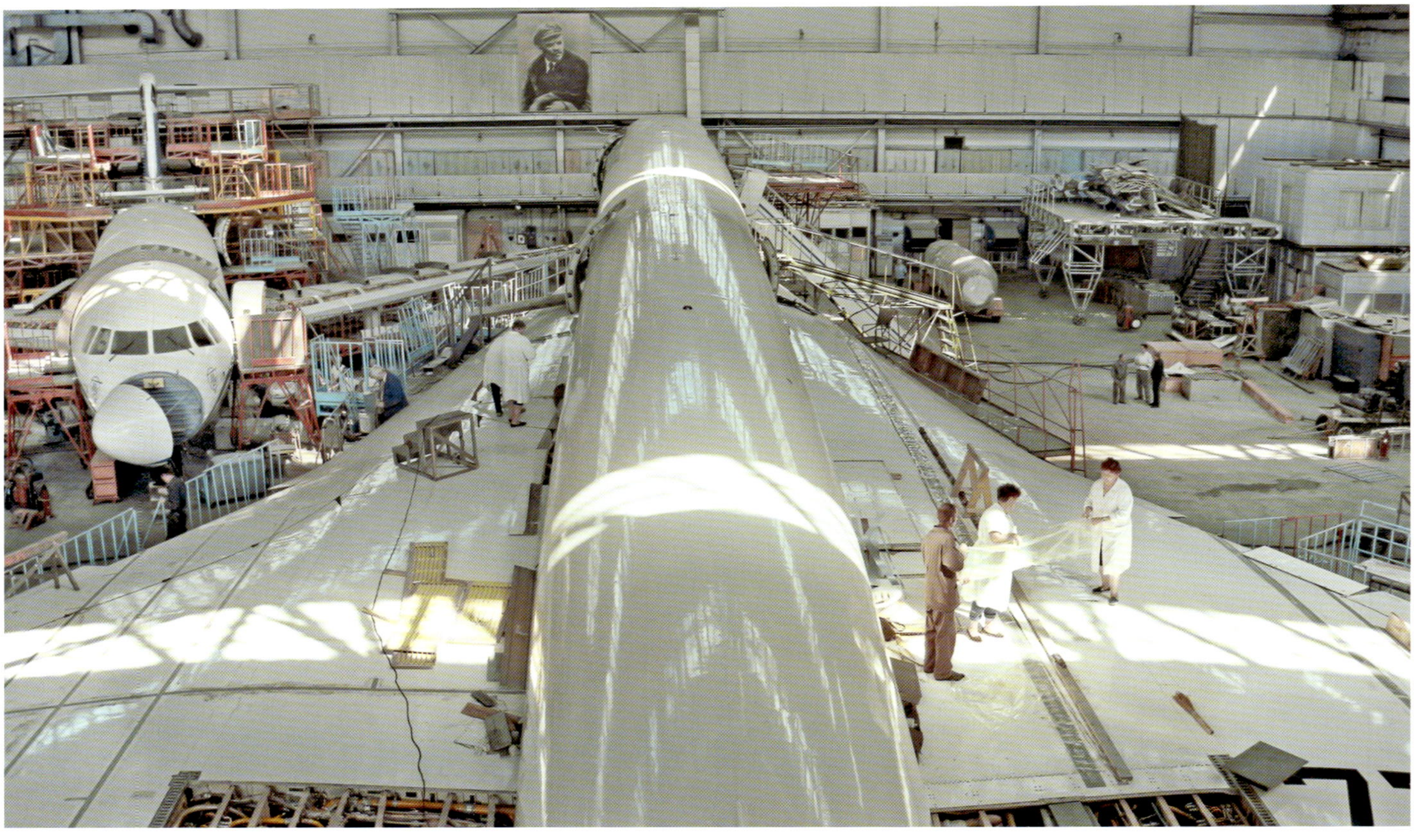

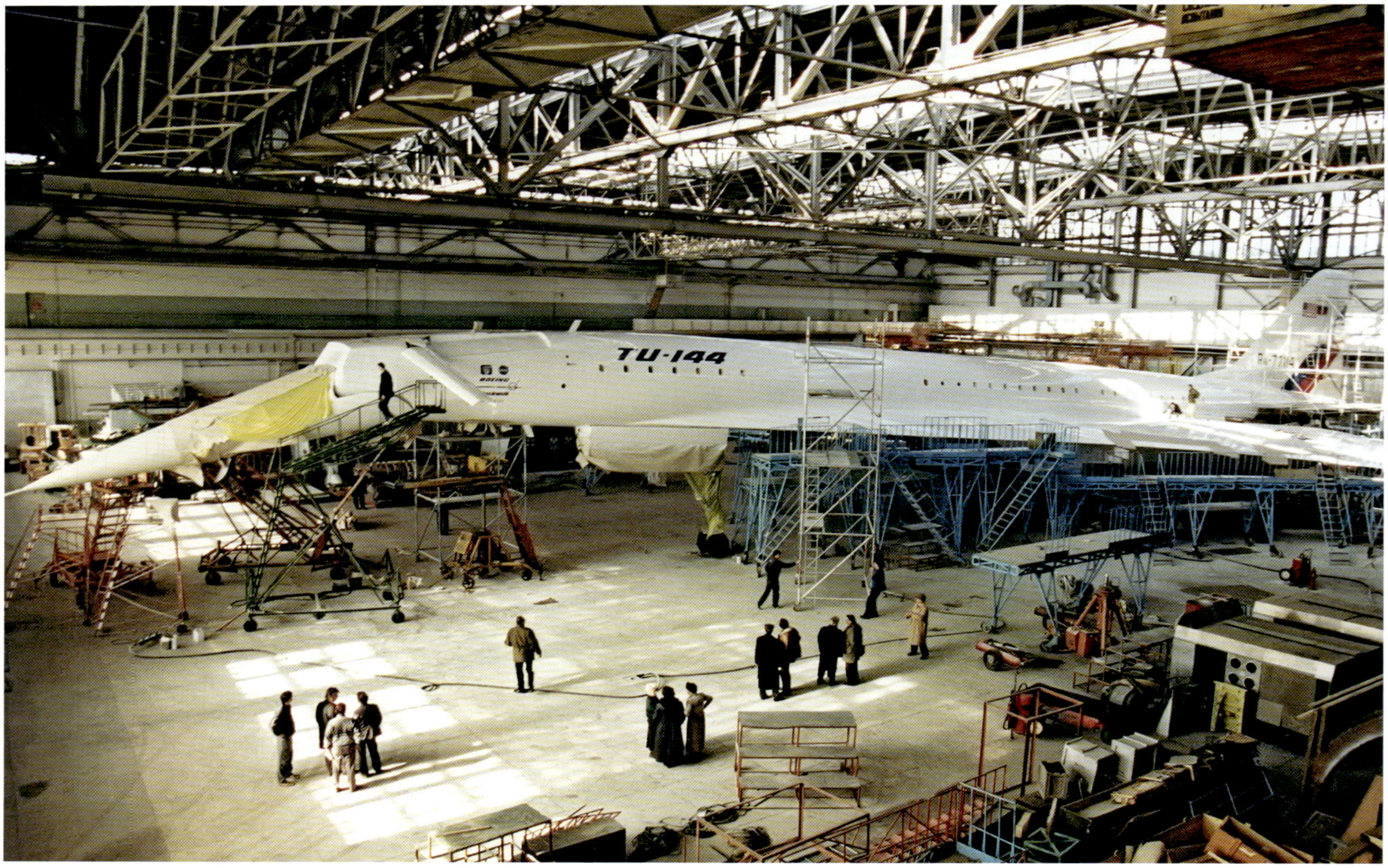
TU-144

Chapter 10 - A New Lease of Life: the Tu-144LL Testbed

Left: The Tu-144LL being worked on in the hangar at Zhukovskiy, with the second prototype Tu-334 short-haul airliner (RA-94005) on the left. Note the wiring runs on the starboard wing and the skin panels removed for access to fuel system components.

Below left: The Tu-144LL in the paint shop at Zhukovskiy in March 1996. The logos of ANTK Tupolev, NASA, Boeing, McDonnell Douglas, Rockwell and IBP Aviation can be seen on the nose.

Above right: The NK-321 (NK-32-1) afterburning turbofan.

Right: The Tu-144LL's flight deck. The instrument panel differs from that of the standard Tu-144D (see pages 196-197). Note the emergency escape hatch control panel on top of the instrument panel shroud in the centre.

as the Mikoyan/Gurevich MiG-15 *Fagot* and MiG-17 *Fresco* fighters and the Il'yushin IL-28 *Beagle* tactical bomber.

When it came to SST development, there was co-operation between the East and the West, too. The partnership between the Tupolev OKB and Aérospatiale began at the 27th Paris Air Show in 1965 where both companies unveiled the projects of the Tu-144 and the Concorde. At the show, Aérospatiale President Henri Ziegler and the Concorde's chief designer Pierre Satre had talks with the Soviet Minister of Aircraft Industry Pyotr V. Dement'yev and General Designer Andrey N. Tupolev; the parties agreed on Soviet-French co-operation in the service introduction of the Tu-144 and the Concorde.

After several meetings at the managerial level, working meetings between the engineers doing the actual design work on the Tu-144 and the Concorde started taking place on a regular basis from 1971 onwards. Actually the basis for practical co-operation had been established at the 28th Paris Air Show in 1967 when Pierre Satre arranged a meeting between Aérospatiale's and Tupolev's chief project aerodynamicists, Fage and Cheryomukhin.

At subsequent meetings the Tupolev engineers, obeying instructions from their top brass, would tell their French colleagues *how* they were working but withhold the information on *what* they had achieved. The French did just the opposite – they spoke freely of the results but would not tell how they had been achieved. Gradually, as the design teams got to know each other better, the French engineers realised that 'the Russians' would eventually guess the 'how' while the Soviet engineers conceded that the French colleagues would see the 'what'. Thus, both sides concluded that there was no point in playing hide-and-seek and started sharing information freely, aiding each other immensely.

Later, designers on both sides of the Atlantic Ocean started work on a second-generation successor tentatively called SST-2. Long-term forecasts showed that by 2015 the world's airlines would need as many as 700 high-capacity SSTs, especially on routes 6,000-9,000 km (3,726-5,590 miles) long, to cope with the predicted growth in passenger traffic volumes. In order to be economically viable the SST-2 needed to be more efficient than similarly sized subsonic airliners by making more flights and carrying

Left: Gleaming with fresh paint, the Tu-144LL sits outside the Tupolev hangar during the roll-out ceremony on 17th March 1996.

Below: Another aspect of RA-77114 during the rollout, showing the nozzles of the NK-321 engines with the petals fully closed. The assorted Tupolev aircraft in the background include Tu-144D CCCP-77113, which was unflyable by then and would eventually be broken up in 2001.

Chapter 10 - A New Lease of Life: the Tu-144LL Testbed

more passengers within the same time frame, offsetting its higher fuel consumption. Thus, calculations showed that transporting 100 million passengers within a year would require 1,200 airliners cruising at Mach 0.8 with a 22-g/seat-km fuel burn, or just 350 SSTs cruising at Mach 2.05 with a 45-g/seat-km fuel burn.

Since an SST is an extremely expensive project beyond the means of any single nation, it would have to be an international programme developed on a risk-sharing basis. The US Congress allotted NASA US$ 450 million for SST-2 research up to the year 2000, and it was decided to establish contacts with ANTK Tupolev and other Russian R&D organisations with practical experience of developing SSTs. In 1993 the Boeing Company, which was also involved in the SST-2 programme, set up a research and design centre in Moscow which established contacts with 40 Russian aerospace companies and institutions, including ANTK Tupolev and TsAGI.

To reduce the technical risk, the design methods and actual design features that go into such an aircraft should be verified on flying testbeds if at all possible. The larger the testbed aircraft is and the closer its performance comes to the projected SST-2's design performance, the more valuable it becomes in its research capacity. Such complex issues as calculating the skin temperature of an integral tank filled with cold fuel in kinetic heating conditions, or calculating the heating intensity of the fuel being fed to the engines, can only be checked out in actual supersonic flight which will yield as authentic a result as you can possibly get, allowing errors in calculation methods to be corrected. This is why in the early 1990s ANTK Tupolev started work on a research aircraft designated Tu-144LL (*letayushchaya laboratoriya* – 'flying laboratory') and intended to provide data for the possible SST-2.

The idea of creating such a research aircraft first came up when the aptly designated Tu-244 SST-2 project was launched. The Tu-244 was to be a 300-seat aircraft with a 322-ton (709,890-lb) take-off weight which was to cruise at Mach 2.0, with a range of 9,150 km (5,685 miles). Given appropriate funding, the aircraft could have entered service as early as 2006. However, this project lies outside the scope of this book.

Aleksandr L. Pookhov was the Tu-144LL's project chief. Working persistently, by 1993 ANTK Tupolev engineers had finalised the Tu-144LL's outlook and completed a set of drawings for the modification job. At the 40th Paris Air Show in June 1993 ANTK Tupolev and the US company Rockwell International inked the first international co-operation agreement concerning development of the Tu-144LL research aircraft.

Even as the Russian-US inter-government commission co-chaired by the then Prime Minister of Russia Viktor S. Chernomyrdin and Vice-President Albert L. Gore signed an agreement in Vancouver in June 1993, giving the Tu-144LL official status and allocating funds for the programme, the aircraft remained the subject of controversy. '*Why the Tu-144? Why not the Concorde?*' – some people clamoured. In the USA there was a powerful anti-Russian lobby which maintained that the funds allocated by the US Congress for the development of a supersonic research aircraft should not be given to Russia and that the Concorde should be used as the basis for this programme instead. In 1995, responding to these allegations, Louis Williams, head of NASA's High Speed Research Program, gave several interviews to the world's leading aviation magazines, explaining why the Tu-144 had been selected over the Concorde. The supersonic research aircraft should come as close as possible to the future SST-2 in size, performance and aerodynamic efficiency, said Williams and gave figures to prove his point. The Tu-144's wing area was 507 m² (5,450 sq ft) versus the Concorde's 425 m² (4,570 sq ft); its cruising speed of Mach 2.2 (versus the Concorde's Mach 2.04) came closer to the SST-2's envisaged speed of Mach 2.4, and its lift/drag ratio at Mach 2.0 was 8.1 versus 7.3 for the Concorde. The Tu-144 had a record share of titanium in its structure accounting for nearly 20% of the airframe weight, retractable canards and a unique wing/fuselage structural design. All this made it a better candidate than the Concorde.

On 17th June 1994 NASA and ANTK Tupolev signed a further contract relating to the Tu-144LL programme. The success of the programme was in no small part due to good interaction between the partners. The organisational aspects were handled by IBP Corporation, a US company with strong Russian ties headed by the wealthy businesswoman Judith DePaul.

The Tu-144LL conversion involved primarily a change of powerplant: the Tu-144D's Kolesov RD36-51A non-afterburning turbojets gave way to Kuznetsov NK-321 afterburning turbofans (also rendered as NK-32-1 or even NK-321LL) – a version of the Tu-160's NK-32 engine rated at 13,000 kgp (28,660 lbst) dry and 25,000 kgp (55,115 lbst) reheat. This was a forced measure, as the RD36-51A was long since out of production and the few surviving examples had a remaining service life of just a few dozen hours.

The NK-32 is a three-spool turbofan with a three-stage LP compressor, a five-stage intermediate-pressure (IP) compressor, a seven-stage HP compressor, a multi-burner annular combustion chamber, single-stage HP and IP turbines, a two-stage LP turbine, a core/bypass flow mixer, an afterburner and a convergent-divergent axisymmetrical nozzle. The air intake assembly has a fixed spinner and 18 inlet guide vanes. The HP compressor incorporates bleed valves supplying air for the de-icing system, pressurisation and air conditioning system and so on. Two of the combustion chamber's flame tubes feature igniters. The HP turbine has monocrystalline blades.

A ventral accessory gearbox is mounted near the front end of the engine; it features an integral CSD for the AC and DC generators and hydraulic pump. The NK-32 has a self-contained lubrication system, FADEC and a powerplant monitoring system. The engine is started by an air turbine starter (ATS) using compressed air supplied by the APU or a ground source.

The bypass ratio is 1.36, the overall engine pressure ratio 28.2 and the turbine temperature 1,630° K. The NK-321 is 7.453 m (24 ft 5$^{27}/_{64}$ in) long, with a maximum diameter of 1.7 m (5 ft 6$^{15}/_{16}$ in); dry weight is 3,650 kg (8,046 lb).

The NK-321 engines required new rear portions of the engine nacelles (featuring new engine attachment points) and new rear portions of the inlet ducts to be manufactured; local reinforcement of the wing centre section was necessary to take the more powerful engines. Since the rear portions of the revised nacelles were wider than the standard ones, the inboard elevon sections were cut away at the root to match them, with a 5% reduction in their area. The new engines necessitated installation of the ESUD-32-1 FADEC

(*elektronnaya sistema oopravleniya dvigatelem* – electronic engine control system) and the SKSU-32-1 powerplant monitoring system (*sistema kontrolya silovoy oostanovki*). The standard SUZ-10 air intake control system (*sistema oopravleniya [vozdukho] zabornikami*) gave way to the SUZ-10M version (*modernizeerovannaya* – updated). The existing engine instruments and engine starting control panel were replaced with appropriate items taken from the bomber; new electric fuel shut-off cocks were introduced and their controls on the control panel relocated.

One thing leads to another: major changes to the aircraft's other systems were also made, although the designers understandably strove to retain as much as possible of the existing hardware. In particular, the Tu-144LL had a new electric system having 120-kW GT120NZhCh-12K three-phase AC generators (*ghenerahtor tryokhfahznyy*) with GP-22 CSDs (*ghidroprivod* – hydraulic drive) as the primary power source instead of the Tu-144D's 60-kW GT60MCh-8U generators, no DC generators, new URG-115V automatic overload protection devices, a BKNA-115V device protecting the system from damage by a faulty ground power source, and appropriate changes to the instrument panels. In the fuel system, high-pressure fuel lines were added for driving the jet pumps, an ETsN-134 electric centrifugal pump (*elektricheskiy tsentrobe-*

Chapter 10 - A New Lease of Life: the Tu-144LL Testbed

Left: The Tu-144LL taxies at Zhukovskiy – specifically, on a taxiway near runway 12 known in local slang as The Bottle for its shape (the taxiway is narrower at one end).

Below left: This view shows that the port and starboard engines are momentarily running at different speed, as the nozzle areas reveal.

Right: RA-77114 is towed by a somewhat lop-sided Kirovets K-701 heavy-duty tractor.

Below: The Tu-144 begins its take-off from runway 12. Note the orange colouring of the exhaust plume due to a high nitrous oxide content – a distinctive feature of the NK-32 engines.

zhnyy nasos) was added near the fuel/air heat exchangers, two centrifugal pumps in the service tanks were set to work simultaneously, and the fuel flow meter was deleted. The hydraulic system included modified NP-103-3 engine-driven pumps. A new fire suppression system was installed, with appropriate changes to the fire warning system. The original twin circular brake parachutes were replaced with a brake parachute system borrowed from the Tu-160; it comprised three cruciform parachutes with a total area of 105 m² (1,130.21 sq ft) and two 1-m² (10.76 sq ft) drogue parachutes.

The AFCS was actually downgraded considerably by excluding the go-around mode, automatic route following capability (with inputs from the NK-144 navigation suite) and ICAO Cat II automatic approach capability – only Cat I automatic approach capability was retained. The standard MSRP-64 FDR was replaced by a new MSRP-A-0.1-0.3 FDR capturing 176 one-time commands and 80 continuous parameters. In addition to the existing test equipment left over from previous tests, the SBI test equipment suite (*sistema bortovykh izmereniy* – on-board measurement

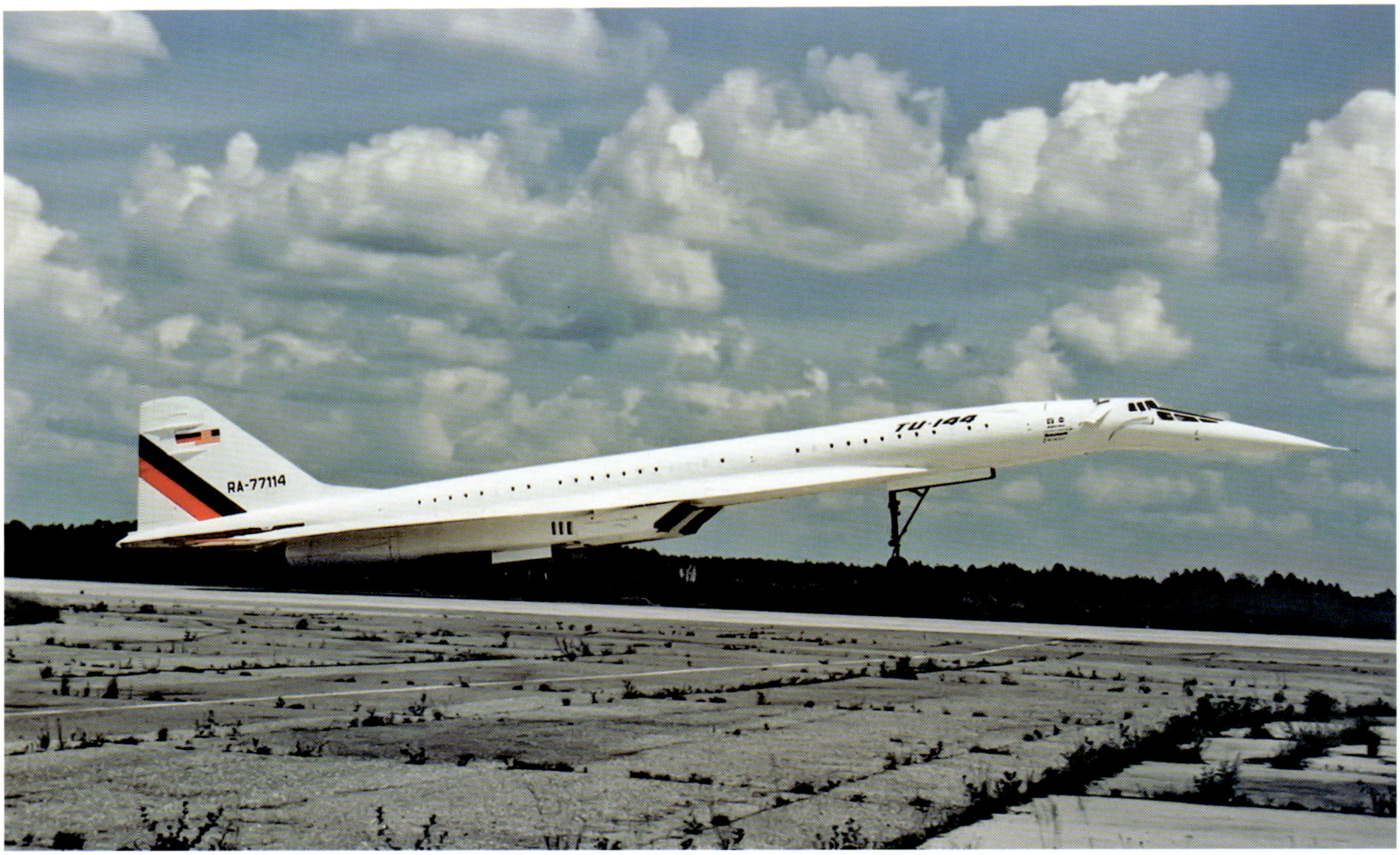
TU-144
RA-77114

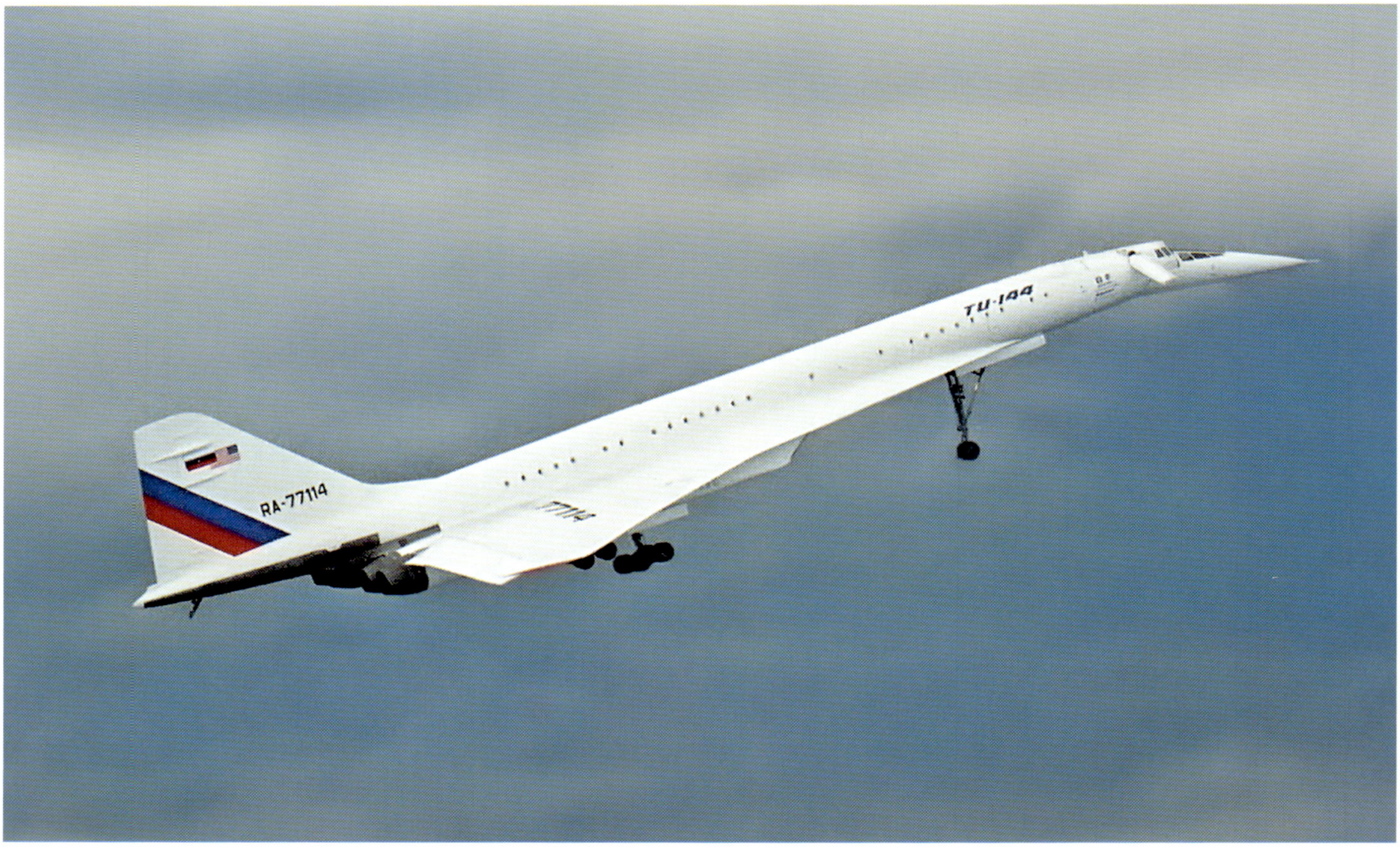
TU-144
RA-77114

Chapter 10 - A New Lease of Life: the Tu-144LL Testbed

system) was installed to the western partners' specifications; it captured 972 flight parameters and 2,028 experimental parameters. The SBI suite included western components, notably the DAMIEN data acquisition system developed by the French company SFIM (*Société de Fabrication d'Instruments de Mesure*, now part of the Safran aerospace industry group).

Due to the aircraft's experimental status, changes were made to the crew rescue equipment and life support equipment. The forward service door on the starboard side could be jettisoned at the captain's orders, allowing the flight crew to bail out. A hatch and chute were provided in the forward cabin floor for the test engineers, allowing them to bail out through the forward baggage door; the latter could be opened electromechanically or manually in an emergency, and safety railings were installed near the hatch to facilitate bailing out and prevent anyone from falling in during normal operations. The overwing emergency exits in the rear cabin were modified to feature emergency depressurisation valves. The pilots' and flight engineer's seats had dished seat pans to take S5-I parachutes (with KP-52M breathing apparatus and ORK-11 oxygen pressure reduction valves), while the seats of the other crewmembers permitted use of PNL-58 backpack-type parachutes with KP-52M breathing apparatus and R-7OA oxygen pressure reduction valves. For high-altitude flights the crew were provided with VKK-6M pressure suits, ZSh-5M 'bone dome' flying helmets (*zashchitnyy shlem* – protective helmet) and KM-34 oxygen masks (*kislorodnaya mahska*).

Deputy Chief Designer Mikhail Ye. Kalmanovich headed the actual design effort. Specific design areas were the responsibility

Left: Seen from the south side of the field at Zhukovskiy, the Tu-144LL rotates for take-off from runway 12...

Below left: ...and begins a steep climb.

Above: Captain Sergey G. Borisov (project test pilot) and co-pilot Boris I. Veremey in the Tu-144LL's flight deck.

Below: The Tu-144LL in high-altitude cruise flight.

Left: The Tu-144LL a few seconds after landing on runway 30 at Zhukovskiy. The nose visor is set at 17°; the elevons are already neutral but the brake parachutes are not yet deployed.

Right: NASA test pilot Charles Gordon Fullerton in the co-pilot's seat of the Tu-144LL.

Below right: Seen from the control tower, RA-77114 completes its landing run on runway 30, streaming the three cruciform brake parachutes.

of A. A. Golubev and V. B. Zakharenkov (the SBI suite), V. A. Tveretskiy (the fuel system), V. P. Kalkanov (the air intake control system), A. V. Gheorgiyevskiy and L. K. Filippova (the AFCS), B. M. Zhirnov (the manual flight control system) and Ye. P. Malyshev (the equipment and the navigation suite).

At that point ANTK Tupolev had three Tu-144Ds in flyable condition – CCCP-77112, CCCP-77114 and CCCP-77115. (Two further examples present at the company's flight test facility in Zhukovskiy, CCCP-77105 and CCCP-77113, were no longer airworthy and were broken up shortly afterwards.) CCCP-77114 (c/n 10082, or 08-2) – the aforementioned record-setting 'aircraft 101' – was selected for conversion. First flown on 13th April 1981 (this date is sometimes reported as the manufacture date), it had logged 82 hours 40 minutes total time since new (including 27 hours 37 minutes supersonic) and 47 total cycles since new – nine flights in 1981, 12 in 1983, five in 1984, 13 in 1986, one in 1987, six in 1988 and one in 1990; on 28th February 1990, the day after the 47th flight, the aircraft was mothballed. CCCP-77112 became a ground test rig in support of the Tu-144LL programme, being used for checking various equipment items (it was declared operational on 14th May 1996), while CCCP-77115 was in 'hot reserve'.

By then CCCP-77114 was 13 years old and had been sitting in storage for four years, with a consequent deterioration in its condition. Therefore, even before the contract with NASA was signed the aircraft was given a thorough check before the conversion job could begin – flight safety was a priority. This was especially the case with the electrics, avionics and instruments, which had to be returned to working condition; they were mid-/late 1970s vintage, and most of the items were no longer in production because the plants that had produced them had either gone bankrupt or been reoriented to producing other products. Thus, operating the aircraft's systems and equipment on a 'technical condition' basis turned into a major headache for the ANTK Tupolev maintenance staff, which had to master the techniques of repairing them in the field. Sometimes the specialists had to sift through dozens of defective avionics or equipment items in order to piece together a serviceable 'undead' item. In so doing a large number of *ad hoc* test benches were built for testing and tuning the reconditioned avionics and equipment items. This technique exacerbated the electromagnetic compatibility problems between the electronic systems, which again had to be resolved in an 'improvise, make do and mend' way. Only the fact that enough specialists with unique skills still remained loyal to ANTK Tupolev and did not quit in those financially lean times made this restoration effort possible.

The airframe structure and aircraft systems were likewise given a thorough inspection. Before the conversion job began, between 21st January and 10th May 1994 the airframe underwent non-destructive testing in accordance with a special list of potential problem areas; some critical structural components were subjected to X-ray checks. During the same time frame all of the aircraft's systems underwent power-on checks to see if they conformed to the specifications; all antenna feeders were tested and their insulation checked for electric resistance.

On 2nd June 1994 ANTK Tupolev issued a document concerning service life extension of the Tu-144LL's systems and equipment. The latter were subdivided into three categories according to the danger they presented in the event of failure: critical items (such as control system components) whose service life could only be extended by their respective manufacturers, involving bench tests and on-board tests; off-the-shelf components whose service life could be extended in the system they were part of; and components designed in house whose service life could be extended after checks in ANTK Tupolev's own laboratories and on the aircraft (as part of the respective systems).

The conversion took place at the Tupolev flight test facility in Zhukovskiy between May 1994 and 19th September 1996. In addition to the company's own quality control department, the Ministry of Defence's quality control inspectors were called upon in May 1996 to assist with the checks. In parallel, the flight manual and maintenance manual were being drawn up. On 17th April 1996 an expert panel convened to judge if the aircraft was safe to fly

Chapter 10 - A New Lease of Life: the Tu-144LL Testbed

and drew up a list of documents that were to be submitted to MAP for obtaining clearance for the Tu-14LL's first flight. TsAGI and LII filed reports for each stage of the conversion job, approving the results; LII's last report concerning the flight/navigation suite and the flight deck equipment was signed on 26th November 1996 – three days before the first flight.

Working out the flight test programme and getting it approved by all participants, including the US partners, the engine manufacturer (SNTK Trood) and LII, was a task in itself. The customer's appetites, the aircraft's capabilities and the supersonic flight time limits (dictated by the size of the test area and its avenues of approach) all had to be taken into account. After a deal of negotiating the programme was approved on 17th April 1996; it comprised 32 flights – 21 test flights to check the modified aircraft's conformity to the airworthiness regulations and determine the difference in flight performance from the Tu-144D, plus 11 research flights. Six flight experiments were agreed upon for Stage 1 of the programme, and a further two were added during Stage 2. These were:

• Experiment 1.2 – defining the aircraft's temperature balance (measuring the equilibrium temperature of the aircraft skin); the purpose was to determine the hottest areas with a view to selecting the appropriate structural materials for the SST-2 or choosing alternate methods of cooling these areas.

• Experiment 1.5 – exploring the powerplant temperature in various flight modes and forming a data base on this; the main purpose was to evolve a design concept for jet engines able to withstand the inevitable strong heating in sustained supersonic cruise.

• Experiment 1.6 – exploring the influence of ground effect on low aspect ratio wings; this was a key factor affecting the aircraft's handling during final approach and landing.

- Experiment 2.1 – measuring the structure's acoustic loads and cabin noise levels; the purpose was to determine the conditions when the slipstream around the fuselage generated additional noise and acoustic loads, with a view to evolving effective ways of reducing these unwelcome factors.
- Experiment 2.4 – checking the aircraft's stability and handling; the objective was to assess the behaviour of the current SST-1 in order to make the larger future SST-2 as much of a 'pilot's aeroplane' as possible.
- Experiment 3.3 – measuring the friction factor and pressure factor characterising the wings' boundary layer; the purpose was to verify the calculation results with an accuracy allowing future SSTs to match the designers' estimates as closely as possible.
- Experiment 4.1 – exploring the flexure of the wings in all flight modes: the purpose was to develop more accurate methods of calculating the structural design and structural strength of the SST-2's wings.
- Experiment 5.0 – participation of American test pilots assessing the aircraft's stability and handling.

The ANTK Tupolev employees supervising the experiments were M. N. Gheneralova (1.2 and 1.5), A. L. Kroopnik (1.6 and 3.3), E. V. Andrianov and Igor' B. Ginko (2.1), Oleg Yu. Alasheyev and Yu. I. Didenko (2.4), I. K. Kulikov (4.1) and Edgar F. Krupyanskiy (5.0).

The first power-on test took place on 15th December 1995 when the Tu-144LL was still incomplete – the engines and many systems components were still missing. Yet this made it possible to start verifying the SBI suite on the actual aircraft; by then the SBI had undergone a large scope of bench testing at ANTK Tupolev's head office in Moscow and flight test facility in Zhukovskiy.

Above: The Tu-144 extends the landing gear during a low pass over runway 30.

Left: This shot shows the auxiliary blow-in doors open and the nozzle petals closed.

Opposite page: The Tu-144LL's Russian-US crew deplanes after a test flight; captain Sergey G. Borisov is foremost. Note the different set of logos – the McDonnell Douglas and Rockwell logos are gone, but TsAGI's airfoil logo has been added.

Chapter 10 - A New Lease of Life: the Tu-144LL Testbed

The aircraft, which had been stripped of its Aeroflot livery during the conversion, was rolled out for the first time (for the benefit of the American partners) in bare metal guise on 20th January 1996 – still incomplete. Painting the aircraft at that time was impossible because of the cold weather – the paint would not have dried properly in the cold hangar. The 'real' rollout took place on 17th March 1996, the Tu-144LL being placed on the Russian civil aircraft register as RA-77114 that same day; by then the aircraft had gained a predominantly white colour scheme with a blue/red diagonal stripe on the tail (representing the Russian flag), sporting the Russian and American flags and the logos of the companies participating in the programme (Tupolev, Boeing, McDonnell Douglas, Rockwell, NASA and IBP Aircraft – a division of IBP Corporation). (Speaking of which, this set of logos changed over time.) Even so, the aircraft was not yet ready to fly – changes to the engine nacelles, fuel and oil systems were being made continuously on a 'cut and fit' basis, and deliveries of many off-the-shelf items were running late.

On 18th-20th March, immediately after the rollout, the management of ANTK Tupolev had briefings with the American partners to discuss programme progress. Speaking at one of the briefings, NASA High-Speed Research (HSR) programme director Louis J. Williams said: *'The first flight date doesn't matter; safety matters. Experience with the Space Shuttle has taught us that.'* Williams was referring to the tragic demise of Space Shuttle *Challenger* (OV-099) with all hands on 28th January 1986.

A lot of bugs had to be eliminated before test flights could begin. The production team under Viktor I. Borod'ko worked round the clock in spite of power failures, shortages of hydraulic fluid and lubricants (which were delivered late) and, last but not least, the fact that the workforce's wages were several months overdue – a common problem in Russia in the 1990s.

On 19th September 1996 RA-77114 was formally turned over to the flight test facility and the ground test phase began. It took more than a month to rectify the remaining defects, ground-run the engines and check the systems. On 1st November the aircraft made two high-speed taxi runs and was then hangared for another two weeks for elimination of the defects that had cropped up at this stage.

The Tu-144LL's ground test team numbering 123 men had been assigned as early as 27th December 1995; it was headed by Edgar F. Krupyanskiy, who had returned to ANTK Tupolev after 17 years of work at MAP. It included operations chief Aleksey Amelyushkin, technicians Ghennadiy A. Kopylov and Aleksey K. Korupayev (both of them old hands with the Tu-144), powerplant technician Nikolay I. Perfilov, equipment technician Nikolay I. Ruzanov. The SBI was the responsibility of technicians Aleksandr S. Sudakov, Sergey L. Boormistrov and Sergey G. Gavrilin; unlike the other technicians, they were constantly monitored by specially assigned representatives of the US companies and by the Tupolev employees in charge of the flight experiments. Flight plan preparation and test data analysis was performed by a group under Vladimir I. Sysoyev. The team also included representatives of SNTK Trood and MIEA (the latter institute was responsible for the automatic control systems).

Krupyanskiy later recalled that many of the colleagues he had previously worked with on the Tu-144 programme before quitting

the OKB tried to dissuade him from embarking on the Tu-144LL project, thinking the whole idea pointless. Their reasoning was that the airframe was old and spares for it were unavailable, the co-operation ties once involved in operating the Tu-144 had been broken, many of the specialists who had worked with the aircraft were gone etc. Moreover, they did not believe that the USA would actually provide the funding for the project.

The flight test team had been assigned on 6th June 1995, comprising test pilots Boris I. Veremey, Vladimir N. Matveyev and Sergey S. Popov (the latter had no prior experience with the Tu-144). Viktor V. Solomatin, Anatoliy V. Krioolin and Ivan Gvozd' were the flight engineers (main and back-up); again, Gvozd' had no previous experience with the type. Shortly afterwards, however, Sergey G. Borisov (ANTK Tupolev's chief of flight operations since 1995) was appointed the Tu-144LL's project test pilot. Despite his fairly young age, Borisov was a seasoned pilot who was equally proficient with fast jets, having flown the Mikoyan MiG-23 *Flogger* and MiG-25 *Foxbat* supersonic fighters in his Air Force days, and with 'fat jets' (that is, heavy subsonic aircraft), having flown the Tu-95 turboprop bomber and the

Tu-134, Tu-154 and Tu-204 airliners after becoming a Tupolev OKB test pilot. He had also flown as co-pilot on the Tu-22M and Tu-160 supersonic bombers on several occasions. The main and back-up flight crews were finalised on 22nd January 1996.

Flying again
The in-house Methodical Council convened on 25th November 1996 to decide if the aircraft was fit to fly; MAP's Methodical Council followed three days later. Both councils raised no objections.

The Tu-144LL made its 43-minute first flight on 29th November 1996, becoming airborne from runway 12 at 1354 hrs Moscow time; the aircraft was flown by captain Sergey G. Borisov, co-pilot Boris I. Veremey, navigator Viktor I. Pedos, flight engineer Anatoliy V. Krioolin and engineer in charge of the flight tests A. K. Shcherbakov. The landing gear and the canards stayed extended and the nose visor was at the 11° take-off setting throughout the flight. The take-off weight was 140,000 kg (308,650 lb) and the landing weight 125,000 kg (275,580 lb).

The weather almost threw a spanner in the works – on 29th November the cloudbase at Zhukovskiy was only 340 m (1,115 ft) instead of the required 500 m (1,640 ft), and special clearance had to be obtained from MAP's Methodical Council. Yet the first flight was marred more by an incident – the aircraft behaved abnormally, 'seesawing' (rocking fore and aft), which was particularly dangerous during the landing approach, and suffering from directional instability. Pitch and roll oscillations were experienced when certain AFCS modes were switched on. It turned out that the pitch and roll damping sensors of the AFCS had been cross-wired to the wrong channels; the mistake occurred when the sensors were being reinstalled after checks on a test bench. The connectors were identical, and the difficult approach to the sensors' locations was a contributing factor.

Here is how Sergey Borisov described that memorable flight.
'The aircraft quickly accelerated to the required [rotation] speed. I pulled the control yoke back gently. The aerodynamicists were right – very gentle movements of the yoke were needed for rotation. The aircraft raised its nose eagerly; with the [take-off] weight we had, I figured the required pitch angle would be about 25°. The speed was growing very fast: 360... 380... 400 km/h [223, 236 and 248 mph]. I moved the control yoke gently to stabilise the AOA; still, the pitch angle continued to grow. I pushed the yoke a little forward, and the nose went down – all too hastily – instead of simply stopping its upward motion. The speed was 420 km/h [260 mph] – close to the limit (with the gear down – Auth.) *It was time to cancel the afterburners. The nose continued to drop, even though the control yoke was motionless; this was wrong. Apparently the pitch control channel was overly sensitive. I cast a look at the co-pilot; Boris Ivanovich [Veremey] was nonchalant. The nose was approaching the level position, and it was time for us to climb. Well, no, I thought – no more messing with the yoke; let's try another method. For a split second I set the pitch trim thumb switch to "climb". That did the trick – the nose started rising gently. I worked the trim switch again, and the aircraft started climbing at 8-10 m/sec [1,570-1,970 ft/min] – just the right rate, and just at the right time. We entered the clouds and the aircraft rocked back and forth at the slightest turbulence; the oscillations took a lot of time to die down. The hardest part was to resist the urge to give corrective inputs with the yoke. I got the knack of using the pitch trim function for this (it gave more subtle elevon movements), even though it was not intended for this.*

Presently it was time to make a banked turn. I turned the control wheel gingerly, expecting a similarly sharp reaction from the aircraft; to my surprise, the bank indicator showed no change. More vigorous actions [with the wheel] elicited no reaction from the artificial horizon. Eventually all I got by turning the wheel all the way was a bank of some 15°, and even then the machine tended to roll back out of it. I toyed with the idea of adding bank by means of rudder input but common sense warned against it. Afterwards, it turned out that such actions would have been no good anyway. After the turn, things got easier; now we knew what we could do and, more importantly, what we could not. The landing was a bit tricky, when we had to compensate [the pitch change caused by] the change in engine thrust; yet the flight ended safely.'

As mentioned earlier, the flight test part of the programme comprised 21 flights as the Tu-144LL's flight envelope was explored and the functioning of the aircraft systems checked. This phase was further split into two parts (subsonic flights and supersonic flights). In addition to the Tupolev pilots mentioned above, LII's chief test pilot Yuriy P. Sheffer and ANTK Tupolev test pilot Andrey N. Soldatenkov also flew the aircraft from the right-hand seat on three and one occasions respectively.

Given the large scope of research work under Experiments 1.6 (exploring the influence of ground effect during final approach and landing) and 2.4 (assessing the aircraft's stability and handling), ANTK Tupolev took the decision to perform this work as part of the fight test phase insofar as possible. As for the other experiments, the SBI would only be checked so far.

The Tu-144LL's second flight on 11th December 1996, when the landing gear and canards were retracted and the nose visor raised for the first time, brought more spills – the No.2 engine's air intake ramp opened fully of its own accord when the engines were throttled back to cruise thrust. When all attempts to bring it under control failed, the affected engine was throttled back to idle at 7,300 m (23,950 ft) and 670 km/h (416 mph) and the crew carried on with the test mission. The aircraft attained a maximum altitude of 8,250 m (27,070 ft) and a maximum speed of Mach 0.725; the stability and handling characteristics were virtually identical to those of the Tu-144D. On the ground it turned out that a push-pull rod actuating the ramp had become disconnected.

On 5th February 1997 Boeing Company Vice-President (Technical Affiliations) Robert E. Spitzer paid a visit to ANTK Tupolev with a view to assessing the first results obtained on the Tu-144LL; a special report translated into English was prepared for the occasion. Also, NASA representative Glenn Beaver was posted full-time to the flight test facility's experimental equipment section.

The first flights and checks of the SBI showed that the western equipment was not immune against failures, too. Problems arose with temperature measurements under Experiments 1.2 and 1.5 – the UAD-16 modules of the DAMIEN data acquisition system did not get along with the Russian-supplied sensors (thermocouples), which resulted in noise levels as high as 40% of the measurement range. ANTK Tupolev flight test facility specialists offered a measurement technique based on the Russian-made Gamma data acquisition system. After discussions with Boeing and NASA representatives a special interface module was developed for integrating the Gamma and DAMIEN systems, allowing the existing data processing techniques to be retained. This episode shows the close co-operation between the Russian and US partners in the programme.

A close-knit team of testers with responsibility for specific systems and equipment formed at the flight test facility during the Tu-144LL programme. It received much assistance from the design office in Moscow. The principal team analysing the test and research data comprised V. I. Sysoyev, A. D. Derikhov, Ye. G. Demidov, V. V. Velesko, R. A. Sorokina, A. I. Yashukova and a large team of technicians under their command.

The third, fourth and fifth flights on 2nd April, 11th April and 18th April 1997 were also subsonic, with a total time of 10 hours 14 minutes. The main purpose of these flights was to check the engines for surge resistance at 8,000 m (26,250 ft), 6,000 m (19,685 ft) and 4,000 m (13,120 ft) at varying speeds; fuel burn per mile and per hour was also measured and in-flight restart procedures performed. The engines were shut down and restarted one at a time, with 30-second and three-minute cooling-down periods, at 6,000-8,300 m (19,685-27,230 ft) and 520-650 km/h (323-403 mph); a total of 28 restarts were made. Pitch and roll stability in take-off/landing configuration and cruise configuration was assessed at 2,500 m (8,200 ft). The take-off weight in these flights was 155,000 kg (341,720 lb), 165,000 kg (363,760 lb) and 177,000 kg (390,220 lb) respectively, and the landing weight ranged from 113,000 to 115,000 kg (249,120-253,530 lb). In the third flight the Tu-144LL attained Mach 0.925 and an altitude of 10,500 m (34,450 ft).

Between 19th April and 20th May 1997 the Tu-144LL was readied for the supersonic flights. Actually the first of these was to take place at 1330 hrs on 25th April, but the tech staff finally got fed up with their wages being delayed and went on strike. In the sixth, seventh and eighth flights (on 21st May, 30th May and 10th June 1997) RA-77114 attained Mach 1.42, Mach 1.83 and Mach 2.02 respectively, logging 3 hours 52 minutes (including 1 hour 57 minutes supersonic); the take-off weights were 147,000 kg (324,080 lb), 176,000 kg (388,010 lb) and 183,000 kg (403,450 lb) respectively. The maximum altitude attained was 17,800 m (58,400 ft). The aircraft passed the sound barrier at 9,500-9,900 m (31,170-32,480 ft) and took 26 minutes to climb to 14,900 m (48,880 ft); all systems functioned OK in supersonic flight and the fuel burn was as expected. Research work under Experiments 1.6 and 2.4 was performed in these flights, but the measurements under Experiment 1.5 were foiled by the thermocouples failing *en masse*.

On 30th May the aircraft skimmed over the runway for about 20 seconds when landing on runway 30 due to a combination of ground effect and excess engine thrust (and hence increased approach speed) caused by the autothrottle being disengaged at an unfortunate moment. The long runway at Zhukovskiy saved the day, but the aircraft used up all the remaining length of it!

The flights were performed making use of LII's so-called Flight Experiment Control Station (PULE – *poonkt oopravleniya lyotnym eksperimentom*) – actually a network of ground radars, optical tracking stations and telemetry pick-up stations, plus a data processing facility with ten computers connected by a local area network. The Tu-144LL's flight path was traced in real time, using an Ashtech Z-12 GPS receiver integrated with the DAMIEN data acquisition system. Among other things, the PULE made it possible to check the parameters of the engines and the fuel system. It also made it possible to alter the mission plan in real time if complications arose. This was the case on 2nd April 1997 when the crew were instructed to descend from 10,000 to 8,000 m (from 32,810 to 26,250 ft) due to a faulty AOA sensor giving phoney readings.

The flight test phase revealed some peculiarities of the Tu-144LL. Because of the bulkier engines the maximum rotation angle was reduced by some 2°; this, in turn, brought about an increase of the approach speed from 290 km/h (180 mph) to 315-330 km/h (195-205 mph). Due to the considerable lag between control column movements and the aircraft's response there was a considerable risk of skimming over the runway in ground effect mode at 1-2 m (3-6 ft), the way it happened in the third flight. This was aggravated by the reduced area of the innermost elevon sections, which were the most effective ones for pitch control; therefore the pilots had to work out a slightly different piloting technique as compared to the Tu-144D. The higher available thrust of the new engines had a beneficial effect on longitudinal trim at transonic speeds (Mach 0.9-1.2) – elevon travel for pitch trim was 2°30' versus 3°30' on the Tu-144D – and allowed the Tu-144LL to reach the Mach 2.0 cruise mode much quicker. The aircraft climbed to cruise altitude in 20 minutes over a 355-km (220.5-mile) stretch versus 32 minutes and 740 km (460 miles) for the Tu-144D. The participating American test pilots, who had some experience with the Concorde, were quick to appreciate this.

Analysis of the test results achieved so far showed that the stability and handling of the NK-321-powered Tu-144LL were fairly similar to those of the Tu-144D throughout the flight envelope. Therefore the designers decided to curtail phase 1, reducing it by 13 flights, or more than 60%. After a series of engine checks to cure an oil leak problem, on 25th May 1997 the aircraft was grounded for modifications associated with the next phase – actual research flights in the interest of the US partners (this primarily involved installation and integration of further SBI components).

On 18th-24th August the Tu-144LL had its first airshow appearance, being displayed statically at the MAKS-97 airshow in Zhukovskiy. The then President of Russia Boris N. Yel'tsin paid a visit to the aircraft on 19th August and was so impressed that he gave instructions to the effect that four persons involved in the programme be awarded the Hero of Russia title and seven others be issued other awards. Alas, the process got ensnared in red tape and the awards never reached their rightful owners...

Preparations for the flight experiments under the second (research) part of the Tu-144LL programme under the original contract continued until 24th September 1997, when RA-77114 was rolled out again. During this time frame the missing equipment necessary for Experiments 1.2, 2.1 and 3.3 was installed, and the bugs that had hindered the proper conduct of Experiment 1.5 in the previous flights were ironed out. Some of the sensors were

Above: The Tu-144LL cruises at high altitude.

Below: The gleaming white finish of the Tu-144LL stands out against the deep blue sky of the stratosphere.

Right: Another fine air-to-air shot of the Tu-144LL.

Below right: Russian President Boris N. Yel'tsin poses with the crew of the Tu-144LL after visiting the aircraft at the MAKS-97 airshow.

Chapter 10 - A New Lease of Life: the Tu-144LL Testbed

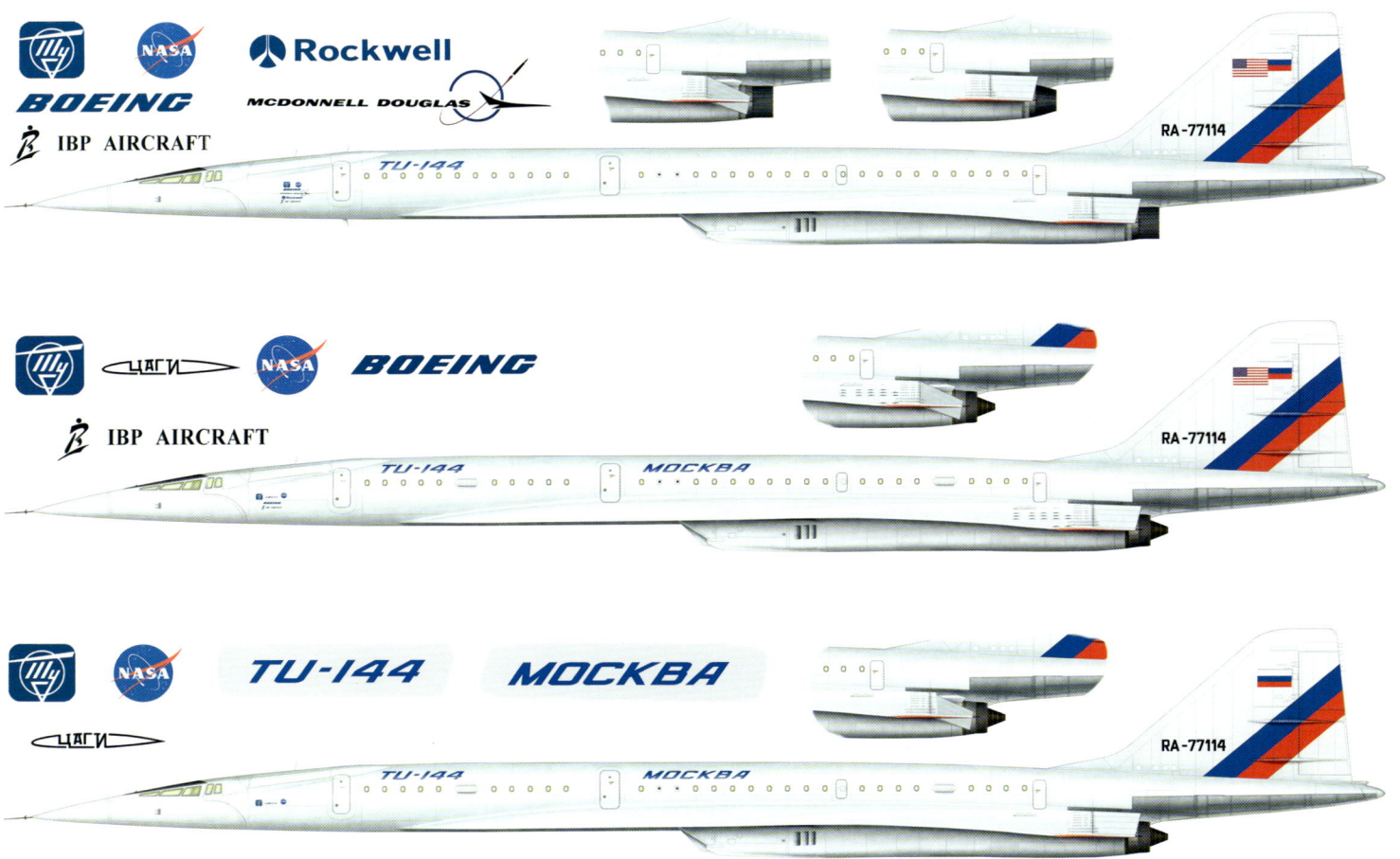

mounted externally on the wings, and the wiring for these was protected by a pink compound, making the aircraft look as if some ill-mannered youngsters had stuck strawberry chewing gum all over it. NASA representatives Glenn Beaver, Don Gallagher and Steve Reese (the latter two were from NASA's Langley Research Centre) and Boeing representative Bob Raquell took part in the installation of the equipment along with the SBI section personnel. The engines, firewalls, fuel lines and critical structural members were also inspected at this stage to check their integrity after the first supersonic flights. (The fuel lines figured in all ANTK Tupolev bulletins concerning the Tu-144LL because of apprehensions that with the engines at full military power, never mind afterburner mode, the fuel quantity in the service tanks might drop to an unacceptably low level and the fuel supply might be cut off.) Some reliability enhancement measures were also taken.

The preparations associated with Experiment 2.1 took the most time. To support this experiment the aircraft was equipped with the American METRUM acoustic data acquisition system, which required a separate operator. Test engineer in charge of the powerplant A. E. Krupyanskiy was assigned this responsibility, part of his responsibilities (monitoring the fuel consumption) being reassigned to engineer in charge of the flight tests A. K. Shcherbakov; the latter was also a back-up operator of the METRUM system. Both men passed a qualification test and were officially cleared by the Americans to operate the equipment. Jumping ahead of the story, it may be said that they coped with the job – none of the measurements were messed up, apart from some minor glitches of the METRUM system itself.

The aircraft was ready for the ninth flight – the first under phase 2 – on 1st October 1997, but adverse weather caused daily cancellations, delaying it by a week. There were other delays and cancellations due to foul weather (the tenth flight was postponed from 24th October to 27th October, there were cancellations on 12th November and 21st November) and fuel shortages at Zhukovskiy (on 15th October, 22nd October and 16th December).

Between 8th October 1997 and 11th February 1998 the Tu-144LL made all 11 flights envisaged by phase 2 of the programme, logging a total of 23 hours 52 minutes, including 6 hours 24 minutes supersonic; the mission on 11th February was the 19th flight. Post-flight inspection after the tenth flight (which involved prolonged Mach 2.0 cruise) revealed damage to the SBI sensors: the pitots were bent, the Nos. 1 and 2 pressure probe arrays were was partly missing (the entire lower half of No.2 was gone) and the No.3 pressure probe array was partially dislodged. The damage had occurred just over one minute after the aircraft had accelerated to Mach 1.93-1.95 and was making a turn. Yet, all necessary data under Experiment 3.3 had been obtained by then, and the mission was considered accomplished.

Left: The Tu-144LL as rolled out on 17th March 1996. The scrap view show the elevons in power-off position (left) and the engines at full military power.

Below left: The Tu-144LL as it looked in 2001 with the RD36-51A engine nozzles reinstalled. Note the different logos on the nose.

Bottom left: The aircraft in even later guise with the US flag, Boeing and IBP Aircraft logos removed.

Right: The Tu-144LL languishing at Zhukovskiy after the programme's completion; note the open cowlings of the Nos. 1 and 2 engines.

Bottom: Another view of the aircraft, showing the legend 'Moskva' added at a late stage of the programme.

There was one major incident on 24th December 1997 when the take-off was aborted at 230 km/h (143 mph) due to a clogged fuel filter warning. It turned out that the inboard engines' fuel filters had become clogged due to fuel contamination – apparently caused by dirty water dripping from the leaky hangar roof into the service tanks which had been opened for modification. It never rains but it pours: the intense heat generated during the emergency braking ruined the wheel brakes, and the nose gear unit received some damage as the aircraft was being towed back to the hardstand. Thus, between 25th December 1997 and 21st January 1998 RA-77114 was grounded for repairs and fuel system flushing.

Post-flight analysis of the experimental data, which was jointly performed by ANTK Tupolev, NASA and Boeing specialists, showed that the research programme insofar as Experiments 1.2, 1.5, 1.6, 2.1, 2.4 and 3.3 were concerned, had been completed in full. The report on the completion of phase 2 (the customer's flight experiments) was duly endorsed by Tu-144LL project chief Aleksandr L. Pookhov on 19th February 1998. The project chiefs in charge of the specific experiments filed separate reports for each experiment.

The programme involved a unique scope of research involving 1,000 separate parameters (700 experimental parameters and 300 associated with the aircraft itself). Experiment 1.2 made use of 265 thermocouples and 18 unique heat flow sensors; the results obtained were used for designing the SST-2's wings and calculating their thermal loads. Experiment 1.5 made use of 109 thermo-

This page and opposite page: The Tu-144LL as it looks today, stored at Zhukovskiy in rather grubby condition and minus US flag on the tail. Note the reinstatement of the RD36-51A engine nozzles (but not the engines proper!), the 21 pressure sensors on the port wing and the blanks with sensors obstructing some of the port side windows.

couples and 60 temperature indicators, yielding all the expected results which were to be used by General Electric and Boeing. The perfectly executed Experiment 1.6 made it possible to refine the analytical theory relating to the landing approach of a delta-wing heavy aircraft; 48 flight parameters were analysed and the altitude was determined with a 10-cm error margin. Experiment 2.1 yielded 10 gigabytes' worth of data on acoustic measurements – the world's largest database of the sort. Experiment 2.4 made it possible to check theories against actual flight conditions. Experiment 3.3 involved an unprecedented number of pressure measurement points (147) and 16 unique friction sensors, again yielding all the expected results which matched the designers' estimates well.

In addition to the huge amount of experimental data, the following results were obtained:

• The Tu-144's stability margins in all three control channels during enforced oscillations with increasing frequencies (0.05-1 Hz) were determined throughout the permitted speed envelope.

• The influence of the ground effect on the aerodynamics of an aircraft with compound-delta wings during landing approach was measured.

• The airflow parameters on the wings and fuselage, the temperatures of the wing and fuselage skin and inside the engine nacelles were measured at speeds up to Mach 2.0. This was done on an unparalleled scale, involving 152 static ports and pitot head

Chapter 10 - A New Lease of Life: the Tu-144LL Testbed

on the wings and no fewer than 399 temperature probes on the airframe (some of them inside the engine nacelles). 95% of the results obtained were declared valid.

• For the first time in world practice, electromechanical and anemometric friction sensors, hitherto used only in wind tunnels, were used successfully in actual flight conditions. There were 21 such sensors, plus the abovementioned 18 heat flow sensors and a number of Kulite pressure sensors feeding data to the METRUM data acquisition system.

• The data were stored in on-board computers which burned CD-ROMs to facilitate transfer of the information to NASA's Dryden Research Centre via Internet. The transfer unfailingly took place within 24 hours after the flight as stipulated by the contract.

• A Z-12 GPS transmitter was used for precision trajectory measurements in real time with an error margin of 10 cm (3^{15}/$_{16}$ in).

This flight test support technique, which had been used successfully with the Soviet space shuttle Buran, made it possible to take immediate decisions, promptly resolving abnormal situations on board the Tu-144LL when these occurred.

• The NK-321 engine's operational envelope was expanded to allow up to 41 minutes' continuous cruise at Mach 2.0; this was attained in the Tu-144LL's 17th flight at 17,500 m (57,410 ft). By comparison, the NK-32's continuous cruise time limit at Mach 2.0 on the Tu-160 was a mere ten minutes at 14,000 m (45,930 ft).

• The maximum weight at which full afterburner rating could be used on take-off was increased from 180,000 kg (396,830 lb) as per the Tu-144LL's flight manual to 190,000 kg (418,880 lb).

• Take-offs and landings were performed in crosswinds up to 12 m/sec (24 kts) versus 10 m/sec (20 kts) as specified by the flight manual.

• Finally, for the first time in Soviet/Russian practice, highly complex avionics and electronic control systems (such as the navigation suite, AFCS, air intake control system and FADEC) were operated on a 'technical condition' basis rather than with rigidly set maintenance intervals. This made it possible to complete the programme while keeping the operating costs to a minimum.

A briefing on the programme's results took place on 23rd-26th March 1998. The American partners rated the results highly. NASA programme manager Russell Barber said: *'It's quite an occasion we may celebrate, five years of partnership. This is not merely a research aircraft development programme, it is an invaluable contribution to the creation of the SST-2. The reports on successful completion of the experiments lead us to use the Tu-144LL further. Congratulations to our partners, and I hope there will be further co-operation.'*

Boeing's high-speed commercial transport programme manager Michael L. Henderson said: *'We had no doubts that the [Tu-144LL] programme would be successfully accomplished, but it is amazing that a capable Russian-US team able to take on any similar issues in the future should come together within such a relatively short time. There are good prospects for further partnership.'*

At the briefing, NASA's Associate Administrator Richard S. Christiansen, Boeing Vice-President Robert Spitzer, IBP President Judith DePaul and ANTK Tupolev Chief Designer Aleksandr L. Pookhov congratulated the people involved in the Tu-144LL programme on the programme's success.

The Americans were as good as their word – on 16th June 1998 IBP Aviation and ANTK Tupolev signed a follow-up contract involving further use of the Tu-144LL. The new programme was divided into four stages. Stage 1 involved maintenance and upgrading of the aircraft, implementation of flight safety measures and pre-flight training with the participation of American test pilots. Stage 2 was concerned with stability and handling assessment (again involving the American test pilots). Stage 3 involved issuing project documents, installing and calibrating the new research equipment. Finally, Stage 4 comprised five more flight experiments. More specific tasks were set out in a further agreement between Boeing, NASA, IBP Aviation and Tupolev on 6th July 1998, and the flight test programme was endorsed by Aleksandr L. Pookhov on 23rd July. Actually Stage 1 began well in advance of the contract signature – it was carried out between 12th February and 18th August 1998.

Shortly afterwards, on 5th September, the two NASA test pilots assigned to the Tu-144LL arrived in Zhukovskiy. One of them was 59-year-old Charles Gordon Fullerton of Dryden Flight Research Centre; he was a highly experienced pilot with more than 14,000 hours' total time on various aircraft. It deserves mention that Fullerton had participated in the free flight tests of Space Shuttle *Enterprise* (OV-101) in 1977 when it was released by the Boeing 747SCA (Shuttle Carrier Aircraft); he had also flown two actual space missions as co-pilot of Space Shuttle *Columbia* (OV-102) on 22nd-30th March 1982 and as captain of Space Shuttle *Challenger* on 29th July/6th August 1985. The other pilot was 47-year-old Robert Alan Rivers of the Langley Research Centre, a former US Navy pilot; he was selected because he had some experience with SSTs, having flown the Concorde. A number of NASA engineers from both research centres and Boeing Commercial Airplane Group engineers headed by Norman H. Princen arrived together with the pilots.

On 5th-14th September the American pilots and engineers took theoretical training on the Tu-144LL's design and systems, studied the flight manual, familiarised themselves with the flight deck and trained in emergency evacuation procedures on the aircraft. After this, C. Gordon Fullerton and Robert A. Rivers were cleared to fly the Tu-144LL as co-pilots.

On 8th September 1998 RA-77114 made its 20th flight in subsonic mode, piloted by Sergey G. Borisov and Andrey N. Soldatenkov, with S. Ye. Solodkov as flight engineer. The Americans watched the flight from the ground on that occasion, but on 15th September they had a chance to fly the aircraft; C. Gordon Fullerton was in the right-hand seat while Robert A. Rivers was an observer on the jump seat. Again, the flight was in subsonic mode and lasted 2 hours 41 minutes. Fullerton's impression was extremely favourable, judging by his comments at the debriefing: *'The best aircraft I have ever flown'*, *'It handles well even in strong turbulence and strong winds'*, *'The aircraft is an avid flyer, performing much better after it "cleans up"'* and so on.

On 18th September the Americans made their first supersonic flight in the Tu-144LL. This time it was Rivers who flew the aircraft from the right-hand seat; the take-off weight was 184,500 kg (406,750 lb). RA-77114 reached Mach 1.95, climbing to 16,400 m (53,810 ft) in 21 minutes; the flight also included a Mach 1 pass at 9,500 m (31,170 ft). Again, Rivers used superlative epithets after the flight: *'It's a real shock! An excellent aircraft!'*, *'Very rapid acceleration – the Concorde doesn't even come close'*, *'The aircraft works well at Mach 1'*, *'The landing went well under the captain's guidance, the brakes are good'*.

The flight scheduled for 23rd September had to be called off. First, the NK-144 navigation suite malfunctioned; then, when it had been fixed, it turned out that Fullerton had accidentally opened the oxygen cock and the oxygen bottle was empty. The second supersonic flight – the final one under stage 2 – took place on 24th September, with Fullerton as co-pilot; the TOW was 184,500 kg (496,750 lb). Again, the Tu-144LL reached Mach 1.95, albeit at slightly lower altitude – 16,200 m (53,150 ft) – and made a Mach 1 pass at 9,000 m (29,530 ft).

At the debriefing C. Gordon Fullerton said: *'We were lucky with the weather all the way. During the first flight there was wind and turbulence; in the second flight the conditions were perfect. We were able to evaluate the aircraft in both adverse and good weather – who could ask for more?'* He went on to say: *'The Mach 1 pass was exhilarating. At Mach 2.0 and altitudes above 14,000 m [45,930 ft] the aircraft behaves very well; it is born to fly at Mach 2.0! [...] The aircraft lands virtually by itself! The ground effect makes for a very smooth landing!'*

At the end of that day, before leaving Russia, C. Gordon Fullerton, Robert A. Rivers and engineers Norman H. Princen, Timothy H. Cox and E. Bruce Jackson presented their preliminary report – in English, of course. The Russian team also filed a report on stage 2 of the programme, which was duly endorsed on 30th September. It may be mentioned that the Russian government saw it as necessary to congratulate ANTK Tupolev specifically on the

Chapter 10 - A New Lease of Life: the Tu-144LL Testbed

completion of this stage – the then Prime Minister Yevgeniy M. Primakov sent an official telegram on 2nd October.

Preparations for the final part of the programme went on from 2nd October 1998 to 3rd March 1999, making slow progress due to late deliveries of the experimental equipment from both TsAGI and the USA. The working conditions in the bitterly cold hangar were horrible (mobile heaters and special tents erected over the Tu-144LL's wings had to be used to provide a degree of comfort); frequent power failures added to the difficulties.

The modifications were as follows. Additional temperature probes were installed on the airframe and connected to the Gamma data acquisition system in support of Experiment 1.2A. As part of Experiment 1.5A, additional temperature sensors were installed on the fuel lines, oil lines, hydraulic lines and air conditioning system ducts; fuel flow meters were added to the port engines, feeding information to specially installed computers in the cabin. Blanks carrying Kulite pressure sensors were installed in four port side cabin windows as part of Experiment 2.1A. Experiment 3.3A involved restoring the sensor arrays damaged in the tenth flight, installing additional equipment (including Preston tubes – a type of pressure sensor – and Orlov friction sensors catered for by a separate computer) and upgrading the pitot/static vent system. Finally, the new Experiment 4.1 (exploring the flexure of the wings) necessitated application of optical marker stripes on the port wing, installation of a strobe light and an optical sensor head, plus appropriate equipment racks.

NASA engineers Steve Reese and Don Gallagher assigned to Experiment 2.1A and Boeing engineer Bob Woclavik assigned to Experiment 4.1 assisted actively with the upgrading and calibration of the SBI at this stage. On 11th March 1999 the Tu-144LL was declared ready to fly the research missions under the final stage of the programme.

The four flights took place between 22nd March and 14th April 1999; on the latter date at 1852 hrs the Tu-144LL touched down for the last time. In these flights the aircraft logged another 8 hours 35 minutes, including 2 hours 50 minutes supersonic.

Additionally, two unique ground experiments associated with the powerplant were performed. These were:
- defining the optimum configuration of an advanced supersonic air intake as regards pressure ratio, airflow irregularity and pulsation;
- Experiment 3.1 – studying the integration of short supersonic inlets and the engines (the SST-2 was to have shorter engine nacelles than the Tu-144). This was done on a special test rig with an RD36-51A turbojet.

The results of the tests made it possible to evolve methods of calculating the thermal load, aerodynamics, acoustic load and so on for the next generation of SSTs and supersonic business jets.

The final briefings with the Americans took place on 3rd-7th June 1999. Boeing's programme manager Dan Smith read a letter from Boeing Vice-President Robert Spitzer: *'Our sincere congratulations! We applaud your unbelievable effort! In spite of all difficulties the mission had been accomplished on schedule and safely! We hope for further co-operation.'* The joint statement issued by ANTK Tupolev, NASA, Boeing and IBP testified that the objectives of the second contract had been attained; 100% of the anticipated data, and often more than 100%, had been obtained in the test flights. The latter had been performed with a high degree of safety thanks to the excellent work of the aircrews and ground crews. The data obtained in the experiments were invaluable for the development of supersonic and subsonic aircraft alike.

Eventually, however, the insurmountable hurdle in the SST-2 programme turned out to be not of a technological nature – it was the environmental issues (primarily the sonic boom) which environmental protection crusaders hyped up to such a degree that flights of SSTs over land were banned altogether. An international association known as the Group of Eight was formed, comprising the Boeing Commercial Airplane Group, McDonnell Douglas, British Aerospace, Aérospatiale, Deutsche Aerospace (as part of the Airbus Industrie consortium), Alenia of Italy, an association of Japanese aerospace companies (Fuji Heavy Industries, Mitsubishi Heavy Industries, Kawasaki and others) and ANTK Tupolev. The Group of Eight came to the conclusion that creating an affordable second-generation SST that would meet the new tough sonic boom limits was technically impossible. If the aircraft were to cruise in subsonic mode on the overland legs of the journey to avoid booming someone, it needed to have a non-stop range of some 12,000 km (7,450 miles) to be economically viable, which was impossible for the time being. Thus, all further attempts to create a successor to the Tu-144 and the Concorde were shelved for many years.

In a feature titled *21st Century: Will We Fly Supersonic?* for the January 2000 issue of the Russian magazine *Grazhdahnskaya aviahtsiya* (Civil Aviation) Aleksandr L. Pookhov wrote: *'Given today's development level of aerodynamics, material science and other aviation-related technologies, creating a technically and economically feasible SST-2 with acceptable environmental impact parameters is impossible – at least in the near term. Yet, if we look at it again, this is just a realistic view of the problem's status quo. We have not given up on the idea of creating supersonic airliners; now we know in what direction to proceed in our scientific and technical research and what hurdles we have to clear.'*

The magazine feature ended in a poem by Pookhov that sounded not exactly optimistic. It loosely translates as follows:

Travelling somewhere, faster than sound,
You feel almost motionless, knowing there might,
Even this early, be someone around
Travelling somewhere faster than light.

At the MAKS-99 airshow (17th-22nd August) the Tu-144LL was again in the static park; this time it wore the legend '*Moskva*' (Moscow) on the fuselage. Later, the Tupolev PLC sought further work for this unique aircraft. In 1999 there were plans to fly it to the USA for the purpose of conducting sonic boom research in Oklahoma; there were also plans to display it at the ILA-2000 airshow in Hannover in March 2000. On 14th-19th August 2001 RA-77114 was displayed at the MAKS-2001 airshow. The Tupolev PLC even toyed with the idea of a round-the-world publicity flight with stops at all major airports. There were reports that the aircraft had been sold to a Texas businessman for US$ 11 million at an internet auction. Yet nothing came of it; the Tu-144LL is now in storage at Zhukovskiy – with RD36-51A engine nozzles (but not the engines themselves!) fitted, – and is no longer airworthy.

Appendix

The following is a list of all Tu-144 airframes built, with brief details of each aircraft. In the case of Voronezh-built examples, both commonly used c/n formats are given. It should be noted that the known manufacture dates stated in official documents are ahead of the first flight dates, which does not make sense; this means they are in reality completion dates or roll-out dates.

F/F = first flight; SOC = struck off charge; TTSN = total time since new; TCSN = total cycles since new

C/n	Version	Registration	Notes
			Tu-144 production list
0	Tu-144 (*izdeliye* 044)	CCCP-68001	C/n also reported as 001 or 00-00 (Batch 00, 00th aircraft on the batch). Co-produced by MMZ No.156 'Opyt' (Moscow), Tomilino branch facility and plant No.64 (Voronezh). F/F 31-12-1968. First supersonic flight (Mach 1.08) 5-6-1969. Last flight 27-4-1973; TTSN 120 hrs (50 hrs supersonic), TCSN 120. Scrapped Zhukovskiy 3-1985
00	Tu-144 (*izdeliye* 044)	none	Static test airframe. Co-produced by MMZ No.156, Tomilino branch facility and plant No.64.
01-1 (10011)	Tu-144 (*izdeliye* 004)	CCCP-77101	Pre-production aircraft/sole *izdeliye* 004 powered by NK-144 engines. Co-produced by MMZ No.156 and plant No.64. F/F 1-7-1971 at Zhukovskiy. Logged 338 hours (56 hours supersonic) and 231 cycles during trials, not counting demo flights. SOC 1975, scrapped Zhukovskiy 1976; rear fuselage used for repairing fatigue test airframe c/n 01-4
01-2 (10012)	Tu-144 (*izdeliye* 004)	CCCP-77102	First production *izdeliye* 004 powered by NK-144A engines. Built 1972; F/F 29-3-1972 at Voronezh-Pridacha. Crashed at Goussainville near Paris-Le Bourget 3-6-1973
01-3 (10013)	Tu-144 (*izdeliye* 004)	none	Static test airframe. Reportedly co-produced by MMZ No.156 and plant No.64. Tested to destruction at TsAGI
01-4 (10014)	Tu-144 (*izdeliye* 004)	none	Fatigue test airframe. Reportedly co-produced by MMZ No.156 and plant No.64. Tested to destruction at SibNIA
02-1 (10021)	Tu-144 (*izdeliye* 004)	CCCP-77103	Mfd 6-1973; F/F 13-12-1973. TTSN 313 hrs (59 hrs supersonic), TCSN 250. Scrapped Zhukovskiy
02-2 (10022)	Tu-144 (*izdeliye* 004)	CCCP-77104	Built 1973-74; F/F 16-6-1974. Possibly had this registration in unpainted guise only during tests; became, see next line
		CCCP-77144	TTSN 431 hrs (95 hrs supersonic), TCSN 265. Struck off charge late 1970s, derelict Zhukovskiy, scrapped after 1987
03-1 (10031)	Tu-144 (*izdeliye* 004)	CCCP-77105	Built 1973-74; never flew as such, converted to, see next line
	Tu-144D		Prototype. F/F 30-11-1974. SOC after 1981; TTSN 314 hrs, TCSN 212. Derelict Zhukovskiy by 1993, scrapped 1995
04-1 (10041)	Tu-144 (*izdeliye* 004)	CCCP-77106	Built 1973-75; mfd 14-2-1975, F/F 4-3-1975. Last flight to Monino 29-2-1980, TTSN 582 hrs, TCSN 320. Preserved Soviet Air Force Museum (now Central Russian Air Force Museum), Monino
04-2 (10042)	Tu-144 (*izdeliye* 004)	CCCP-77108	Out-of-sequence registration. F/F 20-8-1975. Last flight 27-8-1987 to Kuibyshev-Bezymyanka; thence trucked 2-1988 to Kuibyshev-Smyshlyayevka (now Samara-Smyshlyayevka), GIA at Kuibyshev Aviation Institute (KuAI; now Samara State Aviation University, SGAU)
05-1 (10051)	Tu-144 (*izdeliye* 004)	CCCP-77107	F/F 12-12-1975. Last flight to Kazan'-Borisoglebskoye 29-3-1985; to Kazan' Aviation Institute (KAI) as GIA 8-1985
05-2 (10052)	Tu-144 (*izdeliye* 004)	CCCP-77109	F/F 29-4-1976; officially registered 31-10-1977! In Aeroflot service 1-11-1977 to 30-5-1978. Transferred to SibNIA for repeat fatigue tests in the spring of 1981 and tested to destruction by pressurising the fuselage; SOC 20-3-1981
05-3 (10053)	Tu-144 (*izdeliye* 004)	none	Repeat static test airframe. Tested to destruction at SibNIA
06-1 (10061)	Tu-144 (*izdeliye* 004)	CCCP-77110	Last Tu-144 *sans suffixe*. F/F 14-2-1977. In Aeroflot service 1-11-1977 to 30-5-1978. SOC 14-2-1984. Last flight to Ul'yanovsk-Baratayevka 1-6-1984, TTSN 314 hrs, TCSN 212. Preserved Civil Air Fleet Museum, Ul'yanovsk
06-2 (10062)	Tu-144D	CCCP-77111	First production Tu-144D. Mfd 18-4-1978, F/F 27-4-1978. Crashed near Yegor'yevsk 23-5-1978; TTSN 9 hrs 02 min, TCSN 5.
07-1 (10071)	Tu-144D	CCCP-77112	Built 1978-79; mfd 19-1-1979, F/F 23-5-1979. Used ATC call sign CCCP-77339 on 5-10-1981. Stored Zhukovskiy until 2000; sold to Auto- und Technik Museum Sinsheim, Germany, for US$ 500,000. Delivered by river/sea to Sinsheim 11-10/8-11-2000; became an exhibit on 26-3-2011
08-1 (10081)	Tu-144D	CCCP-77113	F/F 2-10-1979. SOC late 1981, TTSN 223 hrs, TCSN 103. Derelict Zhukovskiy, scrapped 2001
08-2 (10082)	Tu-144D	CCCP-77114	F/F 13-4-1981; used for record-setting flights 10-1983 as 'aircraft 101'. Last flight as Tu-144D 27-2-1990, TTSN 82 hrs 40 min, TCSN 47. Converted 1994-96 to, see next line
	Tu-144LL	RA-77114	Registered 17-3-1996; F/F as Tu-144LL 29-11-1996; last flight 14-4-1999. Stored Zhukovskiy
09-1 (10091)	Tu-144D	CCCP-77115	Last Tu-144 completed to flying condition; F/F 4-10-1984; last flight 12-5-1986, TTSN 38 hrs 34 min, TCSN 54. Stored Zhukovskiy as a static exhibit
09-2 (10092)	Tu-144D	CCCP-77116	Built 1984 but not completed; stored Voronezh-Pridacha, scrapped early 1990s